THE DEATHS OF THE POPES

THE DEATHS
OF THE POPES

*Comprehensive Accounts, Including
Funerals, Burial Places and Epitaphs*

Wendy J. Reardon

McFarland & Company, Inc., Publishers
Jefferson, North Carolina, and London

LIBRARY OF CONGRESS CATALOGUING-IN-PUBLICATION DATA

Reardon, Wendy J., 1971–
The deaths of the popes : comprehensive accounts, including
funerals, burial places and epitaphs / Wendy J. Reardon.
p.   cm.
Includes bibliographical references and index.

ISBN 0-7864-1527-4 (illustrated case binding : 50# alkaline paper)

1. Popes—Tombs.   2. Funeral service—Catholic Church—History.
3. Catholic Church—Liturgy—History.   I. Title.
BX958.T7R43   2004   264'.020985—dc22   2004014712

British Library cataloguing data are available

Cover photograph ©2004 Image Source

Manufactured in the United States of America

*McFarland & Company, Inc., Publishers
Box 611, Jefferson, North Carolina 28640
www.mcfarlandpub.com*

FOR MY PARENTS,
WHO SACRIFICED A LOT OF THEIR
TIME, PATIENCE, AND MONEY
TO HELP ME WRITE THIS BOOK
(AND WHO ALSO PUT UP WITH
MY CEMETERY OF DIRTY COFFEE CUPS
AROUND THE COMPUTER)

The westering sun draws near his cloudy bed,
Leo, and gradual darkness veils thy head;
The sluggish life-blood in thy withered veins
More slowly runs its course — what then remains?
Lo! Death is brandishing his fatal dart,
And the grave yearns to shroud thy mortal part:
But from its prison freed, the soul expands
Exulting pinions to the enfranchised lands.
My weary race is run — I touch the goal:
Hear, Lord, the feeble pantings of my soul
If it be worthy, Lord, thy pitying breast
Welcome it unto everlasting rest!
May I behold thee, Queen of earth and sky.
Whose love enchained the demons lurking nigh
The path to heaven; and freely shall I own
'Twas thy sweet care that gained my bliss crown!

— Leo XIII (d. 1903)

Contents

Acknowledgments

I could not have completed this book without the help of many people, including first and foremost my parents, without whose patience and financial help I would never have been able to write this book. I also thank my sister Beth and brother John for their enthusiasm, my late grandmother Marion Low, Marion Kenney, Father Tom Carleton, Father Thomas Buffer, Father Joe Waddas, Joe Chiffriller, Chris Nyborg, Per Einar Odden, Bill Thayer, Anne Ball, Nancy Spies, Brenda M. Cook, Cecilia Gaspochin, George Ferzerco, Stephen Allen, Anne Morgenstern, Julian Gardner, Brenda Bolton, Edward James, Edward Davies, Beverly Kienzle, Kathryn Wildgen, Lory Mondaini, Jon N. Austin, Lino Rulli, Susan Halpert, Melissa Snell, Professor Glenn Mack, Mariser Gascon, Judy Forti, Chad Underkoffler, Father James Garneau, Robert Piperno, Deanna Jurdin, Pierangela Badia, Giuseppe Alfonso, Amy Hirschfield, Father John Goosens, Father Martin Grace and Father Lawrence McGrath (St. John's Seminary), Don Cacace, Elaine Ensor (Chalet Savoy), Father Mario O.P. (Santa Maria Sopra Minerva), Don Sandro Corrandini (San Salvatore in Lauro), Father Fernando Paolone (Santa Maria in Arecoli), Lucrezio Catiani (St. John Lateran), Perrooli Mols (Santa Maria ai Monti), Father Denis O'Brien (San Silvester in Capite), Rosanna Shedid (Santa Susanna), Massalin Renato (St. Balbina Rest Home), Sister Maria Gavarola (San Sisto Vecchio), Nicola Cirone (San Lorenzo fuori la Mura), Stefano and Sara (Verona Cathedral), Don Abubano (Arezzo Cathedral), Clara Bruno (Florence Cathedral), and Francesca and Anna (Papal Palace, Viterbo).

Special thanks are due to John Curran of the Queen's University of Belfast for use of his article, "The Bones of St. Peter?" which appeared in *Classics Ireland* 3 (1996).

Thanks also to the Finnish Academy of Science and Letters for permission to quote translations of papal epitaphs by Iiro Kajanto as published in *Papal Epigraphy in Renaissance Rome* (Helsinki: Suomalainen tiedeakatemia, 1982).

And on a personal note, thanks to: Father Richard Curran (St. Mary's, Hanover, Mass.), Jacquie Martin, Edwin Burgwinkle, Alleyne Brooke, Michael Fennimore, John White, Sidney Iwanter, Katy Henthorne, Nick and Debbie Petaro, Mike Suss, "Big Joe" Woods, Jerry Tilton, Edward Bergin, the Rev. John Coffee, Jack Gantos, Glen Ransden, Karen Quast, RJ Valentine, Bill Brett, Gay Farrington-Pollock.

A Note on the Translators

Many of the Latin epitaphs and exhumation reports in this work were translated into English for the very first time by the following scholars, who worked very hard and sacrificed a lot of their time to help me with this project. They deserve the credit for making this book come alive.

Dr. Phyllis G. Jestice is an assistant professor of medieval history at the University of Southern Mississippi. She specializes in the history of religion in the European Middle Ages. Her work includes the monograph *Wayward Monks and the Religious Revolution of the Eleventh Century* (Brill, 1997); *An Encyclopedia of Irish Spirituality* (ABC-Clio, 2000); and several translations. She is currently editing a three-volume encyclopedia of holy people in the world's religious traditions for ABC-Clio.

Father Rosario Tom Carleton has spent many years in Italy. He is the author of *The Philosophy of Life: The Pope and the Right to Life* and runs the wonderful website www.the-popes.com.

Father Thomas Buffer is professor of theology, dean of men, and director of pastoral formation at the Pontifical College Josephinum, a Roman Catholic seminary in Columbus, Ohio. He holds the degree of doctor of sacred theology from the Pontifical Gregorian University, Rome, and has completed advanced studies in Latin with Father Reginald Foster, Latin secretary to His Holiness John Paul II. He is the translator of *Mary and the Fathers of the Church* by Luigi Gambero (Ignatius Press, 1999).

Samuel J. García received his B.A. in liberal arts from St. John's College, Annapolis, Maryland, in 1999 and his master of theological studies from Harvard University in 2002. He is currently a doctoral student at Yale University (history department). His area of study and interest is the history and historiography of Reformation Europe.

Ruth Yeuk Chun Leung got her B.A. in linguistics and classics from the University of Georgia in 1998, and a master's degree in theological studies at Harvard Divinity School in 2002. Her interests include classical philology, New Testament and early Christianity, and religion and culture.

Bas Jongenelen studied theory and history of literature at the Katholic University of Brabant in Tilburg, the Netherlands. Nowadays he works as a teacher of Dutch language and literature in a secondary school. He has published articles on Dutch literature in several magazines and on CD-Roms. In his spare time he is writing a dissertation about the Middle Dutch translations of *Le chevalier délibéré* by Olivier de la Marche.

PHILLIP HABERKERN is working towards his doctorate in history at the University of Virginia. He previously attended Harvard Divinity School and the University of North Carolina–Chapel Hill, where he studied the history of Christianity.

Preface

Many people have asked me why I wrote a book on papal death because it seems like such a strange subject. I have often asked myself the same thing, and I always come up with the same answer: it's fascinating.

For example, Martin IV choked on the pickled eels he was eating; Paul II gorged himself to death on melons (possibly poisoned); John XXI's ceiling collapsed on him; Sylvester II's tomb allegedly rumbled and leaked water when a pope was going to die. How can one not be fascinated?

Unfortunately, almost all extant sources about papal death are in Italian, Latin, German or French. But what about English-speaking people who aren't scholars but who just want to see pictures of the incredible tombs, read the eloquent epitaphs, and enjoy some very unusual anecdotes? This book is for them just as much as it is for the serious scholar of papal history. I tried to get the best of both worlds, and I hope I have succeeded.

Early in my research, I discovered that it would be very hard to get accurate in-formation about popes' deaths because records were often poorly kept, or not kept at all, in the early years of the church, and the records we do have cannot be considered reliable, although they are very interesting. The few accounts that do exist of the first hundred years of the papacy, the *Liber Pontificalis* (*Book of the Popes*) and the *Golden Legend*, conflict at times with the *Catholic Encyclopedia*, which in turn conflicts with the *Oxford Dictionary of Popes*, and so on. It is therefore impossible to guarantee that everything in this book is fact or that popes are actually interred where sources claim they are. This is particularly true of the popes who were re-moved from the catacombs and reburied in San Martino ai Monti, San Silvester in Capite, and Santa Prassade, to name a few. In each entry I have listed every church that claims to have the body of a pope, sometimes several different churches may list the same pope as belonging to them.

Overall, I have done my best to bring rare information and photos to the general public. I have tried to be very careful when

1

indicating what information is alleged and what is known to be true.

Entry Format

The popes (and antipopes) are listed chronologically according to their dates of reign. In each entry, the papal name is followed by the dates of reign; the birth name (if different from the papal name; see below) follows in *italics*. Each entry then provides as much information as possible about the death, funeral rites, and burial of the pope. In every instance where the information is available, the entry lists all epitaphs and other inscriptions for the pope, first in the original language (usually Latin, but the earliest were in Greek) and then in English translation. Most entries also include a list of suggested material for further specific reading and in-depth research.

Papal Names

The first pope to change his name after election was Pope John II (d. 535). Originally named Mercury, he didn't think it appropriate that a pope should have the name of a pagan god, so he took the name John in honor of his predecessor, St. John I (d. 526). Generally, however, the names of popes up until the late tenth century were their birth names, with one or two exceptions.

Adopting papal names became common around the tenth century, when the pope became a symbol of church leadership descended in an unbroken line from St. Peter; the papal name emphasized the continuation of the line. The name change also demonstrated that each pope was starting a new period in his life as well as a new pontificate. Some popes adopted the name of a predecessor as a gesture of honor to that pope; others adopted the name of

a predecessor in an attempt to erase his memory. For example, Clement VII (d. 1534) adopted that name to symbolically eradicate the existence of Antipope Clement VII (d. 1394).

Papal Epitaph and Inscription Typography

The papal epitaphs and inscriptions are rendered in SMALL CAPITALS. Lowercase letters enclosed in parentheses are provided to fill in words that have been represented in the inscription, such as P(ontifex) M(aximi). Lowercase letters not enclosed in parentheses, e.g. "qvae miHI COMPOSVIT mortaliis," are not present in the inscription because (usually) of wear or breakage; they have been interpolated by scholars.

In Latin the letter "V" was often interchanged with "U." The use of one or the other is inconsistent in the sources recording papal epitaphs and inscriptions. On the actual tombs, "V" is most commonly used, while published works sometimes differ (for example, Iiro Kajanto's *Papal Epigraphy in Renaissance Rome* and Renzo Montini's *Le Tombe dei Papi* substitute "U" for "V"). Many of the epitaphs and inscriptions in this book have been transcribed directly from the tombs, while others were taken from published sources. In all cases, transcriptions are verbatim, and the use of "V" or "U" reflects the usage of the source.

Further Reading

Many of the articles cited at the ends of entries as "Further Reading" are from European journals of the nineteenth and early twentieth centuries. While these journals are not all widely available, most can be found in the collections of the British Library in London.

I hope that people reading this book will not only enjoy seeing the beautiful tombs and reading the epitaphs, but that they will get interested, even excited, or at least curious about why a certain pope was smothered or why another purposely swallowed crushed emeralds. Learning about papal death made me want to learn more about the popes themselves—their stories and their motivations. But most of all, I marveled at, and rejoiced in, the strength of the Catholic faith to withstand two thousand years of scandal, war, and attack. Catholic leaders should not shy away from the rich history of the papacy; they should be proud of it. It is true that mistakes were made, people persecuted, and many lives lost in the name of Catholicism over the years—as in every religion. The Catholic church can acknowledge that these things happened without condoning them, and be glad that our way of thinking has evolved since those bad times.

What people often fail to understand is that we cannot criticize the popes of the past with our twenty-first century concepts of what is acceptable for a pope to do and what is not. In studying any aspect of papal history, one must remember to judge those popes by the standards of *their* day, not *ours*. Popes were rulers of the world, and power corrupts. The popes were only human. They lived, and they died, like the human beings they were.

Introduction

Other men die in darkness, in confusion, and amid tears;
the Pope, alone in the world, dies in ceremony.
— James-Charles Noonan, *The Church Visible*

A Brief History of Papal Funerals

The customs and traditions associated with papal death have changed quite a bit since the first burials of popes in the underground catacombs of Rome. Over the centuries various ceremonies, rites, and rituals developed; these were fundamentally similar, but not until the early fourteenth century was a uniform procedure instituted.

It was Pierre Ameil, a fourteenth-century bishop, who wrote this first official papal funeral "Rule Book" (*Ordo*), which began with the pope on his deathbed and ended with his burial in a church. According to Ameil, papal death ceremonies would begin a few days before the actual death. The chamberlain would call together the cardinals, in whose presence the pope would express his last wishes, including his place of burial. He would then profess his faith, and the cardinals would pardon him for any failings in his duty.

During this time the pope could also suggest the name of a successor, if he felt it appropriate. When this and all matters of church business (including an accounting of the church's credits and debts) were accomplished, the bishop-sacristan would administer Extreme Unction.

When the pope drew his last breath, the cardinals were immediately to visit the body and then (according to Amail's *ordo*) promptly "withdraw," leaving the corpse to be washed and dressed.[1]

The next part of Ameil's *ordo* speaks of the people who took care of the body of the pope, including cleaning, embalming, and dressing. Members of the *curia*—penitentiaries, servants, and almoners—carried out these duties.

The process of embalming was necessary because a pope's body must be in a condition to be viewed by the public during the novena (nine days of mourning). The following is a verbatim account of the embalming process from Ameil's *ordo*:

Once the pope is dead, the penitentiaries, with the Friars of the *Bulla*, if there are any, or else of the *Pignotta*, with water, and with good herbs that the servants or aides of the papal chamber must prepare, will wash the body well, and the barber will shave his head and beard. Thus washed, the apothecary and the said Friars of the *Bulla* will close all his apertures tightly with wool or flax; the anus, mouth, nostrils, and ears, with myrrh, incense, and aloe (if it can be had): his body should then be washed again with white wine, warmed with fragrant herbs and good vernaccia, which the servants in waiting or, indeed, the wine stewards, must provide the workers. Then his throat shall be filled with aromatics and especially with wool, and the nostrils with musk. Lastly his whole body shall be rubbed down and anointed with good balsam, even his hands.[2]

Ameil even details the dressing the papal corpse, as Agostino Paravicini-Bagliani describes in *The Pope's Body* (the quotes in the extract below are from Ameil):

The penitentiaries had to redress the pope's body, after "having almost seated it," "with sacred vestments, almost all of red; that is, with white sandals, cincture and belt, fanon, stole, short tunic, maniple, dalmatic, gloves, chasuble, and pallium taken from the body of Peter." They folded the fanon over the pope's head and shoulders as though he were going to celebrate mass, and put the berretta and white miter (without pearls or gold) on his head.[3]

In the second phase of the papal funeral ritual, a ritual procession would bring the papal corpse from the death chamber to the chapel for semi-private visitation of the body by the pope's family and other dignitaries.

The third phase of the papal funeral took place at the church, where the liturgical vigil was held. Here the curialists and religious public could view the pope and see that he was truly dead. In the church the pope's face remained uncovered, as did his hands and feet so that the faithful could only touch his feet.

While the body lay in the church for the faithful to see during the day, it lay by itself at night during the ritual of abandonment (sometimes with unpleasant results, as in the cases of Innocent III and Clement VI).

When all of the ceremonial masses had been said, the corpse was transferred from the church to the Chapel of the Canons, where it was deposited in a coffin of cypress wood, which was enclosed in lead and finally placed in a casket of oak or chestnut. In the inner coffin were laid purses containing coins minted during the late pope's reign, along with a brief history of his chief acts inscribed on parchment and enclosed in a brass tube. The inner coffins were then sealed by the camerlengo and other high officials. In the old St. Peter's (before the reconstruction in the seventeenth century), "when there ceased to be room in the portico in which to bury popes, their sarcophagi were deposited under the floor of the church and monuments raised as close to the remains as the restricted space allowed."[4]

Modern Papal Burial

The funeral of Paul VI (d. 1978) was simple, in keeping with his request. The rites for his successor, John Paul, who died the same year, were likewise understated. Possibly the years to come will see a continued trend toward simplicity. Nevertheless, procedures for a modern papal burial remain fundamentally the same as their historical counterparts. The following is a simplified summary.

When the pope is considered to be on his deathbed, both his family and the College of Cardinals, as well as the cardinals around the world, are notified that they should begin to converge on Rome. The ailing pope is checked as frequently as need be by the papal doctor, who remains near at all times. Meanwhile, various cardinals and the pope's family join around the bed for a final blessing from the dying pontiff. If he is still lucid, the pope will give his confession as well as receive the final Sacrament of Extreme Unction.

When it is believed that the pope has breathed his last, the camerlengo places a silk cloth over the face of the pontiff three times, each time calling out the pope's Christian name because it is thought no man can remain silent when he hears the name his mother gave him. When he has called the name three times with no answer the camerlengo declares, "The pope is dead!" Until 1676, the camerlengo would remove a small silver hammer from a red pouch and tap the pope on the forehead (slightly above the right eyebrow) three times and call out his name to see if he was truly dead. One of those silver hammers can still be seen in the Vatican treasury today. There is conflicting evidence from respectable authors however, about the modern use of the hammer. In *Pontiff*, authors Gordon Thomas and Max Morgan-Witts attest to the hammer being used for Paul VI (d. 1978) and John Paul I (d. 1978), whereas Frances Burkle-Young, in *Passing the Keys*, claims that the silk cloth was used on both.

After the pope is declared dead, the camerlengo removes the fisherman's ring to be broken in front of the College of Cardinals during their first meeting after the death of the pope, after which it will be placed in the pope's innermost coffin. This is done so that no one will be able to falsify documents with the pope's seal. The camerlengo then seals the papal apartments while the word goes out to the world that the pope is dead, and the bell of the Arco delle Campani rings the death knell. The remaining cardinals are then summoned to Rome, upon pain of excommunication, to celebrate the novena (nine days of mourning) as well as to prepare for the coming conclave.

The reasons for the novena, during which time special masses are said for the soul of the dead pope, have their roots deep in the past. First, the exhibition of the body confirmed the empty see and calling of the next conclave; confirming that the pope actually was dead was important in centuries past, when rumors abounded and the appointment of a new pope was sometimes clouded with deceit and trickery. Second, if the pope was thought to be a saint, it was believed that his body would not decay; hence the novena allowed time for his incorruptible nature to be tested. Also, the nine days gave cardinals enough time to reach Rome and guaranteed that the cardinals would not elect a pope before the funeral masses were completed, and that sufficient time would be taken to contemplate who would become the next Holy Father. The nine days also offered enough time for the pope to be venerated liturgically as the pope, and as the man himself.

In earlier centuries it was tradition for Vatican employees to loot the pope's apartments after his death. Papal decrees were issued as early as 633 to prohibit employees from ransacking the pope's belongings and even the body of the pontiff himself:

> When the pontiff was in his death agony, his nephews and servants carried off from the palace whatever they could. Immediately after his death, the officials of the Camera Apostolica robbed the body of anything of value. But in general those closest to the pontiff assaulted him, with impunity, leaving only the bare walls of the room and the body lying on a poor mattress with an old wooden candlestick and a burned-out candle end.[5]

Today, the employees of Vatican City each receive a year's pay at the death of the pontiff in lieu of the looting.

From the late sixteenth century to the early twentieth, 24 hours after the pope

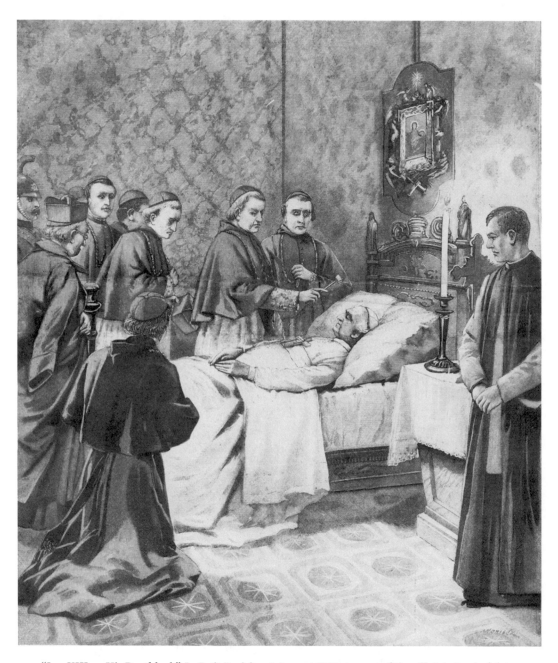

"Leo XIII on His Deathbed," *Le Petit Parisien*, 2 August 1903. As part of the official ritual of the era, a cardinal taps the pope's forehead with a small silver hammer before declaring him dead.

died his body would be washed with rose-water and embalmed, and his heart and viscera would be removed and taken to the Church of SS. Vincenzo e Anastasio in Rome by the *Cappellari Secreti*, who would deposit them in earthen jars behind the walls (see Appendix 6 for more information on this practice).

The embalming process is necessary if the body is to be displayed for the public during the novena, otherwise there could be decided unpleasantness, as in the cases of Pius XII, Paul VI, and John Paul I. The body is then redressed, usually by Franciscans (according to tradition), in a white simar, white alb, cincture, amice, and red and gold chasuble; possibly a golden mitre is placed on his head.

Normally 24 large Paschal candles surround the coffin during the funeral, although there was only one for the funeral of Paul VI (d. 1978) per his request. Members of the papal household and the cardinals then gather in St. Peter's for the final funeral mass, as a deacon, and only a deacon, recites the solemn liturgy of the reception of the dead. The Mass for the Dead and the Absolution are said, and then each cardinal approaches the coffin, censing the altar and body three times. After each individual censing, all of the cardinals chant the versicles and responses. A reading of the Act of Burial is performed, and

A papal coffin being lifted into a burial niche over a door in St. Peter's. From *London Magazine*, 1905.

a copy of the eulogy is put into a brass cylinder in that innermost coffin, along with three bags of coins (of silver, gold, and copper), each containing as many coins as years that the pope reigned. The pope's face and hands are then covered with a veil of white silk, and the body is covered with a crimson pall. The wood coffin is sealed and wrapped with three ribbons before it is placed in the bronze casket, which is then soldered shut.

The bronze casket is then placed in a coffin of elm (the most valuable wood in Rome) and is nailed shut with golden nails. It is wheeled before the high altar and lowered into the grottoes (to be placed in the area chosen by the pope before his death) while clerics chant *In Paradisum*, after which prayers, antiphons, and psalms are recited.

When the sarcophagus is put into its final place, only the pope's family and per-

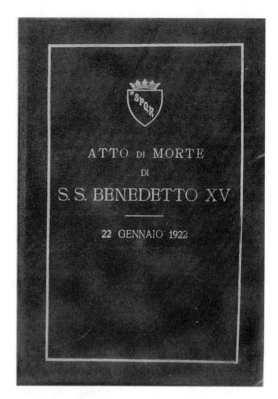

Death certificate for Benedict XV. From *L'Illustration*, February 4, 1922.

sonal friends are allowed to spend time alone with the sarcophagus to say their final goodbyes and offer prayers for the soul of their kinsman and friend.

A Brief History of Papal Tombs

The first popes—excluding Clement I—up until Pope Victor (d. 198) were buried, according to the *Liber Pontificalis*,* "near the body of the Blessed Peter." These popes were simply entombed in coffins of marble, brick, or terra-cotta, and closed with a slab bearing each individual name.

Popes Zephryinus (d. 217) and Callixtus I (d. 222) constructed a vault on the Via Appia — the Cemetery of Callixtus— which was discovered by the great archeologist Giovanni Battista de Rossi in 1854. Sixtus III (d. 440) placed a plaque inside the catacomb that listed the names of those popes buried there: Sixtus II, Dionysius, Cornelius, Felix, Pontainus, Fabianus, Gaius, Eusebius, Melchiades, Stephan, Urban I, Lucius, and Anterus. When these popes died they were wrapped in linen sheets, sprinkled with perfumes and spices, and interred in a *locus* (wall niche) that was then sealed with a stone or marble slab that simply named the interred pope (in Greek letters), with *"episocopus"* and the ivy leaf (the symbol of immortality) added to the name. Pope Damasus (366–384) honored the popes by placing an epitaph in their honor in the papal crypt of the Cemetery of Callixtus:

---

*The *Liber Pontificalis* (*Book of Pontiffs*) is the earliest known collection of papal biographies. It cannot be considered reliable, but it makes for fascinating reading.

HIC CONJESTA JACET, QUAERIS SI, TURBA
PIORUM, / CORPORA SANCTORUM RETINENT
VENERANDA SEPULCHRA, / SUBLIMES ANIMAS
RAPUIT SIBI REGIA COELI. / HIC COMITES XYSTI
PORTANT QUI EX HOSTE TROPAEA, / HIC
NUMERUS PROCERUM SERVAT QUI ALTARIA
CHRISTI, / HIC POSITUS LONGA VIXIT QUI IN
PACE SACERDOS, / HIC CONFESSORES SANCTI
QUOS GRAECIA MISIT, / HIC JUVENES PUERIQUE,
SENES CASTIQUE NEPOTES, / QUIS MAGE
VIRGINEUM PLACUIT RETINERE PUDOREM. /
HIC FATEOR DAMASUS VOLUI MEA CONDERE
MEMBRA, / SED CINERES TIMUI SANCTOS
VEXARE PIONIM

"Here, should you ask, lies a vast company of the righteous gathered together; the venerable tombs preserve the bodies of the saints, but the Kingdom of Heaven has caught up to itself their glorious souls. Here are the companions of Sixtus who bear away the trophies from the enemy, here many of the leaders who serve the altars of Christ, here is laid the Bishop who lived during the long peace, here the holy confessors whom Greece sent, here young men and boys, old men and their chaste grandsons who preferred rather to keep intact their virgin modesty. Here I, Damasus, wished, I confess, to lay my limbs, but I feared to vex the holy ashes of the righteous."[6]

When the papal crypt filled up, popes were buried in other cemeteries— Priscilla, Balbina, Calepodius, Pontian, and Felicitas. St. Celestine (d. 432) was the last known pope to be buried in the catacombs. His successor, Pope St. Sixtus III, was laid to rest in the crypt of San Lorenzo al Verano (now San Lorenzo fuori le Mura) in Rome while the following pope, St. Leo I (d. 461), was the first deceased pope to grace St. Peter's.

Popes were primarily buried in the portico, or porch, of St. Peter's. When that filled up, the southern wall inside the basilica became popular, after which the southern transept was the place for papal burial. The monuments and tombs of the popes came in many shapes and sizes, and some were even interred in altars dedicated to them or perhaps to their favorite saint or

previous namesake. It is interesting to note that until the eighth century, only the bodies of saints were allowed to be buried in porphyry sarcophagi, but during the "dark ages" (probably due to the lack of artisans in Rome), popes began reusing ancient sarcophagi or bathing basins for burial.

The line of papal burials in St. Peter's remained virtually unbroken until Benedict V was interred in Hamburg, Germany, ca. 964. Popes were initially interred in the vestibule, and later inside the church. Of the twelve popes who died in Rome in the twelfth century, ten were buried in the Lateran. Unfortunately, however, the Lateran basilica was destroyed by fires in 1308 and 1361 and no tombs were saved, with the exception of the ornately decorated sarcophagus of Anastasius IV that originally belonged to Emperor Constantine's mother, the Empress Helena (which is on display in the Vatican museum). The charred remains of the other popes were gathered and buried in front of the lower door of the basilica (near the tomb of Innocent III).

In 1185, Lucius III died and was buried in the cathedral of Verona. With this interment began a long line of popes (with a few exceptions) who were buried outside of Rome, in such cities as Perugia, Viterbo, Arezzo, Recanati, Naples, and Pisa, usually for convenience because they were traveling or were in exile. The majority of these were three-tiered wall tombs with a pointed gothic canopy, while the popes of the Avignon papacy were buried in magnificent freestanding Gothic tombs.

With the papacy's return to Rome came the papal tombs. With a few exceptions, all of the popes from Eugene IV (d. 1447) to John Paul I (d. 1978) were originally interred in St. Peter's basilica and crypt, although many were destroyed by Bramante (aptly titled il Ruinate by the Romans) when he tore down St. Peter's in the seventeenth century. Almost all of the tombs (with the exception of Gregory V, d. 999) prior to the thirteenth century that were unfortunate enough to be in Bramante's way were completely destroyed. Luckily, however, some sarcophagi were saved and are on display in the Vatican crypt; other entire tomb monuments were moved to other churches in Rome. Fortunately for the historical record, the church canon and historian Giacomo Grimaldi sketched many of the tombs and their location prior to their dismantling or destruction, and Alphonso Ciacconius took the time to detail several of the tomb monuments that were later destroyed.

Perhaps papal tombs, having come full circle from the simple niches of the catacombs to the simple sarcophagi of Paul VI (d. 1978) and John Paul I (d. 1978), are a reflection of the papal institution coming full circle as well: from the simple spiritual teachings of Jesus Christ, through the excessive temporal powers of the medieval and Renaissance papacy, back to the pure goal of peace, love, and spiritual awareness preached by Pope John Paul II.

THE DEATHS OF THE POPES

St. Peter   (c. 32–67) *Simon*. Died approximately at age 67. Said to have been crucified upside-down by the spot called Naumachia, near the obelisk of Nero on Vatican Hill in the Circus of Caligula and Nero, Rome. His body was probably buried by his friends in a shallow brick crypt on the right side of the Via Cornelia (near the circus) at the point where the road passed on its north side. An obelisk, known as the "terebinth" or turpentine tree, is said to have originally marked the surface, although the exact site is unknown because the obelisk was moved around many times before it was placed finally in the Piazza of St. Peter's.

A small chapel was built by Pope Anacletus (d. 90) over the site. Sixtus II (d. 258), during Emperor Valarius' persecution, allegedly transferred the bones of Peter and Paul to an underground burial place on the Via Appia *ad catacumbes* (where the church of St. Sebastian now stands) on June 29, so that is the day celebrated as the day of Peter's martyrdom. Pope Silvester (d. 335) later brought Peter's remains back to the Vatican Hill and preserved them in a silver (later bronze) shrine.

The Golden Legend (which contains fantastic stories of the saints and early popes) offers an interesting story pertaining to the bones of Saints. Peter and Paul. It claims that some Greeks stole the bodies of Peter and Paul "in the time of Pope Cornelius" (251–253). The power of God made the stone pagan idols yell that the bodies of the gods were being carried away. The Christians took that to mean the apostles' bodies were being stolen, while the pagans thought that the statues of *their* gods were being stolen, which resulted in both Christians and Pagans chasing after the Greeks, who became scared and tossed the bodies in a well near the catacombs. The bones were retrieved by the Christians, but now no one knew which bones belonged to whom. They prayed for and received an answer from heaven: "*The larger bones belong to the preacher, the smaller to the fishermen.*" The bones were then separated and weighed, each set of bones going to its respective church, either St. Peter's or St. Paul's. Emperor Constantine and his mother Helena placed a gold cross weighing 150 pounds over the tomb of Peter, along with an inscription: "Constantinus Augustus and Helena Augusta have adorned this royal house, which is enclosed in a hall of the same splendor."

For years the bones of Peter were thought to still reside under the confessio of St. Peter's basilica, but no one knew for sure because legend had it that whoever disturbed the bones of Peter would die. Finally, when

The original shrine to St. Peter, a small chapel built by Pope Anacletus. By permission of the Houghton Library, Harvard University

the tomb niche for Pius XI was being carved out of the grottoes, the workmen stumbled into an ancient catacomb. The story of what happened next is well told by Professor John Curran of the Queen's University in Belfast, Ireland. His story begins with the death of Peter:

> It is believed by many historians, Christians and non–Christians, that Saint Peter died in Rome at the hands of Nero.
>
> One of Nero's friends, the writer Seneca, records in a letter that he had seen criminals being crucified upside down at around the time of Peter's alleged execution. A generation later, Saint John's Gospel contained a passage in which Christ prophesied Peter's death: "When you are old, then you will stretch out your hands and another will bind you and take you where you do not want to go [John 21:18].
>
> The phrase "to stretch out one's hands" is found in literature of the time referring to crucifixion. Certainly the Christian church at Rome claimed Peter as a martyr and founder along with Paul as early as the end of the first century A.D. And another Roman tradition which we can trace back to the third century A.D. added the detail that Peter asked his persecutors to turn his cross upside down, because he was unworthy to die in the same manner as Jesus.
>
> These literary fragments may not seem impressive, but it must be borne in mind that no challenge was ever mounted to the tradition of Peter's residence and martyrdom in Rome prior to 1324, despite the fact that the authority of the bishops of Rome was a constant battleground in the early church. No one disputed the claim that Peter had died at Rome. As a condemned criminal, Peter, like Christ, did not merit a normal burial. His body, like the bodies of executed villains, should have been dumped in the Tiber or thrown into a convenient rubbish pit. But we know the early Christians often took particular care to recover the bodies of their dead for veneration.
>
> Certainly from a very early date, both the apostles, Peter and Paul, were receiving special attention in the Roman Church. Around A.D. 200, a Roman churchman called Gaius wrote to a correspondent: "I can point out the trophies of the apostles. For if you would go to the Vatican, or to the Ostian Way, you will find the trophies of those who founded this church."
>
> For the first time in the written record, the name of Peter was explicitly associated with the Vatican Hill, situated northwest of the main area of the city of Rome.
>
> It was very widely known that ancient remains filled the soil on which the Renaissance and Baroque masterpiece of St. Peter's basilica stood. In the work to complete the great church, laborers had frequently uncovered ancient artifacts. One notorious discovery in 1626, for example, was the coffin of a man called Flavius Agricola whose final advice to the living was: "Mix the wine, drink deep and do not refuse to pretty girls the sweets of love, for when death comes earth and fire devour everything."
>
> Pope Urban VIII was so appalled by the pagan sentiment that he ordered the sarcophagus broken up and thrown into the Tiber. But objects had continued to turn up, especially as a result of burials in the crypt of Saint Peter's, an area of the church known as the Vatican grottoes. The grottoes lie beneath the nave of the basilica and contain the bodies of some notable Catholics, including James II and a number of popes.
>
> When Pope Pius XI died in February 1939, he was buried in the grottoes alongside his predecessors. The new pope, Pius XII, decided that the time was right to reorganize the space into a proper underground chapel. Under the direction of Monsignor Kaas, administrator of St. Peter's, the Vatican's architects and engineers estimated that the modifications could best be accommodated by lowering the level of the grottoes by three feet.
>
> As soon as the digging started, the anticipated hoard of ancient sarcophagi began to turn up. But at a depth of some two and a half feet, the workmen hit something unexpected. Traces of the top of a walled enclosure were uncovered. The roof of the enclosure had been crudely sliced off, however, and the interior had been packed with earth. Intrigued by the building, the workmen began to dig down through the compressed fill. Fifteen feet down, they finally reached

the floor of what was clearly a Roman mausoleum. Four inscriptions placed below funerary urns identified the owners as a family called the Caetennii. But there were indications that this mausoleum was not alone; it seemed likely that there were in fact other tombs on either side of it. The excavators informed the pope, and Pius XII abandoned the plan to create an underground chapel. Instead, he put together a team of Vatican officials who were to explore the site further. Two Jesuit archaeologists, Antonio Ferrua and Englebert Kirschbaum, undertook most of the work; the Vatican architect, Bruno Apollonj-Ghetti, and the inspector of catacombs, Professor Enrico Josi, oversaw the project, and all four were under the authority of Monsignor Ludwig Kaas, the administrator of St. Peter's, answerable to the pope himself. Pius XII commissioned them to investigate further but laid down one condition: They were not to encroach on the area beneath the high altar.

Work began in 1941 and within months it had become clear that a major area of archaeological importance had been discovered. A whole street of tombs came to light, some 300 feet long, with tombs on both sides. Some were simple structures, small and unadorned; but others were sumptuously decorated with wall paintings, stucco decoration and even expertly finished mosaics. In these tombs, the Vatican excavators found hundreds of burials. Over half were cremation-burials, the rest inhumations, and many of the dead were named. Their names proved to be an important means of dating the street. It seems that the burial area was dominated by freedmen and their families. Slaves customarily took the names of their former masters on manumission, and a small but significant number of the freedmen buried in the street of tombs had been owned by Roman emperors of the second century. There was evidence also that Christians had used the street of tombs. In one tomb, the excavators found a breathtaking golden mosaic which depicted Christ driving a chariot across the sky, a motif borrowed straight from depictions of the sun god Sol or Helios.

But two striking finds convinced the investigators that they were on the verge of some great discovery: First, they noticed the way in which the street of tombs had been destroyed. The roofs of many of the tombs stretching eastwards down the Vatican Hill had been crudely hacked off. Some of the tombs themselves had had buttress walls inserted into them, running north to south; and all had been filled in with a vast quantity of earth, estimated at 1 million cubic feet.

The excavators knew well that the emperor Constantine had built a church in honor of Saint Peter in the 320s A.D., and the transverse walls inside the tombs were clearly part of the foundations of that church. But the way in which the tombs had been damaged and filled in indicated that Constantine had been determined to build his church on precisely that alignment on the Vatican Hill. He had in effect sawn off the top of the hill and deposited it further down to create a vast platform on which to build his basilica. But there could only be one reason for this: there was something on the hill that he wanted to preserve and place in the focal point of his church. The excavators had discovered that the street of tombs which Constantine had destroyed was leading straight under the high altar.

The second important discovery made by the Vatican investigating team was a graffito on the wall of another tomb. Some ancient hand, perhaps belonging to one of Constantine's workmen, had scrawled in charcoal: *Petrus roga Christus Iesus pro sanctis hominibus Chrestianis ad corpus tuum sepultis* ("Peter, pray Jesus Christ for the holy men buried near your body"). For the first time, evidence in this ancient street pointed to the presence of Peter's remains in the vicinity.

These developments, communicated to the Pope, caused him to change his mind about the scope of the excavations. He ordered the team to penetrate the zone beneath the high altar of Saint Peter's basilica. Once again, however, a stern command was issued: not a breath of their activities was to be communicated to the public until the work had been completed and a full report published. Thus, while the Second World War ravaged Europe, Monsignor Kaas and his colleagues burrowed unnoticed under one of the most revered sites in Catholic Christendom.

This phase of the excavators' work presented the greatest difficulties. There was absolutely no question that the basilica of Saint Peter could be closed for the duration of the project, and yet its progress had to remain secret. The present high altar of the basilica was very carefully supported through the skill of Vatican engineers, and the drainage problems were solved by hydrologists. The excavators themselves had been forbidden to use power tools and had to conduct the investigation with trowels and spades and an army of *Sampietrini* (Vatican workmen).

Three years of digging, first from the west, then the south and north, finally brought this part of the street of tombs to light. Directly beneath the area of the high altar of Saint Peter's basilica lay a paved courtyard, 7 meters by 4. The westernmost limit of this courtyard was provided by a thick red brick wall to which the excavators gave the name the *muro rosso*, the Red Wall. Built into this wall was a structure rising to a height of about 2 meters from the floor. Although its upper portions had been badly damaged, its overall shape could be reconstructed. It had an upper and a lower niche; a pediment topped the upper niche and the lower was framed by two short columns. The remains of a slab of marble lay on top of the two columns. Because of its appearance, the excavators called this structure the *aedicula*, the "little temple."

On the floor of the courtyard, at the point where the *aedicula* met the Red Wall, a second slab of marble had been set into the ground. It had come from another tomb in the area and a rectangular hole had been cut into it. To the right hand (or north) side of the *aedicula*, a small buttressing wall had been placed in front of a crack in the Red Wall at a date after the completion of the *aedicula* itself. This wall had been faced with plaster which had been scratched and scored by ancient visitors to the site. Also, the builders of this wall, which the excavators called "the Graffiti Wall," had inserted into it a small marble-lined space to which the team gave the name the "*loculus.*"

The crucial question was the date of this little complex. The investigators regarded the courtyard and the four tombs around it as being constructed at the same time. These tombs around the courtyard yielded names, but nothing strictly datable. However, when the archaeologists explored the sloping alleyway on the western side of the Red Wall they discovered that someone had installed a drain to carry away the rain on the hill. The drain had been made with bricks from a Roman workshop, and five of them bore the same maker's stamp. They came from a factory in production between A.D. 147 and 161.

The excavators concluded then that the basic structures at this end of the street of tombs had been laid down in the middle of the second century A.D. They had in fact discovered the structure which the churchman Gaius described when he was writing around the year A.D. 200. But although this evidence indicated an impressively early date for the *aedicula* and the courtyard, it was still at least three generations later than the traditional date of the death of Saint Peter. Was there anything earlier? The excavators decided to push down through the floor level of the courtyard.

Directly beneath the marble slab set into the pavement at the point where the *aedicula* joined the Red Wall, the archaeologists discovered what was clearly a grave. A cavity, measuring only 72 cm from side to side and approximately 1.4 m deep, was clearly visible. Several attempts had been made to line this cavity with simple stone walls to protect its sides, but it had still been badly damaged. Innumerable ancient coins from all over Christian Europe lay all around the floor of this space and indicated that a large number of pilgrims had visited this site, dropping coins into the grave through the little rectangular window in the marble slab over it.

Of bones, however, there was at first no sign; the grave seemed to be empty. But when Kirschbaum looked more carefully inside the cavity, he noticed that right at one end, where the grave stretched underneath the Red Wall, there was a small pile of bones. The Vatican excavators summoned the pope immediately, and shortly after the closing of the basilica, Pius XII seated himself on a stool beside the cavity and watched Englebert Kirschbaum slowly hand out the fragments of bone to his colleagues. Most of the fragments were small but some were larger.

Part of a breastbone was handed out, and then half of a shoulder blade. There was no skull. This absence of the remains of Peter's head did not disturb Pius XII or the excavators; on the contrary, it actually confirmed one of the great traditions of the medieval church. All those present, the pope and the excavators, knew that a skull in the basilica of Saint John Lateran since at least the ninth century was widely believed to be that of Peter. Obviously, the skull had been taken from this grave at some stage in the early medieval period to adorn the parish church of the pope himself.

The bones recovered from the niche beneath the *aedicula* were carefully placed in a number of lead-lined boxes and given for formal identification to Pius XII's personal physician, Dottore Galeazzi-Lisi. There was, however, as the team knew very well, no actual indication of the date of this grave. Among the coins of all ages which had covered the floor of the cavity, there were several which were much too early, including one from the reign of Augustus, who had died in A.D. 14, when Peter was only a boy. So the coin evidence could not be conclusive. The excavators turned their attentions to other burials within the vicinity of what they took to be Peter's grave.

Two proved to be particularly important. Two meters below the floor of the courtyard the excavators unearthed a child's grave, which they called Gamma. The small sarcophagus had been placed in a short trench from which, leading to ground level was a narrow lead tube. Pipes of this kind were a common feature of pagan tombs; on the anniversary of the child's death the family of the deceased would gather at the grave and pour a little wine down the tube as an offering to the departed shade. At the point where the pipe emerged from the earth, a crude altar had originally been constructed, again with a pagan cultic purpose, but the makers of the *aedicula* had destroyed most of it in building their own monument. Lastly, the child's grave had a distinctive orientation, slightly off a true west-east axis.

The same orientation was notable in the second important grave, to which the excavators gave the name 'Theta'. This was a much humbler burial. The corpse had been placed in the earth and covered over with brick tiles, leaning together like a roof. Crucially, for the excavations, one of these tiles bore a maker's stamp. It had been manufactured in a Roman workshop during the reign of Vespasian, emperor from A.D. 69 to A.D.79, and well within a generation of Peter's death.

Now when the excavators looked closely at the *aedicula*, and more specifically, when they examined the slab of marble that had been set into the floor of the courtyard where the *aedicula* met the Red Wall, they noticed that it too was slightly off the perpendicular. Its orientation was in fact exactly the same as the early burials Gamma and Theta. Also, when they looked again at the foundations of the Red Wall, they discovered that whoever had constructed it had made a curious rise in the foundations at precisely the point where it met the cavity. It seemed to the excavators that the builders of the Red Wall, who we know carried out the task in the second century, had, during the work of laying the foundations, come across something in the ground which they did not want to disturb. Furthermore, those who placed the marble slab on top of the remains marked by the *aedicula* placed it in line with a body that was not lying perpendicular to the Red Wall. That body was in fact in alignment with the earliest burials at the site, one of which had apparently taken place between A.D. 69 and 79.

To the excavators, the task seemed complete, and their confidence turned to joy several months later when Dr. Galeazzi-Lisi reported back on the remains discovered beneath the *aedicula*. They were the bones of a powerfully built man who had been 65 or 70 years of age at the time of his death. But it is a tribute to the professionalism of the excavators and the caution of Pius XII himself that the pope reported the discoveries to the world in the following terms in his Christmas broadcast on 23rd December 1950:

> Has the tomb of Saint Peter really been found? To that question the answer is beyond all doubt yes. The tomb of the Prince of the Apostles has been found. Such is the final conclusion after all the labor and study of these years. A second question, subordinate to the first, refers to the relics of

Saint Peter. Have they been found? At the side of the tomb remains of human bones have been discovered. However, it is impossible to prove with certainty that they belong to the apostle. This still leaves intact the historical reality of the tomb itself.

One reason for the Pope's caution was the absence of any physical reference to Peter in the vicinity of the *aedicula*. But that evidence arrived in startling circumstances just after the excavators had sent their final report to the Vatican publishers. Antonio Ferrua was visiting the site on his own one evening when he noticed that a piece of plaster from the wall on the right hand side of the shrine had worked itself free from the back of the wall, where it was placed against the crack in the Red Wall. Ferrua looked carefully at the fragment and noticed that some unknown hand had scratched two lines of Greek. On the upper line only the letters pi, epsilon, tau and rho were still visible, while of the lower line only epsilon, nu and part of a vertical line survived. Ferrua, however, with his grounding in Christian epigraphy, immediately restored the missing letters in his mind, so that the short inscription read "Petr[os] en[i]" ("Peter is here within"). He believed that at last, and through a stroke of fate that was almost miraculous, a crucial reference associating Peter with the *aedicula* had been found.

As we saw, Pope Pius XII had been cautious in his Christmas broadcast of 1950 about the identification of the bones found in the space beneath the *aedicula*. Those bones had been entrusted to Dr. Galeazzi-Lisi for examination, and he had identified them as the bones of a powerfully built man who had been 65 or 70 years of age at the time of his death. Dr. Galeazzi-Lisi was no specialist, however, but a general physician. The papal authorities, in the interests of proper scientific procedure, sought a second opinion. The remains were passed on to Venerando Correnti, professor of medical anthropology at the University of Palermo and a well respected anatomist. Subjected to thorough examination throughout the 1950s, the bones conveyed a very different conclusion to Correnti.

They were the remains not of one man, but of three people, one of whom was a woman. She was elderly; Correnti estimated her age at death to be 70–75 years. The men were not quite so aged; both were in their fifties at the time of death; one was robust, but the other was not. And just to complicate matters further, included in the hoard of bones had been animal remains: pieces of cockerel, pig and horse were found.

Elsewhere, skeptics had seized on Antonio Ferrua's "Petros" *graffito*. They did not dispute its existence or the letters that had survived, but they argued for very different restorations of the short text. Some believed that it should be read "Petr[os] en[dei]" or "Petr[ou] end[ei]", meaning "Peter is not here," a notice for those who believed that the body of the apostle was beneath the *aedicula* but were wrong. These skeptics pointed out that the Church of San Sebastiano on the Via Appia had long been associated with Peter and Paul; the name it had borne in antiquity had been the *basilica apostolorum*, the "basilica of the apostles." There were ancient remains beneath this old church, too, and Ferrua's critics argued that this was the site of Peter's burial, not the Vatican.

Thus the conclusions of the Vatican excavators had come under strong attack from medical and epigraphic experts. There was nothing conclusive to indicate that Saint Peter had been buried at the site of the *aedicula* or even that the *aedicula* had ever acted as a focus for any kind of ancient cult associated with Peter.

The introduction of a new expert to the whole investigation, however, opened a fresh chapter in the history of the excavations. Professor Margherita Guarducci held the chair of Greek epigraphy at the University of Rome. Like almost all members of her profession, she had heard of the excavations, and she had read the excavators' report when it first appeared in 1950. She had noted in particular the excavators' discovery of a Christian *graffito* in one of the tombs and the strange wall beside the *aedicula* which the Vatican team had found covered with scratches and names and into which a small recess or *loculus* had been built. In 1953, she was invited to inspect the site of the excavations personally. She was greatly intrigued by what the excavators had called the "Graffiti Wall" and secured permission to make a thorough study of it.

The task was daunting. The plaster was deeply scored, and an impenetrable tangle of names and scratches defied her as it had defied the original excavators. They, in fact, had considered it to be of little importance and had looked into the possibility of demolishing it to gain better access to the *aedicula*. But after months of study, Guarducci solved the extraordinary puzzle of the Graffiti Wall with a brilliant and controversial interpretation. Her results astonished the excavators and swept away the argument of skeptics that the site had no demonstrable connection with Saint Peter.

What Guarducci discovered was that the Graffiti Wall was covered with cryptic symbols linked together to signify spiritual and theological beliefs. Woven around the names of early Christians who had scratched their names on the wall was a complex of significant letters and monograms. *Alpha* and *omega* combinations were present, as references to Christ, but they were also found in reverse order, signifying Christ's role as the gateway to eternal life. *Alpha* and *omega* might also be separated from each other and connected by a thin line. Other letters signified other mysteries: *tau* indicated the cross, *epsilon* stood for Eden and *nu* for "nika," victory. But most important of all, curious combinations of *rho* and *pi* were references to the apostle Peter. Not only did Guarducci uncover the spiritual richness and hunger of those who visited the Graffiti Wall; she revealed that there were no fewer than twenty references to Peter on it.

Guarducci's labors took the best part of five years to complete, and they established a new standard for the investigation of ancient Christian inscriptions. But in the course of her work she made another discovery, and this time it was one that cast a dark cloud over the work of the original excavators.

As we saw earlier, the Vatican team had been put together and placed under the control of Monsignor Ludwig Kaas, the administrator of Saint Peter's basilica. Kaas was not an archaeologist himself, and from the start of the investigations he was not of the same mind as the excavators. They were left to get on with the work, and Kaas did not share the painstaking and difficult labor of excavation. He was, in fact, rather romantically inclined,

and he had expected to see realized the medieval tradition that Saint Peter had been buried in a great bronze coffin. The finds of the excavators disappointed him, and he did not approve of what he thought was their cavalier attitude towards the human remains they exhumed. After only a few months, communications between Kaas and the excavating team all but broke down. The archaeologists rarely met him, and when they did, the meetings were formal reports of progress. Kaas, for his part, took to visiting the scene of the excavations in the evening or early in the morning, when the team had gone home. During these visits, he relied on the knowledge of senior *Sampietrini*, who had been helping the excavators during the day.

In 1953, several months after Kaas had died, Margherita Guarducci was working at the site of the Graffiti Wall when she met Giovanni Segoni, a foreman of the *Sampietrini* and an experienced worker on the site who had shown Kaas around the remains many times. Offhandedly, Guarducci pointed to the *loculus* in the middle of the Graffiti Wall, the *loculus* which the Vatican excavators had said was empty, save for a few chips of bone. She asked him if there really had been nothing else in it. Segoni replied that one evening in 1942, he had been showing Monsignor Kaas around the site just after the wall had been uncovered by the excavators. The team had unearthed the wall and the *loculus* in it, but had not yet investigated it fully. Kaas, however, thought that they had. He ordered Segoni to peep inside the *loculus* to see if anything was there. When Segoni reported that he could see some fragments of bone, Kaas thought that the excavators had uncovered another routine burial which they would treat with scant respect. He told Segoni to empty the *loculus*, and the remains were deposited in a lead-lined box in a room in the Vatican complex. Only several days later did the excavating team return, and no one noticed that the *loculus*, which they had not examined properly, was empty. They reported in their final published account of the excavations that it had held only a few fragments of bone. Segoni knew where these bones were stored, but at the time of his conversation with Guarducci, the bones which the excavators had found beneath the *aedicula* were with Venerando Correnti. Guarducci was reluctant to interfere and waited for the results of Correnti's tests on these bones.

As we saw, however, Correnti's analysis of the bones given to him by Pius XII showed that the remains were not those of a single man but of two men and a woman. When Guarducci learned of these findings, she began to wonder again about the bones Segoni had removed from the *loculus* in 1942. Fortunately, Correnti was a thorough scientist. He had decided to test his conclusions on the *aedicula* bones by comparing them to others found in the vicinity, and he selected those taken from the *loculus*. Guarducci was anxious to draw the attention of the papal authorities to the significance of the *loculus* bones but was aware that by doing so she would be bringing to light an unfortunate mistake in the conduct of the original excavations. While Correnti carried out his experiments on the second collection of bones, Guarducci agonized over the dilemma.

Then, on June 21, 1963, Cardinal Giovanni Battista Montini was elected to the papacy, taking the name Paul VI. He was an old friend of the Guarducci family, and in an audience with him in November 1963 Guarducci finally alerted him to the importance of the *loculus* bones. He immediately gave his blessing to the work of Correnti and told her that the research was very close to his heart.

Through late 1963 and into 1964, Correnti worked on the *loculus* bones. Paul VI gave permission for the alleged head of Peter deposited in the Lateran to be examined as well. The one condition which he laid down was that Correnti was to publish nothing himself; the Vatican would decide when and under what circumstances the final report would appear. That task fell finally to Guarducci herself, who produced a book entitled *The Remains of Saint Peter* in 1965. The manuscript incorporated Correnti's findings and had been given to five leading scholars prior to publication. This book was to be the bedrock upon which Paul VI based his momentous public statement in 1968.

The *loculus* had contained 135 fragments of bone. Most of the fragments were small but several were larger; in particular the left

and right femurs and the left and right tibias had survived basically intact. Fragments of skull were present, and the tests carried out on the Lateran skull showed that it did not come from this body. All areas of the body were present, with the exception of the feet. Most important of all, however, Correnti identified the remains of an elderly man, aged between 60 and 70, of robust stature. The bones also had traces of earth clinging to them, showing that they had once been interred in the ground. When Correnti carried out tests on the soil beneath the *aedicula* it provided a perfect match. And finally, mingling with the bones from the *loculus* were the slightest traces of a distinctive garment: purple in color and containing fine strands of gold thread.

Based on these findings, Guarducci concluded that the bones of Peter had been found. The bones were not complete; the feet were missing. But Guarducci argued that the old Roman tradition of Peter being crucified upside down was accurate. His executors had hacked the body off his cross by severing the legs at the ankles. The remains which Peter's followers received were then interred on the Vatican Hill, which became a sacred place for the Christian community in Rome. At some time in the second century A.D., a proper enclosure was built over Peter's grave, featuring an *aedicula* and a marble slab placed over the remains which preserved the original alignment of the grave. But for some reason it became necessary at a later date to move these remains, perhaps because the area was being flooded. Under Constantine, early in the fourth century, the bones were taken out, wrapped in an expensive purple and gold cloth as a sign of their revered status. A special repository was constructed for them by building a new wall (the Graffiti Wall) and a short inscription was added for the faithful, informing them that Peter's remains were henceforth to be found in the Graffiti Wall.

Guarducci's theory was decisive in securing papal agreement that the bones from the *loculus* were those of the apostle. Paul VI shared his knowledge and his joy with the world on 26 June 1968. On the evening of the 27th, at a ceremony before the *aedicula* attended by the pope and professors Guarducci and Correnti, the bones were restored to the *loculus* in the Graffiti Wall. A short prayer was said, and the shrine to Peter was closed off from the street of tombs by a heavy wrought iron gate.

No one who examines the evidence carefully and dispassionately can accept the statement offered by Paul VI in 1968. The truth is that the papal announcement inhibited further debate. On the one hand, there were those who regarded every utterance of the pope as, by definition, untrue. And on the other hand, many Catholic scholars felt uneasy about contradicting the findings of the Vatican authorities. It is important, however, to keep a sensible perspective on the opinions of Paul VI on this matter:

> ...*while belief in the primacy of the Roman pontiff as Saint Peter's successor is part of the Catholic faith, and while respect is always due from Catholics to the Pope's judgment in all matters, no doctrinal issue whatsoever is involved in so relatively secondary a question as that of the precise site in Rome of Saint Peter's burial.*

Aside from documenting the occasions leading up to the finding of the bones, Professor Curran also puts forth the case that perhaps these bones did not belong to Peter. He asks:

> ...was the humble *loculus* and a hastily scribbled graffito *really* the best a Christian emperor could provide for the prince of the apostles? Constantine's *church* is a better guide to the emperor's intentions, and it focused on the *aedicula*, not the *loculus*. And even if the remains were moved at some later date, why weren't they restored to the *aedicula*?

There was of course a reason why the bones from the *loculus* were never restored to the *aedicula*: they had never been in it in the first place. The soil clinging to the *loculus* bones proves only that they had originally been buried in the vicinity of the *aedicula*, and we know that over two dozen people were. The purple and golden fabric may signify status, but the status need not be that of an apostle; it could be a bishop, or a senator, or a wealthy merchant. And as for the missing feet, the whole area beneath the floor of the courtyard was a confusion of bones. The

loculus bones (probably) belong to someone who was originally buried near the grave of Peter but moved by someone else who took the space. But because the bones were clearly old, this second person deposited them in the wall and still near the apostle.

So where is Peter? The *aedicula* was clearly built over an old grave, and the alignment of this grave with graves *Theta* and *Gamma* suggests that it dates to around the same time: the last third of the first century. In the second century, the Christians of Rome built something grander. But the complex had a flaw; a crack soon developed in the Red Wall, and so in the second or third century the Graffiti Wall was built to support it. On this wall pilgrims scratched very abbreviated, symbolic and perhaps secretive messages (off and on during the second and third centuries there were outbursts of persecution). One of these visitors expressed the immanent presence of Peter in the *aedicula* by writing "Peter is in here." The persecutions came to an end in 312 when Constantine captured Rome, and he marked the site of the burial of Peter by building a huge church over the *aedicula*.

But the excavators basically found the grave of Peter empty; so at some point the remains were moved. If the remains were moved by Christians, then it seems odd that they were never restored; it is possible that the whole body might have been broken up to make relics, but there is no trace of this in the medieval sources. But what if those who moved the bones were not Christians? Rome was sacked twice between the fifth and ninth centuries. On the second occasion, when Saracens broke into the city in 846, pontifical records tell us that they carried out "unspeakable acts" of desecration at the site. As a barbaric act of destruction, they may have opened the grave and destroyed the remains.

But did they really succeed? When the excavators opened the grave, they found that the bones inside had been shoved to one end, into a little space beneath the Red Wall. Someone had made an attempt to protect the relics, although over the course of time the remains of Peter had been invaded by some of the many bones from other burials in the surrounding soil. Peter is (probably) one of the two men whom Correnti identified to the dismay of the excavators in 1960. And is it possible, finally, that the remains of a woman found in Peter's grave were those of his wife?[7]

FURTHER READING: F. Cancellierei, *Memorie storiche delle sacre teste dei SS. Apostoli Pietro e Paola*, Rome, 1806; H. Grisar, "Le teste dei SS Apostoli Pietro e Paolo," in *Civilta Cattolica*, LVIII 1907; E. Kirschbaum, "Die Reliquien der Apostelfursten und ihre Teilungen," in *Xenia Piana*, Rome, 1943; Virgilio Cardinal Noe, *Le Tombe e i Monumenti...*, Rome, 2000.

The casket containing the bones of St. Peter in the *confessio* of St. Peter's basilica. Note open grill doors. By permission of Steven Baldwin.

St. Linus (c. 67–c. 78) Allegedly martyred by Emperor Titus Flavius Domitian and buried September 23, supposedly on Vatican Hill near St. Peter. His sarcophagus was made of either marble, brick, or terracotta and had his name inscribed. In 1615, a burial slab was found near the body of St. Peter with the name "Linus" on it, and since that name is very rare in Christian writings it has been assumed that slab belonged to this Linus. However, there were other letters around "Linus" which meant the name could have actually been *Aquilinus* or *Anullinus*. Linus was venerated as a martyr although there was no known persecution during his time as pope.

Dante puts Linus in Heaven in *Paridiso* 28: 40–42:

The spouse of Christ has never nurtured been
On blood of mine, of Linus and of Cletus
To be made use of in acquest of gold....

The feast day for Linus originally was September 23, but it was suppressed in the Roman Calendar in 1969.

St. Cletus (c. 79–c. 91) Allegedly martyred and possibly buried on Vatican Hill near St. Peter. His sarcophagus would have been made of marble, brick, or terracotta with his name inscribed. It is a matter of debate whether his name is *Anacletus* or *Cletus*. Dante places Cletus in Heaven in *Paridisio* 28: 40–42 (see St. Linus, above). He was allegedly buried on April 26, which is also his feast day.

St. Clement I (c. 91–c. 100) Allegedly drowned with an anchor around his neck in the Black Sea near Crimea. St. Clement refused to offer sacrifice on the order of Emperor Trajan and so was exiled to the marble quarries of the Cherson on the Isle of Crimea (then called Chersonesus Taurica). Because the people in the surrounding villages were converting to Christianity, the governor, who didn't want them to regard Clement as a kind of saint or god, had an anchor tied around Clement's neck and ordered him tossed into the ocean. According to legend, the people prayed and the sea receded two miles, exposing the incorrupt body of Clement in a church "not made by hands." The sea would recede annually for seven days so that the faithful could venerate the saint except during the reign of the Emperor Nicephorus in Constantinople, when the sea did not recede for fifty years.

In 868, when St. Cyril, "guided by Christ," prayed with the people, Clement's relics rose to the surface of the sea at midnight and were translated to the Church of the Holy Apostles. Cyril brought some of Clement's relics back to Rome, where Pope Hadrian II (d. 872) deposited them with the relics of St. Ignatius of Antioch in the high altar of the Basilica of San Clemente on October 26.[8] His head was transferred by the holy Prince Vladimir to the Tithe church of Kiev, where a side-chapel was constructed in Clement's honor.

Today it is possible to go down into the dank subterranean church underneath San Clemente (strongly believed to have been where Clement's house stood) and see the original wall painting showing the body of St. Clement being returned to Rome.

Clement's feast day falls on November 23 in the West, and November 24 or 25 in the East.

FURTHER READING: *Acta SS Mart.*, II, Antwerp, 1668; P. Franchi dei Cavalieri, "La leggenda di S. Clem. Papa e martire," in *Note Agiografiche*, fasc. 5, Studi e Testi 27, Rome 1915; F. Dvornik, *Les legends de Constantin et de Methode vues de Byzance*, Prague, 1933; C. Amati, "Due importanti documenti del sec IX sull'invenzione delle reliquie di S. Clem. in Chersona," in *Not. di Arch., Storia e Arte*, II, 1941.

St. Evaristus (c. 100–c. 109) Allegedly martyred under Emperor Trajan in Rome. Possibly buried on Vatican Hill near St. Peter on October 27. Feast Day: October 26.

St. Alexander I (c. 109–c. 116) Although it was unlikely that he was martyred, legend states that he was beheaded and buried on the Via Nomentana, Rome. Probably the beheading story resulted from confusion with a martyr named Alexander whose tomb was discovered on the Via Nomentana in 1855.

Pope Eugene II (d. 827) brought Alex-

ander's body to the church of Santa Sabina, Rome, and placed it near Sts. Sabina and Seraphia. The basilica of San Pelino at Valva (Sulmona), Italy, however, claims to possess the relics of Alexander in a stone tomb with the following inscription:

HIC ALEXANDRI SVNT OSSA RECONDITA SANCTI / PAPAE QVI PETRO QVINTVS SVCCESSOR HABETVR[9]

("Here are buried the bones of Pope St. Alexander, fifth successor to Peter.")

At the base of the tomb:

NON HIC IN DIVI SED ENIM TRANSLATA PELINI / CONTEGIT ARA RECENS NOMINE STRUCTA SVO / A.D. MDCLXXXX

("[His bones] are not here but indeed have been moved to Peligni where an altar recently built in his name preserves them."—*Trans. Sam Garcia*)

In Peligini the relics are said to be enshrined in an urn under the high altar of the basilica, although the *Catholic Encyclopedia* claims that in 834 his relics were translated to Freising, Bavaria.

Alexander's feast day is May 3, the date of his burial.

FURTHER READING: G. Belvederi, "La basilica e il cimitero di S. Alessandro al VII miglio sulla via Nomentana," in *Riv. di Archeol. Crist*, Rome, XIV, 1937; G. Anichini, "La Memoria Martyrum, al VII miglio della via Nomentana," in *Boll. degli Amici delle Catacombe*, Rome, VII 1937; P. Fumasoni-Biondi, "Ficulea e la basilica cimiteriale di S. Alessandro," in *Roma*, Rome, XXI, 1943.

St. Xystus (Sixtus) I (c. 116–c. 125) Possibly martyred in Alatri, Italy, and allegedly buried near St. Peter on Vatican Hill. During the translation of his body from Rome to Alife, where he was to be buried, the mule carrying the relics stopped in Alatri and refused to go any further. As a result the relics were interred in the Alatri Cathedral, leaving only a finger of the saint for the people of Alife. Legend claims that in 1132, Pope Innocent II, upon the request of the people of

Alife, bestowed Sixtus's remains to them. Papal tomb historian Renzo Montini, however, claims that in 1156 Antipope Anacletus brought the entire body of Sixtus I to the Cathedral of Alatri, although some claim he brought the remains of Sixtus II, not Sixtus I.[10] Yet the historian Butler, in *Lives of the Saints*, claims that Clement X (1670–1676) gave some of the relics of Sixtus I to Cardinal de Retz, who put them in the Abbey of St. Michael in Lorraine, France.

Dante places Sixtus in Heaven in *Paridiso* 28: 43–45:

> But in acquest of this delightful life
> Sixtus and Pius, Urban and Calixtus
> After much lamentation, shed their blood.

Sixtus's feast day falls on April 3, the same day he was buried.

FURTHER READING: L. De Persiis, *Del pontificato di Sisto I e della Traslazione delle sue reliquie da Roma in Alatri*, Alatri, 1881; Igino da Alatri, O.F.M. Cap., *Alatri e il suo celeste Patrono S. Sisto I Papa e Martire*, Veroli, 1932; O. Jozzi, *Il corpo di Sisto I Papa e Martire rivendicato alla Basilica Vaticana*, Rome, 1900.

St. Telesphorus   (c. 125–c. 136) Martyred ("bore witness gloriously") by either Emporer Antonius Pius or (more likely) Emperor Hadrian. He was the only second century pope whose martyrdom is confirmed. He was allegedly buried near St. Peter at Vatican Hill on January 2, although his feast day is January 5 in the West, February 22 in the East.

St. Hyginus   (c. 138–c. 142) Possibly martyred and buried near St. Peter on January 11, which is also his feast day.

St. Pius I   (c. 142–c. 155) Possibly but unlikely martyred and allegedly buried July 11 (also his feast day) on Vatican Hill near St. Peter. He was first mentioned as a martyr in the martyrology of Ado of Vienne, which was composed in 858. Dante places Pius in Heaven in *Paradiso* 28: 43–45:

> But in acquest of this delightful life
> Sixtus and Pius, Urban and Calixtus
> After much lamentation, shed their blood.

St. Anicetus   (c. 155–c. 166) Allegedly martyred and buried near the tomb of St. Peter, although the *Liber Pontificalis* states he was originally buried in the Cemetery of Callixtus on either April 16, April 17 (his feast day), or April 20. In 1604, the urn (once used as a sepulcher for Alexander Severius) containing Anicetus's remains was placed in the sarcophagus below the altar in the chapel of the Altemps Palace (in the Piazza Navona) by Pope Clement VIII (1592–1605), who also placed an epitaph there[11]:

MARTYRIS OSSA ANICETI PAPAE / AB ARENARIO
QVOD POSTEA CALLISTI / COEMETERIVM
APPELLATVM EST / AVCTORITATE CLEMENTIS VIII
TRANSLATA / IOANNES ANGELVS AB ALTEMPS DVX /
SACELLVM OBTVLIT / CORPVS EIVSDEM MARTYRIS /
IN LABRVM QVOD ALEXANDRI SEVERI IMP. /
SEPVLCHRVM FVIT COLLOCAVIT D. / ANNO
DOMINI M.D.C. XVII

("[Here are] the bones of pope and martyr Anicetus, moved by the authority of Clement VIII from the sand-pit later called the cemetery of Callixtus. Joannes Angelus, leader from another time, dedicated a chapel and placed the body of this martyr in this trench, formerly the sepulcher of emperor Alexander Severus. D.1617." — *Trans. Sam Garcia*)

FURTHER READING: *Vita S. Aniceti Papae et Martyris a Joanne Angelo Duca ab Altemps colleta*, Rome, 1617, Moroni, II.

St. Soter   (c. 166–c. 174) Possibly martyred and originally buried near the Cemetery of Callixtus, Rome, on April 22, although his body may have been confused with a martyr of the same name who was buried in the Cemetery of Callixtus in 304.[12] It was also rumored that his remains were moved to the Church of St. Silvester, then to the Church of St. Sixtus, although it is thought that some of his remains ended up in Toledo, Spain. Whatever the case, what were thought to be his remains were translated to under the altar of San Martino ai Monte by Sergius II (844–847) to save them from the invading Lombards. Feast day: April 22.

St. Eleutherius

St. Eleutherius (c. 174–189) Legend states that he was martyred by being dragged by horses and burned over a grill while Emperor Commodus watched. He was either buried near the tomb of St. Peter on May 24 or buried in San Giovanni della Pigna on a date unknown. His relics were eventually translated to Santa Susanna (the American Church of Rome) in 1591 by Camilla Peretti, the sister of Pope Sixtus V. He was first mentioned in the martyrology of Ado of Vienne (composed in 858). Feast day: May 26.

St. Victor I (189–198) Possibly martyred and buried near St. Peter on Vatican Hill on July 28, which became his feast day.

St. Zephyrinus (198 or 199–217) Possibly martyred, and the first pope to be buried (August 25) in the Cemetery of Callixtus on the Appian Way, Rome, although in a sepulchral chamber separate from the Crypt of the Popes. He was allegedly transferred to the Church of San Silvestro in Capite in the ninth century to protect his remains against the invading Lombards. His feast day was kept on August 26 until 1969, when it was suspended.

FURTHER READING: A. Ferrua, "Iuxta cymiterium Calisti," in *Rendic. Della Pont. Acc. Rom. di Archeologia*, serie III, XX 1944; De Rossi, *Roma sotterranea*, II, Rome, 1867; Marucchi, "La questione del sepolcro del papa Z. e del martire Tarsicio," in sequito ad un'ultima scoperta, in *Nuovo Bull. Arch. Crist.*, XVI 1910.

St. Callixtus I (217–222) Drowned in a well on orders of the Emperor Alexander in the Trastevere section of Rome. According to *The Golden Legend* (fantastic stories of the early saints), Callixtus had been captured by Emperor Alexander and ended up baptizing his guards whom Alexander then beheaded. The emperor kept Callixtus for five days without food or water, but the saint only became stronger despite the fact that he was flogged every day, thrown from a window, then finally chained to a large stone and dropped down a well on August 25. The priest Asterius raised his body from the well shortly afterward and interred him in the Cemetery of Calepodius on the Via Aurelia because the emperor's guards had the papal crypts under surveillance (although it is possible that he had laid out his own burial place there). In the eighth century the Church of San Callixtus was built over the well to mark his place of martyrdom. The well is still preserved in the church, although the church itself has been closed to the public for some time.

Despite the fact that his name appears in a fourth century calendar of martyrs, it is unlikely that Callixtus died a martyr in the strict sense of the word because there were no persecutions under Alexander Severus.

In the fourth century, Pope Julius I (337–352) erected a proper tomb for him in the Cemetery of Calepodius. He had the tomb decorated with frescoes showing Callixtus's martyrdom. This tomb location was discovered in 1960, although without his bodily relics; these had been translated in 790 by Pope Hadrian I to Santa Maria Trastevere, Rome, to protect them from the Lombard invasions.

Dante places Callixtus in Heaven in Paridisio. 28: 43–45:

> But in acquest of this delightful life
> Sixtus and Pius, Urban and Calixtus
> After much lamentation, shed their blood.

Callixtus's feast day is October 14.

FURTHER READING: A. Silvagni, "La topgrafia cimiteriale della via Aurelia," in *Miscellanea citta di Roma*, II, Rome, 1942; E. Josi, "Note di Aurelia," in *Miscellanea G. Belvederi*, C.d. V. 1954–55.

Antipope St. Hippolytus (c. 217–c. 235) Died in exile on Sardinia, the "Isle of Death," from harsh conditions imposed on him by Emperor Maximinius Thrax. The historian Prudentius wrote a hymn entitled "Peristephanon" in which he places the scene of the martyrdom at Ostia or Porto, and describes Hippolytus as being torn to pieces by wild horses, a scene evidently drawn from stories of the ancient Hippolytus, son of Theseus.[13]

Although an antipope, Hippolytus is considered "reconciled" with the church because Pope Fabian, his rival, brought his remains back to Rome and had them solemnly interred in the Cemetery of Hippolytus on August 13, in either 236 or 237. Orazio Marucchi's *Christian Epigraphy* records the following inscription written by Pope Damasus (d. 384) in his honor:

HYPPOLYTVS FERTVR PREMERENT CVM
IVSSA TYRANNI / PRESBYTER IN SCISMA SEMPER
MANSISSE NOVATI / TEMPORE QVO GLADIVS SECVIT
PIA VISCERA MATRIS / DEVOTVS CHRISTO PETERET
CVM REGNA PIORVM / QVAESISSET POPVLVS
VBINAM PROCEDERE POSSET / CATHOLICAM
DIXISSE FIDEM SEQVERENTVR VT OMNES / SIC
NOSTER MERVIT CONFESSVS MARTYR VT ESSET /
HAEC AVDITA REFERT DAMASVS PROBAT
OMNIA CHRISTVS

("Hippolytus is said, while the commands of the tyrant pressed hard upon us, to have ever remained as a presbyter in the schism of Novatus. At the time when the sword severed the holy flesh of our mother, when, devoted to Christ, he was seeking the kingdoms of the just, and the people had asked him where they should proceed, he is said to have replied that they should all follow the Catholic faith. Thus, having made his confession, he deserves to be our martyr. Damasus reports these things which he has heard: Christ proves all things."— *Trans. Orazio Marucchi*)

Hippolytus's feast day is June 30 in the East and August 13 in the West.

St. Urban I (222–30) Possibly martyred by beheading and buried in the Cemetery of Callixtus (the Urban listed as buried in the catacomb of Praetextatus is a bishop of another city who died at a later time[14]). Because it is unclear whether Pope Urban's remains were later transferred to the crypt of the popes in the Cemetery of Callixtus, there is debate as to whether the slab containing the Greek words OYPBANOC E[pivskopoV] ("Urban, Bishop") belongs to the Pope Urban or the other Bishop Urban.

According to *The Golden Legend* (fantastic stories of the early saints), Urban was found hiding in a cave by the emperor's general Carpasius, who brought him before the Emperor Alexander, who had him imprisoned and lashed with lead-studded whips. When Urban spat on an idol that he was being forced to pray to, the idol fell over and crushed 22 pagan priests. He was then beheaded immediately, after which Carpasius was seized by a demon and strangled despite his desperate attempt to suddenly disavow his pagan beliefs. Urban was buried by St. Tiburtius.

Another story of Urban's death is that he was killed by the prefect Almenius, and that his body was recovered by the emperor's mother and buried in the Cemetery of Callixtus. (Rendina, p. 29)

Urban's feast day in the sarum missal and other medieval English calendars was May 25, and so it continued until 1969, when it was suppressed.

Dante places Urban in Heaven in *Paradisio*. 28: 43–45:

But in acquest of this delightful life
Sixtus and Pius, Urban and Calixtus
After much lamentation, shed their blood.

FURTHER READING: C. Cecchelli, *La Chiesa delle catacombe*, Rome, 1943; G. Wilpert, *La Cripta dei Papi nel cimitero di Callisto*, Rome, 1910.

St. Pontianus (July 21, 230–September 235). Died from exposure and beatings on Sardinia, the "Isle of Death." He had abdicated the papacy on September 28, 235, and died with Antipope Hippolytus. His body was brought back by Pope St. Fabian in 237 and was buried in the papal crypt in the catacombs of St. Callixtus on November 12. In 1909, fragments of the grave slab were found engraved in Greek letters ΠONTIANOC EIII M[αρτυ]ρ (Pontianus Bi[shop] M[arty]r). An engraving in front of the papal crypt read: ΕΝΘΕΩ ΜΕΤΑ ΠΑΝΤΩΝ [αγιων 'Επισχοπων] ΠONTIANE ZHCHC "Mayest thou live, Pontianus, in God with all." His feast day is now celebrated on August 13 along with that of St. Hippolytus.

FURTHER READING: Marucchi, "Osservazioni sull'iscrizione del papa Ponziano recentemente scoperta e su quelle degli altri papi del III secolo," in *Nuovo Bull. Arch. Crist.*, XV 1909.

St. Anterus

St. Anterus (November 21, 235–January 3, 236) The *Liber Pontificalis* claims that "because of a certain priest Maximus he was crowned with martyrdom" as a result of his causing the acts of the martyrs to be collected by notaries and deposited in the archives of the Roman Church. More likely he died from natural causes as his name was not included on early martyr lists. The more reliable fourth-century *Liberian Catalogue* says that St. Anterus "fell asleep in the Lord" (an expression used for popes meaning that they died a natural death). He was the first pope to be buried (allegedly on January 3) in the exclusive papal crypt of the Cemetery of Callixtus, Rome. His slab inscription reads, in Greek letters, ANΘΕΡΩC EIII. ("Anterus, Bishop.") The inscription was broken and so it is supposed that the missing portion told of his martyrdom. The site of his sepulcher was discovered by famed archeologist Giovanni Battista de Rossi in 1854, although his relics had been translated for protection to under the high altar at the Church of San Silvestre in Capite, Rome, during the Lombard invasions of the ninth century. Feast day: January 3.

St. Fabian

St. Fabian (January 10, 236–January 20, 250) Beheaded. He was the first pope to die under the reign of Emperor Decius. His original tomb location was discovered by the famous archeologist of Rome, Giovanni Battista de Rossi, in 1854 in the papal crypt in the Cemetery of Callixtus. The *Liber Pontificalis* (the *Book of Pontiffs*) claims that his body was placed by Sergius II (844–847) under the altar at San Martino ai Monte for protection during the Lombard invasions of the ninth century. Church historian Petrus Mallius, however, claims that Fabian's remains are in a sepulcher at Saint Peter's with those of Pope St. Sixtus II. In 1915 a sarcophagus bearing the inscription ΦABIANOC EIII MP ("Phabianos Bi[shop] M[arty]r"; "Fabian, Bishop and Martyr"), and containing the remains of St. Fabian, was found in the Church of San Sebastiano in Rome. Burial and feast day: January 20.

FURTHER READING: F. Grossi-Gondi, *Fabiano papa e matire: la sua tomba e le sue spoglie attraverso I secoli*, Rome, 1916.

St. Cornelius

St. Cornelius (March 251–June 253) Beheaded. He had been exiled to Centumcellae (modern-day Civitavecchia; the port of Rome) by the Emperor Decius, who ordered that the saint's mouth be beaten with lead-weighted lashes. Cornelius was then brought to the Temple of Mars, where he was to make a sacrifice to the god Mars. A soldier at the temple asked Cornelius to pray for his paralyzed wife, which he did, and she was healed. Upon seeing the miracle all of the soldiers immediately converted to Christianity, but as a result, all (along with Cornelius) were beheaded at the Temple of Mars. The Roman matron Lucina, along with the clergy, retrieved the saint's body at night and buried him in the crypt of Lucina, close to the Cemetery of Callixtus. In 1849, the archeologist Giovanni Battista de Rossi found a fragment of a marble slab with the letters "...ELIVS MARTYR" on the Appian Way. In March of 1852 a crypt was discovered on the border of the Appian Way that contained the missing fragments of Cornelius' inscription: "CORNELIUS MARTYR EP [iscopus]." He had been buried here instead of in the Crypt of the Popes in the Cemetery of San Callixtus because Lucina's property contained the Cornelius family vault, and his family wanted the prestige of a pope in their vault.

Cornelius's papal inscription was the first in Latin, another acknowledgment by his family that he came from an old and noble line of the Roman Republic. Pope Damasus wrote an epitaph in the saint's honor (lowercase letters are reconstructions by de Rossi and recorded by Orazio Marucchi, *Christian Epigraphy*):

Aspice descensu extrucTO TENEBrisQue FVGATIS / Corneli monumenta vides tVMVLVmque SACRATVM / hoc opus aegroti DaMASI PRaesTANTIA FECIT / esset ut accessus meliOR POPVLISQ PARATVM / auxilium sancti et VALEAS SI FVNDERE PVRO / corde preces Damasus MELIOR CONSVRGERE POSSET / quem non lucis amOR TENVIT MAGE CVRA LABORIS

("Behold now that a way of descent has been made and the darkness put to flight, you see the monument of Cornelius and his consecrated grave. The watchful care of Damasus in his sickness has completed this work, that there might be a better mode of access, and that the help of the saint might be procured for the people, and that if you prevail to pour forth prayers from a pure heart, Damasus may rise stronger, though it is not love of light that keeps him here, but rather care for his work." — *Trans. Orazio Marucchi*)

The fourth century *Liberian Catalogue* claims that Cornelius "died gloriously" (a term often used to describe a martyrdom), yet he was not regarded as a martyr and was not listed in the fourth century *Deposito Martyrum*. His remains were allegedly translated to Santa Maria Trastevere during the Lombard invasions of the ninth century. Feast day: September 16.

FURTHER READING: Wilpert, *Die rom. Mosaiken und Malereien etc.*, Freiburg, 1917; Styger, *Rom. Martyrergrufte*; Franchi dei Cavalieri, "La persecuzione di Gallo in Roma," in *Note agiografiche*, fasc. VI, S. and T. 33, Rome, 1920.

Antipope Novation (March 251–258) Possibly martyred at age 58. Novation had himself proclaimed pope when Cornelius was elected but was not popular because he wished to excommunicate all Christians who lapsed during the persecutions (while Cornelius simply reinstated them). The fifth century *Martyrology of Jerome* mentions a Novation among the martyrs, and in 1932 a tombstone was discovered on the Via Tiburtina in Rome with an inscription to the "blessed martyr Novation." The inscription, however, lacks the word "bishop," making it difficult to verify as the inscription for this antipope.

In this small chapel in the crypt of Santa Cecilia in Trastevere, Rome, the sarcophagus of St. Lucius I is the middle of three sarcophagi placed behind the altar screen shown here.

St. Lucius I (June 25, 253–March 5, 254) The *Liber Pontificalis* (*Book of Pontiffs*) claims he was beheaded, although the more reliable

Liberian Catalogue attributes his death to natural causes. Lucius's body was buried in the papal crypt in the cemetery of Callixtus with the inscription "Lucius, Bishop" (written in Greek: ΛΟΥΚΙΣ). His body was translated to Santa Cecilia in Trastevere in the ninth century (to protect his remains from the invading Lombards) and interred behind an altar in a small chapel in the dank yet fascinating area beneath the church, along with St. Cecilia. (To get to this chapel, you must request the assistance of a nun or sacristan, who will either hand you the key or unlock the iron-grated door for you.) The *Catholic Encyclopedia* states that relics of St. Lucius were brought to the Church of San Silvestro in Capite by Pope Paul I (757–767), or to the Basilica of St. Praxedes by Pope Paschal I (817–824). There are inscriptions in both churches claiming that Lucius is there. Feast day: August 2.

St. Stephen I (May 12, 254–August 2, 257) Probably died a natural death, although the *Liber Pontificalis* (*Book of Pontiffs*) claims he was beheaded under the rule of Valerianus and thus treats him as a martyr. The *Roman Calendar of 354*, however, lists him simply as a deceased bishop, not a martyr. Buried first in the papal crypt in the Cemetery of Callixtus, his body was transferred by Sergius II (844–847) to under the altar of San Silvestre in Capite, Rome. (There was a rumor, however, that Stephen's body was transferred by Paul I in 762 to the oraculum, where it was put on display.) In 1160 it was moved to Santa Maria Colonna; finally in 1682 it was moved by the grand duke of Tuscany, Cosimo III, to the Cavalieri in Pisa, where he is still venerated.[15]

FURTHER READING: G.C. Guarnieri, *Cavalieri di S. Stefano*, Pisa, 1928.

St. Xystus (Sixtus) II (August 257–August 6, 258) Beheaded at the Cemetery of Praetextatus, Rome. He had been celebrating mass in the Cemetery of Praetextatus

(because it was usually not watched by the police) when he was caught and beheaded by Emperor Valarian's men. Six of his deacons who were with him (Felicissimus, Agapitus, Januarius, Magnus, Vincent, and Stephen) were also beheaded. The bloodied chair Sixtus had been sitting in when he was martyred was placed in the chapel of the Cemetery of Callixtus. Inscription on *loculi* in the Cemetery of Callixtus: XYSTI PON ("Sixtus, Pope").

The Golden Legend (fantastic stories of early saints), however, claims that Sixtus had been arrested and was en route to a location where he was going to be forced to sacrifice to the god Mars. His friends saw him and called out to the soldiers, saying that they had already given all of his possessions and money away. Hearing that, and realizing that they wouldn't be getting any spoils, the soldiers decided it wasn't worth going through the formalities of sacrifice and beheaded him where he stood.

Pope Paschal I (d. 824) moved the saint's body to an oratory in St. Peter's, just in front (to the east) of the southern part of the entrance screen to the *confessio*, which was dedicated to both Sixtus II and Pope Saint Fabian (236–250). Sixtus's relics were translated in the ninth century by Leo IV (d. 855) to San Sisto Vecchio in Rome. This church is normally closed to the public but the sisters of the attached convent sometimes allow visitors to enter and see the inscription to the martyrs, which is located at the back of the church on the left side of the nave. The following epitaph, which hung in the Cemetery of Callixtus, was written in metrics by Pope Damasus (366–384) for Sixtus II:

TEMPORE QVO GLADIVS SECVIT PIA VISCERA MATRIS / HIC POSITVS RECTOR CAELESTIA IVSSA DOCEBAM / ADVENIVNT SVBITO RAPIVNT QVI FORTE SEDENTEM / MILITIBVS MISSIS POPVLI TVNC COLLA DEDERE / MOX VBI COGNOVIT SENIOR QVIS TOLLERE VELLET / PALMAM SEQVE SVVMQVE CAPVT PRIOR OBTVLIT IPSE / IMPATIENS FERITAS POSSET NE LAEDERE QVEMQVAM / OSTENDIT CHRISTVS REDDIT QVI PRAEMIA VITAE / PASTORIS MERITVM NVMERVM GREGIS IPSE TVETVR[16]

("At the time when the sword severed the holy flesh of our mother, I, the ruler, seated here was teaching the divine laws. Those come suddenly who are to seize me on my throne. Then the people offered their necks to the soldiers who were sent. But when the elder knew who wished to bear away the palm, he offered himself and his life first of all of his own accord, lest their impatient fury should injure anyone. Christ who awards the prize of life shows the merits of the shepherd: He himself keeps safe the number of the flock."[17])

The feast day of Sixtus II is August 6.

St. Dionysius (July 22, 260–December 26, 268) Unknown cause of death, but not martyred, as the *Liber Pontificalis* (the *Book of Pontiffs*) claims. His identity was confused with several Roman martyrs of the same name. The *Roman Calendar of 354* includes him in the list of Episcopal burials, but not of martyrs. He was buried in the papal crypt of the Cemetery of Callixtus on December 27 although no trace of a tomb or monument has been found. In the ninth century his relics were allegedly translated to San Silvestre in Capite, Rome, to protect them from the invading Lombards. Feast day: December 26.

St. Felix I (January 3, 269–December 30, 274). According to the *Liber Pontificalis* (*Book of Pontiffs*) he was decapitated as a martyr, but there is no proof of his martyrdom. He was buried in the papal crypt in the Cemetery of Callixtus on May 30. Legend claims that he may be buried with Pope Felix III (II) in the "Cemetery of the Two Felixes," although the exact location of this cemetery is unknown. The *Roman Calendar of 354* includes him in a list of Episcopal burials, not of martyrs. Feast day: May 30.

FURTHER READING: Kirsch, *Le memorie dei martiri sulle vie Aurelia e Cornelia*; Silvagni, *Topografia cimiteriale*.

St. Eutychian (January 4, 275–December 7, 283) Unknown cause of death, though not martyred as claimed in the *Liber Pontificalis* (*Book of Pontiffs*). He was the last pope to be buried in the papal crypt in the Cemetery of Callixtus. His inscription was written in Greek on a marble slab: EYTYX-IANOC EIIIC ("Eutychian, Bishop"). Because he was a native of Luni, Italy, his remains were translated to the Abbey of Luni in Sarzana in 1659, although his bones were translated to under the main altar in the Sarzana Cathedral in Italy.[18] Feast day: December 8.

St. Caius (Gaius) (December 7, 283–April 22, 296) Buried near the crypt of St. Eusebius, in the Cemetery of Callixtus (not in the papal crypts as stated in the old *Catholic Encyclopedia*), on April 22. The tomb inscription was written in fine Greek marble with unusually large letters:

Ι [ΑΙΟ]Υ ΕΙΙΙ[ϹΚΟΠΟΥ] / ΚΑΘ /
[ΠΡΟ Ι] ΚΑΛ ΜΑΙΩ[Ν]

("The deposition of Caius, Bishop, the 22nd day of April."[19])

His relics were translated to San Silvestre in Capite in the ninth century to protect them from the Lombard invasions. In 1631 his remains were placed under the main altar in the church that had been built over his original house, but when that house was demolished in 1881 his remains were transferred to the private chapel of the Barberini princes, Rome. Feast day: April 22.

FURTHER READING: G. Schneider-Graziosi, "Osservazioni sopra la triplice deposizione del papa Gaio nel cimitero di Callisto," in *Nuovo Bull. Di Archeol. Crist.*, XIII, 1907.

St. Marcellinus (June 30, 296–304[?]; d. October 25, 304). Allegedly beheaded during the persecution of Diocletian. According to the *Liber Pontificalis* (*Book of Pontiffs*) Marcellinus was forced to offer incense to pagan gods. He made the offering but afterwards repented and refused to further worship the idols. He was therefore beheaded, and his body lay in the street for 25 days to serve as an example to other Christians. The next pope, Marcellus (there is debate as to whether Marcellinus and Marcellus are actually the same person), acquired the body and buried it in the Cemetery of Priscilla (then the private property of Acilii Glabrioni) on the Via Salaria because the Cemetery of Callixtus had been confiscated by the emperor. The *Catholic Encyclopedia*, however, claims that Marcellinus probably died a natural death because no "trustworthy" sources of the fourth or fifth century list him as a martyr, nor did the church historian Eusebius. Feast day: June 2.

St. Marcellus I (November or December 306–January 16, 308). Allegedly died from overworking in a stable. The *Liber Pontificalis* (*Book of Pontiffs*) claims that the widow Lucina opened her house as a church to the saint, but Emperor Maxentius heard about this and arrested Marcellus at the house (although there is debate as to whether the previous pope Marcellinus and Marcellus are actually the same person). The emperor then turned the house into a barn and forced Marcellus (who wore only a hair shirt) to work "in servitude to the animals" until he died of exhaustion. The Church of San Marcello is believed to be built over the stable, although the *Oxford Dictionary of Popes* claims that Maxentius banished Marcellus to an unknown location for being a "disturber of the peace." He was buried on January 16 in the Cemetery of Priscilla, Rome. His remains were translated to under the main altar in the basilica of San Silvestro in Capite, Rome, probably in the ninth century to protect them from the invading Lombards. Pope Damasus wrote an inscription in the saint's honor that was found in the Cemetery of Priscilla:

VERIDICVS RECTOR LABSOS QVIA CRIMINA
FLERE / PRAEDIXIT MISERIS FVIT OMNIBVS
HOSTIS AMARVS / HINC FVROR HINC ODIVM

SEQVITVR DISCORDIA LITES / SEDITIO CAEDES
SOLVVNTVR FOEDERA PACIS / CRIMEN OB
ALTERIVS CHRISTVM QVI IN PACE NEGAVIT /
FINIBVS EXPVLSVS PATRIAE EST FERITATE
TYRANNI / HAEC BREVITER DAMASVS VOLVIT
COMPERTA REFERRE / MARCELLI VT
POPVLVS MERITVM COGNOSCERE POSSIT[20]

("The truth-telling ruler, because he commanded the lapsed to weep for their crimes, became a bitter enemy to all these unhappy men. Hence followed rage and hate, discord and strife, sedition and slaughter. The bonds of peace are loosed. On account of the crimes of another who denied Christ in time of peace, he was driven from the borders of his fatherland by the cruelty of the tyrant. Damasus wishes to tell these things which he has found out briefly, that the people may know the merit of Marcellus."[21])

The feast day of Marcellus I is January 16.

FURTHER READING: Marucchi, "La iscrizione del papa M.," in *Nuovo Bull. di Archeol. Crist.*, XIV 1908.

St. Eusebius (April 18–October 21, 310). Died of unknown causes (probably harsh treatment) while in exile on the island of Sicily. Emperor Maxentius had exiled Eusebius to Sicily because of the tension in Rome about lapsed Christians. His catacomb in the Cemetery of Callixtus was discovered in 1873, with an inscription written in Greek: "Eusebius of blessed memory died in peace on the eleventh day before the Kalends of September."[22] His epitaph by Pope Damasus reads:

DAMASVS EPISCOPVS FECIT / HERACLIVS
VETVIT LABSOS PECCATA DOLERE / EVSEBIVS
MISEROS DOCVIT SVA CRIMINA FLERE /
SCINDITVR IN PARTES POPVLVS GLISCENTE
FVRORE / SEDITIO CAEDES BELLVM DISCORDIA
LITES / EXTEMPLO PARITER PVLSI FERITATE
TYRANNI / INTEGRA CVM RECTOR SERVARET
FOEDERA PACIS / PERTVLIT EXILIVM DOMINO
SVB IVDICE LAETVS / LITORE TRINACRIO
MVNDVM VITAMQVE RELIQVIT / EVSEBIO
EPISCOPO ET MARTYRI[23]

("Damasus the Bishop made this. Heraclius forbade the lapsed to weep for their sins; Eusebius taught the unhappy men to mourn for their crimes. The people are divided into parties, as the madness grew — sedition, slaughter, war, discord, strife. Suddenly both were driven out by the cruelty of the tyrant, and since the ruler had kept the bonds of peace inviolate, he gladly endured exile under the judgment of the Lord, and left this world and his life on the Trinacrian shore. To Eusebius Bishop and Martyr."[24])

In two vertical lines on either side of the Damasan inscription, the writer (most likely the secretary of Pope Damasus) put his own name and an expression of affection for Pope Damasus. On the left side:

FVRIVS DIONYSIVS / FILOCALVS SCRIBSIT

("Furius Dionysius Filocalus wrote this.")

On the right:

DAMASI / SVI PAPAE CVLTOR ATQVE AMATOR.[25]

("Devotee and friend of his pope, Damasus.")

Eusebius was buried on October 12. His feast day is August 17.

FURTHER READING: I. Carini, "Le catacombe di S. Giovanni in Siracusa e le memorie del papa E.," in *Dissertaz. della Pont. Acc. Roma di Archeol.*, Rome, II 1890.

St. Miltiades (July 2, 311–January 10, 314).

Buried in an enormous sarcophagus with a massive roof-shaped cover, Militiades was the only pope interred at the Cemetery of Callixtus during the "long peace." His remains are listed as having been translated to San Silvestre in Capite, probably to protect them from the invading Lombards in the ninth century. Feast day: December 10.

FURTHER READING: G. Schneider-Graziosi, "Studio … sulla tomba del papa M.," in *Nuovo Bull di Arch crist*, XX (1914).

St. Silvester I (January 31, 314–December 31, 335).

Silvester I was originally buried in the basilica of San Silvestro (which was built over the Cemetery of Priscilla) on December 31, although he is listed as having been transferred to San Silvestre in Capite, where his body was put on display in the oraculum and then possibly buried in St. Peter's. Yet the *Liber Pontificalis* (*Book of Pontiffs*) says that Sergius II (d. 847) moved Silvester's body to under the altar in San

The sarcophagus of St. Silvester I, Abbey of Nonantola.

Martino ai Monte from the Cemetery of Priscilla. Papal historian H.K. Mann claims that the marble sarcophagus was "wonderfully bound round with iron and lead" and located near the angle of the south transept, near the *confessio* of St. Peter. When the sarcophagus was opened during the demolition of Old St. Peter's in the early seventeenth century, a body was found dressed in papal vestments, but there was no documentation to indicate who it was, and so the sarcophagus and body were moved to the east end of St. Peter's. Mann also claims that the sarcophagus and body are now missing, but this is untrue; the white marble sarcophagus of Silvester I is in the crypt of the Abbey of Nonantola, in Nonanatola, Italy. It rests under a window behind the altar that contains the remains of Pope Hadrian III (d. 885) as well as Saints Senesio, Teopompo, Anserida, and Fosca.[26]

Original epitaph on sarcophagus:

D. O. M. / MONVMENTVM HOC IN QVO / B. SILVESTRI CORPVS QVIESCIT / GVIDO PEPVLVS COMES / TEST. FACIENDVM MAND. ANN. M D V / IOANNES ET CORNEL. EX PHILIPPO / SICIN. ET FAB. EX HIER. ET RQ. EX ALB. / PIAM AVI PATERNI VOLVNT. AMPLIAM / SVNT EXEQVVTI AN. SA. M D LXXXII / ABB. GVID. FERRERIO S.R.E. CARD. VERC. / PONT. MAX. GREGORIO XIII

(*The numerous abbreviations in this epitaph make it impossible to determine exactly which Latin words were intended. The sense of the epitaph is that the body of Silvester was placed at the command of Count Guido Pepulo in 1505 and was redone in 1482 by Cardinal Guido Ferrerio, in the pontificate of Gregory XIII.— Phyllis Jestice*)

Added inscription on original sarcophagus:

QUESTA ARCA HA CONSERVATO DAL 756 AL 1914 / LE SACRE SPOGLIE MORTALI / DI S. SILVESTRO PAPA / PROTETTORE DI NONATOLA

("From 756 to 1914 this tomb preserved the blessed mortal remains of Pope St. Silvester, Protector of Nonantola."—*Trans. Phyllis Jestice*)

Inscription to Pope St. Silvester in the Church of San Silvestro in Capite, Rome:

EX LAMINA PLVMB. SVB CAPITE B. SYVE. / REPERTA GVIDO FERRER S.R.E. CARD. / VERCELL. VERBA HAEC EXEMPLARI MAND. / ANN. M D LXXXII / HIC REQVIESCIT CORPVS B. SYLVE. / SVM. PONT. CVIVS PRAECIB. DEO CREDITIT / CONSTANT. IMP. MAGNIFICVS DELATVM / AB ANSEL. ABB. P. NONANT. ET AB / AVSTVLFO REGE ITALORVM ET AB ADRIANo / PP CONCESS. / ANN 753 DIE 20 MENS. NOVEMB.[27]

("From the lead plate under the head of blessed Silvester. Discovered by Guido Ferrerio, cardinal of the holy Roman Church. He commanded that this copy of the inscription be made in the year 1582. Here rests the body of Blessed Silvester, highest pontiff, whom Emperor Constantine, believing God's command, magnificently reported by Anselm, abbot of Nonantola, and by Austulf, king of the Italians, and by Hadrian, accepted as father of the fatherland. 20th of November, in the year 753."— *Trans. Phyllis Jestice*)

Papal tomb historian Renzo Montini, in *Le Tombe dei Papi*,[28] asserts that Silvester's remains were placed in an altar dedicated to him, which was located at the inner wall of the south transept of St. Peter's. Montini claims that the remains of Pope Vigilius (d. 557) and Pope Hadrian IV (d. 1159) were also placed in the altar with the following inscription:

ALTARE SANCTI SILVESTRI PAPAE-UBI VIGILII ET ADRIANI IV SEPULCRA

("Altar of Pope Saint Silvester with the sepulcher of Vigilius and Adrian IV."[29])

FURTHER READING: T. F., "La tomba di san S.," in *Boll. Degli Amici delle Catacombe*, Rome, V (1935).

St. Mark (January 18–October 7, 336). Originally Mark was buried in the Cemetery of Balbina in the church that he founded there. In 1145, however, his remains were translated and put in a porphyry urn located under the high altar in the Church of San Marco (probably originally his house which he converted into a church), which is now part of the Palazzo di Venezia in Rome. The historian Duchesne claims that because the inscription on the urn is very general and never mentions the name of "Mark," it may not belong to Pope St. Mark as archeologist Giovanni Battista de Rossi claims.

Pope Damasus (366–384) wrote an epitaph in Mark's honor:

Insons VITA FVIT MARCI QVAM NOVIMVS OMNES /
    Plenus amORE DEI POSSET QVI TEMNERE
MVNDVM / Actis monSTRAVIT POPVLVS QVOD
    DISCERET OMNIS / Parvus HONOR VITAE
GRANDIS CONTEMPTVS HABENDI / Intima sed
    VIRTVS TENVIT PENETRALIA CORDIS /
IustITIAE CVSTOS CHRISTI PERFECTVS AMICVS /
Te colit ET DAMASVS TVMVLO CVM REDDIT
    HONOREM / HIC MARCVS MARCI VITA
    FIDE NOMINE CONSORS / ET MERITIS[30]

("All innocent life was as if new to Mark. Full of love for God and despising the world, his acts showed to the people what he taught, having little honor for this life and a great contempt. But he held intimate virtue in the inner reaches of his heart. Guardian of justice, perfect friend of Christ. Damasus honored you with this tomb. Here Mark was given to Mark, sharer in life, faith, and name."—*Trans. Phyllis Jestice*)

Mark's feast day is October 7.

FURTHER READING: G. Bonavenia, "Carme damasiano alla tomba di papa S. Marco," in *Nuovo Bull. Arch. Crist.*, XVII, 1911; Ferrua, "Antichita cristiane: la basilica di papa M.," in *Civilta Cattolica*, September 4, 1948; Montini, "Titulus Marci," in *Capitolium*, Rome, XXVII, 1952.

Julius I (February 6, 337–April 12, 352). Buried on April 12 in the Cemetery of Calepodius, Rome, although his body was later translated to Santa Maria Trastevere to save it from the invading Lombards in the ninth century. Feast day: April 12.

Liberius (May 17, 352–September 24, 366) Possibly died from dysentery. He was buried in the basilica of San Silvestre (which is over the Cemetery of Priscilla) on September 9. *The Golden Legend* (fantastic stories of the early saints) records a story of a saint named Leo, but there was no Leo at the time of this story, so the saint may be Liberius, who was often referred to as Leo. According to the story, Leo (Liberius?) was arguing with St. Hilarus, because Leo was an unpleasant individual. He told Hilarus that he had to "take care of a need of nature" and that when he got back he'd "take him (Hilarus) down a few pegs," but Liberius was suddenly seized with dysentery and died a miserable, painful death.

The epitaph is a long, 54-line inscription that was found in the Cemetery of Priscilla. Roman archeologist De Rossi says it was for Liberius, but some disagree: The historian Mommsen says it belongs to Pope Felix,[31] and the historian Funk believes it belongs to Martin I.[32]

QVAM DOMINO FVERANT DEVOTA MENTE
PARENTES / QVI CONFESSOREM TALEM GENVERE
    POTENTEM / ATQVE SACERDOTEM SANCTVM
SINE FELLE COLVMBAM / DIVINAE LEGIS SINCERO
    CORDE MAGISTRVM / HAEC TE NASCENTEM
SVSCEPIT ECCLESIA MATER / VBERIBVS FIDEI
    NVTRIENS DEVOTA BEATVM / QVI PRO SE
    PASSVRVS ERAS MALA CVNCTA LIBENTER /
PARVVLVS VTQVE LOQVI COEPISTI DVLCIA VERBA /
    MOX SCRIPTVRARVM LECTOR PIVS INDOLE
FACTVS / VT TVA LINGVA MAGIS LEGEM QVAM
VERBA SONARET / DILECTA A DOMINO TVA DICTA
INFANTIA SIMPLEX / NVLLIS ARTE DOLIS SCEDA
FVCATA MALIGNIS / OFFICIO TALI IVSTO PVROQVE
    LEGENDI / ATQVE ITEM SIMPLEX ADOLESCENS
    MENTE FVISTI / MATVRVSQVE ANIMO FERVENTI
    AETATE MODESTVS / REMOTVS PRVDENS MITIS
    GRAVIS INTEGER AEQVVS / HAEC TIBI LECTORI
    INNOCVO FVIT AVREA VITA / DIACONVS HINC
    FACTVS IVVENIS MERITOQVE FIDELI / QVI SIC
SINCERE CASTE INTEGREQVE PVDICE / SERVIERIS
SINE FRAVDE DEO QVI PECTORE PVRO / ATQVE
ANNIS ALIQVOT FVERIS LEVITA SEVERVS / AC TALI
    IVSTA CONVERSATIONE BEATA / DIGNVS QVI
MERITO INLIBATVS IVRE PERENNIS / HVIC TANTAE
    SEDI CHRISTI SPLENDORE SERENAE / ELECTVS
FIDEI PLENVS SVMMVSQVE SACERDOS / QVI NIVEA
MENTE IMMACVLATVS PAPA SEDERES / QVI BENE
APOSTOLICAM DOCTRINAM SANCTE DOCERES /

INNOCV(IAM) PLEBEM CAELESTI LEGE MAGISTER /
QVIS TE TRACTANTE SVA NON PECCATA REFLEBAT /
IN SYNODO CVNCTIS SVPERATIS VICTOR INIQVIS /
SACRILEGIS NICAENA FIDES ELECTA TRIVMPHAT /
CONTRA QVAMPLVRES CERTAMEN SVMPSERIS
VNVS / CATHOLICA PRAECINCTE FIDE POSSEDERIS
OMNES / VOX TVA CERTANTIS FVIT HAEC SINCERA
SALVBRIS / ATQVE NEC HOC METVO NE ILLVD
COMMITTEREQVE OPTO / HAEC FVIT HAEC
SEMPER MENTIS CONSTANTIA FIRMA / DISCERPTVS
TRACTVS PROFVGATVSQVE SACERDOS / INSVPER
VT FACIEM QVODAM NIGRORE VELARET / NOBILI
FALSA MANV PORTANTES SYMBOLA CAELI /
VT SPECIEM DOMINI FOEDARET LVCE CORVSCAM /
EN TIBI DISCRIMEN VEHEMENS NON SVFFICIT
ANNVM / INSVPER EXILIO DECEDIS MARTYR
AD ASTRA / ATQVE INTER PATRIARCHAS
PRAESAGOSQVE PROPHETAS / INTER APOSTOLICAM
TVRBAM MARTYRVMQVE POTENTVM / CVM HAC
TVRBA DIGNVS MEDIVSQVE LOCATVS HONESTE /
MITTERIS IN DOMINI CONSPECTVM IVSTE
SACERDOS / SIC INDE TIBI MERITO TANTA EST
CONCESSA POTESTAS / VT MANVM IMPONAS
PATIENTIBVS INCOLA CHRISTI / DAEMONIA
EXPELLAS PVRGES MVNDESQVE REPLETOS / AC
SALVOS HOMINES REDDAS ANIMOQVE VIGENTES /
PER PATRIS AC FILII NOMEN CVI CREDIMVS
OMNES / CVMQVE TVVM HOC OBITVM
PRAECELLENS TALE VIDEMVS / SPEM GERIMVS
CVNCTI PROPRIE NOS ESSE BEATOS / QVI SVMVS
HOCQVE TVVM MERITVM FIDEMQVE SECVTI.

("How great were the parents, of such devoted mind for the Lord, who were to bear such a powerful confessor and even a holy priest. A dove without bitterness, a teacher of the divine law with a sincere heart. The Mother Church received your offspring. Devoted, nourishing the blessed boy with the teats of faith, you who endured on behalf of Her all wicked things willingly and [while] a young man you began to speak sweet words. By and by, you were inherently made a pious reader of the Scriptures so that your tongue might sound forth the law even more than the words. [As] an artless child, your words were beloved by the Lord with no malign deceits; by skill the gilded page was painted with such a pure and righteous service of reading, and likewise you were a young man guileless of mind, modest and mature in spirit [even] in an impetuous time of life, collected, prudent, mild, serious, virtuous, and fair. This life was golden to you, an innocent reader, and

hence, he was made a young deacon by merit of his faith. You, who thus honestly, purely, uprightly, chastely shall have been a servant to God without deceit, with a pure heart and for some years you were austere amongst easy living and blessed by such a righteous way of life. Without fail you were worthy by merit [and] unimpaired with respect to the law. Hence in splendor you were elected to the magnificent seat of Christ, full of faith and the highest priest that you who with a snowy mind might sit as the immaculate Pope, who taught well and blessedly the apostolic doctrine, a teacher with the heavenly law for the innocent masses, whose sins, by your leading, did not overflow. A victor in synod, you overcame every foe; the chosen Nicene faith triumphs over the sacrilegious against the many, you alone took the struggle in hand. You guarded every Catholic with encircling faith, your voice of battle was this sincere [and] salutary: 'Neither do I fear this nor do I choose to join together this and that [for] this thing [the Church] was always this, with a firm constancy of spirit.' A priest, hauled out, mangled and who has fled overhead so that he envelops the face with a certain blackness. Nobles bearing symbols of heaven with a false hand that it might dishonor the sparkling sight of the Lord with light. Lo! A year will not suffice for your furious peril [for] overhead you will withdraw, a martyr in exile among the stars and among the patriarchs, foretellers, and prophets, among the apostolic throng and powerful martyrs, and validly found to be worthy and in the midst of this crowd. A priest, you will have worthily [been] sent into the sight of the Lord. Thus to you may such power be conferred by merit that you might lay hands upon those suffering, a sojourner of Christ, to expel demons, cleanse and purge those filled [with evil], and even restore men to salvation and being vigorous in spirit, through the name of the father and son in whom we all believe and with your death, we see this with such. We sustain the hope to be personally blessed and for this reason we have imitated your merit and faith."—*Trans. Phillip Haberkern*)

FURTHER READING: I. Funk, *Historisches Jahrbuch*, Munich, V 1884; Marucchi, "La iscrizione di papa L.," in *Nuovo Bull. di Archeol. Crist.*, XIV 1908.

Antipope St. Felix II (355–November 22, 365). Beheaded close to the city walls, alongside the aqueduct of Trajan. Felix proclaimed Constantius, son of Constantine, to be a heretic and to have undergone a second baptism by Pope Eusebius. In retaliation for such slander, Constantius ordered Felix beheaded. The *Liber Pontificalis* claims he was buried in a church that he built on the Via Aurelia. Feast day: July 29.

St. Damasus I (October 1, 366–December 11, 384). Died at age 79. Originally buried December 11 near his mother, Laurentia, and sister, Irene, in the crypts of the Cemetery of Callixtus. Papal historian Renzo Montini claims in *Le Tombe dei Papi* that the head of Damasus is in St. Peter's in a reliquary donated by Pope Clement VIII (1592–1605).[33] Damasus I's sarcophagus inscription reads:

HIC FATEOR DAMASVS VOLVI MEA CONDERE MEMBRA / SED CINERES TIMVI SANCTOS VEXARE PIORVM

His first epitaph was written by Damasus himself, in metric verse:

QVI GRADIENS PELAGI FLVCTVS COMPRESSIT AMAROS / VIVERE QVI PRAESTAT MORIENTIA SEMINA TERRAE / SOLVERE QVI POTVIT LETALIA VINCVLA MORTIS / POST TENEBRAS FRATREM POST TERTIA LVMINA SOLIS / AD SVPEROS ITERVM MARTAE DONARE SORORI / POST CINERES DAMASVM FACIET QVIA SVRGERE CREDO[34]

("He who stilled the fierce waves of the sea by walking thereon, He who makes the dying seeds of the earth to live, He who could loose for Lazarus his chains of death and give back again to the world above her brother to his sister Martha after three days and nights, He, I believe, will make me, Damasus, arise from my ashes."[35])

In the ninth century, Paul I ordered Damasus's remains to be reburied in San Lorenzo en Damaso to protect them from the attacking Lombards. Epitaph in San Lorenzo en Damaso:

HINC PATER EXCEPTOR, LECTOR, LEVITA, SACERDOS CREVERAT HINC MERITIS

QUONIAM MELIONBUS ACTIS. HINC MIHI PROVECTO CHRISTUS, CUI SUMMA POTESTAS. SEDIS APOSTOHEAE VOLUIT CONCEDERE HONOREM, ARCHIVIS FATEOR VOLUI NOVA CONDERE TECTA ADDERE PRAETEREA DEXTRA LAEVAQUE-COLUMNAS, QUAE DAMASI TENEANT PROPRIUM PER SAECULA NOMEN.[36]

("Hence my father advanced from keeper of the records to reader, and from reader to be deacon and bishop, since he was advanced by his ever-increasing merits. When I was preferred hence Christ, who possesses the supreme power, wished to grant me the honors of the Apostolic Seat. I confess that I wished to build a new hall for the archives and to add columns thereto on the right and on the left, which should keep the name of Damasus as their own throughout all ages."[37])

The feast day of Damasus I is December 11.

FURTHER READING: Wilpert, "Die Entdeckung der Crypta Damasi," in *Rom. Quartaslschr.*, Freiburg, XVII 1903; S. Scaglia, "I cimeteri dei santi Marco e Marcelliano e di papa Damaso," in *Riv. St. Critica delle Scienze Teologiche*, VI 1910.

Antipope Ursinus (September 366–November 367, d. 385?) Murdered, and possibly died in Gaul, to which he had been banished by Pope Damasus.

St. Siricius (December 384–November 26, 399). Possibly martyred, and buried in the basilica of San Silvestre (which was built over the Cemetery of Priscilla) on November 26, although according to Claudio Rendina, Paschal II (d. 1118) had his remains transferred to Santa Prassade. He was omitted from the first edition of *Roman Martyrology* in 1584 because of the criticisms of St. Jerome and St. Paulinus of Nola, although his name was added to the martyrology in 1748 by Benedict XIV, who wrote a dissertation on Siricius' holiness.[38] His is the first authentic papal epitaph (i.e., written at the time of his death):

LIBERIVM LECTOR MOX ET LEVITA SECVTVS /
POST DAMASVM CLARVS TOTOS QVOS VIXIT IN
ANNOS / FONTE SACRO MAGNVS MERVIT
SEDERE SACERDOS / CVNCTVS VT POPVLVS
PACEM TVNC SOLI CLAMARET / HIC PIVS HIC
IVSTVS FELICIA TEMPORA FECIT / DEFENSOR
MAGNVS MVLTOS VT NOBILES AVSVS / REGI
SVBTRAHERET ECCLESIAE AVLA DEFENDENS /
MISERICORS LARGVS MERVIT PER SAECVLA
NOMEN / TER QVINOS POPVLVM QVI REXIT
IN ANNOS AMORE / NVNC REQVIEM SENTIT
CAELESTIA REGNA POTITVS[39]

("Lector and then deacon under Liberius, after
Damasus, he was preeminent among all who
lived in those years, and, being a great priest,
he deserved to sit by the holy font. The entire
populace cried out for peace; this pious, just
man brought happy times. Great defender of
many, with noble daring defending the Church,
he removed the king and deserved a name for
great mercy throughout the world. For fifteen
years he ruled the people with love. Now he
rests in the kingdom of heaven."—Trans. Phyllis Jestice)

FURTHER READING: Marucchi, "La iscrizione di
papa S." in *Nuovo Bull. di Archeol. Crist.*, XIV
1908.

St. Anastasius I

St. Anastasius I (November 27, 399–
December 401) Cause of death unknown,
though he was not martyred. He was buried
on April 27 in the basilica that had been built
atop the Cemetery of Pontian on the Via
Portuensis, Rome (where his son Pope Innocent I [d. 417] would also be buried). The
Liber Pontificalis (*Book of Pontiffs*) states that
Sergius II (d. 847) moved Anastasius's body
to under the altar of the church of San Martino ai Monte in the ninth century to save it
from the invading Lombards. Feast day:
December 19.

St. Innocent I

St. Innocent I (December 21, 401–
March 12, 417). Cause of death unknown,
although he was not a martyr as is sometimes
stated. He was buried on July 28 in the basilica above the Catacombe di Ponziano alongside his father, Anastasius I. The *Liber*

Pontificalis (*Book of Pontiffs*) claims that
Sergius II (d. 847) moved his body to under
the altar of the church of San Martino ai
Monte to save it from the invading Lombards. Feast day: July 28.

St. Zosimus

St. Zosimus (March 18, 417–December 26, 418) Died from protracted illness in
Rome, and buried in the atrium of the
Church of San Lorenzo al Verano (the original basilica that is now San Lorenzo fuori le
Mura), Rome, on December 26. His remains
are listed as having been transferred to San
Silvestre in Capite (probably in the ninth
century for protection against the invading
Lombards), although his sarcophagus was
destroyed by the bombardment of 1943.[40]
Only two fragments of the original epitaph
survive (these are held in the Lateran Museum), although the epitaph in its entirety
had been recorded:

DISCERE SI MErens patRIS MERITVM cupis almi /
HVNC PETRVS Zosimum VERVM SECVM EI
sociavit / SOMNIO PRAEcessis denIS VIX
MENSIB. Anno / NATALI VENERando
advenienTEQ. SACRATO / LAETITIAE POPVlo
ferias CONCEDERE IVSSIT / VIXIT
annos ... M.XI.D. VI[41]

("You desired to teach, deserving merit of a
dear father, Peter, who truly associated Zosimus with himself. His life was cut short by
sleep after a year and ten months, during the
celebration of the nativity. He commanded the
people to keep the festival with holy joy."—
Trans. Phyllis Jestice)

Zosimus was omitted from the fifth
century *Martyrology of Jerome* but his name
does appear in the ninth century *Martyrology of Ado*. His feast day is December 26.

FURTHER READING: G. B. de Rossi, "Dello scavo
fatto nell'antica basilica di S. Lorenzo per col-
locarvi il sepolcro di Pio IX e dei papi quivi
deposit nel secolo quinto," in *Bull. Arch. Crist.*,
VI 1881; Giuseppe da Bra, *S. Lorenzo fuori le
mura*, Rome, 1924.

Antipope Eulalius (December 27, 418–April 3, 419; d. 423). Nothing is known of his death except the year.

St. Boniface I (December 28, 418–September 4, 422) Died from old age and frailty, probably in Rome. He was originally buried beneath the pavement (in the chapel that he built himself) near the portico at the northern end of St. Felicitias, Rome, which still exists today. His tomb slab inscription reads:

BONIFACEII PAPAE I CONFESSORIS

("Pope Boniface I, Confessor")

And his epitaph:

POSTQUAM MORS CHRISTI PRO NOBIS MORTE PERISTI, / IN DOMINI FAMULOS NIL TIBI IURIS ERIT. / PONE TRUCEM RABIEM NON EST SAEVIRE POTESTAS, / AT QUID VICTA FURIS NIL NOCITURA PIIS. / HOC SIQUIDEM MELIUS DEMISSO VIVITUR ORBE, / CUM TAMEN UT VIVAT, HIC SIBI QUISQUE FACIT. / HIC SITA SUNT PAPAE BONIFACII MEMBRA SEPULCRO / PONTIFICALE SACRUM QUI BENE GESSIT OPUS. / IUSTITIAE CUSTOS, RECTUS, PATIENSQUE, BENIGNUS, / CULTUS IN ELOQUIIS ET PIETATE PLACENS. / FLETE ERGO MECUM PASTORIS FUNERA CUNCTI, / QUOS TAEDET CITIUS HIS CARUISSE BONIS.

("After the death of Christ conquered death for those of us in the Lord's family, it no longer has power over you. Your duty was to be in God's service, behind the wild madness [of Rome]. At least you piously survived the evil forces, with no harm. In truth it is better to live humbly in this world, because even as one lives, thus shall it be done to him. Here are buried the remains of Pope Boniface, who bore well the work of the pontifical consecration: guardian of justice, righteous, patient, kind, refined and pleasing in eloquence and piety. Therefore weep with me at the funeral of such a pastor, whose early death grieves those who have been left without this goodness."—*Trans. Phyllis Jestice*)

His feast day is September 4.

St. Celestine I (September 10, 422–July 27, 432) Buried in the basilica of San Silvestre (which was built over the Cemetery of Priscilla) on the Via Salaria. His mausoleum was painted with scenes of the Council of Ephesus, and his sarcophagus inscription, the earliest epitaph found in its entirety on a papal tomb, consists of only eight lines of entirely eschatological references:

PRAESVL APOSTOLICAE SEDIS VENERABILIS OMNI / QVEM REXIT POPVLO DECIMVM DVM CONDERET ANNV̄ / CAELESTINVS AGENS VITAM MIGRAVIT IN ILLAM / DEBITA QVAE SCIS (sanctis) AETERNOS REDDIT HONORES / CORPORIS HIC TVMVLVS REQVIESCVNT OSSA CINISQVE / NEC PERIT HINC ALIQVID D(omi)NO CARO CVNCTA RESVRGET / TERRENVM NVNC TERRA TEGIT MENS NESCIA MORTIS / VIVIT ET ASPECTV FRVITVR BENE CONSCIA CHRISTI[42]

("Caelestinus, protector of the Apostolic See, venerable to all people [over] whom he governed while finishing [his] tenth year, leading his life, migrated to the other [life]. He paid back the debts that you know as eternal honors. Here is the tomb of his body; [his] bones and ashes rest [here]. And nothing from here is lost for the lord; all flesh will rise up again. The earth now covers that which is earthly, but the soul, ignorant of death, yet knowing Christ, greatly delights in his presence."—*Trans. Sam Garcia*)

In 820, Pope St. Paschal I transferred Celestine's body to the Church of Santa Prassade, Rome (although the cathedral of Mantua claims to have his relics as well). There is also a memorial inscription to Celestine in the Church of Santa Sabina, Rome:

CULMEN APOSTOLICUM CUM CELESTINUS HABERET, / PRIMUS ET IN TOTO FULGERET EPISCOPUS ORBE, / HAEC QUAE MIRARIS FUNDAVIT PRESBYTER URBIS, / ILIYRICA DE GENTE PETRUS VIR NOMINE TANTO / DIGNUS AB EXORTU CHRISTI NUTRITUS IN AULA, / PAUPERIBUS LOCUPLES, SIBI PAUPER, QUI BONA VITAE / PRAESENTIS FUGIENS, MERUIT SPERARE FUTURAM.[43]

("When Celestine held the apostolic summit and shone as a bishop in the whole world, a presbyter of the city, Peter from an Illyrian race, a man worthy of so great a name, nourished in the hall of Christ, built these things which you admire, generous to the poor, poor to himself who fleeing from the good things of the present life deserved to hope for a future life."[44])

FURTHER READING: Marucchi, "La iscrizione di papa C.," in *Nuovo Bull. di Archeol. Crist.*, XIV 1908.

St. Sixtus (Xystus) III (July 31, 432–August 19, 440) Buried in the original basilica of San Lorenzo al Verano (today San Lorenzo fuori le Mura), allegedly in the crypt area that now houses Pope Leo IX (d. 1878). His name first appeared in the *Martyrology of Ado* although his cult did not develop until the ninth century. Papal tomb historian Renzo Montini claims that his sarcophagus existed until it was destroyed during the bombardment of 1943.[45] Feast day: March 28.

St. Leo I the Great (August or September 440–November 10, 461) Died around age 90 and was the first pope to be buried in the porch of St. Peter's basilica. Leo's tomb was moved by Sergius I in 688 to the south transept of St. Peter's because it was getting lost amidst the papal tombs filling up the portico. According to church canon and historian Giacomo Grimaldi, papal biographer and later antipope Anastasius Bibliothecarus recorded in the *Vitae of Sergius* that he had a vision telling him where to put the tomb of Leo, after which Sergius adorned it himself. Epitaph (from 688):

HVIS APOSTOLICI PRIMVM EST HIC CORPVS HVMATVM / QVOD FORET ET TVMVLO DIGNVS IN ARCE PETRI / HVNC VATVM PROCERVMQVE COHORS QVOS CERNIS ADESSE / MEMBRA SVB EGREGIA SVNT ADOPERTA DOMO / SED DVDVM VT PASTOR MAGNVS LEO SEPTA GREGEMQVE / CHRISTICOLAM SERVANS IANITOR ARCIS ERAT / COMMONET E TVMVLO QVOD GESSERAT IPSE SVPERSTES / INSIDIANS NE LVPVS VASTET OVILE DEI / TESTANTVR MISSI PRO RECTO DOGMATE LIBRI / QVOS PIA CORDA COLVNT QVOS PRAVA TVRBA TIMET / RVGIIT ET PAVIDA STVPVERVNT CORDA FERARVM / PASTORISQVE SVI IVSSA SEQVVNTVR OVES / HIC TAMEN EXTREMO

IACVIT SVB MARMORE TEMPLI / QVEM IAM PONTIFICVM PLVRA SEPVLCHRA CELANT / SERGIVS ANTISTES DIVINO IMPVLSVS AMORE / NVNC IN FRONTE SACRAE TRANSTVLIT INDE DOMVS / EXORNANS RVTILVM PRETIOSO MARMORE TVMBVM / IN QVO POSCENTES MIRA SVPERNA VIDENT / ET QVIA PRAEMICVIT MIRIS VIRTVTIBVS OLIM / VLTIMA PONTIFICIS GLORIA MAIOR ERIT / SEDIT IN EPISCOPATV ANNOS XXI MENSEM I DIES XIII DEPOSITVS EST III IDVS N(ovembr) ET ITERVM TRANSLATVS HVC A BEATO PAPA SERGIO IIII KAL IVL INDICTIONE I[46]

("The body of this Pope was buried in the basilica of Peter, but not in a burial grave worthy of him. The bones of the fathers and pontiffs had already been gathered to lie here, under the roof of this splendid royal hall. Instead Leo continued to act as porter of the basilica, as when he was alive, to speak from the tomb, a shepherded intent on the care of the sheepfold and the Christian flock, so that the wolf might not devastate the sheepfold of God. The books published in defense of orthodox dogma, which religious souls venerate, attest to this, while the ranks of the adversaries fear them. The bold lion roars and the wild beasts remain terrified, while the lambs docilely obey the voice of their shepherd. Before, his bones were lying near the far threshold of the temple, today almost already filled by the tombs of the pontiffs. The bishop Sergio, moved by divine love, transferred the bones now into the main nave of the Vatican basilica, adorning the tomb with bright marble. Those who pray near this sepulcher report numerous graces; and, as in life, Leo was illustrious with very many miracles, so the glory of this Pontiff shall become ever greater."—*Trans. Father Tom Carleton*)

Leo's remains were placed by Paschal II (1099–1118) near those of Leo II, III, and IV in St. Peter's. In 1580 the actual marble sarcophagus that housed the remains of Leo II, III, and IV was discovered by Gregory XIII, but it wasn't until the final destruction of the basilica in the early seventeenth century that the tomb of Leo I was found. Leo I's remains were then placed with those of Leo II, Leo III, and Leo IV (for further details see entry for Leo IV) in an ancient sarcophagus which was placed under the altar of Our Savior della Colonna with the inscription:

HIC IACVERVNT / CORPORA SANCTORVM
LEONVM I II III / ET IIII SVMMORVM
PONTIFICVM / ET CONFESSORVM

("Here are the bodies of Saints Leo I, II, III, and IV, Highest pontiffs and confessors."—*Trans. Phyllis Jestice*).

In 1714 the relics of Leo I were placed by Pope Clement XI under the altar that bears his name in St. Peter's, and an eyewitness account of the exhumation recorded:

("First, they went through the top coffin, that of Leo II–IV. One of these sets of bones was mostly intact, "although much consumed by age." These bones were put in one part of the coffin, where its skull was, and the dust and ashes in another part, and fragments of the ancient coffin put to the side. Then their coffin was removed, and that of Leo I was opened. Leo's body was intact. He was 7¾ palms tall, "and thus it can be conjectured (although he was much consumed by the length of time and antiquity) that his holy pontiff was slender and thin in body. He was clad in pontificals, specifically a chasuble in antique style colored purple. He bore fragments of a tunic and dalmatic. His right leg and feet could be seen to be reduced to bone. The head was consumed and disintegrated into several fragments of bone. Fragments of a pontifical miter of great antiquity could be seen. Around the neck gleamed a golden cord; the same was on his wrist. There remained above the right humerus a small red cross, which was part of the pontifical pallium; the other cross of the pallium, a little longer, lay on the right side on his chest. In the middle of his chest was seen one gold thorn from the pallium, thrust into the chasuble; of the pallium itself nothing remained."[47]—*Trans. Phyllis Jestice*).

Behind the altar is a marble monument to Leo I, showing him confronting Attila the Hun (sculpted by Alessandro Algardi and Domenico Guidi 1646–1652).

Benedict XIV declared Leo a doctor of the church in 1754, and the following was inscribed on his sarcophagus:

CORPVS / S. LEONIS PONT. ET CONFES. /
COGNOMENTO MAGNI / ET ECCLESIAE DOCTORIS

("The body of Saint Leo, high priest and confessor and doctor of the church.")

Feast day: November 10 in the West; February 18 in the East.

FURTHER READING: L. Sergardi, *Ragguaglio della solenne traslazione del corpo di S. Leone Magno seguita li 11 Aprile 1705*, Rome, 1715; R. Sindone, *Altarium et reliquiarum sacrosanctae basilicae Vaticanae ... descriptio historica*, Rome, 1774; Virgilio Cardinal Noe: *Le Tombe e i Monumenti*, Rome, 2000; Louise Rice, *The Altars and Altarpieces of New St. Peter's: Outfitting the Basilica, 1621–1666*, Cambridge University Press, 1998.

St. Hilarus   (November 19, 461–February 29, 468) Died of old age. On his deathbed Hilarus called for the priest Leontius, telling him to go listen to the crowd outside his window. Leontius returned and reported that he couldn't hear anything. Then a bright, blinding light surrounded Hilarus, and when the light faded, he died. He was buried in the Crypt of San Lorenzo al Verano (San Lorenzo fuori le Mura), Rome, near Pope Sixtus III (d. 440). Feast day: February 28.

St. Simplicius   (March 3, 468–March 10, 483) Died in Rome from a long illness. Buried Near Leo I in the Portico of St. Peter's, although his tomb was destroyed during the demolition of the basilica in the early seventeenth century. Feast day: March 10.

St. Felix III (II)   (March 13, 483–March 4, 493). (Known as Felix III (II) because the second Felix was an antipope, he is the third Felix, but really only the second true Pope Felix). He was buried in San Paolo fuori le Mura, Rome, close to his father, his children, and his wife. Church historian Baronius claims the epitaph of Felix IV (III) belongs to Felix III (II), but papal tomb historian Montini claims it does indeed belong to Felix

IV (III), so the epitaph and translation can be found under Felix IV (III). The *Catholic Encyclopedia* claims, however, claims that the tomb of Felix (III) II is in the crypt of the Church of Santissima Concenzione near the Piazza Barberini.

St. Gelasius I (March 1, 492–November 21, 496) Buried in the portico of St. Peter's. He died penniless because he gave all his money to the poor. Feast day: November 21.

St. Anastasius II (November 24, 496–November 19, 498) Died suddenly of unknown causes, although his critics claimed his death was a "result of divine judgment." He was buried under the pavement in the atrium of St. Peter's. Although the tomb has been destroyed (most likely during the demolition of St. Peter's in the seventeenth century), the epitaph in elegiacs survives:

LIMINA NVNC SERVO QVI TENVI CVLMINA SEDIS / HIC MERVI TVMVLVM PRAESVL ANASTASIVS / PRESBYTERO GENITVS DELEGI DOGMATA VITAE / MILITIAEQVE DEI NATVS IN OFFICIIS / PONTIFICVM CASTO FAMVLATVS PECTORE IVSSIS / OBTINVI MAGNVM NOMEN APOSTOLICVM[48]

("Now the threshold of the servant who held the highest seat, here the bishop Anastasius has earned a tomb. Begotten in the priesthood he chose the tenets of life and born in the office of God's militia, bearing the commands of pontifical servitude with a chaste heart, he won a great and apostolic name."—*Trans. Phyllis Jestice*)

It is interesting to note how differently the same Latin epitaph can be translated yet retain the same essential meaning:

("I, Bishop Anastasius, once held the highest throne; and so I deserve to have my tomb at the threshold [of St. Peter's]. Born in the service of God's army, as a priest I brought forth the dogmas of life, and by having served the pontiffs' commands with a chaste heart, I obtained the great apostolic name."—*Trans. Father Thomas Buffer*)

Dante placed Anastasius in the Inferno because he was seen as a traitor to the cause of the West:

And there, because of the dreadful and outrageous stench which the deep abyss threw up, we drew together behind a lid covering a great tomb, on which I saw writing which said, "I hold Pope Anastasius" (*Inferno* 11: 6–9).

St. Symmachus (November 22, 498–July 19, 514) He was buried in the portico of St. Peter's on July 19, 514, but his tomb was destroyed during the demolition of St. Peter's in the seventeenth century. Feast day: July 19.

Antipope Lawrence (November 22, 498–February 499; 501–506; d. 507 or 508). Pope Symmachus ousted him from Rome, so he settled on a farm belonging to his patron Festus, where he later died.

St. Hormisdas (July 20, 514–August 6, 523) Buried in St. Peter's, although his tomb was destroyed during the demolition of St. Peter's in the seventeenth century. His epitaph was composed by his son (later pope) Silverus:

QUAMVIS DIGNA TUIS NON SIT, PATER, ISTA SEPULCRIS / NEC TITULIS EGEAT CLARIFACATA FIDES, / SUME TAMEN LAUDES, QUAS PETRI CAPTUS AMORE / EXTREMO VENIENS HOSPES AB ORBE LEGAT. / SANASTI PATRIAE LACERATUM SCISMATE CORPUS / RESTITUENS PROPRIIS MEMBRA REVULSA LOCIS / IMPERIO DEVICTA PIO TIBI GRAECIA CESSIT / AMISSAMQUE GAUDENS SE REPARASSE FIDEM. / AFRICA LAETATUR MULTOS CAPTIVA PER ANNOS / PONTIFICES PRECIBUS PROMERUISSE TUIS / HAEC EGO SILVERIUS, QUAMVIS MIHI DURA, NOTAVI, / UT POSSENT TUMULIS FIXA MANERE DIU.[49]

("Although my verses, father, are unworthy of your sepulcher and though your celebrated faith has no need for eulogy, accept, however, these praises, to be read by a pilgrim who for love of Peter, will be coming here from the ends of the world. You healed the body of your native country lacerated by schism, and restored the torn-off limbs to their proper places. Greece, defeated by holy power, submitted herself to you, happy in having regained her lost faith. Africa, captive for many years, rejoices over the bishops she owes to your prayers. I, Silverius, have recorded this, though it causes me sorrow, in order that, engraved on a tombstone, it may defy age."[50])

The feast day of St. Hormisdas is August 6.

St. John I   (August 13, 523–May 18, 526) Martyred by starvation in a prison in Ravenna, Italy. John had been thrown into prison by King Theodoric because of political unrest between the Italians and the Goths. He was buried in the nave of St. Peter's on May 27, and his body soon became the focus of miracles and veneration, although his tomb was destroyed during the demolition of St. Peter's in the seventeenth century. His epitaph reads:

QVISQVIS AD AETERNAM FESTINAT TENDERE
VITAM / HAC ITER EXQVIRAT QVA LICET IRE
PIIS / TRAMITE QVO FRETVS CELESTIA REGNA
SACERDOS / INTRAVIT MERITIS ANTE PARATA
SVIS / MINVS MAGIS VIVENS COMMERCIA
GRATA PEREGIT / PERDIDIT VT POSSET
SEMPER HABERE DEVM / ANTISTES
DOMINI PROCVMBIS VICTIMA CHRISTI /
PONTIFICI SVMMO SIC PLACITVRE DEO[51]

("Whosoever hastens to strive towards eternal life seeks the way permitted to the pious. The footpath having been prepared before by the heavenly powers, the trusting priest enters by his merits. He was poor, [thus] living in even more pleasing circumstances. He died, a high priest of the Lord, a prostrate sacrifice of Christ, so that he might always be able to worship God; thus was this highest pontiff pleasing to God."—*Trans. Phillip Haberkern*)

The feast day of John I is May 18.

St. Felix IV (III)   (July 12, 526–September 22, 530) As he lay dying, Felix surrounded himself with his supporters and gave them an edict nominating his archdeacon Boniface as his successor. He even gave Boniface his pallium (on the condition that it be returned if he recovered). He was buried under the pavement in the atrium of St. Peter's on October 12, although his tomb was destroyed during the demolition of St. Peter's in the seventeenth century. His epitaph reads:

CERTA FIDES IVSTIS CAELESTIA REGNA PATERE /
ANTISTES FELIX QVAE MODO LAETVS HABET /
PRAELATVS MVLTIS HVMILI PIETATE SVPERBIS /
PROMERVIT CELSVM SIMPLICITATE LOCVM /
PAVPERIBVS LARGVS MISERIS SOLACIA PRAESTANS /
SEDIS APOSTOLICAE CRESCERE FECIT OPES[52]

("Good Bishop Felix has certain faith that the heavenly kingdom lies open to the just. He was placed before many proud men because of his simplicity and humble piety. Generous to the poor, giver of comfort to the wretched, he increased the wealth of the Apostolic See, and deserves a lofty place."—*Trans. Father Thomas Buffer*)

Antipope Dioscorus   (September 22–October 14, 530) Died suddenly of unknown causes.

The memory of Disoscorus was officially condemned by Pope Boniface II (d. 532), but Agapitus I (d. 536) solemnly burned this document to reinstate the good memory of Discorus (although the officials of the papal chancery made sure that Discorus's name did not appear in any official list of popes).

Boniface II   (September 22, 530–October 17, 532) Buried in the portico of St. Peter's, although his tomb was destroyed during the demolition of St. Peter's in the seventeenth century. Only a small fragment of the original epitaph remains in the Vatican crypt, although the epitaph has been recorded in its entirety:

SEDIS APOSTOLICAE PRIMAEVIS MILES AB ANNIS /
POST ETIAM TOTO PRAESVL IN ORBE SACER /
MEMBRA BEATA SENEX BONIFATIVS HIC SVA
CLAVSIT / CERTVS IN ADVENTV GLORIFICANDA
DEI / MITIS ADVNAVIT DIVISUM PASTOR OVILE /
VEXATOS REFOVENS HOSTE CADENTE GREGES /
IRAM SVPPLICIBVS HVMILI DE CORDE REMISIT /
DEBELLANS CVNCTOS SIMPLICITATE DOLOS /
EGIT NE STERILIS ROMAM CONSVMERET
ANNVS / NVNC ORANDO FVGANS NVNC
MISERANDO FAMEM / QVIS TE SANCTE PARENS
CVM CHRISTO NESCIAT ESSE / SPLENDIDA
QVEM TECVM VITA FVISSE PROBAT /
SED ANN II DIES XXV DEP IN P XVI KAL
NOV ITER P C FL LAMPADI /
ET ORESTIS VV CC[53]

("Longtime servant of the ancient Apostolic See, holy bishop of all the world, the elderly Boniface enclosed his body here, trusting in God's glorious return. As a gentle shepherd, he reconciled division; with the fall of the enemy he revived the troubled flock. He abated their rage with prayers from a humble heart. With honesty he conquered all deceptions. He drove famine away with supplications and compassion, lest Rome be destroyed by her barren year. O saintly father, who would not recognize that you are with Christ? For all approve that you have lived a splendid life."—*Trans. Ruth Yeuk Chun Leung. The last lines of this epitaph, which appear to refer to dates, are too heavily abbreviated to permit accurate translation.*)

John II (January 2, 533–May 8, 535) Buried in St. Peter's, although his tomb was destroyed during the demolition in the seventeenth century. Epitaph:

MENTE PIA VIVENS XPI (christi) NVTRITVS
IN AVLA / ET SOLA GAVDENS SIMPLICITATE BONI /
BLANDVS IN OBSEQVIIS ET PVRO PLENVS AMORE /
PACIFICAM VITAM IVRE QVIETIS AGENS / QVI
GRATVS POPVLIS ET CELSO DIGNVS HONORE /
SVMPSISTI MERITIS PONTIFICALE DECVS /
COMMISSVMQVE TIBI PASCENS BONITATE
MAGISTRA / SERVASTI CVNCTVM SVB PIETATE
GREGEM / PRO QVO RITE TVVM VENERANS
AGAPETVS HONOREM / PRAESTITIT HAEC
TVMVLO MVNERA GRATA TVO / QVI NVNC
ANTISTES ROMANA CELSVS IN VRBE / SEDIS
APOSTOLICAE CVLMINA SACRA TENET[54]

("Living in a godly spirit, brought up in Christ's hall, and rejoicing only in simply goodness, you obtained the honor of the papacy by your attractive merits of obedience. You pleased the people by leading a peaceful, quiet life full of pure love and worthy of high respect. With goodness and safety you sheltered a whole flock entrusted to you, and for this reason, you held the sacred heights of the Apostolic See as the supreme bishop. Agapitus and the city of Rome rightly venerated your honor by bestowing these pleasing gifts to your tomb."—*Trans. Father Thomas Buffer*)

St. Agapitus I (May 13, 535–April 22, 536) Died of illness in Constantinople while trying to talk the Byzantine emperor out of invading Italy. His body was returned in a lead coffin for burial under the pavement of the atrium of St. Peter's, Rome, on September 20, although his tomb was destroyed during the demolition of St. Peter's in the seventeenth century. Dante places Agapitus in Heaven in *Paridiso.* 6:16–18:

> But blessed Agapitus, he who was
> The supreme pastor, to the faith sincere
> Pointed me out the way by words of his.

His feast day is April 22 in the west and April 17 in the east.

St. Silverius (June 8, 536–November 11, 537; d. December 2, 537) Died from harsh prison treatment. Silverius had been exiled to the island of Palmaria for allegedly supporting the Goths, when all he really wanted was to avoid bloodshed in Rome. The Emperor Justinian had him sent back to Rome to stand trial, but the current pope, Vigilius, arranged to have Silverius exiled back to the island and imprisoned underneath the remains of a monastery (beneath the *picco* of San Silverio), where he later died.

Inscription on the tomb located on the island:

ROMANAE SUPREMUS APEX SILVERIUS AEDIS / OSSA
SUB HOC RETINET MORTUUS EXTRANEO[55]

("Silverius, supreme head of the Roman temple, died in a foreign land. Under this [inscription], [this tomb] holds his bones." — *Trans. Sam Garcia*)

Vigilius (March 29, 537–June 7, 555) Died of gallstones (though it was rumored that he was murdered by the next pope, Pelagius) in Syracuse, Sicily. He was returning to Rome from Constantinople when he died. According to the *Oxford Dictionary of Popes*, he was buried in San Marcello on the Via Salaria in Rome (because of his unpopularity the Romans wouldn't allow him to be buried in St. Peter's). The *Catholic Encyclopedia*, however, claims that Vigilius was buried in the basilica of San Silvestre over the Catacomb of Priscilla, also on the Via Salaria.

His epitaph reads:

MOENIBVS VNDISONIS BELLORVM INCENDIA
CERNENS / PARS EGO TVNC POPVLI TELA PAVENTIS
ERAM / PVBLICA LIBERTAS VIGILI SANCTISSIME
PAPA / ADVENIS INCLVSO SOLVERE VINCLA GREGI /
DE GLADIO RAPIVNTVR OVES PASTORE MINISTRO /
INQVE HVMERIS FERIMVR TE REVOCANTE PIIS /
CORPOREVM SATIS EST SIC EVASISSE PERICLVM /
AT MIHI PLVS ANIMAE NASCITVR INDE SALVS /
ECCLESIAM SVBEO DIMISSA NAVFRAGVS AVLA /
PERFIDA MVNDANI DESERO VELA FRETI[56]

("Perceiving the destruction of war, resounding with waves and fortifications, I, Vigilius, most holy pope, preserved those of the populace who were shaking with fear, as well as public liberty. Breaking the chains of my flock and saving them from the sword, smiting with my arm, I recalled you to enough piety that you evaded this bodily peril. To me, however, it was more important to encourage the well-being of your soul. I supported the power of the Church, fallen away by shipwreck. Deserted by the perfidy of the world, my sails were torn." — *Trans. Phyllis Jestice*)

Vigilius's remains were later moved to the inner wall of the south transept of St. Peter's and placed in an altar (to which the remains of Hadrian IV [d. 1155] were added in 1159) that was dedicated to Saint Silvester with the following inscription:

ALTARE SANCTI SILVESTRI PAPAE–UBI
VIGILII ET ADRIANI IV SEPULCRA

("Altar of Pope Saint Silvester with the sepulcher of Vigilius and Adrian IV"[57])

FURTHER READING: Marucchi, 465 and 514, nonche "Il sepolcro del papa V." in *Nuovo Bull. di Archeol. Crist.*, XIV 1908.

Pelagius I (April 16, 556–March 3, 561) Died of old age and was buried in the atrium of St. Peter's, although his tomb was destroyed during the demolition of St. Peter's in the seventeenth century. Epitaph:

TERRENUM CORPUS CLAUDANT HAEC FORTE
SEPULCRA / NIL SANCTI MERITIS DEROGATURA
VIRI: / VIVIT IN ARCE POLI CELESTI LUCE BEATUS /
VIVIT ET HIC CUNCTIS PER PIA FACTA LOCIS, /
SURGERE IUDICIO CERTUS DEXTRAMQUE
TENETNEM / ANGELICA PARTEM SE RAPIENTE
MANU. / VIRTUTUM NUMERET TITULOS
ECCLESIA DEI / QUOS VENTURA UTINAM
SAECULA FERRE QUEANT / RECTOR APOSTOLICAE
FIDEI VENERANDA RETEXIT / DOGMATA QUAE
CLARI CONSTITUERE PATRES, / ELOQUIO CURANS
ERRORUM SCISMATE LAPSOS / UT VERAM
TENEANT CORDA PACATA FIDEM. / SACRAVIT
MULTOS DIVINA LEGE MINISTROS / NIL PRETIO
FACIENS IMMACULATA MANUS, / CAPTIVOS
REDIMENS, MISERIS SUCCURRERE PROMPTUS /
PAUPERIBUS NUMQUAM PARTA NEGARE SIBI /
TRISTIA PARTICIPANS, LAETI MODERATOR
OPIMUS / ALTERIUS GEMITUS CREDIDIT ESSE
SUOS. / HIC REQUIESCIT PELAGIUS P(A) P(A),
QUI SEDIT ANNOS IIII M(ENSES) X D(IES) XVIII. /
DEPOS(ITUS) (ANTE DIEM) IIII NONAS MARTI.

("Although this tomb covers an earthly body, it will not in the least detract from the merits of the saintly man. He lives in the vault of heaven, blessed in celestial light, but he lives here too, everywhere, because of his pious deeds. He is certain to rise at the Last Judgment. Carried by the hand of the angel, he will be placed at the right hand [of Christ]. May the Church of God enumerate all his good qualities and may the coming generation prove equal to them. As a guardian of the apostolic faith he brought to light the venerable people who had lapsed through the errors of schism, so that their souls might in peace enjoy true faith. He ordained many priests in accordance with the Divine Law, yet his hand was never sullied by bribery. He was eager to redeem his wealth. He shared the sorrows of others, put a limit to his own prosperity, and regarded the sufferings of his neighbors as his own. Here lies Pope Pelagius, who occupied the chair for 4 years, 10 months, and 18 days. His body was deposited in the grave on the 5th of March."[58])

John III   (July 17, 561–July 13, 574) *Catelinus*. He was buried in St. Peter's although his tomb was destroyed during the demolition of the basilica in the early seventeenth century. Historian Petrus Mallius gives this inscription fragment:

> IOANNES PAPA TERTIUS, / QUI COMPLEVIT
> ECCLESIAM PHILIPPI ET IACOBI, / SICUT
> HABETUR IN HOC SEQUENTI VERSU: / PELAGIUS
> COEPIT, COMPLEVIT PAPA IOANNES.[59]

("Pope John III, who completed the church of Philip and James, as is found in the following verse: Pelagius began it, Pope John completed it." —*Trans. Father Thomas Buffer*)

Benedict I   (June 2, 575–July 30, 579) Died from illness and was buried in the vestibule of the sacristy of St. Peter's, although his tomb was destroyed during the demolition of St. Peter's in the seventeenth century.

Pelagius II   (November 22, 579–February 7, 590) Died from plague (that allegedly left its victims to die yawning and sneezing[60]) in Rome. He was buried in the atrium of St. Peter's, although his tomb was destroyed during the demolition of St. Peter's in the seventeenth century.

St. Gregory I the Great   (September 3, 590–March 12, 604) Died at age 64 from gout (and illness because he ruined his health by fasting and eating only cabbages). In a letter to Marianus, Bishop of Arabia (601) Gregory talks about his own death:

It is now a long time since I have had the strength to rise from my bed. For at one time the pain of gout tortures me, and at another a fire of what kind I do not know, spreads itself with pain through my whole body. Usually at one and the same time a painful, burning heat afflicts me, and both body and mind fail me. I am unable to count how many other great distresses of illness are visited upon me in addition to those I have mentioned. In a few words, however, I can say that the infection of a poisonous humor drinks me up to such an extent that it is a punishment for me to live, and I look longingly for death which I believe is the only thing which can provide a cure of my groans. *Gregory, Registrum Episularum 11.20.*[61]

He was extremely unpopular when he died because of a plague outbreak in Rome.

Gregory was originally buried March 12 in the portico of old St. Peter's (against its outer row of columns, where an altar was dedicated to him). His epitaph was written by Pope Sabinian (d. 606). A fragment still exists in the Vatican grottoes:

> SUSCIPE TERRA TUO DE CORPORE SUMPTUM, /
> REDDERE QUOD VALEAS VIVIFICANTE DEO, /
> SPIRITUS ASTRA PETIT, LETI NIL IVRA NOCEBUNT, /
> CUI VITAE ALTERIUS MORS MAGIS IPSA VIA EST. /
> PONTIFICIS SUMMI HOC CLAUDUNTUR MEMBRA
> SEPULCHRO, / QUI INNUMERIS SEMPER VIVIT
> UBIQUE BONIS. / ESVRIEM DAPIBVS SVPERAVIT
> FRIGORA VESTE / ATQVE ANIMAS MONITIS TEXIT
> AB HOSTE SACRIS / IMPLEBATQVE ACTV
> QVICQVID SERMONE DOCEBAT / ESSE VT
> EXEMPLVM MYSTICA VERBA LOQVENS / AD
> CHRISTVM ANGLOS CONVERTIT PIETATE
> MAGISTRA / ADQVIRENS FIDEI AGMINA
> GENTE NOVA / HIC LABOR HOC STVDIVM
> HAEC TIBI CVRA HOC PASTOR AGEBAS / VT
> DOMINO OFFERRES PLVRIMA LVCRA GREGIS /
> HISQVE DEI CONSVL FACTVS LAETARE
> TRIVMPHIS / NAM MERCEDEM OPERVM IAM
> SINE FINE TENES / HIC REQVIESCIT GREGORIVS
> PP QVI SED AN XIII MENS VI D X DP IIII ID MAR
> POST CONS DOM N / FOCAE AVG AN II[62]

("O earth, receive these remains, taken from the body of God who gave it life. May you return them when God gives them life again. Now his spirit is making for the stars; the powers of death will not harm him at all, since for him death is rather the very road to the next life. Enclosed in this sepulcher is the body of the supreme pontiff, who always and everywhere lived in incalculable goodness. He overcame hunger with feasts, cold with clothing, and protected souls from the enemy with holy admonitions. He taught by speaking mystical words and by using his actions as examples. He converted the Angles to Christ with the help of godliness, increasing the hosts of the faith by the addition of the new nation. This was your toil, this was your zeal, this was your concern, O shepherd; you did it so that you might offer many gains to the flock. And having become God's consul by these triumphs, rejoice! For now you hold the reward of your works forever. Here rests Pope Gregory, who reigned 13 years 6 months 10 days D[e] P[ositi]. March 29 in the second year of the consulate of Phocas." —*Trans. Father Thomas Buffer*)

Gregory was buried in a great black and white, oval, oriental granite urn that was surrounded by iron bands and placed in an oratory built by Gregory IV (827–844), which was located in the most southerly aisle of St. Peter's. A large relic of the pope was taken to Soissous in France in 826, and Pius II (d. 1464) had the rest of the remains transferred to an ancient porphyry bathing basin (located where Gregory was initially buried) beneath the recently restored altar that also contained the head of St. Andrew. In 1605, during the demolition of St. Peter's, Gregory's remains, along with the head of St. Andrew, were placed in a reliquary near the tomb of Pius II in San Andrea della Valle until the new coffin for Gregory was completed.

On December 28, 1605, the urn was opened for inspection, though not until January 7 was Gregory's body transferred to a cypress coffin. The following is an eyewitness account by church canon and historian Giacomo Grimaldi.

A group of people gathered at the altar of St. Andrew to be present at the opening of the altar and redisposition of the body of St. Gregory the Great into a new cypress coffin by the cardinal of Cusa, with papal blessing, with proper hymn and prayer to the saint.

The marble slab on the altar was raised, and the sarcophagus opened, upon which three priests put on stoles, and raised the wooden coffin that contained the body.

On January 8, a procession, headed by the aristocracy of Rome and the college of cardinals, brought the remains to the Cappella Clementina, near the entrance to the modern sacristy of St. Peter's. The ceremony was led by Cardinal Priest Evangelista Pallotus and Cardinal Cusentinus. Nine canons carried the body.

The body was borne in the second hour of the night to where the populace stood who frequented the place most often, especially nobles, the best and first of the Romans, recalling the memory of such a great pontiff, not only because of his love for their common homeland, but also truly because of the man's singular sanctity and teaching, which spread an ineffable light over the whole world.

Then the body was placed in the altar:

This was done by a large group led by Cardinal Pallottus, in full vestments, including a cloth-of-gold miter. The body was in a cypress coffin. The altar was closed with a marble tablet with the inscription: "Here rests St. Pope Gregory I the Great, Doctor of the Church."

A new inscription on a lead plate was put on the cypress coffin itself: "The Body of St. Pope Gregory I, the Great, from the altar of St. Andrew in the old church, now moved at the order of Pope Paul V into the new church with a solemn procession and placed beneath this altar in a cypress coffin within a marble container on Sunday, January 8, A.D. 1606" [*trans. Phyllis Jestice*].

Inscription placed on the marble lid:

CORPUS S. MARTIRI GREGORII MAGNI

("The body of Gregory the Great, martyr.")

The marble effigy of Gregory in the Vatican crypt was never part of the original monument but was originally used as decoration on the *ciborium* of Innocent VIII (d. 1492).

Dante places Gregory in Heaven in *Paradiso* 20: 106–108:

For one from Hell, where no one e'er turns
    back
Unto good will, returned unto his bones,
    and that of lingering hope was the reward

Gregory's feast day is September 3.

Sabinian (September 13, 604–February 22, 606). *The Golden Legend* (fantastic tales of early saints) claims that Sabinian died when he was struck on the head by the ghost of Pope Gregory I (his predecessor) in the Lateran Palace, Rome. Sabinian refused to help the starving Romans because he thought the past popes had spoiled them by giving them corn for free or for very low prices, and that Gregory the Great fed them out of his own self-glory rather than to help them. Sabinian offered the Romans corn at inflated prices. The ghost of Pope Gregory visited Sabinian three times to tell him to share the corn, but Sabinian steadfastly refused. Therefore, on the fourth visit, the ghost of Gregory killed Sabinian with a blow to the head from his staff.

Because of the people's anger about the corn, Sabinian's burial, on the day of his death, had to take place in a secret procession. The funeral cortege left from the papal residence at the Lateran and made a wide detour around the city to St. Peter's to avoid the Roman mob, who might have hurled his body into the Tiber River. He was then buried in a tomb under the pavement in the atrium, although his tomb was destroyed during the demolition of St. Peter's in the seventeenth century. Only fragments of the original epitaph remain in the Vatican grottoes, but luckily it was recorded in its entirety:

SAEVA VORAX NIL POSSE TVAS MORS ASPICE
VIRES / VIVIT IN AETERNVM QVEM PEREMISSE
PVTAS / NAM BONA DISTRIBVENS QVI NIL
MIGRANDO RELINQVIT / PER TE POST MISSAS
IRE VIDETVR OPES / HIC PRIMVM SVBITAM NON
SVMPSIT LAVDE CORONAM / SED GRADIBVS
MERVIT CRESCERE SANCTVS HOMO / ATOVE
HOMINVM VITIVM BLANDO SERMONE REMOVIT /
NEC IVDEX CVLPIS SED MEDICINA FVIT /

PRAESVLE QVO NVLLVM TVRBAVIT BELLICVS
HORROR / SAEVA NEC ANGELICI VVLNERIS
IRA FVIT / QVEM FAMIS IRA DAPES QVEM NVDVS
SENSIT AMICTVM / VINCEBAT LACRIMIS OMNIA
DIRA SVIS / HIC REQVIESCIT SABINIANVS QVI
SED ANN I M V D VIIII / DP VIII K MART P C
FOCAE AVG ANNO QVARTO IND VIIII[63]

("O fierce, voracious death, consider: Your power can do nothing. You think that he has perished, but he lives forever; for, distributing his goods and riches, he left nothing behind when he passed from this life. He did not suddenly assume the crown of praise, but step by step he merited to grow into a holy man. And with mild words he removed human vice, not as judge of the guilty, but as a cure. A bishop whom no horror of war could disturb nor cruel angelic wounds anger, whoever he saw hungry or angry, or found naked, he conquered with tears all their terrors. Here rests Sabinian, who reigned one year, five months, nine days, buried 25 March in the fourth year of Phocas."—*Trans. Father Thomas Buffer*)

Boniface III (February 19, 607–November 12, 607) Buried in St. Peter's, although his tomb was destroyed during the demolition of the basilica in the seventeenth century.

His epitaph reads:

POSTQVAM MORS CHRISTI PRO NOBIS MORTE
PERISTI / IN DOMINI FAMVLOS NIL TIBI IVRIS
ERIT / PONE TRVCEM RABIEM NON EST
SAEVIRE POTESTAS / AVT QVID VICTA FVRIS NIL
NOCITVRA PIIS / HOC SIQVIDEM MELIVS
DIMISSO VIVITVR ORBE / CVM TAMEN VT VIVAT
HIC SIBI QVISQVE FACIT / HIC SITA SVNT PAPAE
BONIFATII MEMBRA SEPVLCRO / PONTIFICALE
SACRVM QVI BENE GESSIT OPVS / IVSTITIAE CVS-
TOS RECTVS PATIENSQVE BENIGNVS / CVLTVS IN
ELOQVIIS ET PIETATE PLACENS / FLETE ERGO
MECVM PASTORIS FVNERA CVNCTI / QVOS
TAEDET CITIVS HIS CARVISSE BONIS / HIC
REQVIESCIT BONEFATIVS QVI SEDIT MENSES VII
DIES XXII DEPOSITVS / PRID IDVS NOV IMPERANTE
DOM N FOCA PP AVG ANNO VI INDICT XI[64]

("A soldier of the Apostolic See from youth, afterward holy bishop for the whole world. The blessed remains of the old man Boniface are here enclosed, certain of an advent in God's glory. The humble pastor of his sheep sorted them out, restoring those troubled by the enemy, and the failing, to the flock. He abated his anger at the prayers of the humble in heart, subduing all deceits with his simplicity. He took action lest a barren year should consume Rome, driving away famine, now by prayer, now by his compassion. There is no one who does not know, holy father, that you are with Christ, and approve a splendid life with you."—Trans. *Phyllis Jestice*)

St. Boniface IV (September 15, 608– May 8, 615) Died while in monastic retirement and originally buried in the portico of St. Peter's, although he was brought into the interior of the basilica by Nicholas III (d. 1280). The altar dedicated to him in the Chapel of the Madonna delle Parturienti of the Vatican crypts was restored by Boniface VIII (1294–1303), who also added the last two lines of the epitaph. The first line reads GREGORIO QVARTVS IACET HIC BONIFACIVS ALMVS; according to papal tomb historian Renzo Montini, this line indicates that Boniface IV was buried near his predecessor, Gregory the Great, not that Gregory IV had this altar created for him. Another possibility for the first line is that Boniface IV was the fourth pontiff after Gregory the Great, but because of the inferior medieval Latin used here, it is impossible to interpret the first line with absolute certainty.[65] The rest of the epitaph is very straightforward:

HVIVS Q(ui) SEDIS FVIT AEQVVS RECTOR ET AEDIS: / TEMPORE Q(ui) FOCAE CERNENS TEMPLVM FORE ROMAE / DELVBRA CVNCTORVM FUERANT QUO DEMONIOR(um) / HOC EXPVRGAVIT SANCTIS CVNCTIS Q(ui) DICAVIT: / EIVS NATALIS SOLLEMPNIA QVI CELEBRATIS: / PRIMIS SEPTEMBRIS FERT HAEC LVX QVARTA K(a)L(en)DIS / OCTAVVS TITULO HOC BONIFATIVS OSSA REPERTA / HAC LOCAT ERECTA BONIFATII NOMINIS ARA[66]

("Here lies kind Boniface IV, who was the fair guide of this see and building. He purged this temple and dedicated it to all the saints. This fourth light honors his birthday [feast day] which you celebrate September 1. Boniface, the

eighth of that title, having erected this altar with the name of Boniface, sets here his bones that were found."—Trans. *Father Thomas Buffer*)

An arm of Boniface IV had been taken from his sepulcher and placed with the relics of other saintly popes in the altar of Saint Mary in Cosmedin, and in 1246 other relics of Boniface were translated to the Chapel of St. Sylvester beside the Church of the Quattro Coronati, Rome.

Boniface VIII had the bones of Pope St. Boniface IV that had been originally in the portico of St. Peter's brought into his chapel and placed in a *sacellum* under his sarcophagus. Boniface VIII chose to honor Boniface IV this way because the latter had had a large liturgical following in St. Peter's; also, because Boniface's predecessor, Celestine V, had abdicated and so was not dead, Boniface worried that his legitimacy as a pope might be questioned. By placing the relics of St. Boniface IV in his own funeral chapel, he was demonstrating that he was indeed the legitimate pope and had the "support" of Boniface IV because his own relics would be permanently interred with those of Boniface IV. The following is an inscription from the altar of Boniface VIII that contained the remains of St. Boniface IV:

CORPVS SANCTI BONIFACII PAPAE / QVARTI EX ALTARE SITO IN / VATICANA BASILICA INTER / PORTAS IVDICII ET RAVENNI / ANAM A. BONIFACIO PAPA OCTAVO EIVS / NOMINI DICATO ORNATO / ET DOTATO IN NOVVM / TEMPLVM PAVLI V. PONT MAX / IVSSV HONORIFICE TRANSLATVM / HAC SVB ARA RITV. / SOLEMNI COLLOCAVIT EVANELISTA / PALLOTTVS TITVLI / S. LAVRENTII IN LVCINA CARDINALIS / CONSENTINVS HVIVS / BASILICAE ARCHIPRESBYTER / ANNO MDCVI DIE XVII / IANVARII PRIMIS VESPERIS / CATHEDRALE S. PETRI SEDENTE / PAVLO PAPA V ANNO PRIMO[67]

("The body of the holy Pope Boniface IV, taken from the altar in the Vatican basilica between the portal of judgment and the portal of Ravenna, moved to an altar by Pope Boniface VIII, who was adorned, dedicated, and gifted with his name, was by the command of the supreme Pontiff Paul V transferred with honors to beneath this altar. Evangelista Pallottus of

Cosenza, cardinal of San Lorenzo in Lucina, archpriest of this basilica, placed his body with solemn rites in the year 1606, January 17, during first vespers, as Pope Paul V sat on the throne of St. Peter, during the first year of his pontificate." — *Trans. Father Thomas Buffer*)

The following inscription was attached to the wall (which church canon and historian Giacomo Grimaldi said was badly carved in ancient minuscule letters on a marble tablet that was 4½ palms long):

VITA HOMINVM BREVIS EST CERTA HANC DETERMINAT HORA / SED VITAE AETERNAE INDE PARATVR ITER / QVOD NON INDECORA AVT RVRSVM PERITVRA VIDENTVR / SED PVLCHRVM ATQVE DECENS IAM SINE FINE MANET / DIC IGITVR QVID MORS STIMVLIS AGITARIS INIQVIS / QVID FREMIS INCASSVM QVID FVRIBVNDA GERIS / COMMODA NVLLA TIBI POTERVNT TVA FACTA REFERRE / NEC PRODESSE POTEST IMPETVS ISTE TIBI / GREGORII SEMPER MONITA ATQVE EXEMPLA MAGISTRI / VITA OPERE AC DIGNIS MORIBVS ISTE SEQVENS / QVO HVNC TERRERE PVTANS SVNT HVIVS MAXIMA VOTA / MITTERE AD ASTRA ANIMAM REDDERE CORPVS HVMO / SAVCIA MVLTIPLICI SI QVIDEM NAM MEMBRA DOLORE / RVRSVS IN ANTIQVO PVLVERE VERSA MANENT / QVAE CONIVNCTA ANIMAE STABILITO IN CORPORE SVRGANT / AD VITAM AETERNAM TE PEREVNTE MAGIS / SANCTA FIDES MERITO VITAE CLEMENTIA PATRIS / SPEM CERTAM HANC FAMVLOS IVSSIT HABERE SVOS / HIC REQVIESCIT BONIFATIVS IVNIOR QVI SEDIT ANNOS V MENSES VIII DIES XII DEPOSITVS OCT IDVS / MAII IMPERANTE DOMINO HERACLIO ANNO EIVS SECVNDO[68]

("Man's life is short; a fixed hour determines it. But the journey to eternal life is thereupon prepared, which appears not as something unbecoming nor perishable, but beautiful and comely; it lasts without end. Thus, O Death, whatever you trouble with harmful stings, whatever you roar in vain, whatever madness you bring, your deeds can render you no reward, nor can this impulse of yours benefit you. This is the man who ever follows in laboring life and worthy morals the instructions and examples of his master Gregory, to the end that you deem him frightening. He wishes to dispatch his soul to the stars, to return his body to earth, wounded indeed in pain. His many body parts remain collected together and turn in ancient dust. Conjoined to his soul, let them rise to eternal life in a body made firm rather than in you that perish. The holy faith deservedly commanded her servants to keep this sure hope of life in the mercy of the father. Here lies Boniface the Younger, who was seated five years, seven months, 12 days, and was buried in the eighth ides of May by the command of Lord Heraclio in his year two." — *Trans. Ruth Yeuk Chun Leung*)

Grimaldi reported on the decommissioning of the altar of St. Boniface IV on October 20, 1605. According to Grimaldi, Boniface IV's remains had been moved by Boniface VIII, who had a new epitaph carved on marble and placed on the altar itself. The sense of the epitaph, says Phyllis Jestice, who translated Grimaldi's text, is that Boniface IV was good and just, and drove the demons from the Pantheon and rededicated it to all the saints. When the altar was opened, it was found to contain two ancient pots, one full and one half-full of bones. More bones were contained in an ancient round vase made of glass. It is not clear which of these were Boniface's and which belonged to other saints; Jestice notes in Grimaldi's text a reference to "relics of other saints" in the altar.

The remains were then placed in the altar of St. Thomas the Apostle,[69] although Grimaldi said that what was left of Boniface IV was placed in two vases and then put into a new cypress box, and that a few relics were taken out and put in a "noble crystal vessel" ornamented with flowers. A cardinal put the box into the marble sarcophagus with his own hands, and on the box placed an inscription in lead — "The body of St. Pope Boniface IV" — before the workmen closed it up. This altar can still be seen in St. Peter's, with the following inscription on the sarcophagus underneath:

CORPVS SANCTI / BONIFACII PAPAE IV

("The holy body of Pope Boniface IV.")

The cult of Boniface IV did not develop until the pontificate of Boniface VIII. Feast day: May 25.

FURTHER READING: C. Poggi, "Arnolfo di Cambio e il sacello di B. IV," in *Riv. D'Arte*, Firenze, III, 1905.

St. Deusdedit (St. Adeodatus) (October 19, 615–November 8, 615)

On his deathbed Deusdedit was the first pope to request that his clergy should each get a year's salary upon his death. He was buried at St. Peter's. Feast Day, November 8. An epitaph recorded by Montini for Deusdedit is actually the epitaph for Boniface V (q.v.).[70]

Boniface V (December 23, 619–October 25, 625)

Boniface V was buried in St. Peter's, although the tomb was destroyed during the demolition of the basilica in the seventeenth century. His epitaph reads:

DA MECVM GEMITVM SINGVLTI ROMA DOLORIS /
PLENA SACERDOTIS LVCTIBVS EGREGII / CVR
QVONIAM DEFLERE SOLET MENS ARTA PERICLIS /
PLEBSQVE ORBATA PIIS INSVPER OFFICIIS / HIC
VIR INACCESSIS TENVIT CONTRARIA FACTIS /
HAEC DOCVMENTA BONIS MORIBVS APTA SVIS /
MITIS IN ADVERSIS POSITVS REBVSQVE SECVNDIS /
OMIA GRATA FERENS ALTERA PRESSA TENENS /
PRAEVENIT NE NATA FORENT DELICTA VIRITIM /
ORTA IAM SECVIT CVM PIETATE GRAVI / IN
COMMVNE BONVS BONIFATIVS INDE VOCATVS /
PROPRIA LVCRA PVTANS PVBLICA SVBSIDIA /
MVNIFICVS SAPIENS CASTVS SINCERVS ET
AEQVVS / ISTA BEATORVM SVNT PIA SVFFRAGIA /
NAM VIDVALIS APEX PVPILLORVMQVE
PHALANGES / CAECORVMQVE CHORVS DVX
TIBI LVCIS ERIT / INFREMVIT POST FATA
SVIS MORS SAVCIA TELIS / RESPICIENS
MERITVM VIVERE POSSE VIRVM / CVLMEN
APOSTOLICVM QVINQVE ET BIS MENSIBVS
ANNIS / REXIT ET AD MAGNI CVLMEN
HONORIS ABIT[71]

("O Rome, full of mourning for the outstanding priest, together with me, give out a groan of sobbing sorrow. Why? Because the spirit pressed by trials is wont to weep, as is, besides, a people bereft of religious services. In hard times and in prosperous times, he was gentle, enduring all pleasant things, holding bad things in check. These are the fitting proofs of his good morals. He prevented men's crimes from arising, and those crimes that had already sprung up, he cut down. He was generous toward the common good, and so was called "Bonifatius." Considering his own money as public funds, he was magnanimous, wise, chaste, sincere, and fair. These are pious characteristics of the blessed. For you will be the leader of light to the highest ranks of widows, and the phalanxes of orphans, and the chorus of the blind. Then Death, wounded by its own spears, growled, seeing that a deserving man could live. He ruled the height of apostolic power for five years and two months, has gone away to the height of great honor."—*Trans. Father Thomas Buffer*)

Church historian Baronius recorded this epitaph:

CUR TITULATA DIU TORPUERUNT IURA SEPULCRI /
ET POPULI NULLUS PERSTREPUIT GEMITUS. /
SEGNITIES NON CULPA FUIT QUICUNQUE
REQUIRIS / NAM DOLOR INCLAUSUS PIUS
LACERARE SOLET / PANDE DOLOR GEMITUM
MERITISQUE QUIESCE BEATIS / UT LIBEAT SUMMI
GESTA REFERRE PATRIS. / HIC VIR AB EXORTU
PETRI EST NUTRITUS OVILE. / SED MERUIT SANCTI
PASTOR ADESSE GREGIS / PURA FIDES HOMINIS
VOTIS MANDATA BENIGNIS / EXCUVIANS CHRISTI
CANTIBUS HYMNISONIS. / SIMPLICITAS SAPIENS
VIVAX SOLERTIA SIMPLEX / SERPENTINA FUIT
SIMPLICITATE VIGENS. / CUMQUE QUATER DENOS
COMPLERET PRESBYTER ANNOS / PERFECTUM
NUMERUM TERQUE QUATERQUE GERENS / HOC
TIBI PRO MERITIS SUCCESSOR HONORIVS AMPLIS /
MARMORE CONSTRUXIT MUNUS EPITAPHII.[72]

("Why have the titled rights of the tomb long lain still, and no one clatter and sigh? O you who seek to know, indolence was not to blame, for sorrow kept within is wont to wound more deeply. O Sorrow, unfold your lamentation; be still in your blessed merits, that the deeds of the supreme father might be reported. This man from the line of Peter, nourished within Christ's fold, deserved to be the pastor of the holy flock. His pure faith was founded in kindhearted prayers, and he kept vigil, singing hymns of Christ. Wise simplicity, lively skill; he flourished in serpentine simplicity. Though 40 years of priesthood had passed, his aged mind remained fruitful, his apostolic height he cultivated for nearly three years again and again perfectly sustaining his rank. Your successor, Honorius, has constructed this with marble as an epitaphial tribute for your bountiful merits."—Trans. *Father Thomas Buffer and Ruth Yeuk Chun Leung*)

Honorius I (October 27, 625–October 12, 638) Buried at St. Peter's, although his tomb was destroyed in the demolition of the basilica in the seventeenth century. His original epitaph reads:

PASTOREM MAGNVM LAVDIS PIA PRAEMIA
LVSTRANT / QVI FVNCTVS PETRI HAC VICE
SVMMA TENET / EFFVLGIT TVMVLIS NAM PRAESVL
HONORIVS ISTIS / CVIVS MAGNANIMVM NOMEN
HONORQVE MANET / SEDIS APOSTOLICAE MERITIS
NAM IVRA GVBERNANS / DISPERSOS REVOCAT
OPTIMA LVCRA REFERT / VTQVE SAGAX ANIMO
DIVINO IN CARMINE POLLENS / AD VITAM PASTOR
DVCERE NOVIT OVES / HISTRIA NAM DVDVM
SAEVO SVB SCISMATE FESSA / AD STATVTA
PATRVM TEQVE MONENTE REDIT / IVDAICAE
GENTIS SVB TE EST PERFIDIA VICTA / SIC VNVM
DOMINI REDDIS OVILE PIVM / ADTONITVM
PATRIAE SOLLERS SIC CVRA MOVEBAT / OPTATA VT
POPVLIS ESSET VBIQVE QVIES / QVEM DOCTRINA
POTENS QVEM SACRAE REGVLA VITAE /
PONTIFICVM PARITER SANXIT HABERE DECVS /
SANCTILOQVI SEMPER IN TE COMMENTA
MAGISTRI / EMICVERE TVI TAMQVE
FECVNDA NIMIS / NAMQVE GREGORII TANTI
VESTIGIA IVISTI / DVM SEQVERIS CVPIENS ET
MERITVMQVE GERIS / AETERNAE LVCIS CHRISTO
DIGNANTE PERENNEM / CVM PATRIBVS SANCTIS
POSSIDE IAMQVE DIEM / HIS EGO EPITAPHIIS
MERITO TIBI CARMINA SOLVI / QVOS PATRIS
EXIMII SIM BONVS IPSE MEMOR[73]

("The godly rewards of praise purify the great shepherd who, having acted in Peter's stead, possesses highest things. For the bishop Honorius is distinguished by this tomb, and his magnanimous name and honor remain. For, governing the jurisdiction of the Apostolic See, by his merits he called back those who were scattered and brought in very good revenue. And being mentally shrewd, mighty in holy incantation, this shepherd knew how to lead the sheep to life. For Histria [or Istria, a region near Illyria], long exhausted by savage schism, at your admonition returned to the ordinances

of the fathers. Under you, the perfidy of the Jewish people was conquered; thus you make the faithful flock of the Lord to be one. Your skillful care of the homeland provided the longed-for quiet for the people everywhere. You possessed the honor of the pontiffs by your powerful teaching that consecrated a holy life for you. In you, hallowed teacher, the interpretations of your great words always shone out, and fruitfully, for you walked in the footsteps of great Gregory. And you followed eagerly, you also displayed merit. Possess, as Christ deigns, the everlasting day of eternal light, together with the holy fathers. With this epitaph, I have deservedly made you this verse; by it, may I well remember this exceptional father."—Trans. *Father Thomas Buffer*)

Church historian Baronius also recorded this epitaph:

QUIS MIHI TRIBUAT UT FLETUS CESSENT IMMENSI /
ET LUCTUS ANIMAE DET LOCUM VERA DICENTI /
LICET IN LACRYMIS SINGULATUS VERBA ERUMPANT
/ DE TE CERTISSIME TUUS DISCIPULUS LOQUOR. /
TE GENEROSITAS MINISTER CHRISTI PARENTUM /
TE MUNDA ACTIO THOMAS MONSTRABAT
HONESTUM; / TECUM VIRGINITAS AB INCUNABULIS
VIXIT / TECUMQUE VERITAS AD VITAE METAM
PERMANSIT / TU CASTO LABIO PUDICA VERBA
PROMEBAS; / TU PATIENS IAM PARCENDO
PIE DOCEBAS; / TE SEMPER SOBRIUM; TE
RECINEBAMUS MODESTUM / TU TRIBULANTUM
VERA CONSOLATIO VERAX. / ERRORE VETERI DIU
AQUILEGIA CAECA, / DIFFUSAM CAELITUS RECTAM
DUM RENUERET FIDEM; / ASPERA VIARUM
NINGUIDOSQUE MONTIUM CALLES / CALCANS
INDEFESSUS GLUTINASTI PRUDENS SCISSOS.[74]

("Who will grant me an end to my great weeping? Would that my soul's mourning would leave me room to speak the truth. Even if my words burst forth in sobbing tears, I, your disciple, will most surely speak of you. Servant of Christ, your generosity showed that you were a father; Thomas, your pure living showed that you were honest. Virginity lived with you from the cradle, and truth remained with you to the end of your life. You brought forth chaste words from your innocent lips; you taught in a godly way by being patient and sparing. You were always sober. We used to sing of how you were modest. You were truthful, and consoled the afflicted. Auilegia had long been blinded by ancient error, rejecting the right faith spread from heaven. Treading the rough places of the roads, and the snowy paths of the mountains, untiring, prudent, you reattached those who had been cut off."—*Trans. Father Thomas Buffer*)

Severinus (May 28–August 2, 640) Died from old age and harsh treatment at the hands of imperial soldiers who had surrounded the Lateran Palace for three days demanding that he pay them. Finally they stormed the palace, stole their money and beat the pope, which caused his death several days later. Severinus left the clergy a year's salary upon his death. He was buried in the porch of St. Peter's, but his tomb was destroyed during the demolition of the basilica in the seventeenth century.

John IV (December 24, 640–October 12, 642) Buried at St. Peter's on October 12, although his tomb was destroyed during the demolition of St. Peter's in the seventeenth century. He left a year's stipend to each of the clergy upon his death.

Theodore I (November 24, 642–May 14, 649) Possibly poisoned because he had deposed and excommunicated the patriarch Paul over the *Ecthesis*. He was buried in the atrium of St. Peter's although his tomb was destroyed during the demolition of the basilica during the seventeenth century. Luckily, however, his tomb inscription survived:

INCVBAT EGREGII THEODORI
PRAESVLIS ALMI HOC TVMVLO CORPVS[75]

("The body of Theodore, the kind distinguished bishop, lies in this tomb."—*Trans. Father Thomas Buffer*)

St. Martin I (July 5, 649–September 16, 655) The official Vatican list of popes records that the day of his death in exile—September 16, 655—was the end of his pontificate, not the day that Eugenius I was elected, which was August 10, 654, or the date of his exile, June 17, 653. He died from starvation, cold, harsh treatment, gout, dysentery, or possibly a combination of these while in exile in Chersonesus (near modern Sevastopol), Crimea.

Martin had held a council at the Lateran in Rome that condemned the "error of Monothelitism" (which denies that Christ had a human will), a doctrine that the reigning emperor, Constans II, and his two predecessors approved. Martin had also already displeased the emperor by not awaiting his approval to become pope. Although bedridden with dysentery and gout, he was arrested at the Lateran basilica, brought to Constantinople under military custody, and placed in solitary confinement in a prison called Prandearia until his trial. He was mistreated by his jailers, given food that made him sick, and not allowed to wash for forty-seven days "even in cold water." At his trial he was charged with supporting the Olympius rebellion[76] and corresponding with Muslims. His condemnation of Monothelitism was never mentioned, although it was the real reason he was brought to trial. Martin was found guilty of treason, publicly stripped of his vestments, dragged in shackles through the streets, and flogged in front of the crowd before being thrown into the prison of Diomede for 85 days. He was sentenced to death, but the intervention of Paul II (the patriarch of Constantinople) saved his life. He was banished to Chersonesus in Crimea, where he wrote of his harsh conditions and how he was upset that the Romans seemed to forget about him (they breached papal etiquette by electing another pope while Martin was still alive). He was buried in the Church of Our Lady, called Blachdernæ, near Chersonesus. Today no trace of the church or tomb remains.

Martin was the last pope to be venerated as a martyr[77]; his name was recorded in the *Bobbio Missal* of the eighth century. The *Liber Pontificalis* (*Book of Pontiffs*) states that he "died in peace, like Christ's confessor, and performed many miracles down to our days." His former feast day, November 12, supposedly commemorates the day his relics were translated to San Martino ai Monte in Rome by Sergius II (d. 847). Today his feast day is April 13 in the West, September 20 in the East.

St. Eugenius I (August 10, 654–June 2, 657) Buried in St. Peter's, although his tomb was destroyed in the demolition of the basilica in the seventeenth century. Eugenius was elected as an antipope yet was recognized as pope when Martin I died in 655. He left bequests to his clergy and the people of Rome upon his death. The *Oxford Dictionary of Popes* claims that although Eugenius was ignored by ancient martyrologies, his name was inserted into the *Roman Martyrology* by the church historian Cesare Baronius in the late sixteenth century. His feast day is June 2.

St. Vitalian (July 30, 657–January 27, 672) Buried in St. Peter's, although his tomb was destroyed during the demolition of St. Peter's in the seventeenth century. Feast day: January 27.

Adeodatus II (April 11, 672–June 17, 676) Buried in St. Peter's, although his tomb was destroyed during the demolition of the basilica in the seventeenth century. He left a generous sum to his clergy upon his death.

Donus (November 2, 676–April 11, 678) Buried in St. Peter's on April 15, although his tomb was destroyed during the demolition of the basilica in the seventeenth century.

St. Agatho (June 27, 678–January 10, 681) Died of an epidemic at the age of 107. He left

his clergy a substantial amount of money upon his death. He was buried in St. Peter's, although his tomb was destroyed during the demolition of the basilica in the seventeenth century. Luckily his epitaph has been recorded:

PONTIFICALIS APEX VIRTVTVM PONDERE FVLTVS / VT IVBAR IS RADIAT PERSONAT VT TONITRVS / QVAE MONET HOC PERAGIT DOCTRINAE FOMES ET AUCTOR / FORMAT ENIM GESTIS QVOS DOCET ELOQVIIS / DVM SIMVL AEQVIPERAT VIRTVS ET CVLMEN HONORIS / OFFICIVM DECORAT MORIBVS ARTE GERIT / PRAEDITVS HIS MERITIS ANTISTES SVMMVS AGATHO / SEDIS APOSTOLICAE FOEDERA FIRMA TENET / EN PIETAS EN PRISCA FIDES INSIGNIA PATRVM / INTEMERATA MANENT NISIBVS ALME TVIS / QVIS VERO DINVMERET MORVM DOCVMENTA TVORVM / FORMVLA VIRTVTVM DVM TVA VITA FORET[78]

("The pontifical summit was supported by the weight of his virtues as a star shines, as thunder resounds. What the source and author of teaching advises, he accomplishes. For he forms by his deeds those whom he teaches by his words, while at the same his virtue was equal to the summit of honor [i.e., the papacy]. Endowed with these merits, the supreme bishop, Agatho, adorns his office with his way of life, and administrates it with skill. He holds firm the pacts of the Apostolic See. Behold, his godliness; behold, the pure distinguished faith of the fathers remain inviolate because of your efforts, O caregiver. But who could number the proofs of your morals, since your life was the very model of virtues?"—*Trans. Father Thomas Buffer*)

Agatho's feast day is January 10 in both the West and East.

St. Leo II (August 17, 682–July 3, 683) When Leo II died he left a generous sum to his clergy. He was originally buried in St. Peter's, although Paschal II (d. 1118) placed Leo II's remains with those of Leo III (795–816) and Leo IV (847–855) in a marble tomb under the altar of the Chapel of the Madonna della Colonna. The ornate sarcophagus housing the Leos features Christ giving the scroll of the Law to Saint Peter, who is carrying a cross. On the other side of the Lord is Elias dropping his mantle for his disciple. This tomb was found in 1580 by Gregory XIII (d. 1585). In 1601 the remains of Leo I (d. 461) were added to the sarcophagus when his tomb was found in St. Peter's (for detailed information on the burials and exhumations of the Leos, see Leo IV).

For centuries the people of Ferrara thought that Leo II was enshrined under an altar in the church of San Stefano. The finding of a tombstone by the bishop Giacomo Benzoni from 1509 stating that the Duke Alfonso d'Este and Cardinal Ippolito placed the remains of Leo under the altar was considered proof. After some checking, Benzoni found a notice that in 754 Pope Zacharis donated to King Astolfo, for the Abbey of Nonantola, the bodies of Pope Saint Silvester and Leo II, and that the relics of Pope Leo would be brought in 1006 to Vicoventia, and from there to Ferrara. During the demolition of St. Peter's in the early seventeenth century, the remains of Popes Leo II, III, and IV were found in one sarcophagus, thus proving that Leo II rested at the Vatican. The Apostolic Nuncio then forbade the cult of Pope Leo at Ferrara. The relics under the altar in Ferrara actually belong to a different Leo II who was bishop of Voghenza in 611. Perhaps the rumor was started because for a church to contain the body of a pope, let alone a sainted pope, brought in much revenue from people on pilgrimage to his shrine.

The relics of the bishop Leo are still preserved at the first altar on the right side of the church of San Stefano, in a wooden urn gilded with the inscription:

HIC REQVIESCIT CORPVS S. LEONIS / PONTIFICIS ET SACERDOTIS CHRISTI / TRANSLATVM HVC A VICOVENTIA / SVB GRATIANO FERRARIENSI EPISCOPO A. D. M OCT I 1081[79]

("Here rests the body of St. Leo, pontiff and priest of Christ, translated to this place from Vicoventia under Bishop Gratian of Ferrara. October 1, in the year of Our Lord 1081."—*Trans. Father Thomas Buffer*)

The feast day of Leo II is July 3.

FURTHER READING: *Acta SS Junii*, V. Antverpiae, 1709; *De corpore S. Leonis Papae Ferrariae*; G. A. Scalabrini, *Memorie istoriche delle chiese di Ferrara*, Ferrara, 1773; G. Filangieri di Candida, *Chiesa e Convento di S. Lorenzo Maggiore in Napoli*, Naples, 1883.

St. Benedict II (June 26, 684–May 8, 685) Buried in St. Peter's, although his tomb was destroyed during the demolition of the basilica in the seventeenth century. He left thirty pounds of gold to the clergy, the diaconal monasteries, and the lay sacristans of the church. His epitaph reads:

MAGNA TVIS BENEDICTE PATER MONVMENTA RELINQVIS / VIRTVTVM TITVLOS O DECVS ATQVE DOLOR / FVLGVRIS IN SPECIMEN MENTIS SPLENDORE CORVSCAS / PLVRA SED EXIGVO TEMPORE CAEPTA FLVVNT / CVNCTA SACERDOTVM PRAESTANTIA MVNIA COMPLES / ET QVO QVISQVE BONO CLARVIT VNVS HABES / QVIPPE QVOD A PARVO MERITIS RADIANTIBVS AVCTVS / IVRE PATRVM SOLIVM PONTIFICALE FOVES / NON HOC AMBITIO RAPTI TIBI PRAESTAT HONORIS / INDOLIS EST FRVCTVS QVAM COMITATVR HONOS / ET QVIA SOLLERTER CHRISTI REGIS AGMINA PASTOR / PERCIPE SALVATI PRAEMIA CELSA GREGIS[80]

("O Father Benedict, you are leaving behind your great monuments, your titles and honor of virtues, O sorrow! Like lightning, you flash with mental splendor, but in a small period of time, you accomplished your many projects. You complete with distinction all the official duties of priests, and by yourself you flourish in the good that each one of them has. Because you grew great by your shining merits, you rightly tended the pontifical throne of the fathers. You had no ambition to seize honor, for honor is the fruit of your character. And because you, O shepherd, skillfully ruled Christ's hosts, claim now the lofty rewards of the saved flock."—*Trans. Father Thomas Buffer*)

The feast day of Benedict II is May 7.

John V (July 23, 685–August 2, 686) Died from long-term illness. He left 1900 *solidi* to the clergy and the monasteries serving the poor. He was buried in the atrium of St.

Peter's on August 2. According to papal tomb historian Renzo Montini, his tomb was destroyed during the Saracen raid in 846,[81] but the epitaph had been recorded:

IOHANNEM TVMVLVS VATEM TEGIT ASTRVAT AETAS / OPTIMA COEPTA VIRI SI FORET ET SPATIVM / HIC ET IN EXTREMIS SOLLERS FIDVSQVE MINISTER / CLARVIT ET PRIMVS IVRE LEVITA FVIT / MISSVS AD IMPERIVM VICE PRESVLIS EXTITIT AVCTOR / HVNC MEMORAT SYNODVS PONTIFICISQVE TOMVS / CVM TITVLIS FIDEI VIGILANTIA QVANTA REGENDI / COMMISSAS ANIMAS NE LVPVS HOSTIS OVES / CARPERET AMMIXTVS PREMERETVE POTENTIOR IMAM / IVSTITIAM CVNCTOS VISVS HABERE PAREM / PROVIDVS HVMANVS FIRMVS VERVSQVE SACERDOS / NIL TEMERE ATQVE NIMIS PONDERE CVNCTA GERENS[82]

("This tomb covers John the seer; may time add to the great things he began, if there is room. To the end he was a clever and faithful servant. He was famous, and rightly was the first-ranking priest [literally: Levite]. Sent to the empire in his bishop's stead, he stood out by his actions, for the synod and the book of the pontiff recalls him. Provident, polite, firm, and a true priest, he managed nothing blindly, but handled everything with very great authority."—*Trans. Father Thomas Buffer*)

Church historian Petrus Mallius recorded an epitaph for John V; however, Renzo Montini claims the same epitaph for Marinus I (d. 884). Because the epitaph does not name a specific person, it is impossible to say who is correct. The epitaph reads:

QUAM SOLERS DOMINO PLACUIT, QUAM MENTE MODESTA / PRAESUL APOSTOLICUS ORBIS ET OMNE DECUS / HIC STATUIT TUMULO CLAUDI SUA MEMBRA SUB ISTO / HAEC EADEM SPERANS, UT SIBI REDDAT HUMUS. / ARDUA QUI FULSIT CUNCTIS UT SYDERA CAELI, / AUGUSTIS CHARUS GENTIBUS ET TRIBUBUS. / DOCTRINIS COMPTUS SACRIS ET DOGMATE CLARO / PER PATRIAS SANCTA SEMINA FUDIT OVANS. / NAM GRAIOS SUPERANS EOIS PARTIBUS UNAM, / SCISMATA PELLENDO REDDIDIT ECCLESIAM / PRINCIPIS HIC PETRI SED QUISQUIS TENDIS AD AULAM. / DIC SUPPLEX, ISDEM REGNET UT ARCE POLI.[83]

("How greatly he pleased the Lord by his great skill, by his modest spirit! Apostolic bishop and glory of the world, here he decided that his remains should be enclosed beneath this tomb, hoping that the earth would return those same remains to Him who shone before all, like the burning stars of the sky that are esteemed by honorable nations and tribes. Full of holy doctrines and brilliant teaching, he sowed the holy seed throughout the lands, rejoicing. For overcoming the Greeks in eastern lands, driving away schisms, he returned the Church to unity. But whosoever comes to this hall of Peter the prince, humbly say: May he reign as the our heavenly protection!"—*Trans. Father Thomas Buffer*)

Conon (October 21, 686–September 21, 687) Died after a long illness. He left gold to the clergy, to monasteries serving the poor, and to the *mansionarii*. He was buried on September 21 at St. Peter's, probably in the left nave, although his tomb was destroyed during the demolition of the basilica in the seventeenth century.

Antipope Theodore (687) Never consecrated, he accepted defeat in the papal election and embraced Sergius I as legitimate pope. Nothing more is known of him.

Antipope Paschal (687; d. 692) Although he submitted to Pope Sergius, he was deposed from the archidiaconate for continuing to plot against the pope. He was imprisoned in an unknown monastery on charges of being a magician and died five years later, still unrepentant. He was buried in an unknown location.

St. Sergius I (December 15, 687–September 9, 701) The first pope actually buried in St. Peter's proper, not on the portico, in a "most elegant" tomb that was destroyed during the demolition of the basilica in the seventeenth century. His cult spread not long after his death. Church historian Mallius gives the same epitaph for Sergius I in the

Codex Barbarini Latinus 2733 that Renzo Montini erroneously attributes to Sergius III in *Le Tombe dei Papi*:

LIMINA QVISQVIS ADIS PAPAE METVENDA BEATI /
CERNE PII SERGII EXCVBIASQVE PETRI / CVLMEN
APOSTOLICAE SEDIS IS IVRE PATERNO / ELECTVS
TENVIT VT THEODORVS OBIT / PELLITVR VRBE
PATER PERVADIT SACRA IOHANNES /
ROMVLEOSQVE GREGES DISSIPAT IPSE LVPVS /
EXVL ERAT PATRIA SEPTEM VOLVENTIBVS ANNIS /
POST MVLTIS POPVLI VRBE REDIT PRECIBVS /
SVSCIPITVR PAPA SANCTA SEDE RECEPTA / GAVDET
AMAT PASTOR AGMINA CVNCTA SIMVL / HIC
INVASORES SANCTORVM FALCE SVBEGIT /
ROMANAE ECCLESIAE IVDICIISQVE PATRVM[84]

("Whosoever approaches the dread threshold of blessed Peter, see faithful Sergius and Peter keeping watch. He, by paternal right, was elected and held the apostolic summit when Theodorus died. The pope was driven from the City by John, the wolf himself, who invaded the holy places and scattered the Roman flocks. He [Sergius] was exiled from his homeland for seven years, but, answering the people's prayers, he returned. The pope reclaimed the Holy See as its rightful pastor, and all the throngs rejoiced together. This man put down the invaders of the Roman Church with the sickle of the saints and the judgments of the fathers."—*Trans. Father Thomas Buffer*)

The feast day for Sergius I is September 8.

John VI (October 30, 701–January 11, 705)

Buried in St. Peter's, although his tomb was destroyed during the demolition of the basilica in the seventeenth century.

John VII (March 1, 705–October 18, 707)

Unsupported rumors held that he died at the hands of a jealous husband at his new palace at the foot of the Palatine. He was buried in the Chapel of the Blessed Virgin Mary in St. Peter's, which is now part of the Vatican grottoes.

During the demolition of St. Peter's in the early seventeenth century, church canon

and historian Giacomo Grimaldi recorded a simple epitaph for John VII:

("Here is John VII, a Greek by birth, son of Plato, who held office 2 years, 7 months, 17 days, who died in the year of the lord 705. He is buried before the altar of the oratory that he himself built in the basilica of St. Peter.... Anastasius [the papal biographer and later antipope] says "he is buried in St. Peter's before the altar in the oratory of the mother of God that he himself built." However, in the demolition under Paul V, supreme pontiff, not a single trace of his tomb was found."[85]—*Trans. Phyllis Jestice*)

Close to that place, however, was discovered a very ancient body buried in a marble sarcophagus, believed to be that of John VII. At that site, a fragment of stone was uncovered, with "Mother of God" (Theotokos) carved on it in large Greek letters. Perhaps this is a fragment of his epitaph, which originally said:

IOHANNES SERVIS SCAE MARIAE[86]

("Pope John VII, servant of the Holy Mother of God.")

John is known to have been greatly devoted to the Virgin, and since he was Greek, perhaps his epitaph was in Greek.[87]

Unfortunately that sarcophagus was destroyed in the demolition of the seventeenth century, although there is a mosaic of Pope John VII located in the Vatican grottoes that is thought to be from his original tomb. A more thorough epitaph, also probably located in the old oratory, has also been recorded:

HIC SIBI CONSTITVIT TVMVLVM IVSSITQVE
REPONI / PRAESVL IOHANNES SVB PEDIBVS
DOMINAE / COMMITTENS ANIMAM SANCTAE SVB
TEGMINE MATRIS / INNVBA QVAE PEPERIT VIRGA
PARENSQVE DEVM / HIC DECVS OMNE LOCVM
PRISCO SQVALORE REMOTO / NONTVLIT VT
STVPEAT PRODIGA POSTERITAS / NON POMPAE
STVDIO QVAE DEFLVIT ORBE SVB IPSO / SED
FERVORE PIO PRO GENITRICE DEI / NON PARCENS
OPIBVS PRAETIOSVM QVICQVID HABEBAT / IN TVA
DISTRIBVIT MVNERA SANCTA PARENS / PAVPERIVBS
RELIQVVM MVNVS DEDIT INDICAT HOSPES /

FESSVS AB OCEANO QVI TENVS ORBE VENIT /
CVM VCTVM INVENIET QVO VITAE SERIA SVMAT /
HINC APVD EXCELSVM SPES ERIT ALME TIBI[88]

("Here Pope John wished his own sepulcher and arranged to be laid at the feet of Our Lady, placing his soul under the protection of the Holy Mother, the Mother of God, the intact virgin. To this place, he brought every embellishment, changing the ancient squalor in a way that posterity would be left with amazing gratitude. He did this, not because he desired vain glory, which dies with the end of one's life, but because he was driven by religious ardor for the Mother of God. Not considering the costs, he employed whatever he had that was precious in order to donate it to you, oh Holy Mother. He gave what remained as a gift to the poor. The pilgrims, arriving exhausted from the oceans to the Holy City, when destitute would find food, and with it, what was necessary for life. For these things, oh eminent man, your hope is certain in heaven."—Trans. Father Tom Carleton)

FURTHER READING: G. B. de Rossi, *Musaici cristiani delle chiese di Roma*, Rome, 1899; Virgilio Cardinal Noe, *Le Tombe e i Monumenti*, Rome, 2000.

Sisinnius   (January 15–February 4, 708) Died suddenly from gout, from which he had suffered so badly that when he was elected he couldn't even feed himself. He was buried in the left nave of St. Peter's, although the tomb was destroyed during the demolition of the basilica during the seventeenth century.

Constantine   (March 25, 708–April 9, 715) Possibly died from illness. Buried in the left nave of St. Peter's, although his tomb was destroyed during the demolition of St. Peter's in the seventeenth century.

St. Gregory II   (May 19, 715–February 11, 731) Died at age 62. During his funeral, crowds seized the future Gregory III and elected him pope by popular vote. Gregory II was buried under the pavement in the

atrium of St. Peter's, although his tomb was destroyed during the demolition of the basilica during the seventeenth century. His cult first appeared in the *Martyrology of Ado* in the ninth century. Feast day: February 11.

St. Gregory III   (March 18, 731–November 28, 741) Buried in the oratory that he built and dedicated to Our Lady in St. Peter's. The mosaic decorating this tomb was damaged when, in the eleventh century, the body of Eugenius III was placed there. Although the tomb itself was destroyed during the demolition of St. Peter's in the seventeenth century, copies were made of the simple inscription:

TERTIVS HIC PAPA GREGORIVS EST TVMVLATVS[89]

("Pope Gregory III is entombed here.")

His cult is witnessed by the *Martyrology of Ado* of the ninth century. Feast day: November 28.

St. Zacharias   (December 3, 741–March 15, 752) Buried in St. Peter's, although his tomb was destroyed during the demolition of St. Peter's in the seventeenth century. No early evidence of his cult survives. Feast day March 15 in the West, September 5 in the East.

FURTHER READING: D. Bartolini, *Zaccaria papa*, Ratisbona, 1879.

Stephen (II)   (March 22 or 23–March 25 or 26, 752) Died from a stroke only three days after being elected and before he was consecrated. He was not included in the official papal roster until the 1500s. The *Annuario Pontificio* then listed him as a pope until 1961; since then, however, his name has been excluded. To accommodate the changes in status of Stephen (II), the next pope Stephen is numbered as Stephen II (III).

Stephen (II) was buried under the pavement in the atrium of St. Peter's, although his tomb was destroyed during the demolition of the basilica in the seventeenth century.

Stephen II (III) (March 26, 752–April 26, 757)

He was buried under the pavement of the atrium of St. Peter's, although his tomb was destroyed during the demolition of the basilica during the seventeenth century. His tomb inscription reads:

SVBIACET HIC STEPHANVS
ROMANVS PAPA SECVNDVS[90]

("The Roman pope Stephen II lies under here.")

St. Paul I (May 29, 757–June 28, 767)

Died from heat exhaustion at San Paulo fuori le Mura, Rome, and was also temporarily buried there. When Paul was dying, Duke Toto of Nepi (brother of the next antipope, Constantine) plotted his murder but was convinced by the chief notary, Christopher, to let the next election evolve on its own. His tomb inscription reads:

HIC REQVIESCIT PAVLVS PAPA[91]

("Here is buried Pope Paul.")

In October 767 his remains were moved to the oratory of Our Lady that he had built in the western angle of the southern transept of St. Peter's. This oratory was enclosed with a bronze railing and was so sacred that women were not allowed to enter.[92] There is no evidence of his cult before the fifteenth century, and his tomb has been destroyed, probably during the demolition of St. Peter's in the seventeenth century. Feast day: June 28.

Antipope Constantine (July 5, 767–August 6, 768; d.?)

Died from harsh treatment in an unknown monastery. Upon the death of Pope Paul I, the Duke Toto of Nepi forced the election of his brother, Constantine. When Stephen III was officially elected, however, Constantine hid in the Lateran. He was dragged from his hiding place and foolishly paraded around the city on a donkey. At a synod on August 6 he was stripped of his papal insignia and formally deposed, then imprisoned in a monastery, where a gang attacked him and gouged out his eyes. Finally, on April 12 and 13, 769, he appeared before a synod held by Stephen III in the Lateran to settle this issue. He claimed that he had been forced to become pope, but he later admitted guilt. Yet at the second session he changed his mind about the relevancy of his election and insisted that he should be pope. Angered by his assertion, the judges roughly abused him before sentencing him to life-long penance in a monastery. Nothing more is known of him.

Antipope Philip (July 31, 768)

Philip was seized one morning by the Lombard king Desiderius from the Monastery of St. Vito in Rome and appointed pope. No one paid any attention to him, and so he was returned later that night to his monastery, where he disappears from history.

Stephen III (IV) (August 7, 768–January 24, 772)

Abbot Hugh of Cluny assisted the pope in his dying days and personally washed and dressed the corpse. He buried Stephen under the pavement in the atrium of St. Peter's, although the tomb was destroyed in the demolition of the basilica in the seventeenth century.

Hadrian I (February 1, 772–December 25, 795).

It is recorded that Charlemagne wept as though he had lost "a brother or child" when he heard of Hadrian's death, and that he sent many charitable offerings in Hadrian's honor. In France he ordered that the name of Hadrian be engraved on marble in golden letters for Hadrian's tomb in Rome. Hadrian was buried in the oratory that he had built to house the Cathedra Petri in St. Peter's Basilica. Nothing remains of the tomb except the epitaph, which was carved on a slab of black marble and is now located in the wall of the portico of St. Peter's. His metric epitaph was written by Alcuin, although it is often attributed to Charlemagne. (The Gregorovius version below spells out the abbreviations in the original epitaph.)

HIC PATER ECCLESIAE, ROMAE DECUS, INCLYTUS AUCTOR / HADRIANUS REQUIEM PAPA BEATUS HABET: / VIR CUI VITA DEUS, PIETAS LEX, GLORIA CHRISTUS, / PASTOR APOSTOLICUS, PROMPTUS AD OMNE BONUM: / NOBILIS EX MAGNA GENITUS IAM GENTE PARENTUM, / SED SACRIS LONGE NOBILIOR MERITIS: / EXORNARE STUDENS DEVOTO PECTORE PASTOR / SEMPER UBIQUE SUO TEMPLA SACRATA DEO, / ECCLESIAS DONIS POPULOS ET DOGMATE SANCTO / IMBUIT, ET CUNCTIS PANDIT AD ASTRA VIAM. / PAUPERIBUS LARGUS, NULLI PIETATE SECUNDUS, / ET PRO PLEBE SACRIS PERVIGIL IN PRECIBUS / DOCTRINIS, OPIBUS, MURIS EREXERAT ARCES, / URBIS CAPUT ORBIS HONOR, INCLYTA ROMA, TUAS. / MORS CUI NIL NOCUIT, CHRISTI QUAE MORTE PEREMPTA EST, / IANUA SED VITAE MOX MELIORIS ERAT. / POST PATREM LACRIMANS KAROLUS HAEC CARMINA SCRIBSI, / TU MIHI DULCIS AMOR, TE MODO PLANGO PATER. / TU MEMOR ESTO MEI: SEQUITUR TE MENS MEA SEMPER, / CUM CHRISTO TENEAS REGNA BEATA POLI. / TE CLERUS, POPULUS MAGNO DILEXIT AMORE, / OMNIBUS UNUS AMOR, OPTIME PRAESUL, ERAS. / NOMINA IUNGO SIMUL TITULIS, CLARISSIME, NOSTRA / HADRIANUS, KAROLUS, REX EGO, TUQUE PATER. / QUISQUIS LEGAS VERSUS, DEVOTO PECTORE SUPPLEX / AMBORUM MITIS, DIC, MISERERE DEUS. / HAEC TUA NUNC TENEAT REQUIES, CARISSIME, MEMBRA, / CUM SANCTIS ANIMA GAUDEAT ALMA DEI. / ULTIMA QUIPPE TUAS DONEC TUBA CLAMET IN AURES, / PRINCIPE CUM PETRO SURGE VIDERE DEUM. / AUDITURUS ERIS VOCEM, SCIO, IUDICIS ALMAM: / INTRA NUNC DOMINI GAUDIA MAGNA TUI. / TUNC MEMOR ESTO TUI NATI, PATER OPTIME, POSCO, / CUM PATRE, DIC, NATUS PERGAT ET ISTE MEUS, / O PETE REGNA, PATER FELIX, CAELESTIA CHRISTI: / INDE TUUM PRECIBUS AUXILIARE GREGEM. / DUM SOL IGNICOMO RUTILUS SPLENDESCIT AB AXE, / LAUS TUA, SANCTE PATER, SEMPER IN ORBE MANET. / SEDIT BEATAE MEM. HADRIANUS PAPA ANNOS XXIII. / MENS. X. D. XVI OBIIT VII KAL. IAN.[93]

("Here has Pope Adrian found his rest—the Father of the Church, the ornament of Rome, the immortal writer. For him, to live was God: Piety was his Law, his glory, Christ; he was an apostolic shepherd, ready for every good deed. He was noble by birth, and sprung from an ancient race; yet nobler far by reason of his holy merits. The devout soul of this good Shepherd burned ever and in all places to adorn the temples dedicated to God. He heaped gifts upon the churches, and imbued the people with the sacred dogmas; to all he opened the narrow way to Heaven. Generous to the poor, unequalled in piety, and instant in devout prayers for all men, he was the glory of the City and the World, by his doctrines, by his treasures, by the walls he built, he raised thy citadels to honor, O noble Rome! Death has not harmed him, since Death was conquered by the Saviour's death—Nay rather, Death has become the gate of a better life. I, Charles, have writ these lines, in tears over my father. O my father, my sweet love, for thee I mourn. O forget me not! My thoughts are ever with thee. Mayst thou abide with Christ in the blissful realms of Heaven! Clergy and People alike loved thee with ardent love; thou alone were loved of all, O best of Pontiffs. Most illustrious of men, I link thy names and titles with my own. I, Charles the King, thou, Adrian the Pope. Ye who may chance to read these lines, say, with devout and suppliant heart, "Have pity upon them both, most merciful God!" May this thy body rest in peace, beloved Father, and may thy gentle soul joy with the saints of God, yea, till the last trump shall sound in thine ears. Then rise with Peter, Prince of the Apostles, to behold thy God. Thou wilt hear, I know, thy judge's clement voice, 'Enter now upon the great joys of thy Lord!' Then, most loving Father, be mindful, I beseech thee, of thy son! And say, 'Let this my son gain entrance with his father!' O Blessed Father, seek Christ's heavenly Kingdom, and thence aid with thy prayers thine earthly flock! While yet the ruddy sun shines forth from his flaming chariot. Thy praise, Holy Father, shall never cease on earth. Pope Adrian, of blessed memory, reigned 23 years 10 months.[94])

FURTHER READING: De Rossi, *L'inscription du tombeau d'Hadrian I*, in Melanges, VIII, 1880; Virgilio Cardinal Noe: *Le Tombe e i Monumenti*, Rome, 2000.

St. Leo III (December 26, 795–June 12, 816) Died from illness in Rome and was buried in St. Peter's. Paschal II (d. 1118) placed the bodies of Popes Leo II, Leo III, Leo IV in the same marble tomb, which was found in 1580 by Pope Gregory XIII and later destroyed in the demolition of the basilica in the seventeenth century. In 1601 the remains of Pope Leo I were found, and all four Leos were put into an ancient sarcophagus underneath the altar of our Savior della Colonna in the new St. Peter's (Leo I was later removed and is under his own altar in St. Peter's). Leo III's cult dates from the tenth century, but he was not canonized in 1673. Feast day: June 12. For more information on Leo III's burials and reburials, see Leo I, Leo II, and Leo IV.

St. Stephen IV (V) (June 22, 816–January 24, 817) Buried in St. Peter's, although his tomb was destroyed during the demolition of the basilica in the seventeenth century.

A. Vultus imaginum suppleti ex aliis eorumdem temporum.
B. Historia renouata ad exemplum ab Antiquariis olim exceptum cum deflueret.
C. Tabula nullis notata litteris exceptorum incuria.
D. Nomen Pontificis desideratur.
E. Inscriptas tabellae acclamationes seruauit Angelus Massarellus.
F. Ædificij descriptio verbis Anastasij Bibliothecarij.
G. Instaurati operis monumentum.

The original tomb of Pope St. Leo III in St. Peter's. By permission of the Houghton Library, Harvard University.

St. Paschal I (January 24, 817–February 11, 824) Because of his harsh reign, Paschal had many enemies and was so unpopular in Rome that when he died the Romans would not allow his body to be buried in St. Peter's. Consequently, his body was left unburied until his successor, Pope Eugenius II (824–827), allegedly had him buried in the chapel of St. Zeno (beneath the oratory in the south transept) of Santa Prassade,[95] where Paschal's mother had been buried. However, research undertaken in the seventeenth century on the presbytery of Santa Prassade confirms that Paschal's remains were never buried in that church.

The *Liber Pontificalis* (*Book of Pontiffs*), however, reports that Paschal was in fact buried in St. Peter's, in the altar of the oratory of Saints Processus and Martiniano (which he had constructed). But when the oratory was moved in 1548, and again in 1605, no trace of his tomb was found. His name was included in the catalogue of saints in the late sixteenth century.

Feast day: May 14, but suppressed in 1963.

FURTHER READING: P. Brezzi, *Roma e l'Impero medioevale*, Bologna, 1947; B. Davanzati, *Notizie al pellegrino della basilica di S. Prassede*, Rome, 1725.

Eugene II (June 5 [?], 824–August 27 [?], 827) Buried in St. Peter's, although his tomb was destroyed during the demolition of the basilica in the seventeenth century.

Valentine (August–September 827) The *Liber Pontificalis* (*Book of Pontiffs*) claims that he died from "bodily trouble." He was buried in St. Peter's, although his tomb was destroyed during the demolition of the basilica in the seventeenth century.

Gregory IV (late 827–January 25, 844) Buried in St. Peter's, although his tomb was destroyed, most likely during the demolition of St. Peter's in the seventeenth century.

Antipope John (January 844) Pope Sergius II spared his life although he had tried to usurp the papal throne. He was confined to a monastery. Nothing more is known of him.

Sergius II (January 844–January 27, 847) Died suddenly of unknown causes. Probably buried in the altar of Pope Paschal's chapel of Saints Sixtus and Fabian in St. Peter's, although if he were, his burial place would have been destroyed during the demolition of St. Peter's in the seventeenth century.
Epitaph:

SERGIVS EN IVNIOR PRAESVL ET PLEBIS AMATOR / HOC TEGITVR TVMVLO QVI BENE PAVIT OVES / SPES PATRIAE MVNDIQVE DECVS MODERATOR OPIMVS / DIVINIS MONITIS NON FVIT ILLE PIGER / ROMANOS PROCERES NON TANTVM FAMINE VERBI / REBVS ET HVMANIS NOCTE DIEQVE FAVENS / VTQVE LEO SANCTVS DAMASVS QVOQVE PAPA BENIGNVS / HIC RITVM TENVIT

INSTITVITQVE GREGEM / EGENTVM SEMPER STVDVIT RECREARE CATERVAM / PROQVE POLI VT CAPERET CAELICA REGNA LIBENS / IAM IAM PRO TANTO TVNDAMVS PECTORA PVGNIS / PASTORE AMISSO VIVAT VT AXE POLI / NECTITVR ECCE PIIS FAVIANO ET CORPORE XISTO / PRAESVLIBVS QVORVM SPIRITVS ASTRA MICANT[96]

("See, the young bishop Sergius who loved the people, who pastored his sheep well, is covered by this tomb. He was the hope of his homeland, ornament of the world, the very best governor, and he was not lazy when it came to divine teachings. He favored both night and day the Roman nobles who were deprived, not only of good words, but of human goods as well, for like Saint Leo and Pope Damasus, he maintained religious rites and taught the flock. He was always zealous to refresh the hungry crowd and willing that the people should attain the heavenly kingdom. Now let us beat our breasts with our fists for the loss of so great a shepherd. See, in the body, he is entwined with the pious Fabian and Xystus. May he live in the heavens."—*Trans. Father Thomas Buffer*)

St. Leo IV (April 10, 847–July 17, 855) He was buried in St. Peter's, under the altar of Our Savior della Colonna, with his predecessors Leo I (who was removed in the seventeenth century and placed under his own altar), Leo II, and Leo III. Feast day: January 17 (now suppressed). Also see Leo I, Leo II, and Leo III. Altar inscription:

HIC. IACVERVNT. CORPORA. SANCTO / RVM. PONTIFICVM. LEONVM. I. II. / III. ET. IIII. VSQVE. AD. AN. MDCVII. / AD. ALTARE. DEIPARAE. VIRG. IN. / COLVMNA. HVIVS. BASILICAE. PAV / LI. V. IVSSV. SOLEMNITER. TRANS / LATA.[97]

("Here the bodies of the holy popes Leo I, II, III, and IV lay until the year 1607. By the command of Paul V, they were solemnly transferred to the altar of the Virgin Mother of God, by a pillar of this basilica."—*Trans. Father Thomas Buffer*)

Archeologist Rinaldo Lanciani claims that the altar was actually destroyed on May 26, 1607.[98] Church canon and historian Giacomo Grimaldi describes the location and

Original tomb of Leos I–IV. Drawing by Joan Reardon.

appearance of the altar where the remains of Leo I–IV were placed (translated by Phyllis Jestice):

> The oratory or chapel of Pope St. Leo I was situated next to the oratory of the lord Pope Hadrian I and in the area of the altar of St. Mauritius, in the right part of the basilica toward the middle, on the side of the apse with the greater altar of the prince of the apostles, in the lattermost division of the apse. [Antipope] Anastasius Bibliothecarius quotes in the Vita of Sergius that Sergius had a vision telling him where to put the tomb, after which he adorned it himself. Anastasius also quotes in the Vita of Leo III that the tomb was decorated with 119 pounds of silver. And in the Vita of Leo IV, Anastasius quotes that there was silver crown hanging above the tomb. Paschal II had bodies of all four Leos put together there.

Church historian Peter Mallius writes:

> that the altar contained the bodies of the first three Leos, and more recently that of Leo IV, who himself restored and ornamented the oratory, as Anastasius says in the Vita of Leo IV. Before the altar of the mar-

tyr St. Mauritius … is the oratory of St. Pope Leo IV. In which, as we accept from our predecessors (Cenzius and Peter Christianus), Pope Paschal II of blessed memory re-interred the bodies of blessed Popes Leo I, II, III, and IV. The tomb of Leo the Great was situated in the depths of the sarcophagus. Within it was an ancient coffin of pine, with another one of lead enclosed within it, with a cross carved on top with the inscription "The Body of St. Pope Leo I" at the foot. Afterwards, four transverse bars of iron were placed in the middle of the sarcophagus, upon which was placed a cypress coffin containing the holy bodies of Leo II, III, and IV [*trans. Phyllis Jestice*].

The following inscription was engraved on a lead plate on the cypress coffin:

> The bodies of Sts. Leo I, II, III, and IV, high pontiffs, moved from the right side of the basilica to the side of the greater altar of the prince of the apostles, beneath the altar of the old oratory which was protected by the construction of the pavement. This was carried out at the order of Paul V, pontifex maximus, and with the agreement of Evangelista Pallottus, cardinal priest in the title of

St. Lawrence in Lucina, archpriest of this basilica, who bore them to the new church with a solemn procession and placed them here beneath the altar in the same southern part. 27. May, the Sunday within the octave of the feast of the Ascension, 1607, in the third year of that same pontificate.[99]

Benedict III
(September 29, 855–April 17, 858). Buried in the narthex of St. Peter's, immediately to the right of the central door, although his tomb was destroyed during the demolition of St. Peter's in the seventeenth century. Epitaph:

QVISQVIS HVC PROPERAS CHRISTVM PRO CRIMINE POSCENS / QVAM LACRYMIS DIGNVS SIT ROGO DISCE LOCVS / HAC GELIDA PRAESVL BENEDICTVS MEMBRA QVIETE / TERTIVS EN CLAVDIT QVAE SIBI REDDAT HVMVS / QVODQVE FORES TECTVS SERVAT SVB TEGMINE SAXI / INDIGNVM SANXIT SE SOCIARE PIIS[100]

("You who hasten hither begging Christ for pardon, I pray you, learn how this place is worthy of tears. Lo! This cold and quiet place encloses the limbs of the prelate Benedict III which the earth gave him. He felt he was unworthy to be in the company of the godly, although the roof [of St. Peter's] preserves his doors beneath a covering of stone."—*Trans. Father Tom Carleton*)

Antipope Anastasius Bibliothecarius
(August–September 855). He was less then 55 years old when he died, and it is unclear what he died from or where he is buried.

St. Nicholas I
(April 24, 858–November 13, 867) Died from stress-induced illness at age 40. He was buried in a beautiful white marble tomb in the atrium before the doors of St. Peter's, near his predecessor, Benedict. Fragments of the epitaph have been preserved in the Vatican grottoes. The version below was recorded by Montini[101]; church historian Peter Mallius also recorded the epitaph but omitted the first four lines.[102]

scire volens cur trISTE GENVS MORTALE REPENTE / quisquis adhuc propERAS EOIS

PARTIBVS AVLAE / templa vel occiduIS POLLENS AVSTROQVE BEATAE / axe vel a gelido CARMEN SCRVTARE MEMENTO / conditur hoc aNTRO SACRI SVBSTANTIA CARNIS / praesulis egregii NICOLAI DOGMATE SANCTO / qui fulsit cuncTIS MVNDVM REPLEVIT ET ORBEM / intactis nituit mEMBRIS CASTOQVE PVDORE / quae docuit veRBIS ACTVQVE PEREGIT OPIMO / siderea plenuS MANSIT DOCTVSQVE SOPHIAE / caelorum claRIS QVEM SERVANT REGNA TRIVMPHIis / ut vernet solIS PROCERVM PER SAECVLA VATVm

("Whosoever cometh to this temple hall suddenly from eastern or western lands, or from the south or the cold North Pole, wishing to know why the mortal race is still sad, carefully examine this poem, and remember: The substance of the holy flesh of the outstanding bishop Nicholas is preserved in this grotto. By his holy teaching he shone out before all men. He filled the world and shone by his chastity, his members unstained. What he taught in his words he accomplished by his abundant action. He remained full of light and was learned in wisdom. The starry kingdom of heaven preserves him with brilliant triumphal processions, so that the throne of the noble prophets [popes] might flourish through the ages."— *Trans. Father Thomas Buffer*)

Hadrian II
(December 14, 867–November or December 872) Died at age 75 and was buried on the right-hand side of St. Peter's between one of the intercolumniations, in the area of the sacristy. Fragments of the following epitaph are preserved in a hallway to the left as one walks through the Vatican grottoes (lowercase letters are added for completion):

qvae miHI COMPOSVIT MortaliIS PONDERA CARNIS / hADRIANVS PraeSVL HIC SVA MATER Humus / in cinERES MERSIT quiCQVID DE PVLVERE SVmpsit / ast aNIMA CAELO REDDIDIT OSSA solo / vir pius et PLACEDVS FVERAT SVPER AEThera clarus / pauperibVS LARGVS DIVITIBVSQVE simul / omnibus et MEDIVS NVLLIS NISI CARVs habendus / dapsilis AegREGIVS RECTVS vbique bonus / pro quo IVRe deum LACRImis veNErabere visor / uT SIT CVm domino iam super astra suo / QVI

LEGIS HOS versus compuncto dicito corde /
cum christo vivas o hadriane deo[103]

("Here mother earth buried in ashes whatever
she took from the dust, but gave his soul to
heaven. He was a pious and peaceful man,
brighter than the sky, generous to the poor and
rich alike. And moderate to all, for everyone
held him dear. Bounteous, eminent, upright,
and good everywhere for which reason, onlooker, by right you should implore God with
tears that he may now be with his Lord above
the stars. You who read these verses, say with
stung heart: O Hadrian, may you live with
Christ our God!"—*Trans. Father Thomas Buffer*)

John VIII   (December 14, 872–December
16, 882) Poisoned and clubbed to death.
When he excommunicated powerful bishops
who he suspected were going to overthrow
him, the bishops persuaded a family member to poison him. When the poison failed
to work quickly enough, members of his own
entourage clubbed him to death with a
hammer. He is the first "officially" assassinated pontiff, and it is interesting to note that
Pope Formosus (d. 896) was involved in the
conspiracy to kill him. John was buried in
an ancient sarcophagus in the portico, or
possibly the more southerly left nave of St.
Peter's, although his body is lost and his
tomb was destroyed during the demolition of
the basilica in the seventeenth century. There
is some confusion, however, over an ancient
sarcophagus at the church of S. Saba in
Rome. Pope John XVII was allegedly interred
in S. Saba, yet the historian Hulsen suggests
that the sarcophagus in the atrium could
possibly belong to John VIII, having been
transferred there in 1375.[104] The epitaph
reads:

PRAESVLIS OCTAVI REQVIESCVNT MEMBRA
IOHANNIS / TEGMINE SVB GELIDO MARMOREI
TVMVLI / MORIBVS VT PARET FVLSIT QVI MENTE
BEATIS / ALTISONIS COMPTVS ACTIBVS ET MERITIS
/ IVDICII CVSTOS MANSIT PIETATIS AMATOR /
DOGMATIS ET VARII PLVRIMA VERBA DOCENS /
DE SEGETE CHRISTI PEPVLIT ZIZANIA SAEPE /
MVLTAQVE PER MVNDVM SEMINA FVDIT OVANS /

DOCTIloquus PRVDENS VERBO LINGVAQVE
PERITVS / SOLLERTEM SESE OMNIBVS EXHIBVIT /
ET NVNC CELICOLAS CERNAT SVPER ASTRA
FALANGES

("The body of Bishop John VIII rest beneath
the cold cover of a marble tomb. As he is
adorned by his lofty acts and merits, he shone
by his blessed morals. A guardian of judgment,
he remained a lover of piety, teaching many
words to different kinds of doctrine. He often
drove the weeds out of Christ's field and sowed
many seeds throughout the world, rejoicing.
Speaking learnedly, prudent with his words,
and skilled with his tongue, he showed himself
clever in all things. And now may he behold
the hosts of heaven, above the stars!"—*Trans.
Father Thomas Buffer*)

FURTHER READING: F. Matz–F. von Duhn, *An-
tike Bildwerke in Rom*, II, Leipzig, 1881; Huel-
sen, *Le chiese di Roma nel M.E.*, Firenze, 1927.

Marinus I   (December 16, 882–May 15,
884) Originally buried in the portico of St.
Peter's, although his tomb was destroyed
during the demolition of the basilica in the
seventeenth century. Luckily his epitaph was
recorded in its entirety:

QVAM SOLLERS DOMINO PLACVIT QVI MENTE
MODESTA / PRAESVL APOSTOLICVS ORBIS ET
OMNE DECVS / HIC STATVIT TVMVLO CLAVDI
SVA MEMBRA SVB ISTO / HAEC EADEM SPERANS
VT SIBI REDDAT HVMVS / ARDVA QVI FVLSIT
CVNCTIS VT SYDERA CELI / AVGVSTIS CARVS
GENTIBVS ET TRIBVBVS / DOCTRINIS COMPTVS
SACRIS ET DOGMATE CLARO / PER PATRIAS
SANCTA SEMINA FVDIT OVANS / NAM GRAIOS
SVPERANS EOIS PARTIBVS VNAM / SCISMATA
PELLENDO REDDIDIT ECCLESIAM / PRINCIPIS
HIC PETRI SED QVISQVIS TENDIS AD AVLAM /
DIC SVPPLEX ISDEM REGNET AB ARCE POLI[105]

("How greatly he pleased the Lord by his great
skill, by his modest spirit! Apostolic bishop and
glory of the world, here he decided that his
remains should be enclosed beneath this tomb,
hoping that the earth would return those same
remains to Him who shone before all, like the
burning stars of the sky that are esteemed by
honorable nations and tribes. Full of holy doctrines and brilliant teaching, he sowed the holy

seed throughout the lands, rejoicing. For overcoming the Greeks in eastern lands, driving away schisms, he returned the Church to unity. But whosoever comes to this hall of Peter the prince, humbly say: May he reign as our heavenly protection!"—*Trans. Father Thomas Buffer*)

FURTHER READING: A. Reumont, *Geschichte der Stadt Roms*, Berlin, 1867.

St. Hadrian III (May 17, 884–September 885) Possibly poisoned. En route to France to meet with Charles the Fat, who was planning to depose some bishops, he died suddenly in San Cesario sul Panaro, near Modena, Italy. Although his father was still alive, his body was never taken back to Rome, which suggests that he was not popular there. He was buried in the crypt altar in the Abbey of Nonantola, in Nonatola, Italy. His inscription reads:

Altar containing the remains of Hadrian III, Abbey of Nonantola, Italy.

HADRIANI III / PONT MAX / OSSA MIRIFICA

("The miracle-working bones of Supreme Pontiff Hadrian III.")

Leo XIII recognized Hadrian as a saint in 1891 and decreed that the clergy of Rome and Modena, Italy, must celebrate his mass on his feast day, September 7.

Stephen V (VI) (September 885–September 14, 891) Interred in the portico of St. Peter's, although his tomb was destroyed in the demolition of the basilica in the seventeenth century.

His epitaph reads:

ACCEDIS QVISQVIS MAGNI SVFFRAGIA PETRI / COELESTIS REGNI POSCERE CLAVIGERI / INTENTIS OCVLIS COMPVNCTO CORDE LOCELLVM / CONSPICE PERSPICVVM QVO PIA MEMBRA IACENT / HIC TVMVLVS QVINTI SACRATOS CONTINET ARTVS / PRAESVLIS EXIMII PONTIFICIS STEPHANI / BIS TERNIS ANNIS POPVLVM QVI REXIT ET VRBEM / ET GESSIT DOMINO QVAE FVERANT PLACITA / SVSCEPIT TELLVS CONSVMPTVM PVLVERE CORPVS / AETHERA SED SCANDIT SPIRITVS ALMVS OVANS / VNDE PETO CVNCTI VENIENTES DICITE FRATRES / ARBITER OMNIPOTENS DA VENIAM STEPHANO[106]

("Whosoever draws near to beg the aid of great Peter, the key-bearer of the heavenly kingdom, with attentive eyes and stung heart, look upon the obvious little place in which this tomb holds the godly remains, the sacred limbs of the extraordinary pontiff, Bishop Stephen the Fifth, who ruled the people and city for six years and did what was pleasing to the Lord. The earth has received his body, devoured by the dust, but his kind spirit, rejoicing, climbs the heavens. Whence I entreat all brothers who come here, say: 'Almighty Judge, grant forgiveness to Stephen!'"—*Trans. Father Thomas Buffer*)

FURTHER READING: G. Quattrini, *Del culto a papa A. III nell'augusta badia di Nonantola*, Modena, 1870; *Del pontificato e del culto di Sant'A. III*, ivi 1892.

Formosus (October 6, 891–April 4, 896) Died of illness at age 80 and was buried in

St. Peter's. Formosus was the defendant (of sorts) in the infamous "Cadaver Synod." Pope Stephen VI (VII) (896–897) claimed that Formosus had two bishoprics when he was pope, although canon law states that the pope can be only the bishop of Rome and no other see. Stephen used this as an excuse to humiliate his former rival in one of the most bizarre events in papal history: Nine months after Formosus died, Stephen had him exhumed and his rotting corpse dressed in full pontifical vestments. Stephen assigned the corpse a defense lawyer (who did not speak) and Formosus was found guilty of holding two bishoprics, as well as other petty charges. As punishment, Stephen cut off Formosus' three fingers of the benediction and tossed his naked, rotting corpse into the Tiber River. Suddenly, just as the Cadaver Synod was ending, a giant earthquake struck Rome and destroyed part of the Lateran Palace. Taking this as a sign from God, the Roman mob turned on Stephen, imprisoned him in Castel Sant' Angelo for a few months, and finally had him strangled. Meanwhile, a monk had taken pity on the corpse of Formosus, fished it from the river, and buried it with respect in a shallow grave. A few months later Formosus was reinterred in St. Peter's by Pope Theodore II (897), who also presided over a synod renouncing the Cadaver Synod. Sadly, after all this, Formosus' tomb was destroyed in the demolition of St. Peter's in the middle of the seventeenth century, but his epitaph had been recorded:

PRAESUL HIC EGREGIUS FORMOSUS LAUDIBUS ALTIS / EVEHITUR CASTUS PARCUS SIBI LARGUS EGENIS / BULGARICAE GENTI FIDEI QUI SEMINA SPARSIT / DELUBRA DESTRUXIT, POPULUM COELESTIBUS ARMIS / INSTRUXIT, TOLERANS DISCRIMINA PLURIMA, PROMPTUS, / EXEMPLUM TRIBUENS, UT SINT AVERSA FERENDA, / ET BENE VIVENTI METUENDA INCOMMODA NULLA.[107]

("Formosus, the bishop, distinguished with high praises, pious, frugal, bountiful to the needy, is carried up. He scattered the seeds of faith to the Bulgarian people, destroyed pagan shrines, drew up his people in array with heavenly arms as he endured countless dangers, res-olute, showing example, so that adversity might be overcome, and no trouble might be rendered to whoever leads a good life."—*Trans. Ruth Yeuk Chun Leung*)

Boniface VI (April 5–20, 896) Possibly murdered, although he did suffer severely from gout. He was buried in the portico of St. Peter's, although his tomb was destroyed during the demolition of the basilica in the seventeenth century. Luckily his epitaph has been preserved in its entirety:

ATRIA MAGNIFICIS (quae) SUNT (iam) PLENA SEPULVRI (s) / SEDIS APOSTOLICAE BONIFATI PRAESULIS ALMI / (suscipiunt corpus, etc.) / HINC SUBIT AD MODICUM VATES BONIFACIUS ALMUS / TER QUINOS HIC IN ARCE DIES EXPLEVIT HONORIS / CULMINA MOX MUTANS SUPERAT FASTIGIA CELSA / INQUE BREVI SPATIO QUAESITA CACUMINA SCANDENS / INTER APOSTOLICI PROCERES ADSCRIBITUR ALBI[108]

("These halls, which are full of magnificent sepulchers, received the body of provident Boniface, bishop of the Apostolic See. Here the wise priest Boniface reigned for a short amount of time. He filled up fifteen days here in the citadel, soon exchanging these heights of honor for a better place. He soars above the lofty pediments, climbing the utmost desired peaks, for he is enrolled among the nobles of the apostolic registry."—*Trans. Father Thomas Buffer*)

Stephen VI (VII) (May 896–August 897) Strangled. It was Stephen who orchestrated the Cadaver Synod in which the corpse of Pope Formosus [d. 896] was put on trial. (See Formosus.) When a major earthquake rocked Rome immediately at the end of the synod, the Roman took it as a sign from God that Stephen had committed a great wrong. They forcibly deposed Stephen, abused him, and imprisoned him in Castel Sant' Angelo, where he was later strangled. He was buried in the portico of St. Peter's, although his tomb was destroyed during the demolition of the basilica in the seventeenth century. His epitaph has been preserved:

HIC STEPHANI PAPAE CLAVDVNTVR MEMBRA
SACELLO / SEXTVS DICTVS ERAT ORDINE QVIPPE
PATRVM / HIC PRIMVM REPVLIT FORMOSI
SPVRCA SVPERBI / CVLMINA QVI INVASIT SEDIS
APOSTOLICAE / CONSILIVM INSTITVIT PRAESEDIT
PASTOR ET IPSI / LEGE SATIS FESSIS IVRA DEDIT
FAMVLIS / CVMQVE PATER MVLTVM CERTARET
DOGMATE SANCTO / CAPTVS ET A SEDE PVLSVS
IN IMA FVIT / CARCERIS INTEREA VINCI
CONSTRICTVS IN IMO / STRANGVLATVS
VBI EXVERAT HOMINEM / POST DECIMVMQVE
DIEM REGNANTI TRANSTVLIT ANNVM /
SERGIVS HVC PAPA FVNERA SACRA COLENS[109]

("Here the members of Pope Stephen, called the sixth, are enclosed in a shrine, for he was sixth in the order of fathers. He first rejected the baseness of the proud Formosus, who usurped the high Apostolic See; then he set up a council and presided as pastor and, by law, gave rights to the servants who had been abused. And though this father struggled for holy doctrine, he was seized from his throne and struck down into the depths of despair. Then in the lowest part of prison he was dishonored, bound with chains in a small cell, and strangled. Ten years later Pope Sergius celebrated his sacred funeral rites here." — *Trans. Father Thomas Buffer*)

Romanus (August–November, 897; d.?) Allegedly poisoned. Before he died he was forcibly deposed and imprisoned in a monastery, where it is said he was poisoned for favoring Formosus. He was allowed burial in St. Peter's, but his tomb was destroyed in the demolition of the basilica in the seventeenth century.

Theodore II (November 897) Died suddenly from unknown "foul play" (most likely poison) after only twenty days in office. He was buried in St. Peter's, although his tomb was destroyed during the demolition of the basilica in the seventeenth century. His epitaph (in verse) (possibly written by Flodoard of Reims) reads:

DILECTUS CLERO THEODORUS, PACIS AMICUS /
BIS SENOS ROMANA DIES QUI IURA GUBERNANS /
SOBRIUS ET CASTUS, PATRIA BONITATE REFERTUS /

VIXIT, PAUPERIBUS DIFFUSUS AMATOR ET ALTOR. /
HIC POPULUM DOCUIT CONNECTERE VINCULA
PACIS / ATQUE SACERDOTES CONCORDI UBI
IUNXIT HONORE / DUM PROPRIIS REVOCAT
DISIECTOS SEDIBUS, IPSE / COMPLACITUS
RAPITUR DECRETA SEDE LOCANDUS[110]

("Theodore, beloved by the clergy and a friend of peace, governed the Roman jurisdiction for twelve days. Pious and chaste and filled with goodness, he lived in the fatherland. A generous lover and foster-father to the poor, he taught the people to unite under the bonds of peace. He joined the priests together in honor and harmony while he recalled the scattered dissenters back to their own sees. He, very pleased, was seized to be placed in the throne decreed for him." — *Trans. Father Thomas Buffer*)

John IX (January 898–January 900) Probably murdered on orders of Theodora Theophylact, the powerful senatrix of Rome, although it is possible he died from gout. He was buried in the portico, or possibly the more southerly left nave, of St. Peter's, although the *Catholic Encyclopedia* claims he was buried just outside St. Peter's. At any rate, the elegant sepulcher was destroyed during the demolition of the basilica in the seventeenth century. John's epitaph reads:

ECCLESIAE SPECIMEN CLARISSIMA GEMMA
BONORVM / ET MVNDI DOMINVS HIC IACET
EXIMIVS / IOHANNES MERITIS QVI FVLSIT IN
ORDINE NONVS / INTER APOSTOLICOS QVEM
VEHIT ALTITONANS / CONCILIIS DOCVIT TERNIS
QV(I) DOGMA SALVTIS / OBSERVARE DEO MVNERA
SACRA FERENS / TEMPORIBVS CVIVS NOVITAS
ABOLITA MALI(GNA) EST / ET FIRMATA FIDES
QVAM STATVERE PATRES / QVI MORITVRVS ERIS
LECTOR DIC PAPA IOHANNES / CVM SANCTIS
CAPIAT REGNA BEATA DEI[111]

("Here lies a model for the church, a most brilliant jewel of goodness and lord of the world, the extraordinary John the ninth, who shone by his merits among the apostolic men, whom the Almighty drew up, who taught the doctrine of salvation in three councils, giving gifts to God for the observance of the sacred rites. In his days wicked novelty was abolished and the faith the Fathers established was strengthened.

Reader, you who are bound to die, say: 'Pope John, with the saints, may you reach the blessed kingdom of God!'"—*Trans. Father Thomas Buffer*)

Benedict IV (May or June 900–August 903) Murdered. Supporter of Formosus (see Pope Formosus, d. 897), he called his own synod to condemn the Cadaver Synod. As a result of his pro–Formosus stance, he died from 'mysterious causes'. He was buried in St. Peter's near the gate of Guido, in a marble mausoleum that became damaged by weather over the years and was finally destroyed during the demolition of the basilica in the seventeenth century. His epitaph reads:

MEMBRA BENEDICTI HIC QVARTI SACRATA QVI-
ESCVNT / PONTIFICIS MAGNI PRAESVLIS EXIMII /
QVI MERITO DIGNVS BENEDICTVS NOMINE
DICTVS / CVM FVERIT LARGVS OMNIBVS ATQVE
BONVS / HIC GENERIS DECVS AC PIETATIS
SPLENDOR OPIMVS / ORNAT OPVS CVNCTVM
IVSSA DEI MEDITANS / PRAETVLSIT HIC
GENERALE BONVM LVCRO SPECIALI / MERCATVS
CAELVM CVNCTA SVA TRIBVIT / DESPECTAS
VIDVAS NEC NON INOPESQVE PVPILLOS / VT
NATOS PROPRIOS ASSIDVE REFOVENS / INSPECTOR
TVMVLI COMPVNCTO DICITO CORDE / CVM
CHRISTO REGNES O BENEDICTE DEO[112]

("Here rest the members of Benedict the Fourth, a great pontiff, an outstanding bishop, who, being worthy, was rightly called Benedict by name since he was generous and good to all. He was an ornament of his race and a rich glory of godliness. He adorned his every work by meditating on God's commands. He acquired Heaven by using his private wealth the public good; for he gave away all his possessions and continuously cared for despised widows and helpless orphans, whom he treated like his own children. You who look upon this tomb, say with stung heart: 'O Benedict, may you reign with Christ our God!'"—*Trans. Father Thomas Buffer*)

Leo V (August–September 903; d.early 904) Strangled. A supporter of Formosus (see Pope Formosus, d. 897), he was consequently overthrown and imprisoned by antipope Christopher—who was strongly anti–Formosus—before being strangled on the order of Cardinal Sergius (later to become Pope Sergius III). Leo's body was allegedly cremated and the ashes thrown into the Tiber River[113]; the solid remains were buried in St. Peter's. Another version has Leo being buried, whole, in St. John Lateran.[114] Either way, the tomb has been destroyed and no epitaph recorded.

Antipope Christopher (September 903–January 904) Strangled. Overthrown three months after he overthrew and imprisoned Pope Leo V (903–904), he was subsequently incarcerated in the same prison as Leo when Pope Sergius III (904–911) conquered Rome. Sergius had Christopher strangled and buried in St. Peter's, although the tomb was destroyed during the demolition of St. Peter's during the seventeenth century. Church historian Peter Mallius gives a fragment of the epitaph:

CHRISTOPHORUS PAPA / HIC REQUIESCIT
IN ECCLESIA BEATI PETRI DE QUO HABETUR
HOC EPITAPHIUM. / HIC PIA CHRISTOPHORI
REQUIESCUNT MEMBRA SEPULTI.

("Pope Christopher rests here in the Church of blessed Peter. Of him this epitaph is found: Here buried rest the godly remains of Christopher."—*Trans. Father Thomas Buffer*)

Sergius III (January 29, 904–April 14, 911). Died mysteriously while in exile. He was forced into exile because of his stance opposing Pope Formosus (See Formosus, d. 897) and his plan to call a synod to renounce Pope Theodore's (897) synod, which had renounced the Cadaver Synod of 897. He was the father of Pope John XI, by Marozia Theophylact, daughter of the powerful Roman senatrix Theodora Theophylact. He was buried in St. Peter's, although the tomb was destroyed during the demolition of the basilica in the seventeenth century. Some historians claim the epitaph of Sergius I belongs to Sergius III.

Anastasius III   (c. June 911–c. August 913) Probably poisoned on the order of the senatrix Theodora Theophylact because he tried to be independent of her. He was buried in the pavement of the atrium St. Peter's, although his tomb was destroyed during the demolition of the basilica in the seventeenth century. His epitaph has been recorded in its entirety:

VATIS ANASTASII REQVIESCVNT MEMBRA
SEPVLCRO / SED NVMQVAM MERITVM PARVVLA
CLAVDIT HVMVS / SEDEM APOSTOLICAM BLANDO
MODERAMINE REXIT / TERTIVS EXISTENS ORDINE
PONTIFICVM / AD CHRISTVM PERGENS PECCATI
VINCVLA SPERAT / SOLVERE CLEMENTER OMNIA
POSSE SIBI / LIMINA CVRRENTES AD TEMPLI
VNDIQVE HVIVS / VT PRAESTET REQVIEM
POSCITE CORDE DEVM[115]

("The remains of the priest Anastasius rest in this tomb, but a little earth will never cover his merit. With excellent administration he governed the Apostolic See, being the third in order of pontiffs [with that name]. Reaching Christ, he hopes to be able to loose from himself all the bonds of sin. All ye who run to the thresholds of this temple from every place, beg God in your heart to give him rest."—*Trans. Father Thomas Buffer*)

Lando   (c. August 913–c. March 914) Probably murdered on the orders of the Roman senatrix Theodora Theophylact so that her lover John could become Pope John X. He was buried in St. Peter's, although his tomb was destroyed during the demolition of the basilica in the seventeenth century.

John X   (March or April 914–928; d. 929) Either smothered with a pillow in the prisons of Castel Sant' Angelo, Rome (as told by Liutprand of Cremona, known for his sensationalism), or died from anxiety as re-

corded by historian Flodoard of Reims. Guy, Marchese of Tuscany, had marched on Rome; under the orders of his wife, Marozia Theophylact, the powerful Roman senatrix (and daughter of Theodora Theophylact), he had Marozia's stepfather, John X, deposed, imprisoned, and murdered so he and Marozia could gain control of Rome and the papacy by putting her son (fathered by Sergius III, d. 911) on the papal throne as John XI. To dispel the rumors of a violent death, Marozia allowed John X an honorable burial in St. John Lateran (near the middle door at the foot of the nave). He was the first pope to be buried within the city walls of Rome (St. Peter's was outside the walls of the city), although his tomb was destroyed in the fire of either 1308 or 1361. The charred remains were collected and buried in a polyandrum near the lesser door of the basilica (the entrance near the tomb of Innocent III, on the right side of the nave).[116] His tomb inscription reads:

PONTIFICIS SVMMI PAVSANT
IBI MEMBRA IOHANNIS[117]

("The humble body of the highest pope John.")

His epitaph was written by Flodoard of Reims:

SURGIT ABHINC DECIMUS SCANDENS SACRA
IURA JOHANNES / REXERAT ILLE RAVENNATEM
MODERAMINE PLEBEM, / INDE PETITUS AD
HANC, ROMANAM PERCOLIT ARCEM / BIS SEPTEM
QUA PRAENITUIT PAULO AMPLIUS ANNIS. /
MUNIFISCQUE SACRAM DECORANS ORNATIBUS
AULAM / PACE NITET, DUM PATRICIA DECEPTUS
INIQUA / CARCERE CONICITUR, CLAUSTRISQUE
ARTATUR OPACIS / SPIRITUS AT SAEVIS RETINERI
NON VALET ANTRIS, / EMICAT IMMO AETHRA
DECRETA SEDILIA SCANDENS[118]

("The body of supreme pontiff John rests here. John X rises hereafter, ascending the sacred law. He had governed the people of Ravenna, thence by request came and adorned the Roman arch 14 times, by which he surpassed Paul. As he generously embellished the sacred court, he advanced in peace until he was deceived by his rival patrician, thrown into prison, and confined in a shadowed den. Yet his spirit, strong enough not to be restrained by the hostile caves, sprang forth, ascending to the decreed seat of heaven."—*Trans. Ruth Yeuk Chun Leung*)

Leo VI (May–December 928) Possibly murdered on orders of Marozia Theophylact, the powerful Roman senatrix, so that she could install her own son (fathered by Sergius III, d. 911) as John XI. He was buried in St. Peter's, although his tomb was destroyed during the demolition of St. Peter's in the seventeenth century.

Stephen VII (VIII) (December 928–February 931) Likely murdered on the orders of Marozia Theophylact, the senatrix who ruled Rome at the time, because she wanted her own son (by Sergius III, d. 911) to be Pope John XI. The unfortunate Stephen was buried in St. Peter's, although his tomb was destroyed during the demolition of the basilica in the seventeenth century.

John XI (February or March 931–December 935 or January 936) Poisoned. John XI was the son (with Pope Sergius III, d. 911) of the Roman senatrix Marozia Theophylact, who had several previous popes murdered so that her son could become pope. Marozia planned for John XI to crown her husband, Hugh, as emperor of the West, a title only a pope could bestow. In her scheming, however, she failed to reckon with Alberic, her son from a previous marriage. Hugh and Alberic did not get along; in fact, Hugh often humiliated Alberic in public, with Marozia doing nothing to stop it. Events came to a head at the dinner ceremony at Castel Sant' Angelo where the pope was to crown Hugh emperor. Forced to be a servant, Alberic carried water to Hugh but accidentally spilled some, causing Hugh to slap him and belittle him in front of everyone. As the dinner guests laughed, Alberic ran out into the streets— where he roused the Roman mob against Hugh and Marozia, convincing them that Hugh was nothing but a tyrant who would rule them with an iron fist. The mob stormed Sant' Angelo and captured Marozia and the pope while Hugh slipped through a window and escaped. Alberic had his mother and half-brother jailed, though he later freed John and allowed him to remain pope as long as he dealt only with spiritual matters of the church. Finally, Alberic tired of John and had him poisoned so that he could appoint Leo VII as pope. John XI was honorably buried in St. Peter's, although his tomb was destroyed during the demolition of the basilica in the seventeenth century.

Leo VII (January 3, 936–July 13, 939) Died of unknown causes, though it was rumored that he died of a heart attack during sex. He was buried in St. Peter's, although his tomb was destroyed during the demolition of the basilica in the seventeenth century.

Stephen VIII (IX) (July 14, 939–late October 942) Died from mutilation injuries in Castel Sant' Angelo, Rome. He would not be a puppet to Alberic, the ruler of Rome, so Alberic had him jailed, mutilated, and disfigured. He was buried in St. Peter's, although his tomb was destroyed in the demolition of the basilica in the seventeenth century.

Marinus II (October 30, 942–early May 946) Died suspiciously. If he was murdered it was probably on orders of Alberic, the ruler of Rome, because Marinus rebelled against him. He was buried in St. Peter's, although his tomb was destroyed in the demolition of the basilica in the seventeenth century.

Agapitus II (May 10, 946–December 955) Died mysteriously of unknown causes. Agapitus was made to swear to Alberic that upon Agapitus's death, Alberic's son would be elected pope as John XII. Agapitus was buried behind the apse of St. John Lateran, although his tomb was destroyed in the fire of either 1308 or 1361; the remains were collected and buried in a polyandrum (community tomb) near the lesser door of the basilica (the entrance near the tomb of Innocent III, on the right side of the nave).[119]

John XII (December 16, 955–May 14, 964) Strangled in his mid-twenties. The son of the ruler Alberic, he was forced to assume the papacy when the previous pope, Agapitus, died. John was widely reviled as a rabble-rouser whose many vices included gambling and drinking, and no one was surprised when he was caught in bed with a married woman named Stefanetta. The pair was discovered by Stefanetta's husband, who immediately strangled John and tossed him out the window. However, before his death John had been deposed by the Emperor Otto and replaced by Leo VIII, so technically he was not pope at the time of his death. He was buried in St. John Lateran, but his tomb was destroyed in the fire of either 1308 or 1361; his remains were collected and buried in a polyandrum (community tomb) near the lesser door of the basilica (the entrance near the tomb of Innocent III, on the right side of the nave).[120]

Leo VIII (December 4, 963–March 1, 965) Died suspiciously. Originally seen as an antipope, he was declared a legitimate pope during the revision of the official papal list in 1947. There had been questions about his legitimacy because he was appointed by the Emperor Otto rather than by anyone in Rome. However, if Leo VIII is a legitimate pope, that would make Benedict V (the following pope) an antipope because he reigned as pope for a month in 964, although they both now hold the title of legitimate popes.

It is thought that Leo VIII was buried in St. Peter's, and if this is the case, then his tomb was destroyed, probably during the demolition of the basilica in the seventeenth century.

Benedict V (May 22–June 23, 964; d. July 4, 966). Died from brain trauma after being struck on the head with a papal scepter. Otto I installed Leo VIII as pope after the death of John XII, but Leo went to rejoin Otto after he left the city. The Romans then elected Benedict as pope, since they felt that Leo had abandoned them. This so infuriated Otto that he started a siege on Rome. Rome submitted a month later, and Leo VIII became the legitimate pope once again. Leo demoted Benedict V to deacon, stripped him of his papal vestments, and struck him so hard

Tomb of Benedict V, once in the Cathedral of Hamburg, Germany. From P. Lambeck, *Chronologia libri I Rerum Hamburgensium*, 1609.

over the head with his pastoral staff that it broke. He then exiled Benedict to Hamburg, Germany, where he died two years later as a result of the beating.

Benedict was originally buried in the old cathedral at Hamburg, Germany. It has been speculated that possibly he was brought back to Rome and buried in St. Peter's, although no trace of his tomb can be found. A monument was erected in his memory several centuries after his death in Hamburg but has since been destroyed. Luckily a drawing exists of the tomb, which was a lateral sarcophagus with an effigy of the pope on the top and the twelve apostles on the left side, with the annunciation, the prediction of Christ, the crucifixion, and the universal judgment on the right side. His epitaph (which curiously, incorrectly states he died in the year 800, though actually he died in 966) reads:

BENEDICTVS PAPA QVI DE SE / DE APOSTOLICA PER VIOLENTIAM AMOTVS ET POST CVM REVOCARETVR / OBIIT HAMBVRGI ANNO DOMI / NI DCCC QVADRAGESIMO PRIMO QVINTO NONAS IVLI SEPVLTVS EST HIC[121]

("Pope Benedict, who was violently removed from the Apostolic See and afterwards recalled. Died in Hamburg in the year of the Lord 800 and was buried here on the ninth of July."— *Trans. Phyllis Jestice*)

FURTHER READING: P. Lambeck, *Chronologia libri I Rerum Hamburgensium*, in Lindenbrog, *Scriptores rerum germanicarum septemtrionalium*, 1, 1609; O. Sperlingius, *Monitum Hamburgense ... seu de inscriptione et tumulo B.V*, Kiel, 1673; E. Muntz, "Les tombeaux des Papes en Allemagne," in *Revue de l'Art Chrétien*, Lille, 1896; Osservatore Romano, September 16, 1949, *Sarebbe stata rinvenuta ad Amburgo la tombadi papa B. V.*

John XIII   (October 1, 965–September 6, 972) Buried in the basilica of St. Paul fuori le Mura, although his tomb no longer exists. That tomb had images of Saints Peter and Paul writing on the sides, in vertical columns, D[OMINUS] IOH[ANNE]S TERTIVS

DECIMVS PAPA" ("Pope John XIII"). His epitaph is extant in the Abbey Museum of the basilica:

PONTIFICIS SVMMI HIC CLAVDVNTVR MEMBRA IOHANNIS / QVI PRVDENS PASTOR P(er)SOLVENS DEBITA MORTIS / ISTIC PREMONVIT MORIENS SVA MEMBRA LOCARI / QVO PIETATE DEI RESOLVTVS NEXIBVS ATRIS / EGREGII PAVLI MERITIS CONSCENDAT IN ETHRA / INTER APOSTOLICOS CAELORV̄ GAVDIA METAT / GAVDEAT EXVLTET SOCIATVS COETIBVS ALMIS / DICITE CORDE PIO RELEGENTES CARMINA CVNCTI / XPE TVI FAMVLI MISERTVS SCELERA PVRGA / SANGVINE QVI SANCTO REDEMISTI CRIMINE MVNDVM / HIC VERO SVMMVS PONTIFEX IOHANNES IN APOSTOLICA SEDE / SEDIT ANNOS VII DEPOSITIONIS EIVS DIES VIII IDVS SEPTEMBRIS / AB INCARNATIONE DNI ANNI DCCCCLXXII[122]

("Here are enclosed the remains of the highest pontiff John, who, prudent pastor paying his debt to death, admonished beforehand that, dying, his body should be placed in this gloomy place, that with the merits of the distinguished Paul he might ascend to the heavens. May he be gathered up among the apostles in the joy of heaven. May he rejoice and exult in the society of that sweet assembly. Speak such songs with pious heart, oh Christ, who had compassion on your followers and purged of evil, you who with your holy blood redeemed the crimes of the world. Here truly is the high pontiff John, who held the Apostolic See seven years and died on the eighth day before the ides of September in the year of the Lord 972."— *Trans. Phyllis Jestice*)

FURTHER READING: Margarini, *Inscriptiones antiquae basilicae S. Pauli*, Rome, 1645; G. B. Ladner, *I ritratti dei Papi nell'antichita e nel medio evo*, I, C. d. V. 1941.

Benedict VI   (January 19, 973–July 974) Ordered strangled by Crescenzio,[123] son of the powerful and ruthless Theodora the Younger, on the orders of Antipope Boniface VII. Benedict was under the protection of Emperor Otto I, but when Otto died and his successor, Otto II, was involved in turmoil in Germany, the powerful Crescentii family of Rome had Benedict imprisoned in Castel

Sant' Angelo. They put their own man on the papal throne as Boniface VII, who thought it best that the competition be eliminated and so ordered a priest named Stephen to strangle Benedict. He was buried in St. Peter's, but his tomb was destroyed in the demolition of the basilica in the seventeenth century.

Benedict VII (October 974–July 10, 983) Buried in the wall of the nave, on the right side of the entrance of Santa Croce in Gerusalemme, Rome, because he once went to the Holy Land and brought back a piece of the true cross. The original metric epitaph can still be seen in the church:

HOC BENEDICTI PP QVIESCVNT MEMBRA
SEPVLCHRO / SEPTIMVS EXISTENS ORDINE
QVIPPE PATRVM / HIC PRIMVS REPPVLIT
FRANCONIS SPVRCA SVPERBI / CVLMINA
QVI INVASIT SEDIS APOSTOLICAE / QVI
DOMINVMQVAE SVVM CAPTVM IN CASTRO
HABEBAT / CARCERIS INTEREA VINCLIS
CONSTRICTVS IN IMO / STRANGVILATVS VBI
EXVERAT HOMINEM / CVMQVE PATER MVLTVM
CERTARET DOGMATE SCO / EXPVLIT A SEDE
INIQVVS NAMQVE INVASOR / HIC QVOQVE
PREDONES SCORVM FALCE SVBEGIT / ROMANE
ECCLESIE IVDICIIS QVAE PATRVM / GAVDET
AMANS PASTOR AGMINA CVNCTA SIMVL / HICCAE
MONASTERIVM STATVIT MONACHOSQ: LOCAVIT /
QVI LAVDES DNO NOCTE DIEQVAE CANVNT /
CONFOVENS VIDVAS NEC NON ET INOPESQ
PVPILLOS / VT NATOS PROPRIOS ASSIDVE
REFOVENS / INSPECTOR TVMVLI COMPVNCTO
DICITO CORDE / CV XPO REGNES O BENEDICTE
DO D. X. M. IVL IN APL SEDE / RESIDENS VIIII
ANN OBIIT AD XPM INDIC. XII[124]

("In this sepulcher the bones of Pope Benedict rest; indeed, the seventh [of that name] arising in the order of the fathers. This one first drove back the foul acts of the arrogant French who invaded the heights of the Apostolic See, and who held his lord captive in a fortress. Indeed, he was bound with the fetters of prison, where the man was despoiled, and when the father matched many with dogma, the evil invader expelled [him] from the see. This man reaped with the scythe the plunderers of the Roman church, which rejoices with

the judgments of the fathers. Once this shepherd, loving the blind multitudes, built this monastery, he established the monks who sing praises night and day, sheltering destitute women and also helpless orphans, thus continually restoring appropriate successors. Inspector of the tomb, having been prompted by the speaking of his heart, Benedict, you reigned until the tenth day of the month of July, residing nine years in the apostolic throne, you died." — *Trans. Phillip Haberkern*)

FURTHER READING: A. Colsanti, "L'epitaffio di B. VII," in *Nuovo Bull. di Arch. Crist.*, VIII, 1902; A. Silvagni, "Note di epigrafia medievale," in *Arch. Soc. Rom. St. Patria*, Rome, XXXII, 1909.

John XIV (December 983–August 20, 984) *Peter Canepanova.* Starved in Castel Sant' Angelo. He had been named pope by the German emperor Otto II, who died soon after. Antipope Boniface VII, exiled in Constantinople, heard of Otto's death and returned to Rome to claim the papacy for himself. He had John XIV thrown into a prison at Castel Sant' Angelo and severely beaten, with his eyes, nose, lips, tongue and hands cut. John was buried in St. Peter's, although his tomb was destroyed during the demolition of the basilica in the seventeenth century. His epitaph was written while his murderer, Antipope Boniface, was still alive, so there are no details on his gruesome death:

PRAESVLIS EXIMII REQVIESCVNT MEMBRA
IOHANNIS / QVI PETRVS ANTEA EXTITERAT /
QVIPPE SEDEM PAPIAE BLANDO MODERAMINE
REXIT / IMPERATORI OCTONI DVLCIS FVIT
ATQVE PRECLARVS / COMMISSVM POPVLVM ROM.
IN OMNIBVS INSTRVENS / DVLCIS IN ELOQVIO
CVNCTIS PRAECLARVS AMICIS / SVBIECTIS
PLACIDVS PAVPERIBVSQVE PIVS / DEFVNCTVS EST
IOANNES PP ROMANVS M. AVG. D. XX[125]

("Here rest the remains of the outstanding bishop John, who earlier was [named] Peter. Indeed, he was famous, for he ruled the see of Pavia with smooth skill and was dear to the Emperor Otto. The Roman people entrusted his instruction in all things because he was pleasant in speech, a brilliant friend to all, gentle to his subjects and kind to the poor. John the Roman pontiff died August 20."—*Trans. Father Thomas Buffer*)

Antipope Boniface VII (June–July 974; August 984–July 20, 985) *Franco*. Poisoned. In 974 Boniface had the legitimate pope, Benedict VI, strangled. When the Roman populace discovered the murder, their own dislike of Benedict was overcome by their disgust at the actons of Boniface, who had to hide out in Castel Sant' Angelo for fear of reprisals. He eventually escaped to Constantinople but returned in 984 with Byzantine henchmen, who helped him imprison the current pope, John XIV, in Castel Sant' Angelo. There, John eventually starved to death. The angry Romans so hated the antipope that when he died they seized his body, stripped it of papal vestments, dragged it through the streets of Rome, threw it at the feet of the statue of Marcus Aurelius on horseback, then trampled and stabbed his naked body with knives and spears. After the gruesome night several clerics carried away the body and gave it a decent burial in an unknown location.

John XV (mid–August 985–March 996) Died from fever. He was buried in the oratory of St. Mary in St. Peter's, although his tomb was destroyed in the demolition of the basilica in the seventeenth century. Tomb inscription:

> CLAVDITVR HOC TVMVLO
> VENERABILIS ILLE (IOHANNES)[126]

("Buried in this tomb is the venerable John.")

Gregory V (May 3, 996–February 18, 999) *Brunone dei Duchi di Carinzia*. Rumored poi-

Tomb of Gregory V, Vatican grottoes. From H.K. Mann, *Tombs and Portraits of the Popes*, 1927.

soned, though more likely died of malaria, at age twenty-six. Gregory's tomb was found on August 14, 1607, under the pavement of St. Peter's, in the outer left nave, close to Gregory the Great. He was exhumed and reburied on January 15, 1609, in a fourth or fifth century white marble Christian sarcophagus sculpted with common scenes. The left side features Jesus curing a blind man and a woman who touched the hem of his garment. The right side shows the denial of St. Peter, and in the center is Jesus giving the scroll of the law to St. Peter. This sarcophagus, the only tomb monument from the tenth century to survive, can be seen today in the Vatican grottoes. The tomb inscription reads:

GREGORIVS PP V

The epitaph reads:

HIC QUEM CLAUDIT HUMUS, OCULIS VULTUQUE DECORUM, / PAPA FUIT QUINTUS NOMINE GREGORIUS, / ANTE TAMEN BRUNO FRANCORUM REGIA PROLES, / FILIUS OTTONIS DE GENITRICE IUDITH. / LINGUA TEUTONICUS VUANGIA DOCTUS IN URBE, / SED IVVENIS CATHEDRAM SEDIT APOSTOLICAM. / AD BINOS ANNOS ET MENSES CIRCITER OCTO, / TER SENOS FEBRUO CONNUMERANTE DIES. / PAUPERIBUS DIVES, PER SINGULA SABBATA VESTES / DIVISIT, NUMERO CAUTUS APOSTOLICO. / USUS FRANCISCA, VULGARI, ET VOCE LATINA / INSTITUIT POPULOS ELOQUIO TRIPLICI. / TERTIUS OTTO SIBI PETRI COMMISIT OVILE, / COGNATIS MANIBUS UNCTUS IN IMPERIUM. / EXUIT ET POSTQUAM TERRENAE VINCULA CARNIS / AEQUIVOCI DEXTRO SUSTITUIT LATERI. / DECESSIT XII KAL. MAI.1[127]

("He who rests here, of noble eyes and countenance, was once called Gregory, fifth of the name. His early name was Bruno, of the royal Frankish race, the son of Otto and of Judith his spouse. A German in speech, he was brought up in the city of Worms; yet he mounted the apostolic throne, when young in years. [He reigned] two years and almost eight months, [dying] when February had numbered thrice six days. Generous to the poor, each Sunday he gave out vestments among them, careful to observe the apostolic number. Familiar with the vulgar tongue and the French and Latin languages, his threefold eloquence instructed the

peoples. The third Otto entrusted him with the sheepfold of Peter, and he was anointed to the empire by his kinsman's hand. And when he put off the chains of our human flesh, Otto laid him to rest at his namesake's right hand. He died on the 12th day before the Kalends of March."[128] — *Trans. Father Tom Carleton*)

Here is another translation of Gregory's epitaph:

("He whose eyes and face are properly closed with earth was Pope Gregory, the fifth of the name. Formerly Bruno of the Franks, of royal blood, son of Otto by his mother Judith. A German in tongue, he taught in the city of Liège. But at a young age he sat on the apostolic throne. After two years and about eight months a tertian fever brought an end to his days. On every Sabbath, he distributed rich garments to the poor, dividing them carefully in accordance with the number of apostles. In the vulgar Frankish tongue and in Latin he instructed the populace with threefold eloquence. Otto III put him over Peter's flock, and by his relative's hands he was anointed as emperor. Afterward, he escaped from the earthly chains of the flesh, and for uncertainty exchanged a place at God's right hand. Died on the 12th day before the calends of March." — *Trans. Phyllis Jestice*)

The church canon and historian Giacomo Grimaldi recorded the opening of Gregory's tomb on January 15, 1609, during the demolition of St. Peter's (translated by Phyllis Jestice):

The tomb of Pope Gregory V in St. Andrew's chapel was opened. The bones were in a marble container, with the epitaph stuck among them. They were moved from there to a new place under the vault of the new pavement of the church and placed in a marble sarcophagus sculpted with holy images and the pontiff's old epitaph attached.

FURTHER READING: Virgilio Cardinal Noe, *Le Tombe e i Monumenti*, Rome, 2000.

Antipope John XVI   (February 997–May 998; d. August 26, 1001) Died from effects of mutilation. John wanted to abdicate before he was officially deposed by Otto III, but he was handed over to Otto while hiding in a castle. With the permission of the pope and emperor, John was blinded and disfigured; his hands, tongue, lips, and nose were cut before he was placed on an ass and paraded around Rome and ritually stripped of his papal robes. The Romans tossed him in a local monastery, where quietly lived out the rest of his life. He was buried in an unknown location.

Silvester II (April 2, 999–May 12, 1003) *Archbishop Gerbert of Rheims*. He died "in great agony" (possibly poisoned) at age 58 while celebrating mass in the church of Santa Croce in Gerusalemme, Rome. He was buried in a white marble sarcophagus and interred in St. John Lateran, although his tomb was destroyed by the Lateran fire of 1308. His charred remains were collected and buried in a polyandrum near the lesser door of the basilica (the entrance near the tomb of Innocent III, on the right side of the nave).[129] The *Liber Pontificalis* (*Book of Pontiffs*) relates an amusing story about the circumstances surrounding his death:

The well known chronicle of Martinus Polonus relates this in all the simplicity of conviction. Gerbert, urged on, as it was believed, by ambition and love of power, won first Rheims and then Ravenna by means of bribery, and finally secured the Papacy by the help of the devil, but on the condition that after death his soul should become the possession of him whose cunning had won him such exalted honor. When Gerbert enquired of the Fiend how long he would enjoy the Papal dignity, the Enemy of Mankind replied, "If thou dost not set foot within Jerusalem thou wilt live long." Now it so happened that in the fourth year, the first month, and on the tenth day he celebrated the Holy Office in the Basilica of Santa Croce in Gerusalemme. Here he suddenly bethought him of his destiny and of his coming end; full of repentance, he confessed his errors to the assembled people, exhorting them to beware of ambition and devilish lusts, and to lead a good and holy way of life.

He then besought those present to dismember his body after death, according to his deserts, then to place it in a two-wheeled chariot, give free rein to the horses and bury him at the spot to which chance might lead them. The legend goes on to relate, that, at the bidding of Divine Providence, which sought to convince evildoers that a place of pardon lay ever open for them if they did but repent, the horses went of themselves to the Lateran Basilica, and there the corpse was duly interred.[130]

Pope Sergius IV (d. 1012) had the original epitaph engraved for Silvester on a slab of white marble. The slab can still be seen in the cenotaph located on the right side of the central nave in St. John Lateran. It reads:

ISTE LOCUS MUNDI SILVESTRI MEMBRA SEPULTI VENTURO DOMINO CONFERET AD SONITUM. / QUEM DEDERAT MUNDO CELEBRE DOCTISSIMA VIRGO, ATQUE CAPUT MUNDI CULMINA ROMULEA, / PRIMUM GERBERTUS MERUIT FRANCIGENA SEDE REMENSIS POPULI METROPOLIM PATRIAE. / INDE RAVENNATIS MERUIT CONSCENDERE SUMMUM ECCLESIAE REGIMEN NOBILE, SITQUE POTENS. / POST ANNUM ROMAM MUTATO NOMINE SUMPSIT, UT TOTO PASTOR FIERET ORBE NOVUS. / CUI NIMIUM PLACUIT SOCIALI MENTE FIDELIS, OBTULIT HOC CESAR TERTIUS OTTO SIBI. / TEMPUS UTERQUE COMIT CLARA VIRTUTE SOPHIAE, GAUDET ET OMNE SECULUM, FRANGITUR OMNE REUM / CLAVIGERI INSTAR ERAT CAELORUM SEDE POTITUS, TERNA SUFFECTUS CUI VICE PASTOR ERAT. / ISTE VICEM PETRI POSTQUAM SUSCEPIT, ABEGIT LUSTRALIS SPATIO SECULA MORTE SUI. / OBRIGUIT MUNDUS DISCUSSA PACE TRIUMPHUS AECCLESIAE NUTANS DEDIDICIT REQUIEM. / SERGIUS HUNC LOCULUM MITI PIETATE SACERDOS, SUCCESSORQUE SUUS COMPSIT, AMORE SUI. / QUISQUIS AD HUNC TUMULUM DEVEXA LUMINA VERTIS OMNIPOTENS DOMINE, DIC, MISERERE SUI. / OBIIT A. DOMINICAE INCARNATIONIS MIII. INDICTIONE I. / MENSIS MAI DIE XII.

("This spot will yield up the remains of Silvester when the Lord cometh at the last trump. This famous man was given to the world by a most learned virgin, and the seven-hilled city of Romulus, head of all the world. At first Gerbert was deemed worthy to rule the metropolis of Rheims, filling a Frankish see, and later to acquire the chief sway over the noble city of Ravenna, thus waxing powerful. After a year, under an altered name he acquired Rome, and became the new shepherd of the world. He to whom this loyal and friendly mind were all too dear — Otto, third Caesar of the name — has raised this tomb. Each of the two sheds luster on the age by his conspicuous virtue and wisdom; the whole age rejoiced, and every guilty thing was shattered. Like the apostolic bearer of the keys, he gained a place in heaven, having thrice been chosen to fill his place on earth. After filling the see of Peter for the space of five years, death carried him into eternity. The world was stupefied by the loss of its peace, and, wavering, unlearned its repose and the triumphs of the church. Sergius the priest, his successor, has adorned this humble tomb with gentle piety, and as a sign of love. Thou who may'st chance to turn thy gaze upon his tomb, pronounce the prayer, 'Almighty God, have mercy on him!' He died in the year of our Lord's Incarnation 1003, in the first indiction, on the twelfth day of the month of May."[131])

Silvester's sarcophagus was unearthed during reconstruction of the basilica in the seventeenth century, as reported by Lateran Palace historian Rasponi[132]:

> In the year 1648, while new foundations were being laid for the left wing of the church, the corpse of Silvester II was found in a marble sarcophagus, twelve feet below the surface. The body was entire, and clad in pontifical robes; the arms were crossed, on the breast; the head crowned with the tiara. It fell into dust at the touch of our hands, while a pleasant odor filled the air, owing to the rare substances in which it had been embalmed. Nothing was saved but a silver cross and the signet ring.[133]

The famous sculptor Francesco Borromini created a monument for Silvester on orders of Pope Alexander VII (d. 1657), which consisted of the original epitaph at the base, above which was a large cross in a wreath and topped with Silvester's Coat of Arms.

In 1910 Hungarian artists Gzila Nalder and Giuseppe Damko unveiled a modern monument to Silvester that incorporates not only the original epitaph, but also a relief of the Hungarian king kneeling before Pope Silvester as well as a lunette with the Madonna as the queen of Hungary. The new cenotaph epitaph reads:

SILVESTRO SECVNDO ROMANO PONTIFICI QVI SANCTVM STEPHANVM / HVNGARORVM GENTIS DVCEM REGIA DIGNITATE ET APOSTOLIC LEGAT / MVNERE CORONA ET CRVCE MISSA INSIGNIVIT EAQVE RATIONE ECCLESIAE / ET REIPVBLICAE IN HVNGARIA FIRMA FVNDAMENTA STABILIVIT HVIVS / FAVSTI EVENTVS ET ILLLVSTRIS PONTIFICIS MEMORIAM NOVEM POST / SAECVLA GRATO ANIMO RECOLENTES PRAESVLVM HVNGARIAE CONSILIVM / BASILICAE LATERANENSIS CAPITVLO ANNVENTE HOC PIETATIS MONVMENTVM / POSVIT GVILELMVS FRAKNOI ABBATIAE SACRAE DEXTERAE SANCTI / STEPHANI REGIS HVNGARIAE COMMENDATOR ANNO REPARATAE SALVTIS / M C M I X[134]

("For Silvester II, Roman pontifex, who invested St. Stephen, duke of the Hungarians, with royal and apostolic dignity, distinguishing him with the gift of crown and cross for the sake of the church and firmly establishing the foundations of the Hungarian state. The Hungarian council of bishops recall anew after centuries with grateful heart this fortunate event and the memory of this illustrious pontiff. William Franknoi, commendator of the monastery of the holy right of St. Stephen, king of Hungary, placed this monument of piety in the chapter house of the Lateran basilica, in the year of restored salvation 1909." — *Trans. Phyllis Jestice*)

One of the most interesting legends dealing with deceased popes is found in the allegedly prophetic original tomb of Silvester II. Although there was no moisture anywhere near the tomb (no streams, springs, water runoffs, or anything similar), legend claims that the tomb would give off so much moisture when a pope was going to die that the area would flood. If only a cardinal or high member of the church was going to die, the area would just turn to mud. It was said that the amount of water flowing from the tomb was directly proportionate to the importance of the one who would die. This probably derived from a misreading of the second half

Left: The original seventeenth-century monument to Silvester II by Francesco Borromini, St. John Lateran, Rome. Drawing based on photograph in Montini, *Le Tombe dei Papi. Right:* Cenotaph to Silvester II, St. John Lateran, Rome.

of the first line of the original epitaph which alludes to the sounding of the trumpet on the day that "when the lord cometh."

FURTHER READING: Montini, "Un'opera perduta di Francesco Borromini: il monumento a papa S. II in laterano," in *Palladio*, Rome, n.s. V, 1955; p. Portoghesi, "I monumenti borrominiani nella basilica Lateranense," in *Quaderni dell'Ist. di St. dell'Architettura*, Rome, 1955; De la Salle de Rochemaure, *Gerbert-Silvestre II,* Rome and Paris, 1914; A. Graf, "La leggenda di un Pontefice," in *Miti, leggende e superstzioni del Medio Evo*, Turin, 1925.

John XVII (May 16–November 6, 1003) Buried either in San Paulo fuori le Mura or in the portico of the Lateran. (If it was the Lateran, then his tomb was destroyed in the

fire of either 1308 or 1361; the charred remains would have been collected and buried in a polyandrum near the lesser door of the basilica (the entrance near the tomb of Innocent III, on the right side of the nave).[135] Church historian Ciaconnius, however, claims that John was buried in Santa Saba on the Aventine. Whatever the case, an inscription survives:

CERNITVR HIC TVMVLVS QVI PRAESVL
DICITVR ESSE / SVMMI IOHANNIS
SIC QVOQVE DICTVS ERAT[136]

("This tomb which is thought to be that of a bishop is said to be that of the pontiff John."— *Trans. Phyllis Jestice*)

FURTHER READING: M. Armellini, *Le chiese di Roma*, Rome, 1942.

John XVIII (December 25, 1003–June or July 1009) *Giovanni Fasano.* John XVIII had abdicated the papal seat — possibly he was forced down by the powerful Crescenti family — and was forced to retire as a monk in a monastery. He was buried in either St. John Lateran or San Paulo fuori le Mura, though no trace of his actual tomb exists in either place. His tomb inscription, however, has been preserved in the abbey museum:

DOMS IOHS XVIII PAPA[137]

("John XVIII, Pope")

Sergius IV (July 31, 1009–May 12, 1012) *Peter "Buccaporci"* (a nickname meaning

Cenotaph to Sergius IV in the Lateran, Rome. From *Le Tombe dei Papi.*

"pig's snout"). Possibly murdered. He was buried near the left entrance in the Lateran, although his tomb was destroyed in the fire of either 1308 or 1361; the charred remains were collected and buried in a polyandrum near the lesser door of the basilica (the entrance near the tomb of Innocent III, on the right side of the nave).[138] A cenotaph on the right side of the main nave by famed sculptor Francesco Borromini exists, complete with the original epitaph plaque, which reads:

QVISQVIS AD HEC TENDIS SVBLIMIA LIMINA LECTOR / ET CAPERIS TANTE NOBILITATE DOMVS / INTENTIS OCVLIS AVLE PERCVRRERE RARAS / DESINE MATERIAS ARTE IVVANTE MANVS / LVMINA CVM GRESSV PRVDENS ARGVTA COHERCENS / RESPICE SOLLICITVS QVIT VELIT HIC TITVLVS / HIC TVMVLATA IACENT PASTORIS MEMBRA SERENI / QVEM DEVS ECCLESIE CONTVLIT OMNIPOTENS / PAVPERIBVS PANIS NVDORVM VESTIS OPIMA / DOCTOR ET EGREGIVS QVI FVIT IN POPVLO / IVRA SACERDOTI LETAS DVM VIDIT ARISTAS / CETIBVS EQVAVIT NAVIGER ANGELICIS / ALBANVM REGIMEN LVSTRO VENERABILIS VNO / REXIT POST SVMMVM DVCITVR AD SOLIVM / IN QVO MVTATO PERMANSIT NOMINE PRESVL / SERGIVS EX PETRO SIC VOCITATVS ERAT / DVCTVS MENTE PIA IH̅V DIC PARCE REDEMTOR / VTQVE VICEM CAPIAS DIC D̅S HVNC HABEAS / Q. SEDIT A̅N̅I. II ET M. VIII ET DIE XII OBIIT M̅. MDI DIE XII INDI. X / AN. D̅N̅ICE INCARN. MILLESIMO TERTIO X[139]

("Whosoever comes to this lofty threshhold with eager eyes, and is amazed by the nobility of such a great house, cease gaping at the rare treasures that have been shaped skillfully by hand, and be prudent. Keep your footsteps within the gleaming lights and carefully read what this verse wishes to say. Here lie entombed the remains of the serene shepherd whom Almighty God bestowed upon the Church. He was an outstanding teacher to the people, for he clothed the naked and gave bread to the poor. When he saw the abundant ears of corn, he made the rights of the angelic priest equal to the throngs. This venerable man ruled the Alban realm for five years and then was led to the supreme throne on which he remained bishop, though his name was changed. Thus, formerly Peter, he was called Sergius. O you, led here by your religious spirit, say, 'Spare, O

Redeemer!' and so that you may obtain a change [into a better life], say, 'God, take Sergius!' He reigned two years, eight months and twelve days. He died on May 12, in the tenth indiction, in the 1012th year of Our Lord's incarnation."—*Trans. Fr. Thomas Buffer*)

FURTHER READING: G. C. Argan, *Borromini*, Milan, 1952.

Benedict VIII   (May 17, 1012–April 9, 1024) *Teofilatto dei Conti di Tuscolo*. Buried in St. Peter's, although his tomb was destroyed during the demolition of basilica in the seventeenth century.

Antipope Gregory VI   (May–December 1012). Resigned the papacy and died of unknown causes in Hamburg, Germany. No details of any funeral or monument exist.

John XIX   (April 19, 1024–October 20, 1030) *Romano dei Conti di Tuscolo*. Buried in St. Peter's, although his very elegant tomb was destroyed during the demolition of the basilica in the seventeenth century.

Benedict IX   (October 21, 1032–September 1044; March 10–May 1, 1045; November 8, 1047–July 16, 1048) *Teofilatto dei Conti di Tuscolo*.[140] Date of death uncertain, although the tradition passed on by Abbot Luke, who died around 1085, tells of a "youthful pontiff turning from his sin and coming to the fourth abbot of Grottaferrata, St. Bartholomew, for a remedy for his disorders." Bartholomew advised him to resign the pontificate, which he did, and lived the rest of his life in penitence at the abbey.[141]

On March 4, 1739, an ornate tomb slab was found under the pavement with a picture and mosaic of the arms of Conti which was from a twelfth century monument to the pope.[142] This was placed in the wall of the abbey, but it was destroyed during the Allied bombardment in World War II, as was a tomb inscription in white marble that had been located near the third pilaster on the right of the central nave:

SEPULCRUM / BENEDICTI IX. / P. M.

("Sepulcher of Benedict IX, supreme pontiff")

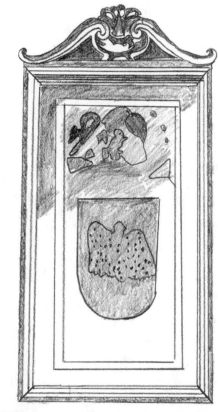

Funerary wall plaque honoring Benedict IX in the Abbey of Grottaferrata. Drawing based on photograph in Montini, *Le Tombe dei Papi*.

The epitaph on the tomb slab reads:

LAPIS SEPULCRALIS / BENEDICTI IX PONT. MAX. / GENTILITIO STEMMATE ET SACRIS EMBLEMATIS / INSIGNIS / NE PENE DETRITUS ABSUMERETUR OMNINO / ET VENDICATUM EJUSD. PONT. NOMEN OBLIVIONI DARETUR / E TUMULO AREAE VERMICULATAE PROXIMO / AD LAEVAM TEMPLI / UBI MARMOR SIGNATUM CONSPICITUR / ANNO JUBILAEI MDCCL / HUC TRANSLATUS JUSSU / EMI D. CARD. GUADAGNI COMMENDATARII / URBIS VIC. ET EPISC. TUSCULANI[143]

("Funeral stone of Benedict IX, supreme pontiff, of noble birth and distinguished with holy emblems. Lest perhaps it fall into utter ruin and the vindicated name of this pontiff be lost to oblivion, it was brought from the tomb near the area of Vermiculatae to the left side of the church, where, marble-sealed, it is admired in the year of jubilee 1750. Transferred to this place by order of the eminent lord Cardinal Guadagna, vicar of the city and bishop of Toscolano." — Trans. Phyllis Jestice)

FURTHER READING: G. Piacentini, De sepulchro Benedicti IX Pontificis Maximi in templo monasterii Cryptae ferratae detecto, Rome, 1747; A. Rocchi, La Badia di Grottaferrata, 2nd ed., Rome, 1904; G. Tomassetti, La Campagna romana, IV, Rome, 1926; St. Benedict and Grottaferrata, Rome, 1895.

Silvester III (January 20–March 10, 1045; d. 1063) *John of Sabina*. Died in Sabina, Italy. Because he had abdicated (or was formerly dethroned by the synod of Sutri in 1046 — see note 140), there is much debate on whether he should be considered an antipope, although in the revision of popes in 1947 he was declared legitimate.

Gregory VI (May 1, 1045–December 20, 1046; d. late 1047) *John Gratian*. Died of illness in Cologne, Germany, after abdicating in Sutri, Italy (or being officially deposed; see note 140). Legend says that because so many people died when Gregory was pope, his cardinals told him they could not bury his body in St. Peter's. He then told them that when

he died they were to place his body outside the doors of St. Peter's, and if God didn't open the doors for him, then they were to leave his body there to rot. This was done, and the door was bolted shut. Just then a strong wind miraculously blew the doors open, and so Gregory was interred in St. Peter's. Whatever the facts of the burial, Gregory's tomb was destroyed during the demolition of the basilica in the seventeenth century.

Clement II (December 24, 1046–October 9, 1047) *Abbot Suidger*. Died of lead poisoning, possibly by those loyal to Pope Benedict IX (who had been deposed while Clement was pope — see n. 140). Clement had been en route to the Marches because of the social and political upheaval in the north of Italy, but he died suddenly in the Abbey of San Tomasso in Pesaro. He was buried in the choir of St. Peter in the Bamburg Cathedral, Bamburg, Germany, because he had been abbot there before he became pope. The original tomb had a canopy, angels, and a recumbent figure of the pope lying atop the ornamented stone sarcophagus decorated with the allegorical figures of Justice, Fortitude, Prudence, Temperance, and Liberty. The cover of the sarcophagus disappeared when the tomb was desecrated by Protestants in the sixteenth century. It was replaced with a simple stone top in which an epitaph was carved.

The tomb inscription from 1741 reads:

R. MVS IN CHRO PATER / ET DNS D. SVIDGERVS A MAYENDORFF SAXO ET EPS / BAMB. POSTEA / SVMM. PONT. CLEM. 2DVS DICT. OBIIT ROMAE 10 OCTOB. AN. 1047[144]

("Father of Rome in Christ and lord under God, Suidger of Mayendorff of Saxony and bishop of Bamberg. Afterwards the highest pontiff, called Clement II. Died in Rome, 10. October, in the year 1047." — Trans. Phyllis Jestice)

The sarcophagus was opened on October 22, 1731, and it was discovered that Clement had been a very tall blond man. It was reopened again on June 3, 1942, when his ornate tomb was salvaged from the destruction of World War II in Bamburg. Tests on Clement's bones determined that they had a very high concentration of lead, meaning he was murdered by lead poisoning.

FURTHER READING: A. von Reitzenstein, "Das Clemensgrab im Dom zu Bamberg," in *Munchner Jahrbuch der bildenden Kunst*, Munich, n.s. VI, 1929; W. Noack, "Ein Engel vom Bamberger Papstsarkophag," in *Kunst hronik*, Leipzig, n.s., XXXIII, 1921–1922.

Damasus II (July 17–August 9, 1048) *Poppone*. Died from malaria (although his contemporary Cardinal Benno claimed he was poisoned) in Palestrina, Italy, where he had gone to escape the heat of Rome. He was buried in a beautifully carved medieval sarcophagus that was placed on the right side of the portico of San Lorenzo fuori le mura (St. Lawrence Outside the Walls), Rome, and can still be seen there today.

For FURTHER READING: J. Gardner, *The Tomb and the Tiara*, Clarendon Press, 1992; A. Muñoz, *S. Lorenzo f. le M.*, Rome, 1944; F.H. Taylor, "The Sarcophagus of S. Lorenzo," in *Art Bulletin*, New York, X, 1927.

St. Leo IX (February 12, 1049–April 19, 1054) *Bruno of Egisheim*. Died from illness. Having long been prepared for death (he slept with his coffin in his bedroom), when he knew the end was near, Leo had himself brought on a litter from the Lateran Palace to St. Peter's, where his stone sarcophagus waited for him. Leo flung himself on the sarcophagus, and according to the eyewitness Libuin, "signed it with the sign of the cross, and prayed that on the day of retribution it might present him before the throne of resurrection, [and he cried in German,] 'For I know that my Redeemer liveth!'"[145] He was originally buried in the east wall of St. Peter's, close to the altar of Gregory I, and his relics were enshrined in 1087. His original epitaph reads:

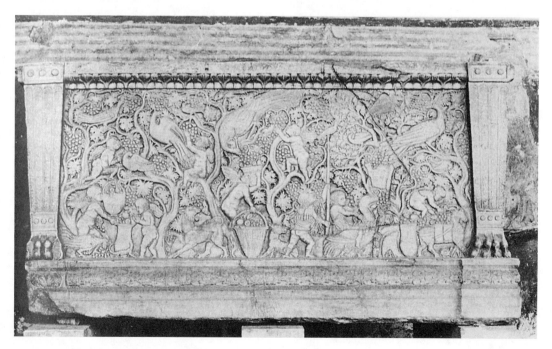

Sarcophagus of Damasus II in the portico of San Lorenzo fuori le mura, Rome. By permission of Julian Gardner, from his book *The Tomb and the Tiara*.

VICTRIX ROMA DOLET NONO VIDVATA LEONE, /
EX MULTIS TALEM NON HABITURA PATREM.

("For her ninth Leo mourns victorious Rome, many shall fade, ere one like him shall come."[146])

Leo's coffin was opened on January 11, 1606, during the demolition of St. Peter's, and a cross and certain parts of his body were taken as relics. What was left was placed in a fresh coffin of cypress wood, which was inscribed with the recording of this translation of his body and placed into a white marble sarcophagus beneath the altar of Saints Marziale and Valeria in St. Peter's. Altar inscription:

CORPVS SANCTI LEONIS PAPAE IX[147]

("The holy remains of Pope Leo IX.")

Within 40 years, 70 miraculous cures took place at the altar.

Church canon and historian Giacomo Grimaldi wrote of the opening and reburial of Leo IX — *Trans. Phyllis Jestice*): "The reverend lord Joseph Dominici, wearing a stola, descended into the vault and reverently began to put together the holy bones of the aforementioned holy pontiff Leo enclosed in a lead coffin within one of cypress, after they had been blessed by the illustrious lord cardinal." According to Grimaldi they took a tibia, tailbone, shinbone, two vertebrae, and one tooth. They searched for an arm bone, because the cardinal very much wanted one to put with his arm of Gregory Nazianzus, but they couldn't find one, although Thomas Carrotius, "doctor of arts and medicine," inspected all the bones. The rest of the bones were replaced in the same lead (inner) and cypress (outer) coffins, closed, and sealed by the cardinal with a lead seal. The cypress coffin was then carried by priests with candles to the choir of Sixtus IV. Grimaldi relates the measurements of the marble sarcophagus in which the coffin rested as 9⅚ palms long, with the side measuring 4 palms and 5 inches, the height 4½ palms. "The body was of great stature, for from the feet to the top of the head, as the reverend Joseph measured, was nine palms. The feet were toward the Silver Door, and the head toward the Ravennian."

According to Veggius, canon of St. Peter's in the time of Martin V (1417–1431), one of St. Leo IX's "great and long" arm bones was donated to the diocese of Suessano, in the kingdom of Naples, and other bits of the body were taken from the saint to put in a reliquary in the chapel of John Chrysostom. On January 18, 1606, Leo's body was deposited in an altar in the second hour of the night. Cardinal Cusentinus officiated, with golden cope and miter. First he blessed the marble sarcophagus, and the cantors sang the hymn "This Confessor." Then the cardinal recited the prayer of the saint, as Grimaldi records

Then the cypress coffin was opened and upon the lead coffin was placed the following inscription, carved in lead, and read aloud to the people standing there in a loud voice: "The body of St. Leo IX, pope, marked with the glory of virtues and miracles, situated under the altar of the dead in the Vatican basilica between the Silver and Ravennian doors...." Another lead plaque was placed on the fragments in the corner of the cypress coffin and another similar one on the fragments behind the marble sarcophagus with these words: "Fragment of the wooden coffin in which this holy body was contained." Then the cardinal, standing with his miter, sealed the aforementioned coffin in which the body of the most holy Leo IX rests with his own cardinal's seal. He admitted the other priests with stoles into the marble sarcophagus, blessing and praising almighty God and giving glory and honor to such a pontiff. Then the builders laid a marble tablet inscribed with these words: "The body of St. Pope Leo IX."

FOR FURTHER READING: E. Muntz, "Recherches sur l'oeuvre archeologique de J. Grimaldi." in *Bibl. De l'eC. Franc. de Rome*, Paris, 1877; Louise Rice, *The Altars and Altarpieces of New St. Peter's: Outfitting the Basilica, 1621–1666*, Cambridge University Press, 1998.

Victor II (April 13, 1055–July 28, 1057)
Gebhard dei Conti di Dollnstein-Hirschberg.

He died from either fever or poison,[148] near Ravenna, Italy. Some of his entourage wanted to take his body back to the Cathedral in Eichstätt, Germany, where he had been a bishop, but the citizens of Ravenna seized the body and interred it in the church of Santa Maria Rotunda (the previous mausoleum of the Ostrogothic king Theodoric, which had been converted to a church). Another version of the story is that the Leo's entourage was robbed near Ravenna and was forced to bury his body in Santa Maria Rotunda, in a tomb that is now lost. There is no trace of his specific tomb at the mausoleum of Theodoric, although the mausoleum had clearly been transformed into a Christian church. There is, however, on the second level of the very empty structure a large sarcophagus resembling a bathtub. It probably did not belong to Victor, or even to Theodoric, but one can at least see the inside of the Mausoleum. Some claim Victor was buried in San Reparata, Florence (the original church upon which the current *Duomo* was built), although there is no evidence of this either.

For FURTHER READING: U. Morini, "Tombe di Pontefici in Firenze e in Toscana," in *Firenze*, Florence, IV, 1935.

Stephen IX (X) (August 2, 1057–March 29, 1058) *Frederick of Lorraine.* Died from malaria in Florence, Italy, and was interred in San Reparata, Florence (the original church upon which the current *Duomo* was built). His tomb was discovered in 1357 when the foundations were being laid for the new *Duomo*, and found in the coffin were a gem-encrusted papal brooch with a gold clasp, a miter, and a ring. The public can view the ruins of San Reparata by going into the crypt of the *Duomo*, but no one knows exactly where the tomb of Stephen IX was located.

Antipope Benedict X (April 5, 1058–January 1059; d. after 1073) *John Mincius.* Died of unknown causes. Benedict had vol-

untarily resigned any claim to the papacy and retired to his family home near Santa Maria Maggiore, Rome, but the Archdeacon Hildebrand (later Pope Gregory VII), afraid Benedict would try to reclaim the papacy, had him jailed. In April of 1060 Benedict was tried for usurping the papal throne, found guilty, degraded, and finally confined to the hospice of Sant' Agnese on the Via Nomentana, where he later died. Despite his earlier hostilities, Hildebrand insisted that Benedict be interred with honor in the Church of Sant' Agnese in Agone. His body is still there, located in the crypt of the church, which is not open to the public.

Nicholas II (December 6, 1058–July 19 or 26, 1061) *Gerard di Borgogna.* Died in Florence, Italy, at age 51 and was originally buried in San Reparata, Florence (the original church upon which the current *Duomo* was built). The historian Peter Mallius, however, claims that Nicholas's remains were buried in the outer left aisle of St. Peter's. In any case, there are no traces of his tomb in either Florence or Rome.

Alexander II (September 30, 1061–April 23, 1073) *Anselmo da Baggio.* Died from illness and was buried either somewhere in St. John Lateran or St. Peter's, but no evidence of a tomb survives in either church.

Antipope Honorius II (October 28, 1061–May 31, 1064; d. 1071 or 1072) *Peter Cadalus.* Died at age 62 in Parma, Italy, claiming until the end that he was the legitimate pope.

St. Gregory VII (April 22, 1073–May 25, 1085). *Hildebrand.* Died in exile at age 65 reportedly from despair and a broken spirit, while in Salerno, Italy. His last words were, "Because I have loved justice, and hated inequity, I die here in exile." In response to his last words, a bishop standing near answered, "In exile, thou can'st not die; for, in the stead of Christ and His Apostles, thou hast received from God the Gentiles for thine inheritance, and the ends of the earth for thy possession."[149] He was buried in the Church of St. Matthew (because he had consecrated the church the year before he died) in an ancient marble sarcophagus carved with garlands and ox skulls. This was discovered in 1573, and the sarcophagus was opened in 1578:

> The body of the aforesaid pope [was found] as it had been, entirely intact, with the nose, teeth, and other members of the body. He was wearing a simple pontifical miter, to the bands of which crosses were attached. For vestments he had a silken stole woven with gold, with golden ornaments, in which were inscribed some letters, to wit, *Pax Nostra* [Our Peace]. He had gloves woven of silk, of admirable beauty, of gold and pearls, with a cross above, and on his ring finger he had a gold ring without a gem. He wore a red chasuble woven of gold, a silken tunicle, frayed stockings, these too woven of gold and silk, with crosses over the feet, that reached almost to the knee. He had a golden cincture, and a veil placed over his face. There appeared still to be some vestiges

of the pallium, and many crosses were attached to his clothes, in such a manner that nothing necessary to the pontifical garments appeared to be lacking.[150]

Archbishop Mark Anthony Colonna had Gregory reburied in a new white marble sarcophagus (which had originally belonged to Robert Guiscardo). The sarcophagus is now located beneath the altar erected by John of Procida in the Salerno Cathedral. The epitaph reads:

GREGORIO VII SOANEN. / PONT. OPT. MAX. /
ECCLESIAE LIBERTATIS VINDICI ACERRIMO
ASSERTORI CONSTANTISSIMO / QUI DUM ROM.
PONT. AUCTORITATEM ADVERSUS / HENRICI
PERFIDIAM STRENUE TUETUR / SALERNI SANCTE
DECUBUIT / A. D. M. LXXXV VIII KAL. JUN. /
M. ANT. COLUMNA MARSIL. / BONONIEN.
ARCHIEPIS. SALERN. / CUM ILLIUS CORPUS POST
QUINGENTOS CIRCITER ANNOS / SACRIS
AMICTUM AC FERE INTEGRUM REPERISSET /
NE TANTE PONTIFICIS SEPULCHRUM
MEMORIA DIUTIUS CARERET / M. P. /
GREGORIO XIII BONONIEN. SENDENTE /
A. D. M D LXXVIII PRID. / KAL. QUINCTIL.[151]

("In honor of Gregory VII, highest and greatest pontiff, who, to vindicate the liberty of the Church, asserted bitterly and with constancy, who strenuously defended the authority of the

Sarcophagus of Gregory VII, Salerno Cathedral. Drawing by Joan Reardon.

Roman pontiff against the perfidy of Henry. He was laid to rest piously in Salerno in the year of the Lord 1085, on the 8th of the calends of June before the column of Marsilius, by Bononius, archbishop of Salerno. When his body was discovered after about fifty years the holy amice was nearly whole. This is erected lest the tomb in memory of such a pope be left untended too long. In pious memory. In the pontificate of Gregory XIII of Bologna, in the year of the Lord 1578, not long before the calends of July." — *Trans. Phyllis Jestice*)

Gregory's tomb was opened again on December 5, 1605, and his head was taken as a relic to the Cathedral of Soana (where he was born).[152] On May 4, 1614, the archivist Lucio Sanseverino translated the corpse to under the altar of the chapel of the *Crociata*, where a statue of Gregory was erected by Archbishop Beltrano (1606–1611). The papal tomb historian H.K. Mann says of the tomb, "Altogether, the whole memorial is utterly unworthy of one of the noblest heroes of the Church of the world."[153]

The chapel was restored in 1856 on the orders of Pius IX (d. 1878), and in 1954, the thousand-year anniversary of the translation of the remains of the apostle Matthew to the church, Gregory's original sarcophagus was put in the transept of the cathedral for all to see while a sort of mannequin or effigy of Gregory was dressed in papal vestments and enclosed in a crystal coffin that replaced the Colonna coffin under the altar. There is no word on the whereabouts of the Colonna coffin.

Gregory's name was added to the Roman martyrology in 1583, and in 1728 Pope Benedict XIII extended Gregory's May 25 feast to all countries.

FURTHER READING: M. Pinto, "St. Gregory VII nel Duomo di Salerno," in *Osserv. Romano*, July 27, 1954; B. Odescalchi, "La tomba di Ildebrando in Salerno," in *Impresioni di storia e d'arte*, Rome, 1895; G. Pesenti, *San G. VII*, Roma-Alba, 1935.

Antipope Clement III (June 25, 1080; March 1084–September 8, 1100) *Guibert*. Died of unknown causes at age 75, at Civita Castellana, Italy.

Blessed Victor III (May 24, 1086; May 9–September 16, 1087) *Daufer (Desiderius)*. Died at age 60 from sudden illness. Victor was elected pope on May 24, 1086, but he left Rome because of political strife and returned to his life in Monte Cassino as a monk. Almost a year later he was persuaded to return to Rome as pope and was consecrated on May 9, 1087. He died, however, just a few months later — at the Benedictine monastery that was his true home. He was originally buried in the apse of the chapter house (in

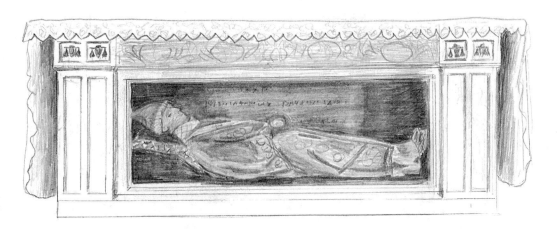

Gregory VII, in the Cathedral of Salerno, Italy. Drawing by Joan Reardon.

Reliquary housing the remains of Victor III, in San Paulo fuori le mura, Rome. Drawing by Joan Reardon.

the fourth chapel on the left, which had been decorated with scenes of Victor's life, painted by Luca Giordano) in a tomb that he had prepared for himself. His cult began about 60 years after his death. In 1515, his tomb was moved to the right of the altar in the chapel of St. Bertharius in the church of the monastery. Sometime between the sixteenth and nineteenth centuries, the remains were moved to underneath the altar in the Chapel of St. Victor. On August 29, 1892, Victor's relics were found in a lead case that was transferred during World War II to San Paulo fuori le mura in Rome so that they wouldn't be destroyed during the aerial bombing of Monte Cassino.

Victor's original epitaph read:

QUIS FUERIM, VEL QUID, QUALIS, QUANTUSQUE DOCERI, / SI QUIS FORTE VELIT AUREA SCRIPTA DOCENT. / STIRPS MIHI MAGNATUM, BENEVENTUS PATRIA, NOMEN / EST DESIDERIUS, TUQUE CASINE

DECUS: / INTACTAM SPONSAM, MATREM, PATRIAMQUE PROPINQUOS / SPERNENS HUC PROPERO, MONACHUS EFFICIOR. / ABBAS DEIN FACTUS, STUDUI PRO TEMPORE TOTUM, / UT NUNC ADSPICITUR, HUNC RENOVARE LOCUM. / INTEREA FUERAM ROMANA CLARUS IN URBE / PRESBYTER ECCLESIAE PETRE BEATAE TUAE. / HOC SENIS LUSTRIS MINUS ANNO FUNCTUS HONORE, / VICTOR APOSTOLICUM SCANDO DEHINC SOLIUM, / QUATUOR ET SENIS VIX MENSIBUS INDE PERACTIS. / BIS SEX LUSTRA GERENS, MORTUUS HIC TUMULOR. / SOLIS VIRGINEO STABAT LUX ULTIMA SIGNO, / CUM ME SOL VERUS HINC TULIT IPSE DEUS.[154]

("He who may seek to know who, what, and how great I have been, may learn it from these letters of gold. My lineage was princely: my home was Benevento; Desiderius was my name, and thou, Monte Cassino, my glory. Leaving in contempt my unwon bride, my mother, my kin and country, hither I hastened to don the monkly garb. Then chosen abbot, I was ever zealous to restore the whole convent, as ye behold it now. Meantime I had grown famous in the city of Rome, as presbyter of thy blessed Church, O Peter. For six lustres save one year, I filled this honorable office, then mounted, as Victor, the apostolic throne. Scarce four months had passed, and I now rest in this grave, at the age of twice six lustres. The sun was already deserting the sign of Virgo, when God, the true Sun, bore me hence."[155])

FURTHER READING: E. Gattola, *Ad historiam abbatiae Casinensis accessiones*, Venice, 1785.

Blessed Urban II   (March 12, 1088–July 29, 1099) *Oddone di Chatillon.* Died at age 64 at the Palazzo dei Pierleone in Carcere, Italy. His body was moved secretly through Trastevere so that his enemies would not disrupt the funeral procession. He was originally buried at the south transept near Hadrian I in St. Peter's, although church historian Gregorovius claims that the tomb could have been in either the Lateran or St. Peter's. Urban's was the first tomb destroyed during the demolition of St. Peter's in the seventeenth century. He was beatified by Leo XIII in 1881.

Paschal II (August 13, 1099–January 21, 1118) *Rainerius.* Died of harsh treatment in Castel Sant' Angelo by orders of Emperor Henry V, although Joachim Prinz, in *Popes from the Ghetto,* claims that Paschal was killed during a street riot. During a religious ceremony early in Paschal's pontificate someone gave Bishop Alberto of Alatri a card with the words *quarter quatemi ternique,* which means "nineteen" (four times four plus three). He quickly showed Paschal the card and said, "That which you see, I see by the grace of God; and you too will see it, so long as you live"—and Paschal indeed reigned for 19 years. Before he was buried (on the right aisle of St. John Lateran), his corpse was covered with balsam and dressed in sacred vestments according to the funeral ordo. The very elegantly sculpted marble tomb was probably destroyed in the fire of either 1308 or 1361, and the charred remains collected and buried in a polyandrum near the lesser door of the basilica (the entrance near the tomb of Innocent III, on the right side of the nave).[156]

Antipope Theodoric (September 1100–January 1101; d. 1102) Died of unknown causes at the La Trinita monastery in La Cava, Italy (having been banished there by Pope Paschal II). He was buried in the community cemetery with the words "Theodoric, 1102" on his tombstone.

Antipope Albert (Adalbert) (1101–?, d. ?) Died at the monastery of San Lorenzo in Aversa, Italy. The supporters of Antipope Clement III had elected Theodoric, but when he was arrested and imprisoned they elected Albert as pope. The Romans rioted, which caused Albert to flee to the safety of a "patron" who was bribed to hand him over to Pope Paschal. Albert was publicly humiliated, stripped of all signs of office, and imprisoned in the Lateran Palace for a few days, after which he was confined for life at the monastery of San Lorenzo.

Antipope Silvester IV (November 18, 1105–April 12, 1111; d. ?) *Maginulf.* Nothing is known about his death or burial. After being ordered by King Henry V to submit to the legitimate Pope Paschal II, Silvester renounced all claims to the papacy, living the rest of his life under his patron, Count Werner of Ancona.

Gelasius II (January 24, 1118–January 29, 1119) *John of Gaeta (Giovanni Caetani).* Died of pleurisy at the abbey church of Cluny, France. Because Antipope Gregory VIII had him attacked during mass at Santa Prassade in Rome, he fled to France and lived the rest of his life in Cluny. On his deathbed he allegedly took his pontifical insignia off, put on his simple frock, and requested to be buried in the ground.[157] He was, however, buried in a Tuscan-style tomb of bright marble located between the cross and the altar (behind the choir) in Cluny's great abbey church. Both the tomb and the church were destroyed in 1792 during the French Revolution.

Antipope Gregory VIII (March 8, 1118–April 1121; d. c. 1140) *Maurice "Burdinus"* (a nickname meaning ass). Most likely died from injuries inflicted by the Roman mob. The residents of Sutri, Italy, handed him over to the troops of the legitimate pope, Callistus II, who let the Roman mob have their way with him. The mob seated Gregory backwards on a camel and paraded him through the streets of Rome while the crowd pelted him with food and rocks. He was jailed in Rome, Passerone, and Rocca Iemolo (near Monte Cassino), but in 1125 he was imprisoned in Castel Fumone, near Alatri, and in August of 1137 he was finally jailed in La Cava, where his trail runs cold. Nothing is known about his burial or death.

Callistus II (February 2, 1119–December 14, 1124) *Guido of Borgogna.* Died at age 74 from Roman fever. The *vita* of Callistus records that before he died he made confession and arranged all his affairs. He was buried in St. John Lateran, next to Paschal II, although his tomb was destroyed in the fire of either 1308 or 1361; his charred remains were collected and buried in a polyandrum near the lesser door of the basilica (the entrance near the tomb of Innocent III, on the right side of the nave).[158]

Honorius II (December 21, 1124–February 13, 1130) *Lamberto Scannabecchi of Ostia.* He died from Roman fever in the Gregorian Monastery in the Caelian, Rome, although the rumor was that Honorius' powerful cardinal chancellor Aimeric had been planning to kill the dying pontiff, steal his corpse, and bury him immediately so the next election could be carried out right away, thus avoiding much political strife. When he knew the pope's end was near, Aimeric ordered him to be brought from the Lateran to the monastery of St. Gregorio in the Caelian in Rome so that he could be quickly and quietly buried when he died. The people clamored at the walls of the monastery, demanding to see if their pope was still alive, so Aimeric brought the pope to the window, propped him up with pillows, and made the pope bless the crowd by lifting the pope's arm himself. Honorius died overnight and was quickly buried in a grave at the monastery. Proper funeral rites were not performed, as the *vita* of Honorius states that the body was dressed in only a shirt and sleeves, there were no sheets in the coffin, and the body was brought from the monastery to the Lateran by "lay hands."

After Innocent II was elected, Honorius was exhumed and properly interred in the Lateran. In fact, the two popes, living and dead, entered the Lateran at the same time, Honorious being quickly buried while Innocent prepared himself for the coronation. Unfortunately, Honorious's tomb was destroyed in the fire of either 1308 or 1361; the charred remains were collected and buried in

a polyandrum near the lesser door of the basilica (the entrance near the tomb of Innocent III, on the right side of the nave).[159]

Antipope Celestine (II) (15 or 16 December 1124; d. 1125 or 1126) *Teobaldo Boccapecci.* Died from a severe beating. During his consecration, Celestine's enemies (the Frangipane troops) broke in and severely beat the elderly man until he resigned. He died two days later from his injuries. Because he had not been consecrated or enthroned, he is considered an antipope.

Innocent II (February 14, 1130–September 24, 1143) *Gregorio Papareschi.* When he died in Rome he was originally buried in the elegant porphyry sarcophagus of Emperor Hadrian, which he had brought from Sant'-Angelo to the Lateran specifically for his own

Monument to Innocent II, Santa Maria in Trastevere, Rome.

burial. After the fire of 1308, Innocent's damaged tomb was placed outside the vestibule of the Lateran, although nothing remains of the original tomb itself save the inscription in St. John Lateran. During the fifteenth century, Innocent's bones were placed underneath a simple tomb slab (which can still be seen today) in the Church of Santa Maria in Trastevere, Rome. Historian Duchesne claims Innocent was first interred in the Lateran, then in 1148 moved to Santa Maria Trastevere (where the tomb of Antipope Anacletus [d. 1138] had stood[160]), then back again to Lateran, and then, after the fire of 1308, back to Santa Maria Trastevere.[161] In 1869, Pius IX erected an exquisite marble tomb monument (probably designed by Vespignani) that now houses his remains. The epitaph on the tomb monument incorporates the words of the original inscription, shown here in brackets:

INNOCENTII II PONT. MAX. / OSSA / OLIM IN BASILICA CONSTANTINIANA PERNOBILI SEPVLCRO CONDITA / ET POST ILLIVS INCENDIVM SVB CLEMENTE V HVC DEDVCTA / VT IN AEDE VIRGINI SACRA / VIRGINIS CVLTOR ETIAM MORTVVS VIVERET / SIMPLICI AC NVDO SVPERIMPOSITO LAPIDE DIV TECTA QVIEVERVNT / HAC TANTVM INSCRIPTIONE NOTA / [HIC REQVIESCVNT VENERABILIA OSSA SANCTISSIMAE MEMORIAE / D. INNOCENTII PAPAE II DE DOMO PAPARESCORVM / QVI PRAESENTEM ECCLESIAM AD HONOREM DEI GENITRICIS MARIAE / SICVT EST A FVNDAMENTIS SVMPTIBVS PROPRIIS RENOVAVIT / S. A. D. MCXL ET AN. D. MCXLVIII] / TAM PRAECLARO PONTIFICI / AD IMPERIVM ORBIS CHRISTIANI SOLA VIRTVTIS VOCE EVOCATO / TAMQVCAM RELIGIONIS VINDICI DEFENSORI ECCLESIAE / SCHMISMATIS DEVELLATORI / RELIGIONE IN DEVM BENIGNITATE IN PAVPERES / PRVDENTIA AC SOLERTIA AGENDI INCOMPARABILI / REGIBVS CAESARIBVS ALIISQ. CVIVSQ. ORDINIS HOMINIBVS / PER XIII ANNORVM MENSIVM VII DIERVM VII SPATIVM / PROBATO / HVIVS BASILICAE CAPITVLVM ET CANONICI / ACCEPTI BENEFICII MEMORES / PARENTI BENEMERENTISSIMO / CVLTAE IN VIRGINEM PIETATIS MONVMENTVM / OBSEQVENTISSIMI RESTAVRARVNT AN. SAL. MDCLVII[162]

("The bones of Innocent II, supreme pontiff, formerly in the Constantinian basilica, pre-

served in a noble sepulcher. After it was burned, they were brought here under Clement V so that in the temple of the virgin this devotee of the virgin should lie in death as he lived. They rest with a simple and plain stone placed above, with this inscription: [Here rest the venerable bones of the lord pope Innocent II of the Papareschi family, of most holy memory, who restored from its foundations this church in honor of God's mother Mary, with appropriate lavishness AD 1140 and AD 1548. In memory of such a preeminent pontiff, called to rule over the Christian world by the voice of virtue alone. Defender of religion and defender of the Church; puller-down of schism, benign toward paupers in God's religion; incomparable in prudence and skillful in action with kings and caesars and all other orders of men, he was tested through the period of 13 years, 7 months, and 7 days.] The chapter of this basilica accepted the memory of this beneficent father with deepest veneration. They restored the monument in piety to the cult of the virgin, with greatest submission, in the year of salvation 1657."—*Trans. Phyllis Jestice*)

An epitaph written by Pius IX in Santa Maria Trastevere reads:

INNOCENTIO II PONTIFICI MAXIMO / E REGIONE TRANSTIBERINA GENTE PAPARESCO / CVIVS CORPORIS EXVVIAS / QVAE IN LATERAN, BASILICA PRIMITVS REQVIEVERANT / EAQVE DIRO INCENDIO CONFLAGRANTE / ANNO MCCCVIII IN HANC TRANSLATAE FVERANT / IAMPRIDEM NVTV EIVS / IN AMPLIOREM FORMAM A FVND. REFECTAM ET EXORNATAM / PIVS IX P. M. E. VETERI LOCVLO / IN MONVMENTVM SVA IMPENSA PERFECTVM / INFERRI IVSSIT ANNO MDCCCLXIX

("For Innocent II, supreme pontiff, from the Trastevere district, of the Papareschi family, the remains of whose body, which at first rested in the Lateran basilica (which burned in a great fire in 1308), were transferred to this place, which, long ago, was rebuilt in more ample form and adorned thanks to his care. Supreme pontiff Pius IX took his remains from their old place and placed them at his expense in a perfect monument. He ordered this to be done in the year 1869."—*Trans. Phyllis Jestice*)

FURTHER READING: G. Marchetti Longhi, *I Papareschi e I Romani*, Rome, 1947.

Antipope Anacletus II (February 14, 1130–January 25, 1138) *Pietro Pierleoni.* Although no document recorded how Anacletus died, it is known that he was buried in his family church of Santa Maria in Trastevere. Joachim Prinz, in his book *Popes of the Ghetto,* surmises that they must have erected a tombstone for Anacletus that read: "Anacletus II, Pontiff of the Roman Catholic Church from 1130 to 1138." Soon after Anacletus's death (which ended the prevailing schism), Innocent II entered Rome and ordered that the chuch be torn down because his enemy Anacletus was buried there. Anacletus's tomb was destroyed, and Prinz claims that where Anacletus's tomb stood is now where the tomb of Innocent II stands.[163]

Antipope Victor IV (middle of March–May 29, 1138; d. ?) *Gregorio Conti.* Resigned the papacy to Innocent II. Nothing more is known of him.

Celestine II (September 26, 1143–March 8, 1144) *Guido of Citta diCastello.* Died of old age in a monastery near St. Caesarius on the Palantine and was buried in St. John Lateran, although his tomb was destroyed in the fire of either 1308 or 1361; the charred remains were collected and buried in a polyandrum near the lesser door of the basilica (the entrance near the tomb of Innocent III, on the right side of the nave).[164]

Lucius II (March 11, 1144–February 15, 1145) *Gherardo Caccianemici.* Died from being struck on the head with a large stone while trying to calm the Roman mob and prevent them from storming the forces on the commune on the capitol. He was buried on the left of the central nave in St. John Lateran, although his tomb was destroyed in the fire of either 1308 or 1361; his charred remains were collected and buried in a polyandrum near the lesser door of the basilica (the entrance near the tomb of Innocent III, on the right side of the nave).[165]

Blessed Eugenius III (February 15, 1145–July 8, 1153) *Bernardo Pignatelli.* Died from violent fever in Tivoli, Italy. The corpse was transferred from Tivoli to St. Peter's on the same day as his death; the funeral cortege wound through the center of the city on the public streets. With the death of Eugenius, papal death became an occasion of symbolic mourning for the whole church, not just for the pope as a man. He was buried in the nave of Saint Peter's (where Pope Gregory III was initially buried — the burial of Eugenius greatly damaged the old tomb of Gregory) in a tomb that was made of granite (because of its imperial symbolism and because granite was used as a substitute for porphyry). The mausoleum itself was made of many ancient stones taken from classical Roman monuments and was inscribed:

EUGENIO PAPA TERZO

("POPE EUGENIUS III")

Epitaph:

HIC HABET EVGENIVS DEFVNCTVS CARNE SEPVLCRVM / QVEM PIA CVM CHRISTO VIVERE CVRA FACIT / PISA VIRVM GENVIT QVEM CLARAEVALLIS ALVMNVM / EXHIBVIT SACRAE RELIGIONIS OPVS / HINC AD ANASTASII TRANSLATVS MARTYRIS AEDEM / EX ABBATE PATER SVMMVS IN ORBE FVIT / ERIPVIT SOLEMNE IVBAR MVNDIQVE DECOREM / IVLIVS OCTAVAM SOLE FERENTE DIEM / CONCEPTVM SACRAE REFEREBANT VIRGINIS ANNI / CENTVM BIS SENI MILLE QVATERQVE DECEM[166]

("In this sepulcher lies the mortal remains of Eugene, that divine goodness made to live in Christ. Pisa gave birth to the man; Clairvaux formed the student in the holiness of the religious life. Having passed from this place to the monastery of the martyr Anastasius, from abbot he became universal high priest. In the month of July, when the sun was opening the eighth day it took him, beacon of light and splendor, in the year 1153 from the conception of the Virgin."—*Trans. Father Tom Carleton*)

Because many miracles occurred at the tomb before its destruction in the seventeenth century (during the demolition of the old basilica), Eugenius was beatified by Pius IX in 1872. His feast day is July 8.

FURTHER READING: G. Mercati, "Un epitafio metrico di E. III," in *Studi e docum. Di Storia e di Diritto*, Rome, XX, 1899.

Anastasius IV   (July 8, 1153–December 3, 1154) *Corrado*.

Died of old age and was buried in St. John Lateran, in the tomb that once housed the body of Emperor Constantine's mother, Helena, which he had moved from the Via Labicana for the purpose of his own burial. His excuse for using her particular sarcophagus was that the holy empress's mausoleum no longer contained her mortal remains. This was the only tomb to survive the Lateran fires of 1308 and 1361, and although heavily damaged, it was restored in 1509. In the nineteenth century Pius VI had it moved to the treasury of the Vatican Museum, where it can be seen today.

FURTHER READING: A. Monaci, "Sul sarcofago di S. Elena" in *Arch. R. Soc. Rom. St. patria*, Rome, XXII, 1899; G. Gradara, "I sarcofagi vaticani di S. Elena e di S. Costanza," in *Nuovo Bull. Arch. Crist. Roma*, XX, 1914; A. Westholm, *Zur Zeitbestimmung der Helena-und Constantia-Sarkophage*, Lung, 1934; Julian Gardner, *The Tomb and the Tiara*, Oxford University Press, 1992; Virgilio Cardinal Noe, *Le Tombe e i Monumenti*, Rome, 2000.

Sarcophagus of Anastasius IV, in the treasury of the Vatican Museum. Drawing by Joan Reardon.

Hadrian IV   (December 4, 1154–September 1, 1155) *Nicholas Breakspear*.

Died from illness in Anagni, Italy, at age 59 and was buried in a pagan sarcophagus of Egyptian granite decorated with carvings of oxen skulls and garlands. On his deathbed the English Hadrian requested that the charity of the church of Canterbury take care of his feeble mother.[167] Godfrey of Viterbo wrote a poem which blames Hadrian for that era's schism of the church and gives an unflattering account of his death in stanza twelve[168]:

> 12. The Death of Pope Adrian in the Campagna.
>
> As the pope returns to his estate of Campagna
> And grandly comes to cool springs,
> He uttered various threats against the empire.
> Wherefore he lies constricted, overthrown, without medicine,
> His neck swells, he dies, having left war in place of peace;
> For he himself was the grizzly head of schism.[170]

According to Renzo Montini, Hadrian's remains were later moved to the inner wall of the south transept of St. Peter's and placed in an altar with the remains of Pope Vigilius (d. 557) and Silvester I (d. 331). The altar was dedicated to said Saint Silvester with the following inscription:

ALTARE SANCTI SILVESTRI PAPAE–UBI
VIGILII ET ADRIANI IV SEPULCRA

("Altar of Pope Saint Silvester with the sepulcher of Vigilius and Adrian IV."[171])

This is somewhat confusing. Was the body of Hadrian IV entombed with Vigilius and Silvester in the altar, or was Hadrian's monument only placed in the chapel that contained the altar? Historically it makes more sense that Hadrian's monument was simply located in the same chapel as the altar of St. Silvester, because we do know for a fact (from church canon and historian Giacomo Grimaldi, who recorded the monuments and exhumations of St. Peter's before its demolition) that Hadrian's monument contained

LEG. DE LATERE IN NORVEGIAM MISSVS / AN. DNI. MCLII / CONTENTIONE INTER REGES PACATA / ET ARCHIEPISCOPATV IN CIVIT NIDAROS CONST. / ILLIVS ETIAM TERRAE GENTEM / CHRISTIANA LEGE AC DISCIPLINIS ECCLESIAST / STVDIOSE IMBVIT / AD PETRI VERO CATHEDRAM EVECTVS / NORVEGENSES / AD LIMINA APOSTOLORVM PEREGRINANTES / TVTAVIT / EOSQVE PATERNO FOVIT AMORE / NE TOT BENEFICIORVM MEMORIA EXCIDAT / REG. SOC. ORVEGICA SCIENT. NIDROSIENS. P. / AN SAL. MCMXXIV / DCCCC A CONVERSIONE NORVEGENS AD FIDEM / PER S. OLAVVM REGEM ET MARTYREM

Sarcophagus of Adrian IV in the grottoes of St. Peter's basilica. By permission of Julian Gardner from his book *The Tomb and the Tiara*.

an effigy of the pope and was originally placed against the inner wall of the south transept of St. Peter's. We also know from papal tomb historian H.K. Mann that Hadrian's monument was to the outer north aisle of the eastern half of St. Peter's,[171] although it was destroyed during the demolition of the basilica in the seventeenth century, leaving just the sarcophagus, which can now be seen in the Vatican crypt. Grimaldi witnessed the opening of Hadrian's sarcophagus on Wednesday, November 8, 1606, and described the remains as wearing a black chasuble, dalmatic, and tunic with gold borders, fragments of papal pallium with black crosses, a maniple of pure white, sandals "in Turkish fashion" that were ornamented with marigolds but without crosses, and a gold ring of "polite" work with one emerald. His body was of medium height, intact but corrupted, although his head was reduced to bone. The sarcophagus inscription reads simply

HADRIANVS PAPA IIII

("Pope Hadrian IIII")

although in 1924 the Royal Norwegian Society of Nidaross erected an epitaph in Hadrian's honor that can be seen today in the Vatican crypt:

HADRIANVS IV P.M. / QVI NICOLAVS BREAKSPEAR ANGLVS / CVUM ESSET CARD. EPVS. ALBANENSIS /

("Adrian IV, great high priest. He was the Englishman Nicholas Breakspear, who, being cardinal bishop of Albano, was sent as a legate to the shores of Norway in the year of our Lord 1152. Having pacified the dispute between the kings and having constituted the archiepiscopal see in the city of Nidaross [present day Trondheim], he also formed with care the people of that land in the Christian law and in the discipline of the Church. Raised then to the chair of Peter, he defended the Norwegians, who were coming on pilgrimage to the tombs of the apostles, and protected them with brotherly love. In order that the memory of so many benefits may not be lost, the Royal Norwegian Society of Nidaross, in the year of our Lord 1924, the ninth centenary of the conversion of Norway to the faith by means of Saint Olaf, king and martyr."—*Trans. Father Tom Carleton*)

FURTHER READING: L. Munoz-Gasparini, "Memorie norvegesi nelle chiese di Roma," in *Roma*, Rome, IV, 1926; Julian Gardner, *The Tomb and the Tiara*, Oxford University Press, 1992; Virgilio Cardinal Noe, *Le Tombe e i Monumenti*, Rome, 2000; Brenda Bolton, *Hadrian IV*, Ashgate Publishers, 2003.

Alexander III (September 7, 1159–August 30, 1181) *Orlando (Roland) Bandinelli.* Died in Civita Castellana from illness at age 81. He had been forced out of Rome in 1179 by the Roman Commune and stayed away because of Antipope Innocent II. He was buried in the Lateran, although the Roman mob ruined his tomb with graffiti. His original epitaph read:

LVX CLERI DECVS ECCLESIAE PATER URBIS ET
ORBIS / PRAESVL ALEXANDER CLAVDITVR HOC
TVMLO / LVMINIS EXTINCTI PATTITVR DISPENDIA
CLERVS / CVMQVE SVO DOLET VRBVS ORBE FVISSE
PATREM / NON TAMEN ILLE RVIT QVIA VIRTVS
NESCIA CASVS / CREDITVR HVIC VITAM
PERSPETVASSE VIRO / LARGA MANVS PIA CVRA
GREGIS PVDOR ALMVS HONESTAS / HVIC INTER
SVPEROS OBTINVERE LOCVM / SI QVAERIS QVIS ET
VNDE FVIT NOMEN SIBI QVONDAM / ROLANDVS
PATRIA TVSCIA SENA DOMVS / HVNC FESTIS
IVNXERE SVIS FELIX ET ADAVCTVS / CVM QVIBVS
EST FELIX FACTVS ADAVCTVS ERIT

("Bishop Alexander, light of the clergy, glory of
the Church, father of the city and the world, is
enclosed in this tomb. The clergy, the city, and
the world suffered great loss and sorrow when
his light was extinguished. Such as he was not
cast down for lack of virtue; he had a generous
hand and cared piously for his flock with modesty and honesty. May he obtain a place among
those above. If you seek to know who he was
and whence came his former name, he was
Roldand from Tuscany, of the city of Siena. His
happiness is compounded now that he is in
feast [with Christ] as is the happiness of those
he united." — *Trans. Phyllis Jestice*)

Unfortunately his tomb was destroyed
in the fire of either 1308 or 1361; the charred
remains were collected and buried in a
polyandrum near the lesser door of the basilica (the entrance near the tomb of Innocent
III, on the right side of the nave).[172]
Alexander VII (1655–1667) raised a
huge cenotaph by Francesco Borromini to
Alexander III on the right side of the Lateran. The epitaph on this monument, which
can be seen today, reads:

ALEXANDER III PONT. MAX. / NOBILI BANDINELLA
GENTE SENIS NATO / QVI DIFFICILLIMIS
TEMPORIBVS / EXIMIA PIETATE / SVMMA
PRVDENTIA AC DOCTRINA / ECCLESIAE PRAEFVIT
ANNIS XXII / INVICTA FORTITVDINE ATQVE
CONSTANTIA / APOSTOLICAE SEDIS IVRA /
AVCTORITATEM DIGNITATEMQVE RETINVIT / ET
POST IMMENSOS LABORES / AC SOLLICITVDINES
PACE PARTA / OECVMENICVM LATERANENSE
CONCILIVM / CELEBRAVIT / SANCTISSIMAS DE
ELIGENDO SVMMO PONTIFICE / DEQVE VI ET
AMBITV COERCENDO / LEGES TVLIT / THOMAM

Monument to Alexander III, St. John Lateran,
Rome.

CANTVARIENSEM ANTISTITEM / BERNARDVM
CLARAVALLIS ABBATEM / QVOS VIVENTES
AMICISSIMOS HABVIT / EDVARDVM ANGLIAE
CANVTVM DANIAE REGEM / SANCTORVM
NVMERO / ADSCRIPSIT / PLVRIMISQVE ALIIS
MAXIMIS REBVS GESTIS / VITAE DEMVM ET
GLORIAE CVRSVM CONFECIT / ANN. SAL.
MCLXXXI KAL. SEPT. / ALEXANDER VII PONT.
MAX / NOMINIS ET MVNERIS IN ECCLESIA
SVCCESSOR / PONTIFICI TANTO CIVI SVO /
PIOS CINERES VENERATVS POSVIT[173]

("Alexander III, supreme pontiff. Born to the
noble Bandinelli family of Siena, who in times
of greatest difficulty presided over the Church
for 22 years with exceptional piety and the
greatest prudence and doctrine. Unconquered
in fortitude and constancy, he upheld the laws,
authority, and dignity of the Apostolic See. And
after immense labors and solicitude for the
cause of peace, he celebrated the ecumenical
Lateran council. He issued holy laws on the

election of popes, bringing an end to force and bribery. He added to the number of the saints Thomas, bishop of Canterbury and Bernard, abbot of Clairvaux, who, living, he had held dearest, and kings Edward of England and Canute of the Danes. He accomplished many other great things and deeds in the course of his life of glory. In the year of salvation 1181 on the calends of September, Alexander VII, supreme pontiff, his successor in the Church in both name and office, in the pontificate of his city piously placed these venerable ashes here."—*Trans. Phyllis Jestice*)

Antipope Victor IV (September 7, 1159– April 20, 1164) *Ottaviano.* Died of a short, painful illness in a monastery near Lucca, Italy. Neither the clergy of the Cathedral of Lucca nor that of San Frediano would allow an excommunicated cardinal (whom they in no way considered a pope) to be buried in their churches, so he was buried in the church of a poor monastery outside the walls. The prevailing, legitimate pope, Alexander III, wept when he heard that Victor had died and sternly reproached his cardinals for celebrating the antipope's death. In December of 1187, Pope Gregory VIII ordered Victor's tomb destroyed and the remains tossed out of the monastery church.

Antipope Paschal III (April 22, 1164– September 20, 1168) *Guido of Cremona.* Died in a Castel Sant' Angelo after having barricaded himself inside because he didn't trust the feelings of the Roman mob. No information about his burial is known.

Antipope Callistus (III) (September 1168–August 29, 1178) *Giovanni.* Died in Benevento, Italy. No information about his burial is known.

Antipope Innocent (III) September 29, 1179–January 1180 d. ?) *Lando.* Died in the Benedictine abbey of Trinita in La Cava,

Italy. No information about his burial is known.

Lucius III (September 1, 1181–November 25, 1185) *Ubaldo Allucingoli.* Died at age 75 in Verona after having been run out of Rome by the Roman mob. He was originally buried in a marble sarcophagus in front of the high altar in the *Duomo* of Verona, Italy, although now his bones rest in the Capitol Library of Verona. Church historian Gregorovius gives this as the original tomb inscription:

LUCI LUCA TIBI DEDIT ORTUM, PONTIFICATUM / OSTIA, PAPATUM ROMA, VERONA MORI. / IMMO VERONA DEDIT VERUM TIBI VIVERE, ROMA / EXILIUM, CURAS OSTIA, LUCA MORI.[174]

("O Lucius, Lucca gave thee birth; Ostia, the purple; Rome, the Papacy; and Verona, death. Nay, rather, Verona gave to thee true life; Rome, exile; Ostia, sorrows; and Lucca, death."[175])

Church historian Renzo Montini, however, gives this as the original epitaph:

On top:

O SAISSIM PAT DO LVCIVS PP III / MCLXXXV DIE XXV NOV

On left:

LVCA DEDIT LVCEM TIBI LVCI PONTIFICATVM / OSTIA PPTVM ROMA VERONA MORI

On right:

IMMO VERONA DEDIT LVCIS TIBI GAVDIA ROMA / EXILIVM CVRAS OSTIA LVCA MORI / OBITT S. PATER D. D. LUCIUS PAPA III. A. MCLXXXV. DIE XXV[176]

(*On top:* "O most holy father, lord pope Lucius III. 1185 on the 25th of November." *On left:* "Lucca gave light, the pontificate, to you, Lucius. Placed over Ostia and Rome, he died in Verona." *On right:* "Verona indeed gave light to your joy, Rome. In exile from the cares of Ostia and Lucca he died. The holy father lord pope Lucius III died in the year 1185 on the 25th day."—*Trans. Phyllis Jestice*)

When Bishop Gilberti (1524–1543) restored the cathedral, he had the body of Lucius put beneath the pavement in the middle of the sanctuary, with a slab of red Veronese marble inscribed:

OSSA / LVCII III PONT. MAX. / CVI ROMA OB INVIDIAM PVLSO / VERONA TVTISSIMVM AC GRATISSIMVM REFVGIVM / FVIT VBI CONVENTV CHRISTIANORVM ACTO / DVM PRAECLARA MVLTA MOLITVR E VITA / EXCESSIT[178]

("The bones of Lucius III, supreme pontiff, who, having been driven from Rome by ill will, found at Verona a most dutiful and gracious refuge. This was where, with the coming together of Christians, he built much while preeminent, and exited from life." — *Trans. Phyllis Jestice*)

On February 25, 1879, a great storm damaged the apse of the church and threw a large stone on the tomb, smashing Gilberti's slab to bits and exposing the original tombstone of red Veronese marble. The tomb was recovered and given a new marble slab, although the original slab is built into the wall on the right side of the cathedral near the major altar. The partially counter-sunk reliefs on the tomb consist of two crowning

and censing angels at the head of the pope, with a cleric prostrating himself at the pope's feet.[179] The inscription on the wall tomb was carved to be read from above:

LAPIS CASV FRACTVS DIE XXV FEBRVARII M DCCC LXXIX / AB ARCA SVB CHORO IACENTE HIC NE PERRIRET INFIXVS[179]

("The stone case having been broken on 25 February 1879, it was removed from where it lay in the vault under the choir and fixed in this place lest it be destroyed." — *Trans. Phyllis Jestice*).

FURTHER READING: O. Jozzi, *La tomba di L. III in Verona*, Rome, 1907.

Urban III

Urban III (November 25, 1185–October 19 or 20, 1187) *Umberto Crivelli*. Died of illness in Ferarra, Italy, because the Veronese, who were loyal to the emperor, refused to let him stay in Verona. The original tomb was made of red marble and placed atop four columns. Created in 1305, the original tomb was placed in the duomo of Ferrara, and in 1395 it was moved to behind the high altar of the duomo.

The original tomb inscription, which stated incorrectly that Urban was buried in 1185, read:

HIC JACET SACRE MEMORIE VRBANVS PAPA III NACIONE / MEDIOLANENSIS ET GENERE CRIBELLORVM / SEPVLTVS MILLŌ C. LXXXVII ET REVELATVS MILLŌ CCCV DIE / VIII MENSIS AVGVSTI MENSIS INDICIONE TERTIA / TEMPORIBVS FRATRIS GVIDONIS FERRARIENSIS EPISCOPI / IOHANNIS ARCHIPRESBITERI ET BONAGRACIE PREPOSITI[180]

("Here lies Pope Urban III of holy memory. By nation a Milanese from the Crivelli family. Buried in 1187 and uncovered in 1305 on the 8th of August in the 3rd indiction, in the times of brothers Guido, bishop of Ferrara, of John the archpriest, and of Bonogracio the provost." — *Trans. Phyllis Jestice*)

In 1485 Urban's body was transferred to a marble urn created by Paulo di Luca, the Florentiens Stolfo and Bartolomeo di Bigigio, Battista and Antonio di Dominico da Como, and Sando di Bartolo.[181] In 1636 the

Tomb slab of Lucius III in the Verona Cathedral. By permission of the *Archeologica Christina of Verona.*

Top: The original tomb of Urban III, the *Duomo* of Ferarra, Italy. *Bottom:* Fifteenth-century cenotaph to Urban III, in the *Duomo* of Ferrara.

tomb was moved to another part of the church during its restoration. Nothing of the original tomb exists, but a large cenotaph in Urban's honor was built by G. B. Boffa into the left wall of the choir of the duomo of Ferrara in the fifteenth century (the date of death was corrected to 1187).

FURTHER READING: A. Sautto, *Il Duomo di Ferrara*, Ferrara, 1934; M. A. Guarini, *Compendio historico ... delle chiese ... di Ferrara*, Ferrara, 1621.

Gregory VIII (October 21–December 17, 1187) *Alberto de Morra*. Died of illness in Pisa. Gregory was traveling to Rome via Pisa (stopping at Lucca to order Antipope Victor IV's tomb destroyed) when he became sick. He was originally buried in a beautiful white marble tomb in the first chapel of Our Lady in the duomo of Pisa, which was then moved to the right of the main door in the duomo. Sadly, the monument was destroyed in the fire of 1600.

FURTHER READING: R. Roncioni, "Le Istorie Pisane, lib. VIII," in *Arch. St. it.*, VI, 1844.

Clement III (December 19, 1187–late March, 1191) *Paolo Scolari*. Buried in St. John Lateran, although his tomb was destroyed in the fire of either 1308 or 1361; the charred remains were collected and buried in a polyandrum near the lesser door of the basilica (the entrance near the tomb of Innocent III, on the right side of the nave).[182]

Celestine III (March/April 1191–January 8, 1198) *Giacinto Bobone Orsini*. Died at age 93 of sickness and old age. On his deathbed he asked the cardinals' permission to retire if they would accept his choice as successor, Cardinal Giovanni of Santa Prisca. They refused, so Celestine remained pope for another three weeks until he died. He was buried in St. John Lateran in a white marble sarcophagus which no longer exists, as it was probably destroyed in the Lateran fires of either 1308 or 1361; his charred remains were collected and buried in a polyandrum near the lesser door of the basilica (the entrance near the tomb of Innocent III, on the right side of the nave).[183]

Innocent III (January 8, 1198–July 16, 1216) *Lotario Conti*. Died of sudden fever at age 56. En route to settle a dispute between Pisa and Genoa, he died in Perugia. St. Francis of Assisi was summoned to Innocent's bedside and finally arrived after (legend holds) stopping along the way to give a spoonful of soup to a blind invalid, talk to street Arabs, and help a spider. The funeral was held, "as tradition requires, in the presence of seventeen cardinal bishops, priests, and deacons, and of many other archbishops, bishops, and prelates, and of a multitude of clergy and laity."[184] However, during the ritual of abandonment, when the corpse was left overnight in the San Lorenzo, vandals broke in and stole the valuable burial vestments from the corpse, as recorded by Jacquesde Vitry, cardinal of Tuscolo: "The body was abandoned in the church almost naked."[185] Innocent was left "*fere nudum,*" a Latin phrase meaning in "whiteness." This could mean either that the corpse was stripped nude, or, more likely, that the vandals left him in only his plain white cassock. Whatever the case, Innocent was buried the next day in the Perugia cathedral, in the marble sepulcher located near the window of the altar of the Blessed Herculanus. Sometime during the fourteenth or fifteenth century, when the San Lorenzo was being rebuilt, Innocent's remains were placed in an iron casket along with those of popes Urban IV (d. 1264) and Martin IV (d. 1285), and the casket was placed in the sacristy of San Lorenzo.

Exhumed in 1587, Innocent was found to be wearing an antique chasuble, miter, rings, and other pontifical ornaments. In 1615, Bishop Comitoli had Innocent's remains (his body was well preserved, as were those of Urban IV, but those of Martin IV were just bones because at his request he was not embalmed) placed in a flimsy mausoleum located at the end wall of the right transept of San Lorenzo. In 1730 the mausoleum was moved to the right side of the great chapel which forms the left transept of

Cenotaph to Innocent III, St. John Lateran, Rome.

the Perugia cathedral. In 1891, Leo XIII had the remains of Innocent brought to Rome and placed in St. John Lateran. Sculptor Giuseppe Lucchetti carved a beautiful sarcophagus with a recumbent effigy, which lies atop the door to the Lateran Gift Shop and Museum. Underneath the pope on the left side of the door is the figure of Wisdom, and on the right side is the figure that symbolizes the Western Church. Atop the sarcophagus in the lunette is the figure of Christ flanked by St. Francis and St. Dominic, with an arch of heavenly spirits above it. Inscription:

LEO XIII / INNOCENTIO III / MDCCCXCI

("Leo XIII, Innocent III, 1891")

On the base of the right pilaster is carved

GIUSEPPE LUCHETTI/ARCHITETTO
E SCOLPI/NEL 1891.

("Giuseppe Luchetti, architect and sculptor, 1891.")

FURTHER READING: U. Flandoli, *I. III e il monumento d'onore ereggogli da Leone XIII P. M. nell'Arcibasilica Lateranense*, Rome, 1891; B. LaBanca, *I. III e il suo nuovo monumento in Roma*, Rome, 1892; S. Sibilia, "L'iconografia di I. III," in *Boll. Sez. Anagni della Soc. Rom. di St. patria*, Rome, II, 1953.

Honorius III   (July 18, 1216–March 18, 1227) *Cencio Savelli*. Died of old age. Approximately ten days before his death, Honorius was brought to the window of the Lateran palace, "exhausted and half-dead," and held upright so that he could give his last blessing to the people, who cried and prayed on their knees. The cardinals had an ulterior motive for showing the pope to the crowd: If the people saw that the pope was still alive, they would postpone their plundering of the papal treasures as was custom after the death of a pope. This would give the cardinals time to secure their own palaces just in case.[186]

After the funeral, which was held according to custom on the day immediately following his death, Honorius was buried in an ancient classical porphyry sarcophagus in a monument beside the altar of the manger in Santa Maria Maggiore, Rome. Because miracles were soon reported there, his tomb became an object of public devotion. Today, however, nothing of his tomb remains, not even the sarcophagus.[187]

FURTHER READING: G. Biasiotti, "La basilica di S. Maria Maggiore di Roma prima delle innovazioni del secolo XVI," in *Melanges*, cit. XXV, 1915.

Gregory IX   (March 19, 1227–August 22, 1241) *Ugo (Ugolino) Conti*. Died of heat exhaustion at around age 100 at the Lateran palace. When he was dying he gave an ivory cross to his doctor, Richard, because both the cross and the doctor were dear to him. As he lay dying, Gregory's last words were, "True, Peter's little ship is sometimes caught in a hurricane and driven onto the rocks, but it soon bobs up again among the foaming waves."[188] Several cardinals in Anagni were extremely angry at the Roman cardinals for not participating in Gregory's funeral and later claimed that sickness and quick death of the the subsequent pope, Celestine IV, were caused by the mortally indifferent cardinals. Gregory was buried in St. Peter's, but the tomb no longer exists; no doubt it was a casualty during the demolition of the basilica in the seventeenth century.

Celestine IV   (October 25–November 10, 1241) *Goffredo da Castiglione*. Died from old age and harsh conditions in conclave. He was chosen as pope because the cardinals had been locked in a filthy, fetid palace by the Roman senator Matteo Orsini, and they wanted to quickly choose a pope who would soon die so they could have a freer conclave. Just as they had hoped, Celestine became sick three days after he was elected (which several cardinals ascribed to the lack of interest by other cardinals for the funeral of the previous pope, Gregory IX). He died shortly

Original tomb of Honorius III in Santa Maria Maggiore, Rome. By permission of the Houghton Library, Harvard University.

thereafter, and was buried in St. Peter's the day after his death. Some say he was consecrated on October 28, but he most likely died before he was consecrated. The tomb was destroyed during the demolition of St. Peter's in the early seventeenth century.

Innocent IV (June 25, 1243–December 7, 1254) *Sinibaldo Fieschi (Fieschi Count Lavagna).* Died in Naples, Italy, after hearing that the papal troops had been routed near Foggia, Italy. Salimbene de Adam wrote in his chronicles that Innocent "lay naked on the straw, abandoned by all, following the custom of Roman pontiffs when they die."[189] Humbert of Montauro, archbishop of Naples, erected a beautiful monument to him in 1318 in San Januarius, Naples, which was made up of several stories and was inlaid with mosaics. Almost nothing of the original tomb monument exists today; The recumbent figure and everything above it is

The original tomb of Innocent IV, San Januarius, Naples.

from the sixteenth century, a fact made obvious by the tiara which, in Innocent's time, did not have a round top (the tiara on the effigy incorrectly has a rounded top). The lunette features Innocent kneeling on the left to the Blessed Mother, and kneeling on her right is Archbishop Annibale of Capua. The original epitaph read:

HIC SUPERIS DIGNUS, REQUIESCIT PAPA BENIGNUS, / LAETUS DE FLISCO, SEPULTUS TEMPORE PRISCO. / VIR SACER, ET RECTUS, SANCTO VELAMINE TECTUS. / UT IAM COLLAPSO MUNDO TEMERARIA PASSO, / SANCTA MINISTRARI URBS POSSET QUOQUE RECTIFICARI, / CONCILIUM FECIT, VETERAQUE IVRA REFECIT. / HAERESIS ILLISA TUNC EXTITIT ATQUE RECISA, / MOENIA DIREXIT, RITE SIBI CREDITA REXIT, / STRAVIT INIMICUM CHRISTI COLUBRUM FEDERICUM. / IANUA DE NATO GAUDET SIC GLORIFICATO. / LAUDIBUS IMMENSIS, URBS TU QUOQE PARTHENOPENSIS. / PULCHRA DECORE SATIS, DEDIT HIC SIBI PLURIMA GRATIS. / HOC TITULAVIT ITA UMBERTUS METROPOLITA.[190]

("Here rests, long buried, the kindly Pope, Laetus de' Fieschi, worthy of the heavenly kingdom—a holy and upright man robed in the veil of sanctity. He assembled a council and renewed ancient laws, in order that, when the world was fallen on evil days and suffered every kind of violence, the Holy City might be governed and led in the right way. Heresy was then wiped out and extinguished. He governed the cities and ruled justly what was committed to his charge. He trampled under foot that serpent Frederick, the enemy of Christ. Genoa is proud of her noble son, and thou, too, city of Naples, dost render high praises to his name; beautiful enough in thy charms, thou owest him many a gift. This was inscribed by Humbert the Metropolitan."[191])

The lower epitaph was added, as is made evident by an inscription written by Archbishop Annibale of Capua in the late sixteenth century, which tells how he restored the monument because of decay:

D. O. M. / INNOCENTIO IV PONT. MAX. / DE OMNI CHRISTIANA REP. OPTIME MERITO / QUI NATALI S. JOANNIS BAPTISTAE / ANN. MCCXLI / PONTIFEX RENUNCIATUS / DIE APOSTOLOR. PRINCIPI SACRA CORONATUS / QUUM PURPUREO PRIMUS PILEO /

CARDINALES EXORNASSET / NEAPOLIM A
CONRADO EVERSAM / S. P. RESTITUENDAM
CURASSET / INNUMERISQUE ALIIS PRAECLARE ET
PROPE / DIVINE GESTIS PONTIFICATUM SUUM /
QUAM MAXIME ILLUSTREM REDDIDISSET / ANNI
MCCXLIV / B. LUCIAE VIRGINIS LUCE HAC LUCE
CESSIT / ANNIBAL DE CAPUA ARCHIEP. NEAP. /
IN SANCTISSIMI VIRI MEMORIAM / ABOLETUM
VETUSTATE EPIGRAMMA RESTITUIT.[192]

("To Innocent IV, supreme pontiff, who hath deserved well of the whole Christian republic, who was proclaimed pope on the day of St. John Baptist, in the year 1243, and was crowned on the sacred day of the prince of apostles, and who, having decorated for the first time the cardinals with the purple hat, having secured the restoration to St. Peter of the kingdom seized by Conrad, and having made his reign illustri-

The tomb of Innocent IV, in the *Duomo* of Naples. From H.K. Mann, *Tombs and Portraits of the Popes.*

ous by countless other famous and almost divine achievements, departed from this light on St. Lucy's Day 1244. Annibale of Capua, Archbishop of Naples, in memory of the holy man, has restored this epitaph injured by time."[193])

FURTHER READING: A. De Rinaldis, *Santa Chiara*, Naples, 1920; O. Morisani, *Tino di Camaino a Napoli*, Naples, 1954; R. Causa, *Sculture lignee nella Campania*, Naples, 1950; C. Celano, *Notizie del bello, dell'antico e del curioso della citta di Napoli*, 1856; D Mallardo, "Papa I. IV a Napoli" in *Osservatore Romano*, December 12, 1954; F. Capecelatro, *Storia del Regno di Napoli*, Naples, 1811.

Alexander IV (December 12, 1254–May 25, 1261) *Rinaldo dei Conti, Count of Segni.* He died in Viterbo and was buried in the Cathedral of San Lorenzo, also in Viterbo, although the tomb was destroyed in 1490 during a radical restoration of the cathedral. Nothing remains, not even a description of his tomb.

FURTHER READING: C. Pinzi, *I principali monujmenti di Viterbo*, 2nd ed., Viterbo, 1894; F. Cristofori, *Le tombe die Papi in Viterbo*, Siena 1887.

Urban IV (August 29, 1261–October 2, 1264) *Jacques Pantaleon.* Died in Perugia, Italy, at age 64 and was buried in the city cathedral. Possibly the sculptor Giovanni Pisani made a marble tomb for him (though some say the tomb was for Martin IV), with a notice that there was a fine of 25 lira for anyone "who might dare to offend the sepulcher of Urban IV,"[194] but this was unfortunately destroyed in the late fourteenth century. Nothing is known of that tomb except the epitaph, a fragment of which has been preserved in the Civic Museum of Perugia. The original tomb inscription (possibly written by Thomas Aquinas) read:

ARCHILEVITA FUI, PASTORQUE GREGIS
PATRIARCHA, / TUNC JACOBUS, POSUI MIHI
NOMEN AB URBE MONARCHA. / NUNC CIVIS

EXIGVI, TUMULI POST CONCLUDOR IN
ARCHA, / TE SINE FINE FRUI, TRIBUAS
MIHI SUMME IHERARCHA.[195]

("Archdeacon was I, and shepherd and patriarch of the flock. Once called James [sic]..., I
took the name of the city whose monarch I was.
Then I went out from the city [into exile]; now
I rest within the tomb. Highest lord of the
world, grant that I may enjoy thee without
end."[196])

When the new Cathedral of Perugia was
being built in 1587, Urban's body, along with
those of Innocent III (d. 1216) and Martin
IV (d. 1285) was placed in an iron casket and
interred in the sacristy of San Lorenzo in
Perugia. Urban's body was found to be very
well preserved when it was exhumed in 1587.
His nephew, cardinal Ancher Pantaleon,
erected a church of St. Urban to him, and
the clergy were required to celebrate a mass
every day in his honor.

FURTHER READING: Coffinet, "Recherches his-
toriques et archeologiques sur les restes mor-
tels du pape U. IV" in *Mem. de la Soc. Arch. de
l'Aude*, Troyes, XXI, 1857.

Clement IV   (February 5, 1265–Novem-
ber 29, 1268) *Guy Foulques*. Died in Viterbo,
Italy, at age 63. The funeral service was held
at the Cathedral of Viterbo, but because he
willed his remains should be placed in a
Dominican church, he was buried in the
Dominican church of Santa Maria in Gradi,
Viterbo. Miracles soon occurred at his tomb,
drawing thousands of pilgrims—and their
money—to the church. The bishop of
Viterbo then insisted that the pope be reinterred at the cathedral of Viterbo, which
would then garner all the money and prestige that a papal tomb brings to a church.
And so, while the funeral monument was
being built for Santa Maria in Gradi, the
body was placed in the Church of the Cardinals of Viterbo (seen as neutral territory).
After the monument was completed by
Pietro di Oderisio, it was sent to the cathedral of Viterbo instead of Santa Maria in

Gradi, which angered the Dominicans. After
the next pope, Gregory X, was elected, Cardinals William of St. Mark and Uberto of San
Eustachio ordered Clement's tomb returned
to Santa Maria in Gradi. Despite Gregory X's
support of this order, those at the cathedral
of Viterbo sent Clement's body but not his
tomb, nor the money it would take to rein-
ter the body. This prompted Gregory to write
four letters to the cathedral of Viterbo before
the matter was completely settled and both
the body of Clement IV and his tomb went
to Santa Maria in Gradi.

The original epitaph read:

LECTOR FIGE PEDES ADMIRANS QVAM BREVIS
AEDES / PONTIFICEM QVARTVM CLEMENTEM
CONTEGIT ARTVM / EN DATVR IN CINERES PETRI
SVCCESSOR ET HERES / CVIVS SI MEMORES NON
MVNDI GAVDIA QVAERES / HIC IVDEX PRIMVM
QVEM SI SVCCESSVS OPIMVM / REDDIDIT VT
FERTVR MILES PROBVS EFFICERETVR / TALEQVE
SORTITVS NOMEN IVRISQVE PERITVS / VIRGINIS
VNIVS FVIT VNICVS IPSE MARITVS / QVI VIDVATVS
EA MOX CHRISTI SORTE PETITA / ANICIENSIS ITA
DIGNVS FVIT ARCHILEVITA / PRAESVL IBI FACTVS
POST ARCHIEPISCOPVS ACTVS / PASTOR VT
EGREGIVS NARBONAE PRAEFVIT AVCTVS / VTQVE
DEO GRATVS VIR CARDINIBVS SOCIATVS / PAPATVS
NOMEN CLARVM SVSCEPIT ET OMEN / SIC
SVBLIMATVS SIC DENIQVE CLARIFICATVS /
PERFICIENDO GRADVS CENSETVR AD
ASTRA LEVATVS / ANNIS SEX DENIS OCTO
CVM MILLE DVCENIS / TRANSACTIS CHRISTI
CLEMENS TVMVLO DATVR ISTI / AGHIOS
QVARE QVI TRANSIS CREDE PRECARE / VT
FINALIS EI DET GAVDIA SVMMA DIEI AMEN[197]

("Reader, pause and admire how a small shrine
conceals the pontiff Clement IV, now reduced
to ashes. This successor and heir of Peter did
not seek memorials of worldly joy, although he,
acting as a chivalrous knight, is the judge who
successfully restored wealth. Of such a chosen
name and skillful in laws, he was the sole husband of a single virgin; widowed from her, he
then begged for Christ's lot. Worthily he was
archdeacon of Le Puy. He became bishop there
and afterward archbishop, admirable pastor of
Narbonne. And then, thanks to God, the man
entered the society of cardinals and received
the papacy with untarnished name and auspi-
cious signs. Thus elevated and thus made

bright, ascending a further step, he was raised up among the stars in the year 1268. Clement, passing over to Christ, is here given to his tomb. You who pass may believe that he is to be found among the saints, so that at the last he might receive the highest joy from God. Amen."—*Trans. Phyllis Jestice*)

In 1738, during the reconstruction of the church, the tomb was placed in a little chapel in the church, where it was desecrated in 1798 by French soldiers of the Republic. In 1838, the French ambassador to the Vatican had it repaired, and then inscribed in 1840. The tomb inscription of 1840 reads:

CLEMENTIS PP. IV NATIONE GALLI
ANNO CHRISTIANO 1268 DEFUNCTI /
TITULUM HUNC RESTITUENDUM
CURAVIT / SEPTIMUS DE FAY COMES
DE LA TOUR MAUBOURG / FRANCORUM
REGIS APUD S. SEDEM ORATOR. /
ANNO 1840 / REGNANTE HVMBERTO
I / AD PRISTINAM FORMAM
RESTITVTM / M DXXX XC

("With Pope Clement IV of the nation of Gaul having died in the Christian year 1268, Septimus De Fay, ally of La Tour Mauborg, presided over the restoration of this inscription, [while] an ambassador of the king of the French at the Holy See in the year 1840. In the reign of Humbert I [this tomb was] restored to the original appearance. 1890."—*Trans. Phillip Haberkern*)

In May 1885 the Italian Municipal authorities "scandalously violated" the tomb and turned the convent of Santa Maria in Gradi into a prison. During this "exhumation" of sorts it was discovered that the only remains inside the coffin were lace vestments of silk, a miter, and a ring. The lack of respect for Clement's tomb and memory caused much anger among the people, and so in 1890 it was moved to its final location — the transept on the gospel side of the high altar in the church of San Francesco alla Rocca.

Tomb of Clement IV (after World War II), San Francesco, Viterbo.

Clement's was the first effigy in Italy to depict the pope in death, showing his physical mortality, and the tomb itself is the earliest canopied Gothic tomb in central Italy.[198] As Paravincini-Bagliani writes in *The Pope's Body*, "there is no visible beauty in his features…. His tired and aged face reflects the 'very truth of death.'"[199] The effigy at the bottom of the tomb is that of Clement's nephew, Pierre le Gros. Originally the tomb had beneath the canopy a statue of the Virgin Mary and Child, but during World War II the entire church was gutted by aerial bombardment and these statues were destroyed. Surprisingly, the effigy survived, although the monument itself had to be completely restored.

The post–World War II inscription reads:

CLEMENS IV PONT. MAX. /
29 XI 1268 / REF. 1949[200]

FURTHER READING: P. Toesca, *Il Medioevo*, Turin, 1927; G. Rossi, *Il mausoleo di C. IV*, Siena, 1889; A. Scriattoli, *Viterbo nei suoi monumenti*, Rome, 1920; H. Keller, "Il sepolcro di C.IV in S. Francesco a Viterbo," in *Illustraz Vaticana*; G. Auda, "Le ceneri di C. IV sono tornate a S. Francesco di Viterbo," in *Osservatore Romano*, October 31, 1947; G. Colonna Brigante, "La tomba di un Papa scoperta dale bombe," in *Relata Politica*, Rome, December 29, 1951; A.L. Frothingham, "Two Tombs of the Popes at Viterbo by Vassallectus and Petrus Oderisi," in the *American Journal of Archaeology*, Boston, VII, 1891.

Blessed Gregory X (September 1, 1271–January 10, 1276) *Tedaldo Visconti*. Died of fever in Arezzo, Italy. He was crossing the Alps on his way to Rome, settling disputes in Northern Italy along the way, but became sick and died in Arezzo. He was buried in the duomo of Arezzo in a marble tomb by the sculptor Margaritone (also of Arezzo).[201] The tomb today resembles the original, although the original canopy was once higher because there was a fresco of the pope beneath it, which was probably lost when the tomb was moved around in 1810. There are five medallions beneath the effigy of the pope: the Lamb carrying the cross in the middle and flanked on both sides by the evangelists (Matthew, Mark, Luke, and John). In the arch is the figure of Christ bestowing the benediction. The original tomb inscription (which no longer exists on the monument) read:

GREGORIUS DENUS, VIRTUTUM LUCE
SERENUS / DORMIT IN HAC ARCA,

DIGNUS ROMAE PATRIARCHA, / QUEM GENUIT
PLACENTIA, URBS ARRETINA TENET.[202]

("The tenth Gregory, shining in the light of his virtues, sleeps in this tomb—a worthy Patriarch of Rome. Born at Piacenza, his remains rest at Arezzo."[203])

His current epitaph reads:

HOC SEPVLCHRVM / ARCHITECTVRA SCVLPTVRA
ET PICTVRA / OLIM A MARGARITONE ARRETINO
EXORNATVM / IN QVO CONDITA SVNT GREGORII X
PONT. MAX / EXVVIAE ANN. EXCESSVS EIVS
MCCLXXVI / AMPLIORE INDE CVLTV ALTARI
INLATAE / ANNO MDCCCVII / TVMVLVM
VENERARE MORTALIS / CVIVS SVMMA VIRTVS /
IMMORTALEM PEPERIT GLORIAM[204]

("In this sepulcher, with architecture, sculpture, and pictures provided by Margaritone

The tomb of Blessed Gregory X in the *Duomo* of Arezzo.

Arrentino, were buried the remains of Pope Gregory X. In the year of his demise, 1276, they were further interred with a veneration of the high altar in the year 1807. Revere the tomb of the mortal whose greatest virtue begat immortal glory."—*Trans. Phillip Haberkern*)

Many miracles occurred at the tomb; these were transcribed on a tablet and placed near his tomb. A cult developed at Arezzo as well as in other Italian cities, and Benedict XIV (1740–1758) added his name to the Roman martyrology. His remains are venerated under an altar at the end of the left nave of the church. His feast day (since 1963) has been January 9; previously it was January 10.

FURTHER READING: A. del Vita, *Il Duomo d'Arezzo*, Milan.

Blessed Innocent V (January 21–June 22, 1276) *Pierre of Tarentaise*. Died of sudden fever in Rome at age 52 and was buried in St. John Lateran, although his tomb was destroyed by the fire of either 1308 or 1361; his charred remains were collected and buried in a polyandrum near the lesser door of the basilica (the entrance near the tomb of Innocent III, on the right side of the nave).[205] Charles of Anjou, senator of Rome, ordered that a grand tomb be built for this pope so that it would match the ruined Lateran sarcophagi, but even this tomb is now lost. A statue of a genuflecting pope thought to depict Innocent V and to be taken from his tomb is located in the Chapel of the Crucifix in the Lateran basilica. He was beatified by Leo XIII in 1898, and his feast day falls on June 22.

FURTHER READING: E. Dupre-Theseider, *Roma dal Commune di popolo alla Signoria pontificia*, Bologna, 1952; A. Bartolini, "La tomba del b. I. V. I Laterano e Ancora sulla tomba del b I. V. in *Laterano*," in *Geornale Arcadico*, Rome, Series II, II (1899); L. Frenguelli, "La statua del beato I. V al Laterano," in *Memorie Domenicane*, Florence LIV, 1937.

Gregory X in the Duomo of Arrezo. By permission of Bill Thayer.

Hadrian V (July 11–August 18, 1276) *Ottobono Fieschi.* He died of illness in Viterbo, Italy, having hastily left Rome for the better weather of Viterbo, but to no avail as he died suddenly without ever being ordained, crowned, or consecrated. His wishes were that he be buried in Genoa with his family, but the cardinals in charge of the burial decided he would be buried in Viterbo. Presumably thinking of the money and prestige that would result from having the pope's body in a local church, the cardinals took advantage of a statement in the will that Hadrian should be buried in a local Fransican church until he could be transferred to Genoa to be buried with his family; since the pope's brother was already buried in Viterbo, it could be argued that Hadrian would be buried with family, so the cardinals decided not to move his remains. Hadrian's white marble tomb, originally inlaid with mosaics, was carved by Arnolfo di Cambrio (although some suggest Vassalletus or even a student of de Cambrio[206]) and placed in the Church of San Francisco, Viterbo. This tomb "reproduces the essential elements of a papal funeral at the time of public exposition, including leaving the feet, hands, and face uncovered."[207] A bearded head sits in the apex of the canopy, and atop the capitals are a mourning head and a grinning head. The tomb inscription reads:

Tomb of Hadrian V in the Church of San Francisco, Viterbo, pre–World War II. From H.K. Mann, *Tombs and Portraits of the Popes.*

HIC REQUIESCIT CORPUS SANCTE MEMORIE DOMINI / HADRIANI PAPE V̄ Q̄ PRIUS VOCA / TUS OCTOBONUS DE FLISCO DE JANUA, / TUNC TIT. S. HADRIANI DIAC. CARD.

("Here rests the body in the blessed memory of the Lord of Pope Hadrian V, who first was called Octobonus de Glisco de Janua, then by the title of the Cardinal Deacon of St. Adriano."—*Trans. Phillip Haberkern*)

On the base of the monument:

R. S. I. / HADRIANVS V PONT. MAX. / PRIVS OCTOBONVS FLISCVS IANVEN. / EX COMITIBVS LAVANIAE / AB INNOCENTIO IV EIVS PATRVO / INTER S. R. E. CARDINALES ADSCITVS / DOCTRINA PIETATE PRVDENTIA / CATHOLICAE FIDEI ADMODVM PROFVIT / PLVRIBVS LEGATIONIBVS / AC INNVMERIS LABORIBVS / DE S. SEDE OPTIME MERITVS / AD PETRI CATHEDRAM EVECTVS EST / POST XXXIX DIES XII KAL. SEPTEMBRES MCCLXXVI / VITERBII DEGENS ANIMAM COELO / CORPVS VERO HVIC MONVMENTO TRADIDIT / QVOD TEMPORIS INIVRIA VIOLATVM / PRISTINO DECORI RESTITVENDVM / POSTERI DE FAMILIA FLISCA / VNAMINES CENSVERE / A. D. M DCC XV / CVRANTE FR. JOSEPHO FREZZA DE CRYPTIS HVIVS CENOBII GVARDIANO[208]

("Pope Hadrian V, first Octobonus Fliscus Januen out of the companions of Lavania, from Innocent IV, his uncle adopted among S.R.E. cardinals with doctrine, piety, and prudence. He was useful to the Catholic faith in full measure by his many missions as legate and his innumerable works deserving of the highest Holy See. He was led forth to the cathedral of Peter 39 days after the 12th day of September,

1276. Truly his soul was passing into heaven, while the Viterbans delivered hither his body to this burial monument, which was violated by the ravages of time, [yet] restored to pristine comeliness by the later generations of the Fieschi family, to be judged of one accord. In the year of the Lord 1715."—*Trans. Phillip Haberkern*)

An inscription in black letters over the effigy of the pope, from a restoration in the seventeenth century, reads:

HADRIANVS QVINTVS PONTIF. MAX /
FLISCA E FAMILIA NOBILISSIMA GENVENSI /
MENSIS VNIVS DIERVMQ. IX MAGISTRATVM /
PONTIFICIVM GERENS / XV KAL. OCTOB.
MCCLXXVI / DIEM VITERBII FVNCTVS / HAC
HONORIFICA SEPVLTVRA / DONATVR[209]

("Supreme pontiff Hadrian V from the most noble Fieschi family of Genoa. Having borne the pontificate for a single month and nine days, he died on the fifteenth day before the calends of October in 1276 at Viterbo, and here was honorably entombed."—*Trans. Phyllis Jestice*)

The tomb was heavily damaged by aerial bombardment in World War II and exactly reconstructed in 1949.

FURTHER READING: A. Venturei, "Arnolfo di Cambio," in *L'Arte*, Rome, VIII, 1905; M. Salmi, "Arnolfiana," in *Riv. d'Art*, Florence, XXII, 1940.

John XXI
(September 8, 1276–May 20, 1277) *Pedro Juliao (Peter the Spaniard).* Died at either age 57 or 67 when a newly made observatory ceiling collapsed on him in the papal palace of Viterbo. John was buried six days after his death and interred in a wood coffin that was placed in a porphyry sarcophagus and located near the high altar of San Lorenzo in Viterbo. The original epitaph can be seen today in the Museum of the Palace of the Popes, Viterbo). Note that this epitaph gives an incorrect date of death:

IOANNES LVSITAN / XXI PONT. MAX. /
PONT. SVI / MENS. VIII /
MORITVR / M CC LXIIII[210]

("Pope John XXI of Lusitania [Portugal], who died during the eighth month of his pontificate in 1264 [*sic*]"—*Trans. Phillip Haberkern*)

During the rebuilding of the cathedral in the sixteenth century the porphyry sarcophagus was destroyed and the wood coffin placed in a different stone sarcophagus with an effigy of the pope. This second stone sarcophagus was located at the end of the cathedral, between the middle and the left hand door. There was an attempt to correct the death date on the inscription by putting MCCLXXII in parentheses, but that year (1272) was incorrect as well.

In 1886, the Duke of Saldanha, John's fellow countryman and Portugese ambassador to the Holy See, had John's remains transferred to a new coffin and placed in a new monument sculpted by Filippo Gnaccarini with the following epitaph:

HEIC IN PACE REQVIESCIT / IOANNES XXI P.M. /
QVI VITERBI ELECTVS / IDIB. SEPTEMB. A. M CC
LXXVI / IBIDEM SVPREMVM DIEM OBIT / OCTAVO
SACRI PRINCIPATVS / MENSE VIX ELAPSO[211]

("Here rests in peace Pope John XXI, who was elected in Viterbo in September of the year 1276. In that same place he entered upon his last day with the eighth month of his sacred reign scarcely having elapsed."—*Trans. Phillip Haberkern*)

An inscription at the base of the monument read:

QUI LUSITANI FUERAT LUX MAXIMA REGNI /
EXIGUO JACUIT CONDITUS IN TUMULO /
SALDANHAE HUNC PIETAS / CLARO LOCAT
ECCE SEPULCHRO. / PRAESTAT PONTIFICI,
PRAESTAT ET HOC PATRIAE.[212]

("The great light that came from the kingdom of Portugal lies enclosed in a small tomb, this piety of Saldanha. Behold, it is placed in a noble sepulcher, distinguished in the pontificate and also in this country."—*Trans. Phyllis Jestice*)

Upon exhumation for the transfer to the Gnaccarini tomb, it was discovered that all of the larger bones of the pope were intact. The old sarcophagus with effigy was moved to under the stairs in the cathedral, and the following epitaph was put up over it:

The second tomb of John XXI. The plaque atop it was added when the tomb was moved to under the stairs in the cathedral and a new, more ornate tomb was erected for John. From H.K. Mann, *Tombs and Portraits of the Popes.*

Monument to John XXI, given by the Duke of Saldanha, 1886. Drawing by author based on photograph in Renzo Montini, *Le Tombe dei Papi.*

VETVS JOHANNIS XXI P. M. SEPVLCRVM / ANTEA MEDIAM INTER AC LAEVAM AEDIS / IANVAM COLLOCATVM ELEGANTIORE / AD S. PHILIPPI NERII SACELLVM SVFFECTO / E MARMORE HVC TRANSLATVM EST / A M DCCC LXXXVI

("The ancient tomb of Pope John XXI, previously [located] in the middle and towards the left entrance of the sanctuary, was more fittingly placed, chosen to fill a vacancy in the chapel of St. Philip of Nerius. The body was transferred hither from the marble [floor] in the year 1886."—*Trans. Phillip Haberkern*)

After World War II, when the church was heavily bombed, the wood sarcophagus was moved to the crypt, and the second tomb pieces were gathered and a new monument to John XXI constructed.

Monument to John XXI, cathedral of San Lorenzo, Viterbo.

Nicholas III (November 25, 1277–August 22, 1280) *Giovanni Gaetano Orsini.* Died of stroke or apoplexy in the Castle of Soriano, Viterbo, at either age 60 or 70. When he was dying he gathered all his cardinals and prelates around his bed and expressed his wish to be buried in the Chapel of St. Nicholas in St. Peter's. His funeral took place on August 25 (the delay was due to travel time from Viterbo). He was subsequently buried in a simple sarcophagus in the Orsini chapel of St. Nicholas (in the second nave on the right), though he was transferred on May 16, 1285, when his tomb monument was ready for him. Sadly, the exquisite marble tomb was destroyed during the demolition of St. Peter's in the seventeenth century, leaving only a sarcophagus and bits to be seen in the grottoes. In 1620 Nicholas's relative Cardinal Alessandro Orsini placed Nicholas's remains along with his family members Rainaldo Orsini, cardinal deacon of St. Hadrian (d. 1374), and an earlier Cardinal Rainaldo Orisini, in a Christian marble sarcophagus that can be seen in the grottoes of St. Peter's. Rumor holds that the sarcophagus of Urban VI (d. 1389) is Nicholas's original sarcophagus.[213]

The sarcophagus inscription reads:

NICOLAVS PAPA TERTIVS / VRSINVS /
RAINALDUS CARD. VRSINVS / RAINALDVS
VRSINVS SANCTI / HADRAINI DIAC. CARD.
HVIVS / BASIL. VATIC. ARCHIPRESB.[214]

("Pope Nicholas III, Orsini, cardinal deacon of Saint Adrian, arch-priest of this Vatican basilica." — *Trans. Father Tom Carleton*)

Dante put Nicholas upside down in the eighth circle of Hell (19: 29–114) of *Inferno* and refers to him in the following verse: (19: 73–75):

Beneath my head the others are dragged down
Who have preceded me in simony,
Flattened along the fissure of the rock.

Original tomb of Nicholas III, Vatican grottoes. From H.K. Mann, *Tombs and Portraits of the Popes.*

The sarcophagus of Nicholas III as it looks today in the Vatican grottoes.

Martin IV (February 22, 1281–March 28, 1285) *Simon de Brie (Brion)*. Martin died at either age 65 or 75 in Perugia, Italy, from choking on his favorite dish of brine-pickled eels. In his will, Martin had requested that he not be embalmed and that he be buried in a Franciscan habit. As the executor of Martin's will, the next pope, Honorius IV, honored these wishes. Martin's body remained on display for four or five days, during which time a number of miracles took place, as reported by the chronicler Martinus Polonius:

> People afflicted with various maladies, especially of sight, joints, hearing, and speech, remained prostrated around the bier on which the pope's body had remained for several days. They were seen and assisted by numerous clerics and laity; many were healed. The series of miracles had not yet ended by May 12, the day on which this writing was set down; on the contrary, every day miracles were mercifully performed by God on behalf of the multitude of the faithful who flocked there; and he who wrote these things also saw them.[215]

The burial took place on April first or second[216] in the cathedral of Perugia, although Martin's will had stipulated that he be buried in the Church of St. Francis of Assisi. Giovanni Pisani possibly made the marble tomb for him, though some say the tomb was for Urban IV (d. 1264). This tomb was destroyed either when part of the cathedral was razed to build a new fortress, or during the uprising of 1375; all that remained was a sarcophagus. Upon examination, Martin's body was found intact, which impressed the local people so much that they made a separate monument for him and placed it within the choir of the Perugia cathedral. This monument, however, was broken up in the late fourteenth century by the abbot of Mommaggiore so that he could use the marble for other monuments. Only after he had the monument destroyed did the abbot discover that he would be unable to produce the other monuments, and so the marble was used to make two *ambone*, which are still at either side of the cathedral choir. Meanwhile, Martin's body was to be moved to Assisi so he could be buried there as he had requested.

The people of Perugia did not want Martin's body leaving the city, so they managed to stretch out negotiations with Honorius IV for years until he died in 1287. Martin's remains stayed in his sarcophagus until 1587, when the new cathedral was being built. Then his remains were placed in an iron casket, along with popes Urban IV (d. 1264) and Innocent III (d. 1216), that was located in the sacristy of San Lorenzo.

When Bishop Comitoli opened the sarcophagus in 1615, he noted that although Urban and Innocent remained fairly intact, Martin had disintegrated into bones. The bishop had the following engraved on the sarcophagus:

OSSA / TRIVM ROMANORVM PONTIFICVM /
QVI PERVSIAE OBIERVNT / INOCEN. III.
VRBAN. IV. MARTI. IV / A. MCCXVI A. MCCLXIV

The sarcophagus housing the remains of Popes Urban IV and Martin IV (Innocent's remains were transferred to the Lateran in the late nineteenth century.

A. MCCLXXXII / AB HVIVS TEMPLI SACRARIO /
HVC TRANSLATA / AN. M. D. C XV[217]

("The bones of three Roman pontiffs who died at Perugia — Innocent III, Urban IV, Martin IV. 1216, 1264, 1282 — were transferred to this place from the sacristy of this temple in the year 1615." — *Trans. Father Thomas Buffer*)

Dante placed Martin in Purgatory (24: 22–24), with an allusion to Martin's love for his favorite, yet fatal, dish of pickled eels:

Has held the holy Church within his arms.
From Tours was he, and purges by his fasting
Bolsena's eels and the Vernaccia wine.

The following is a recipe for the eel dish that Martin choked on:

Eels in Vernaccia à la Martin IV[218]
(serves 6)
1½ pounds eel, ¾ cup Vernaccia wine or dry white wine, 3 garlic cloves, one sliced onion, oil and butter for frying, 1½ cups stock, pinch of salt, pepper, one tablespoon flour. Clean and skin the eels, cut them into chunks and leave them to marinate in the Vernaccia. Fry the garlic and onions; add the eels, a few spoons full of marinade and stock as required. Once the fish is cooked, adjust the seasoning and serve the chunks of eel in a warmed dish, covered in Vernaccia cooking sauce thickened with a little flour.

Honorius IV (April 2, 1285–April 3, 1287) *Giacomo Savelli*. Died at age 77 from either gout or a stroke at the Savelli palace on Aventine Hill, Rome. He was so paralyzed when he was elected that he could hold the host only with help, most likely a "mechanical device of wood."[219] His obsequies were performed at his family fortress on the Aventine; afterwards, his body was brought with much ceremony to St. Peter's. His marble sarcophagus was placed in a beautiful mausoleum designed and carved by Arnolfo di Cambrio and located in the north transept of St. Peter's (near Nicholas III). The mausoleum was exceptional because it originally had both an upright statue of the pope and a recumbent effigy. The mausoleum was

The tomb of Honorius IV as it looked when first moved to Santa Maria in Aracoeli. From H.K. Mann, *Tombs and Portraits of the Popes.*

The tomb of Honorius IV, Santa Maria in Aracoeli, Rome.

moved by Pius II (1458–1464) to another part of St. Peter's, only to be destroyed during the beginning phases of the destruction of St. Peter's in the sixteenth century. Luckily Pope Paul III (1534–1549) had the remaining sarcophagus with the recumbent effigy and baldecchio moved to the Savelli chapel in the Church of our Lady of Aracoeli (Santa Maria in Aracoeli, on the Capitol, Rome) in 1545. There they were placed over the sarcophagus of Honorius's mother, Vana Aldobrandini, and near his brother Pandolfo and his father, Luca Savelli. The monument remained intact until 1727, when the baldecchio was destroyed during the reconstruction of the church and was replaced by a plain classical baldecchio.

For FURTHER READING: P. Cellini, "Di fra' Guglielmo e di Arnolfo," in *Boll. D'Arte*, Rome, s. IV, XI, 1955; C. Cecchelli, "I sepolcri della

famiglia Savelli in Araceoli," in *Romana Tellus*, Rome, I, 1912.

Nicholas IV (February 22, 1288–April 4, 1292) *Girolamo Masci.* Died in Rome at age 65. As a Franciscan, Nicholas wanted to be humbly buried in the ground so people could walk over him, and initially his request was honored. An antique urn with his name and title inscribed was placed under an ornamental slab on the floor at the head of the Santa Maria Maggiore, against the minor door. The urn inscription read:

ET INIBI HUMATUM REPERTUM FUERIT CORPUS FELICIS ET S. RECORDATIONIS NICOLAI IV PONT. MAS. / EXISTENS IN QUADAM ANTIQUA URNA CUM SUI MONINIS INSCRIPTIONE ET TITULO.

("And herein is the buried body of Pope Nicholas IV of joyous and blessed memory [now] existing in a certain urn with the inscription and title of honor."—*Trans. Phillip Haberkern*)

The original epitaph on the floor slab read:

HIC TUMULUS TUMULAT HUMILEM, QUI FASCIBUS AUCTUS / SIC MORIENS STATUIT OSSA MANERE SUA. / HUNC FRANCISCUS ALIT, CARDO ET SIT ALMAQUE PETRI / SEDES MAGNIFICAT: GRATIA DIA BEAT. / QUARTUS PAPA FUIT NICOLAUS, VIRGINIS AEDEM / HANC LAPSAM REFICIT, FITQUE VETUSTA, NOVA. / PETRUS APOSTOLICUS SOCIUM FRANCISCUS ALUMNUM / PROTEGAT, OMNIPOTENS, MATRE ROGANTE BEET.

("This tomb contains the humble man who, full of the power while dying, thus erected [this tomb] to hold his bones. The Franciscan maintained this, that it might be made fruitful and a hinge that glorifies the seat of Peter that blesses with divine grace. Nicholas was the fourth pope [who] restored the dilapidated Church of the Virgin, and much that was ancient, he made new. Peter the apostle protects his companions, [and] with Francis, having asked the Mother, the all-powerful blesses his ward."—*Trans. Phillip Haberkern and Sam Garcia*)

During the reconstruction of the basilica in 1572, the urn was discovered, and so

SEPVLCHRVM NICOLAI IV · PONT. MAX · INBASILICA LIBERIANA

NICOLAVS QVARTVS
PONT.OPT.MAX.
etc.pag.262.

Original tomb monument to Nicholas IV, Santa Maria Maggiore, Rome. By permission of the Houghton Library, Harvard University.

the cardinal of Montalto (later Sixtus V, 1585–1590) commissioned a mausoleum for Nicholas that was designed by Domenico Fontana, with Leonardo da Sarzana sculpting the figures. This was placed at the end of the nave on the left (near the high altar) in the original Chapel of the Blessed Sacrament. To the pope's right is the figure of Truth, and to his left is Justice. Interestingly, the pope's right hand is raised not to give the blessing, but to invite the onlooker to approach him. The epitaph reads:

NICHOLAS IV AUSCULANO PICENO / PONT. MAX. CUM IN NEGLECTU DIU / SEPULCHRO FERE

LATUISSET, / FR. FELIX PERETTUS, CARDINALIS DE MONTE ALTO / IN ORDINEM ET PATRIAM PIETATE POSUIT. / MDLXXIV

("Pope Nicholas IV, high priest. Because your sepulcher had been continually neglected, Asculani Piceno, Father Felix Perettus, cardinal of Monte Alto in the order and fatherland, restored it with piety in 1624"—*Trans. Sam Garcia and Philip Haberkern*)

RENOVABITVR   IVSTVS VT VT AQVILA   PALMA FLOREBIT

NICOLAVS IIII ORDINE MINOR. PROFESSVS PHILOSOPHVS ET THEOLOGVS / EGREGIVS CONSTANTINOPOLIM A GREGORIO X MISSVS GRAECOS AD R. E. / COMMVNIONEM TARTAROS AD FIDEM REDVXIT POST BONAVENTVRAM / GENERALIS SANCTITATE ET DOCTRINA ORD. PROPAGAVIT NICOLAI IIII / NVNCIVS INTER FRANCORVM ET CASTELLAE REGES PACEM CONCILIAVIT / SANCTAE POTENTIANAE CARDINALIS LEGATVS HONORII IIII IN GALLIA / SENATORIAM P. R. DIGNITATEM SEDI APOSTOLICAE RESTITVIT

("He shall be renewed as an eagle. The just will flourish like a palm. Nicholas IV of the order of friars minor, philosopher and theologian. Sent by Gregory X to the Greeks of Constantinople for the restoration of communion, he brought the Tartars back to the faith. After Bonaventure he was general of the order with holiness and good doctrine. As legate, Nicholas IV propagated peace between the kings of France and Castile. As cardinal legate of Honorius IV in France he reconciled that state to holy power, and restored the dignity of senator of the Roman people to the Apostolic See."—*Trans. Phyllis Jestice*)

At the base of the monument:

FACTVS PONTIFEX REMP. SVBLATIS DISCORDIIS COMPOSVIT CHRISTIANOS / PRINCIPES SACRO FOEDERE IVNXIT PTOLEMAIDEM COPIIS ADIVVIT / FLAMINIAM IN PONTIFICIS ITERVM DITIONEM

REDEGIT PVBLICVM IN / MONTE PESSVLANO
GYMNASIVM INSTITVIT PROBOS ET ERVDITOS IN /
COGNATORVM LOCO TANTVM HABVIT LATERAN.
ET HANC BASILICAM / STRVCTVRIS ET OPIBVS
AVXIT TANDEM IVSTITIA ET RELIGIONE ORBEM /
TERRAE MODERATVS MAGNA SANCTITATIS
OPINIONE OBIIT PRID. NON. / APRILIS
MCCXCII PONTIFICATVS SVI ANNO V[220]

("Having been made pontiff, he settled the discord between Christian princes and joined them together with a holy alliance. In the pontificate, he supported Ptolemy Flaminia and under his direction founded a public school in Monte Pessulano. Under him all who inhabited the Lateran were upright and learned, and he enlarged this basilica in structure and wealth. Having ruled moderately with justice and religion, he died in great repute of sanctity on the day before the nones of April 1292 in the fifth year of his pontificate."—*Trans. Phyllis Jestice*)

In the late seventeenth century, a cult developed around the tomb of Nicolas IV because some alleged relics of his were found in a box of saint's relics at Santa Maria Maggiore. The inscription on the wrapping of these relics read, "*De P. Nicolao Disepolo di S. Francesco.*" There were pieces of material (thought to be pontifical) with the inscription "*Delle vestimenta di S. Nicolo Papa che fu discepolo di S. Francesco*" ("The vestments of Pope St. Nicholas, who was a disciple of Saint Francis") and some bones inscribed "*Le ossa di S. Nicolo Papa che fu etc.*" ("The bones that were of Pope S. Nicholas"). But because no one knew when or by whom the inscriptions were written, the pope of the time, Benedict XIV (1740–1758), paid them no mind and forbade any public veneration of the relics. On October 24, 1750, he had the monument to moved to its present location in Santa Maria Maggiore.

FURTHER READING: P. De Angelis, *S. Mariae Majoris de Urbe ... descriptio et delineatio*, Rome, 1621; R. Lanciani, "Il mausoleo di Nicolo IV," in *Ausonia*, Rome, I 1906.

Celestine V (July 5, 1294–December 13, 1294; d. May 19, 1296). *St. Peter of Morrone.*

Died at age 86 from an infected abscess (due to harsh treatment in the prison of the Castle of Fumone). The hermit Peter of Morrone had been elected pope as a compromise candidate in 1294. At the time he lived on a mountain in a simple shack and was considered much too lowly for the great cardinals themselves to go and tell him of the news—at least until they recognized the possibility of obtaining favors from this new pope. On the strength of that realization, many cardinals and even the King of Naples himself scrambled up the mountainside, trying to beat each other to the top so they could be the first to influence this naive pope.

After six months in the papal seat, Peter (now Pope Celestine V) had wearied of the politics and pomp, and he abdicated so he could return to his simple life atop the mountain. Probaby this decision was due at least in part to Cardinal Bendetto Gaetani (who became the next pope, Boniface VIII), who browbeat Peter and allegedly went to so far as to whisper to him in his sleep, "This is the voice of God. Abdicate Peter, abdicate!" Gaetani became Boniface VIII when Celestine resigned, but he was afraid that the people would rise up against him in favor of the simple, good monk, so he had Celestine captured while he was fleeing back to his mountain. Celestine escaped, however, traveling through the deserts of the Majella and through the woods of Apulia until he reached the sea, where he sailed for the Dalmatian coast. When a bad storm arose, the ship had to dock at Viesta in the Capitanata, where Celestine was captured.

Celestine was brought to Boniface VIII at Anagni and put in jail supposedly for his own protection at the Castle of Monte Fumone. He said when they took him to his small cell, "I have desired nothing in my life save for a cell, and a cell they have given to me."[221] Celestine died ten months later, and it is said that when he was in his death agony in front of the door of his cell, a golden cross appeared to float in the air, a sign of the holiness of Celestine. It disappeared at vespers the moment Celestine died.

In 1313, Clement V canonized Celestine under his monastic name of Peter, not his pontifical name, and as a "confessor," not as a martyr as King Philip IV of France wanted. Canonization as a martyr would have implied that Boniface had had Celestine murdered, making Boniface look like a monster — which is exactly what Philip, his enemy, wanted. The canonization, however, was still seen as a rebuke of Boniface.

Celestine was originally buried behind the altar in the Church of St. Anthony (allegedly ten cubits down so that it wouldn't be found) near Ferentino, Italy. For fear of desecration by a supporter of Boniface, his tomb was watched day and night for thirty years.

In 1326, the body was moved to the Church of St. Agatha, inside the Ferentino city walls, to protect it against a siege. Inscription:

CORPORA / SS. PETRI COELESTINI PP. / ET / AMBROSY MARTYRIS / DIV / (heic) REQVIEVERVNT[222]

("Inscription of St. Agatha, Ferentino, 1326. The bodies of saints Pope Peter Celestine and the martyr Ambrose rested here a long time." — *Trans. Phyllis Jestice*)

After repeated unsuccessful attempts by the city of L'Aquila to buy the body, two of Celestine's friars, Fra Yacobo de Rogi and Selmontino, stole it and brought it to L'Aquila on January 27, 1327, sparking off a twenty-day festival drawing some 100,000 people. Celestine was interred in the Church of Santa Maria de Collemaggio in a silver chest (made by the Sulmona school) that was placed in a marble mausoleum on August 27, 1517. The mausoleum, commissioned by the Ordine della Lana and executed by Girolamo da Vicenza, was constructed in the sixteenth century at the expense of the guild of wool-workers. It once had many small statues and grotesques, but they have disappeared over the centuries. In the arch is the seated figure of Our Lady and Child between Celestine and St. Benedict. On the back of the tomb is the figure of Our Lord between Saints Maurus and Scholastica. The epitaph reads:

CONDITUR HOC TUMULO PARIO DE MARMORE PETRUS / CUI COELESTINO FUERAT COGNOMEN IN ANTRIS / INQUE HEREMO VIXIT VITAM SINE LABE PEREGIT / QUIQUE TULIT TRIPLICI QUAESITUM EX HOSTE TRIUMPHUM / VIRTUTE HIC SOLA AD SUMMOS ELECTUS HONORES / PONTIFICI DECUS

Monument housing the remains of Celestine V in Church of Santa Maria de Collemaggio, L'Aquila, Italy.

TITULOS QUOS SPREVIT ET INDE / DEPOSUIT
VARIOS RERUM ASPERNATUS HONORES / HINC
NEXUS VINCLIS HINC SAEVO CARCERE CLAUSUS /
OCCUMBIT SAEVAE MORTI MOX SPIRITUS ASTRIS /
REDDITUS HIC POPULO CORPUS VENERATUR
AB OMNI / ANNO 1517 DIE 27 AUG. TEMP.
FRATR. MATURINI PRIORIS

("Contained in this tomb of parian marble is Peter, who took the cognomen Celestine in the cave in which he lived as a hermit, where he pursued his life without blemish, and whence he was sought out triumphantly by strangers and solely for the sake of virtue elected to the highest honors. Fittingly, he rejected the title of pontiff and laid down the honors he spurned. Then, bound in chains, he was kept in a harsh prison. Presently he sank down to savage death, but his spirit rose to the stars. Restored to the people, his body is venerated by all. August 27, 1517, in the priorate of Brother Maturin."— Trans. *Phyllis Jestice*)

In 1683 Cardinal Nicola Ludovisi donated the heart of Celestine to the Church of San Chiara in Ferentino, and in 1705 a plaque was placed at the original resting place of Celestine in Fumone:

LOCULUM IN QUO PER PLURES / ANNOS
CORPUS S. PETR. COELESTINI / PP. V JACUIT
ET TEMPORIS INIURIA PENE / EXESUM REMANEBAT
D. COELESTINUS GUICCIARDINI / ABB. PERPET.
S. EUSEBII AD POSTERORUM DEVOTIONEM /
EXCITANDAM REFECIT / D. 1705

("Celestine Guicciardini, abbot of S. Eusebius, in order to arouse the devotion of future generations, restored the place, which was nearly devoured by the injuries of time, in which the body of St. Peter, Celestine V, lay for many years. 1705."—*Trans. Father Thomas Buffer*)

Celestine's tomb and remains have been stolen three times. The first incident was in 1528, when the Prince of Orange's troops stole the silver casket. In 1799, the French stole the 18th century urn. In April of 1998 a nun noticed the glass casket was empty and called the police. They began trailing two suspicious people who had come through town and who led them unknowingly, just a day and a half after the theft, to Celestine's remains in a graveyard in the town of Ama-

trice, about forty miles away. The pair got away, but the remains were in good shape. Still wearing his miter and robes, Celestine was lying on a red velvet cushion located in a plywood box inside one of the niches of the cemetery.

In 1998, according to the Associated Press (as reported in the *Rocky Mountain News*, August 23, 1998), the Reverend Quirino Salomne said that a CT scan performed on Celestine's mummified remains in 1988 showed a half-inch hole in the left temple, leading him to conclude that Celestine was murdered by a nail driven into his head. Salomne did not offer further details, though at the time he was apparently planning to write a book about this discovery.

Today the mortal remains of Celestine (a skeleton with a wax face), dressed in papal vestments and the slippers he actually wore during his short pontificate, can be viewed in a crystal and silver casket made by the Aquilan goldsmith Luigi Cardilli.

As good and humble a soul as he apparently was, Celestine was condemned by Dante in the *Divine Comedy* for abdicating the papacy. Dante places him at the entrance of Hell (*Inferno* 3 :58–60):

When some among them I had recognized.
I looked, and I beheld the shade of him
Who made through cowardice the great
    refusal.

From 1668 to 1969, Celestine's feast day was celebrated on May 19. It is no longer celebrated.

FURTHER READING: Telera, *Historie sagre degli Huomini Illustri per Santita dei Celestini*, Bologna, 1648; A. Leosini, *Monumenti … della citta di Aquila*, Aquila, 1848; F. Visca, *Il castello di Fumone e gli ultimi giorni di C. V*, Aquila, 1894; L. Serra, *Aquila monumentale*, Aquila, 1912; G. Casali, "Le vicende del corpo di S. Pietro Celestino," in *Osservatore Romano*, C.d. V., September 3, 1949; Giovanni Battista Proja, *Pietro del Morrone da Eremita a Papa*, Vitmar, 1998.

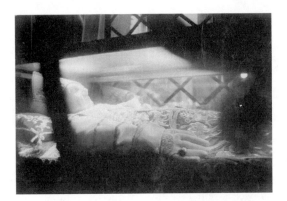

The remains of St. Peter of Morrone (Celestine V) in the church of Santa Maria del Collemaggio. By permission of the Abruzzo World Club.

Boniface VIII (December 24, 1294–October 11, 1303) *Bendetto Gaetani.* Died at age 68 from kidney stones and severe humiliation. (In *The Bad Popes*, E.R. Chamberlain mentions a "rumor spread that he [Boniface] gnawed the flesh from his arms, ultimately killing himself by beating his head against the wall,"[223] and author Malachi Martin claimed that Boniface was: "locked up in the Vatican for thirty-five days where, on the last morning, they will find him dead on the floor, his skull smashed open, his brains on his shoulders and all over the floor."[224] Neither assertion is true.)

Boniface's downward spiral, which would end in his death, began with a fight with King Philip IV of France. Boniface had been captured by the French and held prisoner at Anagni, Italy, but eventually escaped back to the Vatican, where he died shortly after from humiliation and a broken spirit, according to the majority of sources.

Boniface's alleged deathbed scene is recorded in the book *Rings for the Finger*:

> When this pope was dying and was told that he must prepare his soul for the great change, he cast his eyes upon a stone set in a ring he was wearing, and exclaimed, "O you tricky spirits imprisoned in this stone, why have you deceived me to abandon me now in my extremity?"; And so speaking he snatched off the ring and threw it away.[225]

Charles II, king of Naples, respectfully led the funeral procession of knights and nobles to St. Peter's for Boniface's funeral, although another monarch, King Phillip IV of France — Boniface's mortal enemy — drew up a formal indictment of him as a tyrant, sorcerer, murderer, embezzler, adulterer, sodomite, simoniac, idolator, and infidel for a posthumous trial. Boniface was "acquitted" before this came to trial because he died a Catholic.

Boniface had had a funeral chapel built for himself in the southeast angle of the nave of St. Peter's. He had the bones of Pope St. Boniface IV (d. 615), which had been originally in the portico of St. Peter's, brought into his chapel and placed in a *sacellum* under his sarcophagus. Boniface VIII chose to build his chapel in honor of Boniface IV because the latter had had a large liturgical following in St. Peter's. Because Boniface VIII's predecessor, Celestine V, had abdicated and was not dead, Boniface was wor-

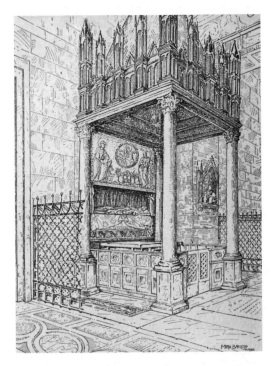

The square chapel of Boniface VIII in the nave of St. Peter's. From Renzo Montini, *Le Tombe dei Papi.*

ried that his legitimacy as pope might be questioned. By placing the relics of St. Boniface IV in his own funeral chapel, he was demonstrating that he was indeed the legitimate pope and had the "support" of Boniface IV, whose relics would be permanently interred with him.

The following is an inscription from the altar of Boniface VIII:

CORPVS SANCTI BONIFACII PAPAE / QVARTI EX ALTARE SITO IN / VATICANA BASILICA INTER / PORTAS IVDICII ET RAVENNI / ANAM A. BONIFACIO PAPA OCTAVO EIVS / NOMINI DICATO ORNATO / ET DOTATO IN NOVVM / TEMPLVM PAVLI V. PONT MAX / IVSSV HONORIFICE TRANSLATVM / HAC SVB ARA RITV. / SOLEMNI COLLOCAVIT EVANELISTA / PALLOTTVS TITVLI / S. LAVRENTII IN LVCINA CARDINALIS / CONSENTINVS HVIVS / BASILICAE ARCHIPRESBYTER / ANNO MDCVI DIE XVII / IANVARII PRIMIS VESPERIS / CATHEDRALE S. PETRI SEDENTE / PAVLO PAPA V ANNO PRIMO[226]

("The body of the holy pope Boniface IV, taken from the altar in the Vatican basilica between the portal of judgment and the portal of Ravenna, moved to an altar by Pope Boniface VIII, who was adorned, dedicated, and gifted with his name, was by the command of the supreme pontiff Paul V transferred with honors to beneath this altar. Evangelista Pallottus of Cosenza, cardinal of San Lorenzo in Lucina, archpriest of this basilica, placed his body with solemn rites in the year 1606, January 17, during first vespers, as Pope Paul V sat on the throne of St. Peter, during the first year of his pontificate." — Trans. Father Thomas Buffer)

Unfortunately the chapel was destroyed during the demolition of St. Peter's in the early seventeenth century, although there exists a mysterious, rare Ciacconius illustration of a round tomb chapel for Boniface VIII. Curiously although this round tomb chapel is not mentioned in any literature or inscription, and it is completely different from his square altar, both illustrations include Boniface's sarcophagus. It remains a mystery where this round tomb chapel was located or whether it even existed. The only certainty is that the sarcophagus in the illustration matches the real sarcophagus, which can be seen today in the Vatican grottoes.

Boniface was exhumed in the seventeenth century during the demolition of St. Peter's. The event was recorded as follows by church canon and historian Giacomo Grimaldi — Trans. Phyllis Jestice):

On Monday, 28 November, 1605, there was said a long prayer, followed by the blessing of the lead coffin. The body was in a wooden coffin eight palms by two palms by five palms. That in turn was in a lead coffin, and it was in pine. Taken from the corpse's finger was a beautiful sapphire ring. The same finger had another ring with a red stone. The body was moved to the chapel of Popes Andrew and Gregory, among the monuments of Pius II and III and Julius III.[227]

Another description by Grimaldi comes from Paravicini-Bagliani's The Pope's Body:

Boniface VIII had on whole stockings that covered his legs and thighs, in accordance with the custom of those times; the inside was colored red, and at the top they had silver buckles. The soutain, instead, was white; the rochet long down to his heels, made of cloth of Cambrai, and on the breast, behind the legs, and at the ends of the sleeves, were gold and silk embroideries representing the mysteries of the life of Jesus Christ, and its length descended to his feet. The stole that he wore at the collar, about five palms long, was bound with a tassel of brocaded fabric with silver and black silk. The maniple of gold and silver fabric, worked in waves, of black silk, and purple, three palms long. The sandals, colored black, pointed according to the gothic style, without crosses, worked in "flower of silk." The pontifical habit of black silk with narrow sleeves, brocaded, with lions of silk cloth and gold in a blue field. The dalmatic of black silk cloth, with similar brocade work, embroidered with roses, with two dogs at the feet. The pontifical socks of black silk. The chasuble broad and long, of black silk with curious designs. The fanon was like the one used today. The pallium of very fine white silk with crosses. The gloves of white silk made with well-done needlework, and decorated with pearls. The hands were crossed, the left placed upon the right, and on the accustomed finger there was a (gold) ring with a sapphire of (quite

A mysterious illustration of a round tomb chapel for Boniface VIII. No such chapel exists today, nor is any mentioned in the literature of the past. By permission of the Houghton Library, Harvard University. Sarcophagus of Boniface VIII, Vatican grottoes.

exceptional size and beauty) and of great value: finally he had on his head the miter of white damask, a palm wide and long.[228]

Boniface VIII must have been unusually tall, for *Rings for the Finger* notes that his body measured '7 palms'; according to the opinion of the doctors he was bald and beardless."[229]

The new tomb plaque for Boniface VIII reads as follows: "Jesus. Body of Boniface VIII of the Caetani family, supreme pontiff. Transferred from the old basilica to the new and reinterred here. This was done on the same day on which he died, the fifth of the ides of October, 302 years having elapsed. The body was discovered whole and incorrupt, in the year of the Lord 1605."—*Trans. Phyllis Jestice.*

Dante insinuates that Boniface will end up in hell in *Inferno* (19: 52–54) when Pope Nicholas III (d. 1280) mistakes Dante for the shade of Boniface:

And he cried out: Dost thou stand there already,
Dost thou stand there already Boniface?
By many years the record lied to me.

FURTHER READING: L.L. Frothingham, "Opening of the tomb of pope Boniface VIII in the basilica of S. Peter in V.," from the *American Journal of Archaeology*, Boston, IV, 1888; C. Scaccia Scarafoni, "Reliquuie artistiche del mausoleo di B. VIII rinvenute" in Boville Ernica, in *Boll. D'Arte*, 1921–1922; A. Loreti, "Osservazioni sulla tomba di B. VIII," in *Osservatore Romano*, C. d. V., March 31, 1951; Julian Gardner, *The Tomb and the Tiara: Curial Tomb Sculpture in Rome and Avignon in the Later Middle Ages*, Oxford University Press, 1992; Virgilio Cardinal Noe, *Le Tombe e i Monumenti*, Rome, 2000.

Blessed Benedict XI (October 22, 1303–July 7, 1304). *Niccolo Boccasino.* Rumored to have died suddenly from eating poisoned figs, although the more likely cause of death was dysentery. He died at age 64 while in exile in Perugia, Italy, and his is the first complete description of a pope's confession in preparation for death. In *The Pope's Body,* Paravicini-Bagliani relays the last moments of Benedict's life:

> The pope confessed himself and received communion in the presence of the cardinals; he called for extreme unction and received it devoutly from the cardinal bishop of Albano; the profession of faith also served implicitly to authenticate the orthodoxy of the pope's action; the dying pope exhorted the cardinals to concord. After the description of the pope's selection of a burial site [the Dominican convent in Perugia], there follows an article dedicated entirely to the cardinals, whom Benedict absolved from every excommunication, irregularity, and sin. Along with other prescriptions concerning the papal *familia,* the goods he had had when he was still a cardinal, and the books in his possession, other elements confirm the general impression of the document as a whole: in its substance and structure, it was indebted to thirteenth-century curial and papal testaments.[230]

Tomb monument of Benedict XI, San Dominico, Perugia.

Benedict was originally buried with "great honor" the day after he died (though the actual funeral rites are unrecorded) under the pavement in the choir of St. Stephen, the Preachers' Church of Perugia, where miracles soon began occurring. These were recorded in a book which has unfortunately been lost, although in honor of his friend, Cardinal Nicholas de Prato had Giovanni Pisano carve an elegant new sepulcher for him. The sepulcher included a gisant (effigy) "taken from life," which was completed about twenty years after Benedict's death. The Blessing Christ is located in the apex of the canopy, underneath which is a triptych containing, from left to right, St. Dominic presenting the genuflecting pope to the Madonna and Child (who are in the middle) and (probably) St. Ercolamo, the patron saint of Perugia, as the bishop in the last section. Between the triptych and effigy (with the curtains of eternity held back by two angels) are reliefs of an unknown apostle, St. Peter, St. Paul, and Peter Martyr. Epitaph:

The ossuary of Benedict XI, Perugia cathedral.

O QVAM LAVDANDVS QVAM DVLCITER EST
VENERANDVS / INCLYTVS ILLE PATER PRIVS
EXTITIT ORDINE FRATER / SANCTI DOMINICI
CHRISTI VIGILANTIS AMICI / LECTOR HONORATVS
PIVS EXTITIT IPSE VOCATVS / EFFECTVS TALIS
FRATRVM QVOQVE DVX GENERALIS / POST RO.
DOCTRINAE POST HAEC FIT CARDO SABINAE /
OSTIA VELLETRI TITVLOS SIBI DANT PIA LAETI /
PERFICIT VNGARIAE LEGATVS IVSSA SOPHIAE / FIT
PATER IPSE PATRIS CAPVT ORBIS GLORIA FRATRIS /
EST MERITO DICTVS RE NOMINE VIR BENEDICTVS /
TREVISII DATVS HIC PRIMO SED PONTIFICATVS /
ANNO DECESSIT SIBI RECTE SVBDITA REXIT / IN
NONO MENSE MORTIS PROSTERNITVR ENSE /
HVNC HOMINEM SANCTVM REDDVNT MIRACVLA
TANTVM / INNVMERIS SIGNIS DANT GRATA IVVAM-
INA DIGNIS / LECTOR HABE MENTI CVRREBANT
MILLE TRECENTI / QVATTVOR APPENSIS DVM
TRANSIIT HIC HOMO MITIS / MENTE DIE SEXTA
IVLII SVNT TALIA GESTA[231]

("Oh, how praiseworthy and how sweet it is to venerate this renowned father, formerly brother of the order of St. Dominic, the vigilant friend of Christ. Honored and pious lector, he himself was called and made master general of such brethren. Following Roman doctrine, after this he became cardinal of Sabina. Joyfully he was sent as legate to Hungary at the command of wisdom. Then the father became head of all fathers in the world, to the glory of the brothers, and the man was called Benedictus in merit and in name. Given to Treviso with this first pontificate, he withdrew after a year in which he had ruled rightly. He was brought down by death in the ninth month. Such great miracles surround this holy man; innumerable worthy signs give grace and aid. Reader, desire in your mind. Thirteen hundred and four years had run their course when this humble man passed away on the sixth day of July."—*Trans. Phyllis Jestice*)

Many of the small sculptures of the tomb had disappeared by 1682, and Napoleon's troops picked apart the valuable mosaics.[232] In 1700, the sepulcher was moved to the left transept of the new Church of San Dominico in Perugia, Italy, while his actual remains were interred in an ossuary in the same chapel as his monument. Benedict was beatified by Clement XIV in 1773.

FURTHER READING: G. B. Vermiglioli, "La tomba del pontefice B. XI nella chiesa di S. Domenico di Perugia," in *L'Album*, Rome, 1841; A. Lupattelli, *Benedetto XI, suo monumento sepolcrale*, Rome, 1903; Ricci, "Il sepolcro del b. B. XI in S. Domenico di Perugia," in *Augusta Perusia*, Perugia, I, 1906.

Clement V (June 5, 1305–April 20, 1314)

Betrand de Got. He died at age 54 from swallowing a dish of emeralds that were supposed to cure his stomach cancer[233] in Roquemaure, Langueduc, France. His relatives came to remove his body, but while they were there, an argument erupted over who should be the next pope. Blows were exchanged by the de Gots (who wanted one of their own elected pope) and the cardinals (who wanted a free election).[234] The cardinals won.

Clement had wished that his body be buried in the parish church at Uzeste, France, although no references to a novena ceremony for his funeral exist.[235] His nephew, the viscount of Lomagne, hired Jehan de Bonneval to create a grand tomb for Clement. De Bonneval's progress was slow, and the heirs of the viscount of Lomagne had to continue to pay for the monument until it was completed in 1359.

On that monument, the full figure of the pope, carved from one slab of white marble, rested on a black marble slab atop the sarcophagus. The effigy (minus the head and hair) was painted a reddish brown. His feet

The remains of the tomb of Clement V in Collègiale, Uzeste. By permission of Julian Gardner from his book *The Tomb and the Tiara.*

rested on a griffon and his head on an embroidered pillow, while small silver columns containing aromatic spices were placed in the coffin. A casket of gold and silver, costing the viscount of Lomagne 50,000 florins of gold, was erected over the top of the tomb, and precious stones adorned the tiara and gloves.[236] Finally the epitaph was engraved on the edge of the slab that supported his sculpted figure[237]:

HIC IACET FEL. REC. D. / CLEMENS PAPA V
FVNDATOR ECCLESIARVM DE ASESTA / ET DE
VILHENDRAVDO QVI OBIIT APVD RVPEM
MAVRAM / NEMAVSENSIS DIOCESIS XX APRILIS /
PONTIFICATVS SVI ANNO IX PORTATVS VERO AD
ISTAM / ECCLESIAM BEATAE MARIAE XXVII AVGVSTI
DIE TVNC PROXIMO / SEQVENTI ANNO DOMINI
MCCCXIIII ET SEPVLTVS / DIE ... ANNO MCCCLIX[238]

("Within lies the body of Clement V, the founder of the collegiate churches of Uzeste and Villandraut, who died at Roquemaure April 20, 1314, in the ninth year of his pontificate. Brought to the church of St. Mary of Uzeste in the following August, the body of the most unfortunate pontiff was buried in 1359."[239])

In 1577, the tomb was ransacked and vandalized by Huguenots, who stole the precious stones and the silver columns, then broke the tomb to pieces and tossed the bones of the pope into the fire. The canons of the church tried to put as much of the tomb back together as they could but it was pretty well destroyed: the face of the effigy was gone, the hands and feet mutilated and the cushion for the head cracked in half, although the griffon against which the feet rested survived.

Clement was originally buried in front of the altar, but the tomb was relocated in 1805 to the wall of the south aisle, and then in 1897 it was placed in the nave behind the altar. Dante placed Clement in Hell in *Inferno* (19: 82–84):

For after him shall come of fouler deed
From tow'rds the west a Pastor without law,
Such as befits to cover him and me.

FURTHER READING: E. Muntz, "Les tombeaux des Papes en France," in *Gazette des Beaux Arts*, Paris, XXVI, 1887; J. De Lauriere, *Le tombeau de C. V.*, Paris, 1889; E. Brun, *Uzeste et C. V*, Bordeaux, 1899; E. Steinmann, "Die Zerstorung der Grabdenkmaler der Papste von Avignon," in *Monatshefte für Kunstwissenschaft*, Leipzig, XI, 1918.

Tomb of John XXII, Cathedral of Notre-Dame-des-Doms, Avignon. By permission of Julian Gardner from his book *The Tomb and the Tiara.*

John XXII   (August 7, 1316– December 4, 1334) *Jacques Dusse.* Died at 90 from old age in the papal palace of Avignon, France. His last words were, "The purified soul would see God face to face immediately after death." His tomb, begun shortly after his death, was made of white fine-grain Pernes limestone and was the first truly Gothic free-standing tomb of the Avignon popes. L. B. Alberty in *Cronica del sec. XV* described the tomb as "quills upon a fretful porcupine."[240] A finely cut sapphire ring was found in his coffin when his bones were being transferred to a golden reliquary in March of 1759. Clement was originally buried in the Chapel of St. Joseph at the Cathedral of Notre-Dame-des-Doms. The monument was moved into the corner of the same chapel in 1759; in the late eighteenth century it was moved to the Chapel of St. Martha; and in 1840 was moved for the last time back to its original position in the middle of the chapel of St. Joseph. The tomb has not escaped desecration: All sixty statuettes have been stolen; the head of the effigy now is the head of a bishop with a miter, not a pope with a tiara; and like most French papal tombs, it was badly mutilated during the French Revolution.[241] All was not lost, however, for two small statuettes of alabaster that once adorned the tomb can now be seen in the Musée du Petit-Palais. One depicts a deacon with a maniple and book; the other, a layman. Both probably formed part of the funeral cortege at the base of the monument. There is no known inscription or epitaph.

Dante places John XXII in heaven in *Paridiso* 18:127–129:

> One 'twas the custom to make war with
>   swords;
> But now 'tis made by taking here and there
> The bread the pitying Father shuts from
>   none.

FURTHER READING: L. Duhamel, *Le tombeau de J. XXII à Avignon*, Avignon, 1887; L. H. Labande, *Le palais des Papes et les monuments d'Avignon au XIV siècle*, Marseille, 1925.

Antipope Nicolas V (May 12, 1328–July 25, 1330) *Pietro Rainalducci*. Died around age 83 in the Church of the Fransiscans, Avignon. He threw himself at John XXII's feet with a rope around his neck and begged for absolution, which he received, and he spent the last three years of his life detained in honor at the papal palace.

Benedict XII (December 20, 1334–April 25, 1342) *Jacques Fournier*. Died at age 62 from "tibial pain" (perhaps linked to his severe obesity). On his deathbed he retracted all the proposals from his last sermons, and there are no references to the novena having been celebrated for his funeral. His original tomb, sculpted by Jean Lavenier at a cost of 600 gold florins (although Lavenier actually received 651 florins)[242] was located in the fourth chapel (of the Guild of Tailors) to the left, in the Cathedral of Notre-Dame-des-Doms, in Avignon, France. The monument measured 13½ feet high, 8¼ feet long, and 4 feet wide.[243]

In 1689 the canopy was removed because it was about to fall down, and in 1765 the monument was removed from the chapel to make room for the burials of members of the Guild of Tailors. It was placed against the north wall of the Our Lady Chapel. The recumbent figure of the pope was destroyed, as were many things papal, in the French Revolution, although the epitaph has been recorded:

HIC SVBSVNT CINERES ET OSSA / BENEDICTI XII
PONT. MAX / QVI FVIT ORIVNDVS EX OPPIDO
SAVARDVNO DIOEC. APAMIENSIS / IN COMITATV
FVXENSI ET APPELLABATVR IACOBVS FVRNERVIS /
MONACHVS CISTERCIENSIS THEOLOGIAE DOCTOR
EXIMIVS / FVIT PRIMVS ABBAS MONTIS FRIGIDI
INDE EPISCOPVS MIRAPICENSIS / DEMVM PRESB.
CARD. S. PRISCAE A IOANNE XXII / CVI IMMEDIATE
IN PONTIFICATV SVCCESSIT CREATVS / VVLGO
CARDINALIS ALBVS DICEBATVR / QVEM OB REI
FAMILIARIS ANGVSTIAM CARDINALIVM PENE
INFIMVM / IN SVMMVM PONTIFICEM OB EIVS
VITAE INTEGRITATEM / ELEGERVNT IN VIGILIA S.
THOMAE APOSTOLI / IN CONVENTV FRATRVM
PRAEDICATORVM HVIVS VRBIS / VBI ETIAM

KALEND. IAN. PER NEAPOLEONEM DE VRSINIS /
DIAC. CARD. CORONATIONIS INSIGNIA SVSCEPIT /
ANNO 1335 / VIR FVIT DOCTRINA ET VITAE
INTEGRITATE PRAESTANTISSIMVS / VIRORVM
BONORVM ET DOCTORVM VALDE STVDIOSVS /
MVLTA PRAECLARA STATVIT TVM AD MORVM /
ET PRAECIPVE CLERI REFORMATIONEM / ET
ECCLESIASTICAM DISCIPLINAM INSTAVRANDAM /
SEDIT PONTIFICATV ANNOS VII MENS. III DIES VI /
VNICA TANTVM HABITA SEX CARDINALIVM /
VIRORVM PRAESTANTISSIMORVM CREATIONE /
DECESSIT IN AVENIONENSI PALATIO QVOD
IPSE FABRICARI IVSSERAT / EX TIBIAE DOLORE
VII KAL. MAII 1342 / FVNVS IN PRAESENTI
ECCLESIA MAGNIFICE CVRATVM FVIT /
OMNIBVS QVI ADERANT OB TANTI PONTIFICIS
OBITVM / COLLACRYMANTIBVS

("Here lie the ashes and bones of Supreme Pontiff Benedict XII, who came from the town of Savardun in the diocese of Apamea in the Fuxensi court, and was named Jacques Fournier. A Cistercian monk, and distinguished doctor of theology, he was first the abbot of Fontfroide, then Bishop of Mirepoix, and finally cardinal-priest of St. Prisca by John XXII, whose pontificate he was soon elected to succeed. The people called him the fortunate cardinal, for on account of the difficulty he had faced as the lowest amongst cardinals, and on account of his integrity, they elected him as supreme pontiff on the Vigil of St. Thomas the Apostle in the assembly of priestly brothers in this city, where, too, in the month of January through Cardinal-Deacon Napoleon of the Ursins he accepted the seal of coronation in the year 1335. A learned man without doubt, he was most eminent amongst doctors and good men in respect to knowledge and integrity. He then set forth countless remarkable tasks according to morals, especially to render clerical reform and ecclesiastical discipline. He was enthroned in pontificate for seven years, three months, and six days, by the election, unique in character, of six most prestigious cardinals in the palace of Avignon, whose construction he himself had decreed. He died of tibial pain on the sixth of May, 1342. His funeral was attended in the present magnificent church by all who came and mourned together for the death of a pope of such greatness."—*Trans. Ruth Yeuk Chun Leung*)

Tomb of Benedict XII, Calvet Museum, Avignon. Drawing based on Montini's *Le Tombe dei Papi.*

Only a few original fragments of the tomb remain and are preserved in the Musée Calvet at Avignon. Both the tomb and effigy we see today, commissioned by Cardinal Jean de Cros, were completed in 1828 by the sculptor Casimir Poitevin.[244]

The modern inscription reads:

HIC IACET / BENEDICTVS PAPA XII / OBIIT / DIE XXV APRILIS / ANNO MCCCXLII

("Here lies Pope Benedict XII who died on the 25th day of April in the year 1342."—*Trans. Ruth Yeuk Chun Leung*)

Clement VI (May 7, 1342–December 6, 1352) *Pierre of Rosier d'Egleton.* Died of a short illness at age 61. He designed his own tomb and planned his own funeral, wishing that his mausoleum be created in the middle of the choir of the La Chaise-Dieu monastery in Avignon, France, where he had once been a monk. His personal physician, Guy de Chauliac (d. 1368), removed his vital organs to embalm him.[245] During the Ritual of Abandonment (when the pope's body is left unattended in the cathedral overnight) one of the candles fell over onto the bier and severely burned his body. Nevertheless, Clement's body was dressed in full pontifical vestments and laid in a marble tomb in the choir of Cathedral of Notre Dame-des-Doms, Avignon, to await the spring thaw so that the path was clear to travel to his final burial spot. After three months Clement's funeral procession of ecclesiastics and family members set out for the month-long journey to the remote Benedictine abbey at La Chaise-Dieu (which he had completely rebuilt to house his tomb). The coffin was covered in a black silk cloth that was embroidered with gold, with his papal arms in red silk adorning the bottom.

The funeral began with the Mass for the Dead, then moved on to the Absolution, when each cardinal censed the altar and the body three times and, after each censing, led the chanting of versicles and responses. Finally the burial took place: the body was taken to the tomb accompanied by clerics chanting *In paradisum*, after which prayers, antiphons, and psalms were recited as the corpse was lowered into the tomb in the monastery. It was then sprinkled with holy water, and the rite concluded with the final orations and psalms, notably the *Miserere mei*.[246]

The black marble monument, costing 3,800 gold florins, featured a fine white marble recumbent effigy of the pope lying in state and was carved by Pierre Boye, Jean de Sanholis, and Jean David at the workshop of Pierre Boye in Villeneuve. Originally it had a canopy containing 44 statuettes, each rep-

Top: The original tomb of Clement VI, La Chaise-Dieu, Avignon, France. From Renzo Montini, *Le Tombe dei Papi.* *Bottom:* The remains of the tomb of Clement VI, La Chaise-Dieu, Avignon. By permission of Anne Morgenstern.

resenting a member of the pope's family who attended his funeral at La Chaise-Dieu.

In 1562, during their wars of religion, the Calvinists exhumed the remains of Clement VI and tossed them onto the bonfire. The bier of the tomb was restored in the seventeenth century, but all that remains now of the monument is the effigy (which was replaced in 1958), lying on a black marble chest. A few of the original tomb ornaments can be found in the library of La Chaise-Dieu.

FURTHER READING: Anne Morgenstern, "Art and Ceremony in Papal Avignon: A Prescription for the Tomb of Clement VI," in *Gesta,* XL/I; M. Faucon, "Eglise de La Chaise-Dieu," in *Bull. Arch. du Comite des Travaux Hist. et Scient.* Paris, II, 1884; E. Deprez, "Les funerailles de C. VI et d'Innocent VI" in *Mélanges,* 1900.

Innocent VI (December 18, 1352–September 12, 1362) *Etienne Aubert.* Died at age 80 from stress due to a plague breakout in Avignon. An honor guard was stationed

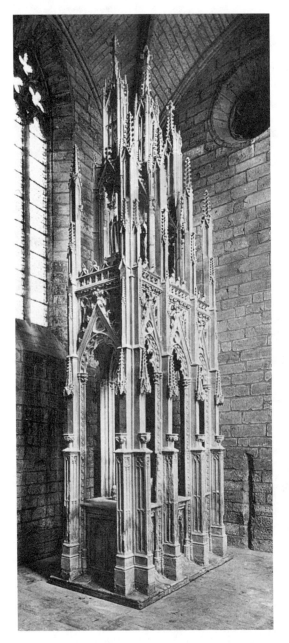

Tomb of Pope Innocent VI, Chartreuse, Villeneuve-les-Avignon. By permission of Julian Gardner from his book *The Tomb and the Tiara*.

around his corpse for the two days it was on display (Sept. 12–14) in the great chapel of the Apostolic Palace. There were no references to a novena, yet the *vita* of the subsequent pope, Urban V, notes that it was celebrated.[247]

Innocent was buried in the Holy Trinity Chapel, in the charter house of Villeneuve-les-Avignon, in a tomb by Beltran Nogayrol. Bartholomew Cavallier was paid 150 British pounds to carve the effigy. It was ransacked in 1790 during the French Revolution, but by 1835 it had been completely restored and transferred to the Chapel of the Hospice at Villeneuve (because the Holy Trinity chapel had fallen into decay). Sadly, the actual remains of the pope are lost. The short epitaph, however, was recorded:

HIC IACET BEATISSIMVS PAPA INNOCENTIVS VI
PRIMVS / FVNDATOR HVIVS DOMVS QVI
OBIIT ANNO MCCCLXII / DIE VERO XII
MENSIS SEPTEMBRIS CVIVS ANIMA /
IN PACE REQVIESCAT AMEN

("Here lies the most blessed pope Innocent VI, the first founder of this house, who died in the year 1362 on the 12th day of September. May his soul rest in peace. Amen.—*Trans. Father Thomas Buffer*)

FURTHER READING: E. Deprez, "Les funerailles de C. VI et d'Innocent VI," in *Mélanges*, 1900.

Blessed Urban V (September 28, 1362–December 19, 1370) *Guillaume de Grimoard.* Died of illness at age 60 in front of the high altar of the Marseille Cathedral while mass was being sung.[248] St. Bridgette of Sweden had warned Urban that he would die if he returned to Avignon from Italy (although it was no longer politically safe in Italy) and indeed, three months after his return to Avignon, he died. According to the *vita* of Gregory XI, Urban's funeral novena was celebrated.

Urban was initially buried in the church of St. Marziale in Avignon, France,[249] but in accordance with his wishes, he was moved when his tomb was ready in 1372 (the same year he was beatified) to an area near the high altar in the Chapel of St. Peter of the abbey of St. Victor in Marseille.[250] Gregory XI commissioned the sculptor Joglarii (who used a very cheap base stone) to create a gothic tomb, which measured 21 feet high by about 11¼ inches wide[251] and was described by medieval papal tomb historian H.K. Mann as follows:

> Gothic in style … the lower half, where there was the recumbent effigy of the Pope, was adorned with a number of little columns supporting ogival and trefoil arches; while the upper half displayed pointed arches, pinnacles, and a frieze, and niches filled with statues. Both parts bear the arms of the Pope. In the tympanum may be seen angels carrying to heaven the soul of the departed pontiff, and placing it at the feet of the Eternal Judge, by whose side is the seated figure of the Mother of God, and around whom are angels in adoration.[252]

The original epitaph reads:

HIC REQVIESCIT VRBANVS PONTIFEX IN ORDINE
QVINTVS / SVMMVS DIVINITVS ROMANORVM
PRAESVL ELECTVS / AVCTOR BONORVM LVX
CENSOR NORMAQVE MORVM / SPECVLVM
CVNCTORVM DOGMA DVX MONACHORVM /
BONORVM DVCTOR MALORVM QVOQVO
CORRECTOR / IVSTITIAE TVTOR STVDIORVMQVE
REPARATOR / NVLLIVS ACCEPTOR DIREXIT
IVSTITIAE LIBRAM / VIRTVTIBVS FVLGENS CVNCTIS
VERA REDDIDIT IDEM / ATQVE SIMONIAM DNI
SPLENDORE FVGAVIT / ECCLESIAE NEMPE
REPARAVIT ROMAE DIVINITVS / APOSTOLORVMQVE
CAPITA TVNC RECONDIDIT / PAVPERES ALENDO
CHRISTI MANDATA COMPLEVIT / HICQVE BONVS
PASTOR AD FIDEM CHRISTI REDVXIT / GRAECORVM
CAESAREM ERRORVM CALIGINE TECTVM /
POST LABORES TANDEM MVLTOS DESVPERQVE
VOCATVS / INTER FRATRVM MANVS ILLA FACTA
MEMBRA RESOLVENS / CHRISTI VICARIVS
TRANSIVIT AD ASTRA BEATVS / QVEM DEVS
MVLTVM EX ALTO PER SIGNA MONSTRAVIT /
QVALIS ENIM FVERIT SIGNA TANTA CLARE
DEMONSTRANT / AD TVMVLVM CVIVS
LANGVENTVM MEMBRA SANANTVR / IN MVLTIS
ALIIS PROVINCIIS QVOQVE CLARE CORVSCAT /
NECNON ITALIA AB IPSO MVLTVM AMATA /
MIRACVLIS LATE HOC IN HISPANIA PATET / AC IN
BOEMIA NOBILIQVE FRANCIA TOTA / GAVDET
PROVINCIA ARELATENSIS SIVE VOCATA / PER TANTA
SIGNA MERITIS VRBANI ORNATA / ERGO MENTE
PVRA TE VRBANO BEATO / PONTIFICI SVMMO
LECTOR DEVOTE COMMENDA / ANNO MILLENO
TRECENTENO QVOQVE SEPTVAGENO / CVRRENTE
DOMINI MENSISQVE DECIMA NONA / DECEMBRIS

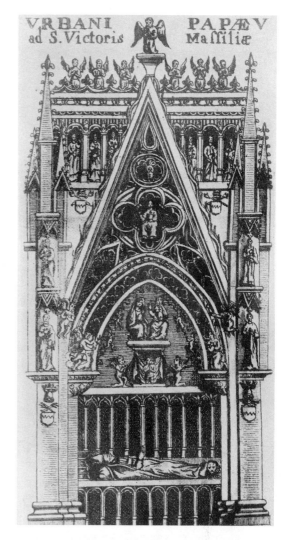

Original tomb monument of Urban V, the Abbey of St. Victor, Marseille, France. From H.K. Mann, *Tombs and Portraits of the Popes.*

ERAT DIES CVM BEATVS ISTE / VRBANVS AD
CHRISTVM TRAMITE FELICE MIGRAVIT

("Here rests Pope Urban V, by divine providence elected the supreme bishop of the Romans. Source of goodness and light, judge and model of morals, leader of all monks, leader of good men and corrector of bad men, protector of justice and restorer of zeal. Shining by all his virtues, he steered the scales of justice so that no one would be regarded unjustly; he restored the truth, and by the Lord's glory he put simony to flight. With God's assistance, he recovered the heads of the apostles for the Roman Church, and then buried them again. By nourishing the poor he fulfilled Christ's commandments. And this good shepherd returned the faith of Christ to the emperor of the Greeks, who had been covered with the darkness of error. Finally, after many labors, called from above, he released his body into the hands of his brothers. The blessed vicar of Christ passed over to the stars, and God exemplified his greatness with signs that clearly showed what kind of man he was, for at his tomb the limbs of the sick are healed. And he shines brightly in many other provinces as well as Italy, which he so greatly loved. This is plain to see by the miracles done in Spain, and in Bohemia, and throughout noble France. The province of Arles rejoices to be adorned by such great prodigies, thanks to Urban's merits. Therefore, with pure spirit, reader, devoutly commend yourself to blessed Urban, the supreme Pontiff. In the year of the Lord 1370, December 19 was the day when blessed Urban happily departed to Christ on a happy road."— Trans. Father Thomas Buffer)

This epitaph has also been translated as follows:

("Here lies Pontiff Urban V, most nobly elected bishop of the Romans, champion of the good, light, censor and standard of morals, mirror to all in teaching, head of monks, leader of the good, corrector of the wrongful, guardian of justice, restorer of learning. Partial to no one, he guided the scale of justice; shining with all virtues, he rendered them all the same. He banned simony with the splendor of the Lord, and indeed restored the Holy See of the Church of Rome and the apostles. He then sheltered the poor, and by nourishing them he fulfilled Christ's commandments. A good shepherd, he returned to Christ's faith the Greek emperor, who was covered by the darkness of his errors. After many toils he was at last summoned from above. The vicar of Christ passed into blessed immortality, which God from above revealed through signs. Such great signs demonstrated clearly what he might have been: Around his tomb diseased bodies were restored to health. In many other provinces also he appeared in a bright flash, especially in Italy, which he loved dearly. By miracles it is known in Spain far and wide, in Bohemia and all of noble France too. The province of Arles rejoices for the signs so

adorned by Urban's merits. Thus, with a pure mind, O reader, commit yourself devotedly to the blessed Urban, the supreme pontiff. In the year of the Lord 1370, the tenth nones of the month of December was the day when the blessed Urban departed to Christ on a favorable path."—Trans. Ruth Yeuk Chun Leung)

Urban's tomb suffered heavy damage during the French Revolution, then was further damaged in the late nineteenth century when choir stalls were placed against it during the secularization of the church. Sadly, the only original remnants remaining are the base and a few fragments, which can now be seen at the Musée Calvet di Avignone.

Like a saint, Urban had a considerable following at his tomb because "an infinite number of wax statuettes were hung before the sepulcher and in almost the entire church of the monastery of St. Victor of Marseilles, that had been brought there by people saved from dangers and sickness who had invoked his name (miracles)."[253] There is now a cenotaph for Urban in the Church of St. Martin in Avignon, although the alabaster figure of the pope can now be found in the Musée Calvet of Avignon with the following epitaph:

URBANUS HUJUS MONASTERII COLLEGII
BENEFACTOR / ABBATIAE CLUNIACENSIS
DECANUS AB INNOCENTIO VI / SI GERMANI
ANTISSIODORENSIS AC POST MODUM SI / VICTORIS
MASSILIENSIS ABBAS CREATUS APLICUS APUD /
MEDIOLANENSES LEGATUS AVENIONE SUMMUS /
PONTIFEX ELIGITUR ANNO AETATIS SUAE LIII
CHRISTI / MCCCLXII POST EXCEPTAM ROMAE
JOANNIS / PALEOLOGI IMPERATORIS
CONSTANTINOPOLITANI FIDEI / PROFESSIONEM
ET IN HAC CIVITATE JOANNIS GALLIARUM / REGIS
OBEDIENTIAM PONTIFICATUS SU ANNO VIII /
MENSE IV MONACHALI QUEM NUNQUAM
DIMISERAT / INDUTUS HABITU MORTUUS IN
METROPOLITANA / AVEN. SEPULTUS XVII
POST MENSES MASSILIAM / TRANSLATUS
MULTIS DIE CLARUIT MIRACULIS[254]

("Urban, benefactor of the community of this monastery, deacon of the abbacy of Cluny, made abbot of [the monasteries of] St. Germain of Antisidore and later of St. Victor of Marseille by Innocent VI, adjunct in Milan, deputy in Avignon, was elected pontiff at the

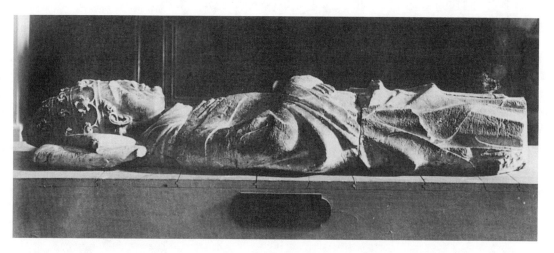

Remains of the effigy of Urban V, in the Musée de Petit-Palais, Avignon. By permission of Julian Gardner, from his book *The Tomb and the Tiara.*

age of 53 in the year of Christ 1362. After the profession of the Constantinopolitan creed of Emperor John Paleologus was received in Rome, and this city was brought under the obedience of King John of the Gauls in the eighth year of his pontificate, the fourth monastic month. Clothed in his habit, which he had never given up, he died and was buried in the capital of Avignon. After 27 months he was brought over from Marseille, and he manifested himself on that day with many miracles."—*Trans. Sam Garcia*)

Because many miracles were reported at Urban's tomb, King Waldemar of Denmark demanded his immediate canonization. Gregory XI promised it as early as 1375, but it did not take place because of the political upheaval at the time. Urban's cult was approved about 500 years later when he was beatified by Pius IX in 1870.

FURTHER READING: E. Muntz, "La statue du pape U. V au Musee d'Avignon," in *Gazette archeol. Paris,* IX, 1886.

Gregory XI (December 30, 1370–March 27, 1378) *Pierre Roger de Beaufort.* Died from exhaustion on a very difficult trip from Marseille to Italy, probably in Anagni, Italy, at age 49. In his last words he gave orders that the next pope should be elected by the

majority of cardinals, not by a ⅔ vote. The pope died on a Saturday, and on the next Monday the corpse was displayed in the choir of St. Peter's, Rome, although the formal exposition took place in Santa Maria Nuova, where his body was transferred on Tuesday.[255] The next pope, Urban VI, held even more funeral services for Gregory, lasting for four days after his election, perhaps to prove the legitimacy of Gregory's death.

Gregory was buried in a plain coffin in Santa Maria Nuova (then known as Santa Francesca Romana in the Roman Forum), which had been his titular church when he was a cardinal. There was originally no monument, but in 1584 the sculptor Pietro Paolo Olivieri carved a relief which can still be seen today (against the wall to the right of the sanctuary near his grave). The relief shows St. Catherine of Siena leading the reentry of the pope into Rome. On either side of this relief are the allegorical figures of Faith and Prudence. The coffin was inscribed with gothic letters:

HIC REQVIESCIT CORPVS
BEATI GREGORII PAPAE XI[256]

("Here lies the body of the blessed Pope Gregory XI.")

The monument epitaph reads:

Monument to Gregory XI, Santa Maria Nuova. By permission of the Houghton Library, Harvard University.

CHR. SAL. / GREGORIO XI LEMOVICENSI / HUMAN-
ITATE DOCTRINA PIETATEQUE ADMIRABILI QUI /
UT ITALIAE SEDITIONIBUS LABORANTI MEDERETUR
SEDEM / PONTIFICIAM AVENIONI DIU TRANSLATAM
DIVINO / AFFLATUS NUMINE HOMINUMQUE MAX-
IMO PLAUSU / POST ANNOS SEPTUAGINTA ROMAM
FELICITER REDUXIT / PONTIFICATUS SUI ANNO VII
/ S.P. Q. R. TANTAE RELIGIONIS ET BENEFICII NON
IMMEMOR / GREGORIO XIII PONT. OPT. MAX COM-
PROBANTE / ANNO AB ORBE REDEMPTO M D
LXXXIIII POS. / JOHANNES PETRO DRACO / CYRI-
ACO MATTHAEIO COSS / JO BAPTISTA ALBERTO
THOMAS BUBALO DE CANCELLARIIS PRIORE[257]

("To Gregory XI, of Limoges, admirable for his
humanity, learning and uprightness. Eager to
rescue an Italy sick to death by reason of her
confusion, and moved by the Holy Ghost and
the rejoicing of mankind, he gloriously restored the Papal See to Rome, after an absence
of seventy years, in the seventh year of his
Pontificate. The senate and people of Rome, in
memory of such great up-rightness and well-
doing, with the approval of Gregory XIII in the
year 1584 after the redemption of the world.
Johannes Petrus Draco, Cyriacus Matthaeus,
Consuls Jo. Battista Alberto Thomas Bubalo De
Cancellariis, Prior."[258])

FURTHER READING: R. Lanciani, "Il panorama di
Roma scolpito da P. P. Olivieri nel 1585" in *Bull.
Comm. Arch. Comun*, Rome, XXI, 1893.

Urban VI (April 8, 1378–October 15,
1389) *Bartolomeo Prignano*. Died at age 71,
allegedly poisoned because of his incredible
cruelty toward his cardinals (it was rumored
that he walled up two or three of his cardinals in Genoa).[259] His original monument
featured a sarcophagus that resembled a tiny
basilica (See Appendix 4 for picture) and was
located in the Chapel of St. Andrew in St.
Peter's. The original epitaph read:

HAC ANIMO MAGNUS, SAPIENS, IUSTUSQUE
MONARCHA / PARTENOPEUS ADEST URBANUS
SEXTUS IN ARCHA. / FERVEBAT FIDEI LATEBRAS
CONFERRE MAGISTRIS / O DECUS HIS FRETUS
SEMPER POST PRANDIA SISTRIS. / SCHISMATIBUS
MAGIS ANIMO MAIORE REGEBAT / OMNE
SIMONIACUM TANTO SUB PATRE TREMEBAT. / QUID
IUVAT HUNC TERRIS MORTALI TOLLERE LAUDE /

PRO MERITIS CAELI SPLENDET SIBI GLORIA
VALDE. / OBIIT ROMAE IDIBUS OCTOB.
ANNO MCCCLXXXIX AETATIS SUAE LXXI[260]

("In this sepulcher lies Urban VI, Neapolitan
prince, magnanimous, wise and just. He loved
to converse of the mysteries of the faith with
the masters. O splendor! He was always intent
after dinner on such melodies. He dominated
the great schisms with still greater courage. All
that which was infected with simony, shud-
dered under so great a pope. But what use is it
to exalt him on earth with human praise? Very
splendid the glory of heaven for the merits
which one has conquered. He died at Rome,
the 15th of October 1389, at 71 years of age." —
Trans. Father Tom Carleton)

As an interesting study of the translation of medieval ecclesiastical Latin, consider
also the following transation. Both transla-
tors used the same Latin epitaph of Urban
VI. They came up with similar concepts but
different wording: "Here the great-spirited,
wise, and just ruler, the Neopolitan Urban
VI, lies entombed. He was fervent in providing refuge for masters of the faith, always
properly supported by these after meals. He
governed schismatics firmly with great spirit,
while every simoniac trembled under such a
father. How can this mortal earth take away
such praise? For his merits, great glory shines
for him in heaven. He died in Rome, on the
ides of October, in the year 1489, at the age
of 72." — *Trans. Phyllis Jestice*.

Interestingly, Douglas Sladen, in *Old
Saint Peter's*, translates the epitaph almost
exactly as Phyllis Jestice does, but he adds in
a line around line five in the English translation: "That gained for him, noble one, a
fatal poison cup at the end of the repast."[261]
Yet there is no reference in the Latin that
could mean "poison cup."

Around 1568, during the preliminary
deconstruction of St. Peter's, Urban's monument was destroyed and his sarcophagus
placed against the left wall. Later it was
removed to make way for an entrance into
the chapel behind it, and it ended up under
the dome for almost 20 years. Just as some
workmen were about to dump Urban's bones

The original tomb of Urban VI in St. Peter's Basilica. By permission of the Houghton Library, Harvard University.

so the sarcophagus could be used as a water trough, church canon and historian Giacomo Grimaldi arrived and ordered the entire sarcophagus and remains be moved to the eastern portion of the Basilica. In 1606 they were moved to the crypt, as Grimaldi notes in his eyewitness account:

Exhumation of the body of Urban VI, 12. September 1606. In the presence of the aforementioned reverend lord Parido, the marble sarcophagus was opened that contained the bones of Pope Urban VI, and with the same sarcophagus were redeposited under the aforementioned vault of the new pavement.... In the year 1588, the masons of the great rotunda wanted to use this sarcophagus to hold water for the building. They brought it to the former buttress full of limestone, and in my presence took that same sarcophagus, which was full, from the earth, and came upon the bones of this same pontiff, with a ring, which James of Porta, the architect, kept; they were buried in the aforementioned marble sarcophagus behind the organ in the old basilica. It stood open to the heavens for many years under the great dome [*trans. Phyllis Jestice*].

Sarcophagus inscription:

HIC JACET URBANUS VI
PONT. OPT. MAX.

("Here is Urban VI, high priest")

Urban's sarcophagus can still be seen today in the Vatican grottoes although somehow the cover of the sarcophagus of (allegedly) Nicholas II (d. 1280) ended up on Urban's coffin. It is obvious that the cover is from another sarcophagus, as it is too long for the coffin, and the tiara on the effigy has only one crown, when two crowns were in use during Urban's time.

FURTHER READING: G. Ciampini, *De sacris aedificiis a Constantino Magno constructis,* Rome, 1747; Julian Gardner, *The Tomb and the Tiara: Curial Tomb Sculpture in Rome and Avignon in the Later Middle Ages,* Oxford University Press, 1992; Virgilio Cardinal Noe, *Le Tombe e i Monumenti,* Rome, 2000; Agostino Paravicini-Bagliani, *The Pope's Body,* Chicago University Press, 1994.

Antipope Clement (VII) (September 20, 1378–September 16, 1394) *Robert of Cambrai,* "the butcher of Cesena." Died in the morning from a fit of apoplexy while in Avignon, France, at age 52, and was temporarily interred in Notre-Dame-des-Doms

Top: The sarcophagus of Urban VI before the construction of the modern grottoes. By permission of Julian Gardner from his book *The Tomb and the Tiara. Bottom:* Urban VI's tomb in the grottoes as it looks today.

Top: Original tomb of Antipope Clement VII. By permission of Julian Gardner from his book *The Tomb and the Tiara. Left:* Remains of the tomb of Antipope Clement VII, in the Musée de Petit-Palais, Avignon. By permission of Julian Gardner, from his book *The Tomb and the Tiara.*

Unfortunately it was destroyed during the French Revolution and all that remains is the head of the effigy, now in the Musée de Petit-Palais, Avignon.

Boniface IX (1389–1404) *Pietro Tomacelli.* Died of kidney stones at age 54. Antipope Benedict XIII had sent a proposal to Rome attempting to end the current schism, but because Boniface was seriously ill, he said he wasn't fit for a meeting. Begrudgingly, he attended the meeting anyway. The angry and violent exchanges hastened the deterioration of his health, and he died shortly after. The Romans held the antipope's envoys responsible for the pope's death and jailed them, releasing them only upon payment of an enormous ransom.[263]

Originally Boniface was buried in a simple grave in the crypt of Saint Peter's until his white marble sepulcher (commissioned by the Count of Sora and carved by

in a canopied tomb thought to have been sculpted by Perrin Morel. On September 8, 1401, the monument was transferred to the chapel of the Celestines, and then in 1658 it was moved to the choir of the church.[262]

Possibly the original monument of Boniface IX. From Renzo Montini, *Le Tombe dei Papi.*

Giovanni Tomacelli) was completed in 1409. The sepulcher was then placed in the Chapel of Saints Peter and Paul, although on August 5 of that year the tomb was transferred to the Chapel of St. Guiles in the basilica. Regrettably, this was one of the first sepulchers destroyed during the demolition of St. Peter's in the seventeenth century. Fragments of the tomb, however, survive in the Chapel of the Crucifixion in the Lateran. Luckily the epitaph, which was most likely carved in Gothic letters, was recorded in its entirety[264]:

BONIFACIUS IX STIRPE TOMACELLUS, GENERE CYBO / EN PETRA PARVA PATREM SUB CELICA SIDERA PRIMUM / CLAUDIT, APOSTOLICA SOLIUM QUI REXIT HABENA / CATHOLICAMQUE FIDEM, SERVANS A TURBINE SANCTUM / REMIGIUM CHRISTI VICTIS VIRTUTE TYRANNIS. / ORTHODOXUS ERAT SUPER OMNES, ARCA SUPERNI / CONSILII, SUA IURA TUENS ET GRANDIA TRACTANS / CESARIS EX ANIMO, FIDEI CLIPEATUS HONORE. / CORPORE CONSPICUUS, ROSEUS FLOS, FAMINE CONSTANS / AUDITORQUE PLACENS, MISERIS MISERATOR OPIMUS. / OSSA IACENT, MENS ALTA POLUM FELICIBUS ALIS / ASCENDENS MICAT ANTE DEUM NOVA LUCIS ORIGO. / GLORIUS ANTISTES QUISNAM BONIFATIUS ALTER / NONUS UT ISTE FUIT QUE CHRONICA SCRIPSERIT UNQUAM. / QUODVE GENUS PARILEM DEDIT EVO NOMEN ET OMNES / DE TOMACELLIS FULGET FULGEBIT IN ANNOS. / PARTHENOPE LUSTRANS TULIT HUNC GENUS OMNE LATINUM / QUICQUID ALIT TELLUS ET QUOD TEGIT OMNIA CELUM. / OBIIT MCCCCIIII DIE I OCTOBRIS PONTIFICATUS VERO EITIS ANNO XV.[265]

("Oh You keys, the cross, the dear tiara, the church who has been bereft of her man, and you famous Rome, shed tears over your champion. Look, a small stone covers the First Father under the stars of Heaven. He ruled with Apostolic reins the seat and the Catholic faith. Defeating the tyrants by his valor, he saved Christ's holy oarsmen from the whirlwind. He exceeded others in orthodoxy, and he was the repository of celestial counsel. Armed with the honor of faith, he defended his rights and did great deeds like an emperor. He had an imposing figure, he was ruddy of face, and his speech was resolute. He was a considerate judge and took great pity on the wretched. His bones lie here, but his soul,

ascending to Heaven on happy wings, shines before God as a new fountain of light. A glorious Pope! Has any other Boniface been equal to the ninth? How impressive is the story of his life! Has any other family given the age a comparable man? The name of the Tomacelli shines and will shine eternally. He died on the first of October in 1404, in the 15th year of his papacy."[266])

The following translation of the same epitaph by Phyllis Jestice shows how the Latin language can say the same thing many different ways: "Weep over your champion, oh keys, cross, and gentle tiara. Oh Church, you and famed Rome alike are widowed. See! A small stone closes in the apostolic father, first under the stars of heaven, who alone held the reins of power. Serving the holy Catholic faith within the storm, rowing with Christ to conquer tyrants, he was orthodox above all, and followed supernal counsel, defending his laws and controlling the mighty. Armed with a shield, honored by Caesar from a spirit of faith, distinguished in body, a rose, a constant flame, he was one who heard, satisfying the wretched with abundant compassion. His bones lie here, his spirit ascending to the highest heaven on wings; he sparkles before God as a new source of light. Oh glorious bishop, who can compare to Boniface IX? Who ever could have written such a chronicle, and what race could give birth to an equal? The name and everything of Tomacelli shines, and will shine throughout the years. Lustrous Naples bore this race for all the Latin world, which nourished those on earth and which covers all heaven. He died in 1404 on the first day of October, in the 15th year of his pontificate."

Antipope Benedict XIII (September 28, 1394–July 26, 1417; d. May 23) *Pedro de Luna.* Died at age 95 from natural causes, though weakened by an earlier failed poisoning attempt in Pensicola, Spain. He reigned for 29 years, more than "Peter's years," which was a major factor in his dethronement and was further cause for damnation by the Council of Constance in 1417. He was originally buried in the chapel crypt in Pensicola, but in 1430, Rodrigo and Juan de Luna got permission from King Alfonso to take his body away. When they opened the tomb a sweet fragrance seeped out, and they saw that Benedict hadn't decayed, although his clothing and a parchment that was placed under his head quickly crumbled away. The de Lunas took Benedict's body through the mountains to his bedroom in the palace of Illueca, Spain, where he was born, and soon his body had mummified under glass and attracted many pilgrims. In 1537, an Italian prelate named Porro smashed his heavy walking stick down on the crystal coffin and ran for his life. The room was then closed by the archbishop of Saragossa, and all visits forbidden, although in the eighteenth century there were reports that lights were seen mysteriously burning in that deserted bedroom.

In 1811 many of the de Luna family were murdered trying to defend their castle during the War of Succession. The French attackers looted Illueca, completely shattering the coffin with their rifle butts and hacking up Benedict's body before tossing it over the castle wall. Fortunately peasants were able to recover Benedict's skull, and it was put on display at the Castle of Illueca, although during the Spanish Civil War in 1936 it had to be buried for protection in the palace of the Counts of Argillo y Morata at Sabinan.

In 1923, the students and teachers of Saragossa commemorated the 500 years since Benedict's death by placing a tablet of gray marble inscribed with Benedict's coat-of-arms and an epitaph, which described Benedict as the grand Aragonese and stated that he lived a generous and clean life which he sacrificed for the idea of knowledge.

On August 23, 2000, the skull was stolen and the Mayor of Illueca, Javier Vicente Inez, received a very badly written letter (with pictures of the kidnapped skull) demanding one million pesetas ($5400) for the safe return of the skull. Otherwise, the letter claimed, it would be thrown in the river. A second badly written ransom note arrived soon after, suggesting a meeting in the city of Zaragoza, Spain, but no one showed up to recieve the money. On September 3, 2000, the Spanish

The skull of Antipope Benedict XIII, in Illueca, Spain. By permission of the Cultural Center of Illueca, Spain.

police arrested a minor and a 22 year old for stealing the skull, which was safely returned in its urn to the Castle at Illueca.[267]

Innocent VII (October 17, 1404–November 6, 1406) *Cosimo Gentile de'Migliorati.* Died from a common cold in the Lateran Palace, Rome, at age 81. His body was transported on the tenth of November to St. Peter's, where he would be buried in the Chapel of Saints Peter and Paul. His novena obsequies lasted until November 18.

Around 1455 the tomb was moved to the foot of the baptismal font in the Chapel of St. Thomas because the Chapel of Saints

Sarcophagus of Innocent VII, Vatican grottoes.

Peter and Paul fell into decay. Church canon and historian Giacomo Grimaldi reports the following epitaph was placed on the tomb:

INNOCENTIO VII. PONT. MAX. / QVVM
NEGLECTI EIUS SEPULCRI MEMORIA
PENE INTERISSET / NICHOLAS V, PONT. MAX /
INSTAVRARI HOC CVRAVIT.[268]

("Innocent VII supreme pontiff. Since he is scarcely remembered because of the neglect of his tomb, Nicholas V, supreme pontiff, caused it to be restored." — *Trans. Phyllis Jestice*)

The following translation by Father Tom Carleton is for the same epitaph, and it is interesting to note the differences in the Latin translations: "To Innocent VII, High Priest. In order that the memory of his neglected tomb might not completely disappear, Pope Nicholas V took the initiative of restoration."

The tomb was opened on September 12, 1606, and Innocent's bones were put in a new marble sarcophagus—a mid–fifteenth century copy of the original—on top of which

was a relief of the original lifelike effigy. Grimaldi witnessed the opening:

Opening of the sepulcher of Innocent VII, 13 September 1606. The body was reduced to bones. He was buried on the epistle side of the chapel of St. Thomas the Apostle, with his epitaph and image placed on the tomb. Found within the tomb were some scraps of parchment worked in the Persian style. Everything was taken, along with his image, and put in the marble container under the vault of the new pavement [*trans. Phyllis Jestice*].

FURTHER READING: Virgilio Cardinal Noe, *Le Tombe e i Monumenti*, Rome, 2000.

Gregory XII (November 30, 1406–July 4, 1415; d. October 18, 1417) *Angelo Correr*. Died at age 92 in Recanati, Italy (as legate of the March of Ancona, *not pope*, because he had resigned the papacy under pressure). He was originally buried near the eastern door of the

The tomb of Gregory XII in the Cathedral of St. Flaviano, Recanati. Drawing by Joan Reardon.

Cathedral of St. Flaviano in Recanati, although in 1623 the cardinal Giulio Roma had the tomb moved to the north of the cathedral, at which time the coffin was opened and the body, found whole, was reclothed. In 1760 the monument was moved to the west of the building, and in 1793 it was moved for the last time to a dark corner near the tomb of Cardinal Angelo Cini, upon whom Gregory had bestowed the red hat. At this time the coffin was opened but revealed nothing but dust. The original epitaph, written in Gothic minuscules, read:

MAXIMVS ECCLESIA PRINCEPS SVMMVSQVE
[*unintelligible*] / ORDINE GREGORIVS BISSENVS
CLAVDITVR ARCHA / HIC PRO PACE DATVS

CAELESTI MVNERE SEMPER / FERBVIT AETHEREOS
SVPERIS VNIRE DECENTER / AST BIS SCISMA
MALVM FACTA HAEC DEMENTIA PISIS / IPSE PIVS
RELEVAT PVRA EST CONSTANTIA TESTIS / CARDINE
BIS SACRO PASTORIS CONSCIA SEDES / MARCHIA
SVSCEPIT RACANATI FLAVIVS AEDE /
SVB ANNO DM M.CCCC.XVII[270]

("Greatest prince of the Church and highest, Gregory XII is enclosed in this coffer. He, given to peace and always seeking heavenly gifts, longed to unite heavenly matters in decency, to resolve this evil madness of Pisa, the stem divided in two. He himself piously revealed the evidence of his pure constancy. Twice seated at the holy threshold of the pastor, he received the church of Flavius Racanate in the year of the Lord 1417."—*Trans. Phyllis Jestice*)

The alleged "original" tomb of Gregory XII as illustrated by Ciacconius. From Cicconius *Vitae*....

Epitaph on plaque:

GREGORIVS XII P. O. M. / VIR SANCTVS A D.
ANTONINO DICTVS / ET PROPTER SVMMAM IN
ADVERSIS CONSTANTIAM / S. STEPHANO MARTYRI
COMPARATVS / RECINETI XV KAL. NOV. AN.
MCCCCXVII DEFVNCTVS / ET IN HAC PRINCIPE
ECCLESIA TVMVLATVS / ANGELI EPISCOPI A SE
CARDINALIS RENVNTIATI / ACCIPIENS DIGNIOREM
LOCVM / SOLEMNI EMORTVALI RITV RENOVATO /
TRANSLATVS EST TERTIO / CVRANTE CAPITVLO OB
NOVI SACELLI / PRO INSIGNIBVS RELIQVIIS A
GREGORIO ETIAM / ELARGITIS ASSERVANDIS
DEDICATIONEM / DIE XVIII IVL. AN. MDCCXCIII[271]

("Gregory XII, the best and greatest pontiff, a holy man according to Don Antonio; for the sake of his utmost perseverance against adversity he was likened to St. Stephen the martyr. He died in Recanati on the 15th of November in the year 1417, and was buried in this church. Though the angelic bishop was forsaken by his cardinals, assuming a more dignified place, as the solemnities for the dead had been renewed, he was translated by the third administrative chapter, on account of the consecration of the new chapel before the distinguished who had been deserted by Gregory, as well as those who gave generously to preserve him, on the 18th day of July, in the year 1417." — *Trans. Ruth Yeuk Chun Leung*)

The "original" tomb illustration by Ciacconius is most likely a fabrication, as stated by medieval tomb historian H.K. Mann: "The author, here cited, affirms positively that the design of Ciacconius was imagined by the editors [F. and A. de Rossi] of the third edition of that book, and was worked out by the well-known engraver Egideo Sadeler [d. 1629]."[271] Another determining factor in the farce that is the Ciacconius illustration is that in the illustration the effigy is wearing a tiara, whereas the effigy on the actual tomb wears a miter. Also, as in the case of the alleged original tomb of Boniface IX, the Renaissance setting gives away the fact that this illustration cannot be a truthful representation of the original tomb.

FURTHER READING: F. Raffaelli, *Il monumento di Papa Gregorio XII*, Fermo, 1874; G. A. Vogel, *De ecclesiis Recanatensi et Lauretana*, Recineti, 1859.

Antipope Alexander V (June 26, 1409–May 3, 1410) *Pietro Philarghi*. Possibly poisoned. Because he died so suddenly in Bologna, some thought he had been poisoned by his rival for the papal throne, Baldassare Coscia (Antipope John XXIII, d. 1419). His body was exposed for eight days after the internal embalming by Dr. Pietro d'Argellata, professor of anatomy at the University of Padua. An observer recorded the embalming:

Nevertheless I relate this method to you as it is the same one used to embalm the highest pontiff, Pope Alexander V. His doctor opened up the abdomen to the pubis, making a straight line incision without injuring the viscera, tying up the colon in two places, cutting it between the two ligatures, leaving out the waste. The rest of the intestines were then removed together with all the viscera. He then used a sponge and washed everything clean with alcohol, and proceeded to pour alcohol into the body. He then used a sponge to dry up any moisture that was left. He then filled the whole abdominal cavity with one pound of aloe, caballainies [a coarse kind of aloe used as a medicine for horses], succatrinol [a syrupy preservative], acaciae [a kind of gum], nucis xuperuni [a kind of nut], Galluae [a sweet-smelling shrub], and muscatae [a fragrant wine]. Then he covered the abdomen with cotton, powder, and more cotton, repeating this until the whole cavity was filled, after which the domestic appeared and sewed the body up in the same manner in which a furrier would sew up furs. They then put powder into the cavity of the esophagus and larynx, and filled it with cotton, adding balsam. They put egg white into the rectum. They then made a few more tufts of cotton and put them into the mouth, nostrils, and ears. After all this they covered the entire body with waxed linen to which a little turpentine was added. They also put his thighs and arms close to the body and covered them with linen. When finished, they put his ornate Papal cloak on him because he had to lie for eight days without giving offensive odor. This method of embalming the Doctors of that era liked best. In this way the putrefaction of the dead body was prevented. The

Monument to Antipope Alexander V in the Church of St. Francis, Bologna. Drawing by Joan Reardon.

face of the Pope was washed with thoroughly salted rosewater.[272]

Alexander's face, hands, and feet were left undressed because they had to be seen at the funeral. The intestines and other viscera were buried immediately in an unknown location.

The existing tomb for Alexander may not be the original, as the account-books for the monastery of St. Francis claim that in the year 1424, there is an entry for stones "for the sepulcher of Pope Alexander."[273] The terra cotta and stucco tomb (stone and marble were particularly difficult to procure in Bologna) was commissioned by the favorite secretary of Alexander V, Leonardi Bruni, and sculpted by Niccolo di Pietro of Arezzo. The effigy was taken from a death mask (which was later preserved in the monastery) with the mouth actually open; it can still be

seen on the colorful tomb. In 1482, payments were made to Sperandio da Mantova, " the famous medallist," to decorate the monument so it would retain the classical style that was popular in the late fifteenth century. Medieval papal tomb historian H.K. Mann writes,

This well-balanced monument may be said to be made up of three parts—a high elaborately decorated basement with two angels resting on shields that display the flaming star of the Pope's arms; a sarcophagus divided by four short pillars into three panels which again display the arms, and with a narrow border or frieze, resting on the pilasters which shows six winged heads (This frieze is said to be the only portion of Sperandio's work which has survived the damage done to the monument by wanton injuries and translations); and finally, the recumbent figure of the Pontiff wearing a pointed triple crown. The couch on which the figure rests is inclined at an angle toward the spectator, and rests beneath a highly decorated ridge on which stands a statue of our Lady bearing her Child, and the statues of St. Francis and St. Anthony on each side of her. In the course of restorations of the monument in 1584 and 1672, seemingly during the former, a drapery in red fresco was painted on the wall behind the mausoleum, and at its top a half-figure of the Eternal Father with outstretched hand above the statue of our Lady."[274]

Originally placed behind the choir of the Franciscan Church of Bologna, the tomb was moved in 1807 to the Certosa outside the walls of Bologna to be repaired (although its restoration wasn't begun until 1837). It was brought back to the Church of St. Francis in 1889 and is now located on the left side of the nave of the church. As one looks straight at the tomb, on the right side of the monument is the original inscription:

SUMMUS PASTORUM ALEXANDER QUINTUS, /
ET OMNIS SCRIPTURAE LUMEN SANCTISSIMUS /
ORDO MINORUM QUEM DEDIT, / ET PROPRIO
CRETENSIS NOMINE PETRUS: / MIGRAVIT,
ANNO DOMINI MCCCCX.[275]

("Greatest of pastors, Alexander V, and most holy light of the whole Scripture, from the Franciscan Order to which he dedicated himself, and Peter of Candia by name, departed to the light from above and blessed thrones, in the year 1410."—*Trans. Ruth Yeuk Chun Leung*)

On the left side:

ALEXANDER V / BONONIENSIS / PONT. MAX. / CRETENSIS. EX. DOMICILIO / CRETENSIS. NVNCVPATVS / HAC NOSTRA IN ECCLESIA / REQVIESCIT / VT QVIBVSCVM / EODEM INSTITVTO / EADEMQVE SODALITATE / IVNCTVS VIXERAT / EISDEM ET DEFVNCTVS / IVNGERETVR / MONVENTVM / EX TEMPLO QVOD FVIT S. FRANCISCI / ANNO MDCCCVII / NVECTVM INSTAVRATVMQVE / ANNO MDCCCXXXVI / CVRA ET IMPENSA / ORDINIS MVNICIP / HVC TRANSLATVM / ET AD VETVS OPERIS EXEMPLAR / RESTITVTVM EST

("Alexander V, supreme pontiff in Bologna, from a Cretan family. Called a Cretan, in this church of ours he rests, so that as he lived and joined himself in brotherhood with whomsoever he had instituted, he may die and join with them. The monument was inferred and renewed from the sanctuary which was in St. Francis in the year 1836, [then] translated here by the administration and expense of the senatorial body [and] restored to the original form."—*Trans. Ruth Yeuk Chun Leung*)

Also on the right side:

HOC MONVMENTVM AN / MCCCCLXXXII SEPVLCRO / ALEXANDRI V PONT MAX / FRANCISCAES IMPOSVERVNT / AD ARCVM PRIMVM ABSIDIS / AVSTRALEM-QVOD OPVS / NICOLAO PETRI ARETINO / GEORGIVS VASARI TRIBVERAM / DEIN SPERANDIO MANTVANO / PROBATA HISTORIAE FIDES / VINDICAVIT-INSTAVRATVM / MDLXXXIII PIETATE ET / IMPENSA IOAN-BAPT PAGANI / ZANETTINI ITERVM A MDCLXXII / A. MDCCCVII TEMPLO AD PROFANA / CONVERSO DIFFRACTVM / PARTESQVE CVM RELIQVIIS / PONTIFICIS IN NOVVM / COEMETERIVM PVBLICVM / ILIATAE SVNT VBIA. MDCCCXXXVI / COAGMENTATVM INCOMPTA / ARTE-HOC POSTEA TEMPLO / NOVARI COEPTO SACRISONE / A MDCCCLXXXVI FELICITER / REDDITO MONVMENTVM / TRIENNIO POST AB ORDINE / MVNIC. CONCESSVM FRANCISCO / BATTAGLINI CARD. ARCHIEP. / PRIMO HONORI

RESTITVENDVM / HEIC REPOSITVM EST / AD PRISTINAM FORMAM / REDINTEGRATVM EX BENIGNIATEM / MVNIFICA LEONIS XIII / PONT. MAX. QVI EODEM CARD / ARCHIEP. ET CVRATORIBVS / TEMPLI INSTANTIBVS / SPLENDIDE PRAESTITIT VTI / RELIQVIAE DECESSORIS / TVTO HONESTISSIMEQVE / CONQVIESCERENT SOLLEMNI / RITV RECONDITAE DIE / X OCT. A. MDCCCXCIII / OVARVM RERVM MEMORIAM / ET VETERES MAVSOLEI / TITVLOS NEOCORI / EXTARE VOLVERVNT

("In the year 1482 the Franciscans laid this monument upon the sepulcher of Supreme Pontiff Alexander V at the main southern arch of Absidis, which work Georgius Vasari assigned to Nicolao Petri Aretino, thereafter defended by Sperandio Mantuano with historical proof, restored in the 1583 by the piety and expense of John-Baptiste Pagani Zanettii and again in the year 1672. In the year 1807, while the temple was turned to the profane, it was shattered, and pieces of it along with the remains of the pontiff were transferred to the new public cemetery in Ubia. In 1836 they were clumped together by unkempt skill. After this, when reconstruction of the temple began, and in the year 1886, 30 years after, by the senatorial body, it was granted with supreme honor to Cardinal Archbishop Francisco Battaglini to repair the monument. Then it was returned to its previous form by the bountiful kindness of Supreme Pontiff Leon XIII, who presented himself splendidly with the cardinal archbishop himself and the curators who were devoted to the temple, so that the remains of the deceased might rest safely and most honorably. When the solemn rite was reestablished on the tenth day of October in the year 1893, they wished to make known the memory of the joyful world and old inscriptions of the tomb decor."—*Trans. Ruth Yeuk Chun Leung*)

Antipope John XXIII (May 17, 1410– May 29, 1415) *Baldaserre Coscia*. Died November 22, 1419, at age 59 from a sickness in Florence, Italy. He had been deposed by the council of Constance in 1415 and was consequently imprisoned in Heidelberg, Germany. He owed his release to his friend and fellow Florentine Cosimo Medici, who paid a high price for his ransom. Because John resigned the papacy to Martin V, he was given the honor of the cardinalate of Tusculum. What Martin did not count on, however, was that his former rival would not only be the recipient of an immense funeral, but would be buried in the prestigious baptistery of the Cathedral of Florence.

But how did an antipope (and one who began his career as a pirate) attain burial in such an esteemed place? More or less by barter: Long ago he had procured the finger of St. John the Baptist and donated it to the Cathedral. That donation had secured his burial in the baptistery.

Because of his commitment to the city of Florence, Coscia was given an unprecedented threefold funeral that celebrated him as pope and cardinal, as civil servant of Florence, and as Baldasarre Coscia, the man. The entire funeral celebration is described in great detail in Sharon Strocchia's *Death and Ritual in Renaissance Florence*; here is a summary: The day after his death, Coscia was dressed in a white miter and cassock and brought to the baptistery at the Cathedral of Florence, where he was placed on the baptismal font. The Office of the Dead was recited, after which the body was moved to a place beneath the pulpit in the baptistery, where it lay for eight days during the novena celebration. The first of the three funeral masses was paid for by Coscia's private estate and was held in the cathedral, although the body remained in the baptistery. Coscia's cardinal's hat lay on the bier in place of the body because this funeral also celebrated Coscia as cardinal. The massive catafalque, decorated with black draperies that bore Coscia's coat of arms, was surrounded by candles and eighty mourners dressed in black, each holding his own lighted candle. City dignitaries, bishops, archbishops, knights, judges, guild captains, and cardinals all attended this portion of the funeral celebration, giving hundreds of torches as well as palls of black and gold as funeral gifts. After the mass was said, the bier carrying Coscia's red hat was transferred to the baptistery.

The second part of the funeral was very similar in ceremonial aspects to the first part, and also took place in the cathedral, but this time the concentration was on John's devotion and civic acts for the city of Florence, and so this portion was paid for by the city. The only cardinal present was Coscia's nephew, Tommaso Brancacci, which further emphasized the civil (as opposed to ecclesiastical) overtones in this dedication of Coscia's devotion to Florence.

Finally, the third requiem paid homage to Baldasarre Coscia, the private man. Of the three ceremonies, this was the only one held exclusively in the baptistery. Coscia's family attended, along with 44 poor men dressed at the state's expense in white, to symbolize Coscia's charitable works. After the bishop of Fiesole performed mass, the participants accompanied Coscia's kin back to their house as was customary in private funerals.

In 1422 Cosimo de' Medici commissioned Coscia's tomb to be sculpted by Donatello and Bartolomeo di Michelozzo; they finished almost six years later. The base of the tomb is sculpted with garlands and Christian cherub heads, and the three niches above the base house three Virtues: Faith, Charity, and Hope. Above the Virtues are three coats of arms; the middle is the arms of the church, the right side is the arms of Coscia as pope (the right side being more important in medieval heraldry), and the left side is Coscia's arms as cardinal. In the lunette, the Virgin and Child welcome the soul of Coscia into eternity.[276] The inscription reads:

JOANNES QUONDAM PAPA / XXIII OBIIT FLORENTIAE / ANNO DOMINI MCCCCXVIIII XI / KALENDAS JANUARII

("John XXIII, formerly pope and Florentine. Died in the year of our Lord 1419, on the eleventh calends of January.")

Pope Martin V (d. 1431) attempted to have the inscription on the tomb changed to reflect Coscia's status as cardinal only, but he was unsuccessful, so the papal inscription remains.

Tomb monument of Antipope John XXIII, Baptistery of the Duomo, Florence.

FURTHER READING: Sharon Strocchia, *Death and Ritual in Rennaisance Florence*, Johns Hopkins University Press, 1992.

Martin V (November 11, 1417–February 20, 1431) *Oddo Colonna*. Died suddenly of apoplexy at age 63 in Rome and was buried in a "pavement" tomb of imported Florentine bronze carved in the basso-relievo style. Most art historians agree the sculptor was Giovanni Ghini, a Florentine goldsmith,[277] but whoever the sculptor he shows the definite influence of Donatello in his work. Thus, Martin's tomb began the renaissance of art in Rome. The tomb originally rested in the middle of the basilica before the heads of the apostles in St. John Lateran (which was also the Colonna family church).

The inscription read:

MARTINVS PP V SEDIT ANNOS XIII / MENSES IIII
DIES XII OBIIT AN. / M CCCC. XXXI DIS XX
FEBRARII / TEMPORVM SVORVM FILICITAS[278]

The tomb of Martin V in St. John Lateran. By permission of the Houghton Library, Harvard University.

("Pope Martin V held the chair for 13 years 3 months and 12 days. He died in the year 1431 on the 20th of February. The happiness of his age."[279])

In 1853, the tomb was placed before the high altar of St. John Lateran with another inscription:

MARTINI V R. P. CONDITORIVM / MARMOREIS
EMBLEMATIBVS ORNATVM / AENEO OCCLVSVM
OPERCVLO / SIMONIS FLORENTINI ARTE
COELATO / ANNO 1433 / PIO IX PONTIFICE
MAXIMO / SECLVSVM ET OPERTVM /
E TESSELLATO ECCLESIAE PAVIMENTO /
HVC TRANSLATVM EST / VI IDVS FEBR. 1853

("The public burial place of Martin V, adorned with marble mosaics, sealed with a bronze lid carved by the art of Simon of Florence, in the year 1433 by Supreme Pontiff Pius IX. It was closed off and concealed with mosaic and pave-

Tomb of Martin V, St. John Lateran. From Ferdinand Gregorovius, *Tombs of the Popes.*

ment of the church, and was translated here on the sixth, the ides of February, 1853." — *Trans. Ruth Yeuk Chun Leung*)

Today the tomb of Martin V, although still in front of the high altar in St. John Lateran, is covered with a Plexiglas cover to protect it from coins that people toss. Unfortunately it cannot be seen at all.

FURTHER READING: Lazaroni and Munoz, *Filarete*, Rome, 1908; F. Martinucci, "Breve commentario intorno le reparzaioni esequite all'altare papale di Martino V," in V. Tizzani's *Del sepolcro di papa M. V,* Rome, 1867.

Antipope Clement (VIII) (June 10, 1423–July 26, 1429; d. 1447) *Gil Sanchez Muñoz.* Died from apoplexy at age 86, having been appointed bishop of Palma by Martin V (to whom he abdicated on July 26, 1429). He is buried in a beautiful monument in the Cappella de la Piedad in the Cathedral of Palma, Spain. He requested, on his deathbed, that his bishop's hat hang over his tomb, and it still hangs there today.

Antipope Benedict (XIV) (November 12, 1425–?: d.?) *Bernard Garnier.* Bernard Garnier was elected pope expressly by Cardinal Jean Carrier, who did it out of spite for not having been included in the election that produced Antipope Clement VIII. Garnier took the name of Benedict XIV and went into hiding, thus receiving the nickname "the hidden pope." Garnier died a few years later, but being excommunicate, he was refused funeral services, and his body was shoveled into a grave at the foot of a rock in Armagnac, Spain. Meanwhile, Jean Carrier elected himself as pope, also taking the name of Benedict XIV, and so became a sort of counter antipope. He was almost immediately arrested, and spent his "reign" in the prison of Castle Foix, France, where he eventually died. The second antipope Benedict XIV is rarely considered important enough even to rate mention.

Eugenius IV (March 3, 1431–February 23, 1447) *Gabriele Condulmaro.* Died of plague at age 64. On his deathbed he confessed that he wished he'd never left his monastery,[280] and he stated that if he died in Rome, he wanted a simple tomb like Eugenius III, along with an equally unpretentious epitaph, because he despised the vain things in the world. After he died, his body was prepared with balsam[281] and presented for public veneration for only a day because of the commotions caused by crowds flocking to see the papal body. His funeral is the oldest example of a "feigned representation of the corpse," meaning that the body was buried and the novena celebrated around an empty catafalque. Yet they kept up the illusion that it was a real funeral by placing two footmen in mourning clothes at the foot of the catafalque, who slowly moved papal fans back and forth to simulate shooing flies.[282]

Eugenius's tomb, commissioned by his nephew Cardinal Peter Barbo (although the epitaph states it was erected by order of another nephew, Francesco Condulmari), was sculpted by Isaia da Pisa and Pellegrino di Antonio da Viterbo. The shell lunette at the top of the tomb is symbolic of the soul's regeneration; the triptych below the shell contains the Madonna and Child in the center, flanked by two angels, while the niches contain statuettes of the doctors of the Church: Ambrose, Augustine, Gregory the Great, and Bonaventure.

Eugenius was originally buried at the western extremity of the outer southern aisle of St. Peter's but was moved to the outer northern aisle in the eastern part of the basilica during demolition of old St. Peter's in the early seventeenth century. Church canon and historian Giacomo Grimaldi recorded the original epitaph:

Tomb of Eugenius IV in San Salvatore in Lauro, Rome. From H.K. Mann, *Tombs and Portraits of the Popes.*

EUGENIUS IACET HIC QUARTUS, COR NOBILE CUIUS / TESTANTUR VITAE SPLENDIDA FACTA SUAE. / ISTIUS ANTE SACROS SE PRAEBUIT ALTER AB ORTU / ALTER AB OCCASU CAESAR UTERQUE PEDES, / ALTER UT ACCIPIAT FIDEI DOCUMENTA LATINAE, / ALTER UT AURATO CINGAT HONORE CAPUT. / QUO DUCE ET ARMENII GRAIORUM EXEMPLA SECUTI / ROMANARN AGNORUNT A ETHIOPESQUE FIDEM, / INDE SYRI AC ARABES

MUNDIQUE E FINIBUS INDI. / MAGNA, SED HAEC ANIMO CUNCTA MINORA SUO. / NAM VALIDA RURSUM THEUCROS IAM CLASSE PETEBAT. / DUM PETIT AST ILLUM SUSTULIT ATRA DIES. / QUI SEMPER VANOS TUMULI CONTEMPSIT HONORES / ATQUE HAC IMPRESSA CONDITE, DIXIT, HUMO, / SED NON QUEM RUBRO DECORAVERAT ILLE GALERO, / NON HOC FRANCISCUS, STIRPS SUA CLARA TULIT, / SUSCEPTIQUE MEMOR MERITI TAM NOBILE QUOD NUNC / CERNIS, TAM PRAESTANS SURGERE IUSSIT OPUS.[283]

("Here lies Eugenius IV. The splendid deeds of his life bear witness to the nobility of his heart. Two emperors presented themselves at his holy feet, one from the East, the other from the West, the one to accept the documents of the Latin faith, the other to crown his head with gold. Recognizing him as the leader, the Armenians, following the example of the Greeks, as well as the Aethiopians, endorsed the Roman faith, then the Syrians, the Arabs, and the Indians from the end of the world. These were certainly great things, but the soul of the Pope yearned for more. He was once again trying to attack the Turks with a mighty fleet when black death swept him off. He had always held the vain honors of the tomb in contempt and said: 'Bury me in this dug-out earth.' But Francesco, his famous descendant, whom he had honored with the red hat, did not tolerate this. Grateful for the benefit, he gave orders to erect the noble and magnificent tomb, which you now see."[284])

This epitaph is not entirely accurate as the attack on the Turks actually happened several years before the pope's death, but praising the pope in all his temporal greatness was more important than historical accuracy when it came to recording the high points of a papacy.[285]

Luckily the monument was moved to San Salvatore in Lauro, Rome, in the early seventeenth century and escaped total demolition during the destruction of St. Peter's. The following epitaph was written when the tomb was brought to San Salvatore in Lauro:

URBS VENETUM DEDIT ORTUM. QUID ROMA? URBIS ET ORBIS IURA. / DET OPTANTI CAELICA REGNA DEUS. / MEMORIAE / EUGENII IIII, / SUMMI ATQ(ue) OPTIMI PONTIFICIS. / HIC IN PACE GRAVIS, IN BELLIS PRO CHRISTI ECCLESIA IMPIGER, / IN INIURIIS PATIENS, RELIGIOSORUM AMATOR AC IN ERUDITOS VIROS MUNIFICUS, / CONCILII BASILEENSIS INSOLENTIAM / ADVERSUS PONTIFICIAM ROMANAM POTESTATEM / CONCILIO, FLORENTIAE CELEBRATO REFRENAVIT AC FREGIT, / IN QUO / IOANNES PALEOLOGUS GRAECIAE IMPERATOR / ROMANUM CAPUT AGNOSCENS / EIUS PEDIBUS SE MULTASQ(ue) EXTERNAS ET REMOTAS NATIONES HUMILL(ime) SUBSTRAVIT. CONGREGATIO CANONICOR(um) S. GEORGII IN ALGA VENET(orum) / FUNDATORI RELIGIOSISSIMO PIETATIS CAUSSA P(onendum) C(uravit)[286]

("The city of the Venetians gave origin. What Rome? Authority over the city and the world. May God grant him his wish and take him into the kingdom of Heaven. To the memory of Eugenius IV, the excellent supreme pontiff. He was venerable in peace, energetic in the wars for the church of Christ, patient with injustices, a friend of the monks and generous towards the learned. At the council held in Florence he checked and broke the insolence of the council of Basel towards the power of the Pope. At Florence John Paleologus, the emperor of Greece, acknowledged the primacy of Rome and very humbly prostrated himself at the Papal feet together with many foreign and remote nations. The congregation of the canons of S. Georgio at Alga in Venice [erected this monument] out of gratitude to their most pious founder."[287])

A rejected epitaph submitted by the Christian humanist Maffeo Veggio for the tomb in San Salvatore in Lauro reads:

DUM STUDET ECCLESIAM PLACIDA COMPONERE PACE, / ACTAQUE PARS VOTI, PARS QUOQUE AGENDA SUI, / EUGENIUS QUARTUS MORIENS HIC OSSA RELIQUIT. / SIC NECE PRAERUPTURN QUOD BENE COEPIT OPUS. / DEBUERANT DURAE TANTISPER FERRE SORORES / TARDIUS ET VITAE SOLVERE PENSA BREVIS. / TUNC UBI PAX TERRIS, QUAM MIRO ARDEBAT AMORE, / REDDITA, TUNC CAELO RESTITUENDUS ERAT. / SED DEUS, ACTUTUM SEDES ORNARE BEATAS / CONSULTUMQUE SUIS MALUIT IRE BONIS.[288]

("While trying to restore undisturbed peace to the church, one part of his wishes realized, another still to be fulfilled, Eugenius IV left here his dying bones. Thus death cut short a promising work. The cruel Fates should have awaited a little and cut the thread of a brief life later. He should have been returned to Heaven only after peace, which he loved with a wonderful zeal, had been restored to the earth. But it was God's will that the abodes of the blessed should have their ornament [i.e., the soul of the Pope] without delay and that care should be taken of his own good people."[289])

The tomb was moved to its final resting place on the left side of the nave in the monastery church next to San Salvatore in Lauro, and access is possible only with the help of the very kind, friendly, and helpful sacristan of the church. (See the next pope, Antipope Felix V, for a poem about the combined grave of Eugene IV with Antipope Felix V.)

FURTHER READING: E. Steinmann, *Rom in der Renaissance*, Leipzig, 1899; F. Burger, *Geschichte des florentinischen Grabmals,* Strassburg, 1904; A. Paolucci, "Monumenti sepolcrali della seconda meta del Quattrocento in Roma," in *Roma,* Rome, X, 1932.

Antipope Felix V   (November 5, 1439–April 7, 1449; d. January 7, 1451) *Amadeus VIII, Duke of Savoy.* He died at age 68 in Geneva, Switzerland, and was buried in Ripaille, France, at the Abbey of Hautecombe (along with a lot of the early counts of Savoy). Unfortunately the abbey was looted during the French revolution and Felix's tomb destroyed. His name now appears on a memorial plaque with those of his family members whose tombs were also destroyed.

Oliver de la Marche wrote in "Le Chevalier delibère" (1483) about a graveyard where Fresche Memoire shows the author the tombs and graves of famous people. One grave had occupants: Pope Eugenius IV and Antipope Felix V:

Dex papes desoubz ung tombeau
Geürent, Felix et Eugene.
Ceulx firent ung scisme nouveau:
Chascun pour faire son plus beau
Voult estre pape en ung temps mesme.
Lèglise en eult douleur et paine,
Maise debile les mist en terre
Et fist la fin de ceste guerre.

(Two popes are lying under one tomb:
Felix and Eugene.
They made a new schism,
Each of them did his very best,
Both would like to be pope at the same time.
The church had grief and pain,
But Disease put them in the ground
And made an end to this war."—*Provided and translated by Bas Jongenelen*)

Nicholas V   (March 6, 1447–March 24, 1455) *Tommaso Parentucelli.* Died from gout and depression over a lack of enthusiasm for a new crusade, at age 52. His marble monument, commissioned by Cardinal Calandini and carved by Mino da Fiesole, was originally located in the left outer aisle by the great sacristy of St. Peter's, although it was later moved during the demolition of St. Peter's in the seventeenth century, to the right outer aisle of the eastern portion of the basilica. The original epitaph (the last to be written in verse) was attributed to Aeneas Sylvius Piccolomini (Pius II, d. 1464):

HIC SITA SUNT QUINTI NICOLAI ANTISTITIS OSSA / AUREA QUI DEDERAT SAECULA ROMA TIBI / CONSILIO ILLUSTRIS, VIRTUTE ILLUSTRIOR OMNI / EXCOLUIT DOCTOS DOCTIOR IPSE VIROS / ABSTULIT ERROREM QUO SCHISMA INFECERAT ORBEM / RESTITUIT MORES MOENIA TEMPLA DOMOS / TUM BERNARDINO STATUIT SUA SACRA SENENSI / SANCTA IOBELEI TEMPORA DUM CELEBRAT. / CINXIT HONORE CAPUT FRIDERICI ET CONIUGIS AUREO / RES ITALAS ICTO FOEDERE COMPOSUIT. / ATTICA ROMANAE COMPLURA VOLUMINA LINQUAE / PRODIDIT, EN TUMULO FUNDITE THURA SACRO. / SEDIT AN(nos) VIII DIES XX, VIX(it) AN(nos) LVII M(enses) IIII DIES VIIII. / PHILIPPUS CARDINALIS BONON(iensis) FRATRI CAR(issimo) P(osuit)[290]

("Here are placed the bones of the pontiff Nicholas V, who gave to you, Rome, the age of gold. Illustrious for good sense, more illustrious for every virtue, he honored the learned men, he being more learned than every other. Having taken away the error with which the schism had poisoned the world, he reestablished good customs, the walls, the churches, the houses. He decreed sainthood for Bernardine of Siena to the honor of the altars, while he celebrated the time of the Holy Jubilee. He placed the crown on the head of Frederick and his spouse, and organized the states of Italy, forming them into a federation. He had many Greek works translated into Italian. Sprinkle incense on this sacred tomb! He sat [reigned] 8 years and 20 days. He lived 57 years, 4 months, 9 days. Philip, cardinal of Bologna, [placed] this [monument] to his brother."—*Trans. Father Tom Carleton*)

This epigram was probably written by the Christian humanist Maffeo Veggio:

PONTIFICUIS SUMMI NICOLAI HIC CONDITA QUINTI / OSSA CUBANT, LIBER SPIRITUS ASTRA COLIT. / AEMULUS ILLE NUMAE, PACEM SED PRAETULIT ARMIS, / PRAETULIT ET DIRIS CANTICA SANCTA TUBIS / MIRO IDEM STUDIO RITUS CULTUSQUE SACRORUM / CURAVIT, MIRA

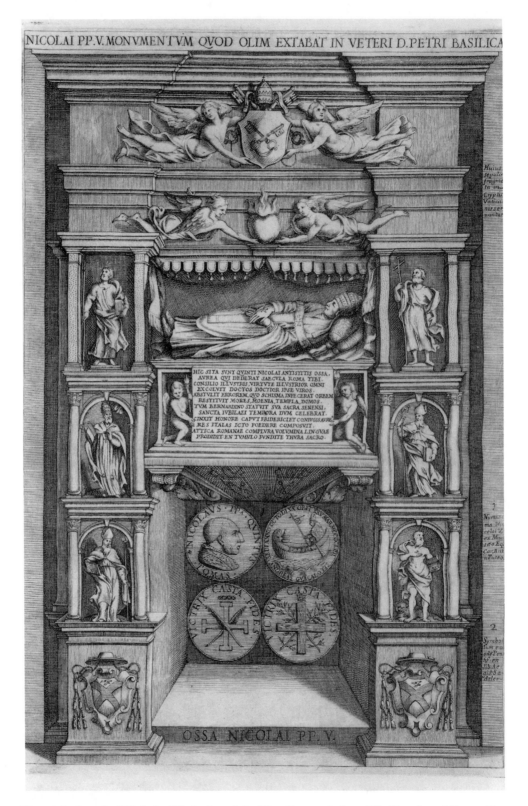

The original tomb of Nicholas V in St. Peter's Basilica. By permission of the Houghton Library, Harvard University.

Sarcophagus of Nicholas V, Vatican grottoes.

DONAQUE SACRA FIDE. / ALTER ET AUGUSTUS DOCTOS DOCTISSIMUS IPSE / EXCOLUIT SUMMA SEMPER ET AUXIT OPE. / EXTULIT ATQUE ALTAE RENOVAVIT MOENIA ROMAE. / EXTULIT INGENTES ET RENOVAVIT OPES, / SAECULA QUI MAGNI IUBILEI LAETA SACRAVIT, / CAESAREUM RUTILO CINXIT ET ORBE CAPUT, / SCISSUM ECCLESIAE PASTOR COMPEGIT OVILE, / AD SUAQUE ERRANTES CLAUSTRA REDUXIT OVES.[291]

("Here lie buried the bones of the supreme pontiff Nicholas V. His spirit, free, dwells in the heights. Rivaling Numa [second king of Rome], he preferred peace to weapons and preferred holy songs to fearsome trumpets. With remarkable zeal he cared for sacred rites and worship, and with remarkable faith, he cared for the holy gifts. Another Augustus, he was most learned, for he cultivated intelligent men, always enriched them with the greatest aid, raised up massive wealth and renewed the high walls of high Rome. He consecrated the year of the great jubilee and girded the chief city of the Caesars with a red-gold ring. He mended the broken flock of the Church and led the wandering sheep back to his enclosure.—*Trans. Father Thomas Buffer*)

Although his monument was destroyed during the demolition of St. Peter's, Nicholas's sarcophagus with the deathbed image of the pope was relocated on Sept 11, 1606, to the Vatican crypt, where it can still be seen today. The sarcophagus inscription reads:

OSSA NICOLAI PP V

("The bones of Pope Nicholas V")

FURTHER READING: E. Muntz, "Les Arts à la Cour des Papes pendant le XV et XVI siècle," I, in *Bibl. Ec franc.*, Paris, IV, 1878; Virgilio Cardinal Noe, *Le Tombe e i Monumenti*, Rome, 2000.

Callistus III

Callistus III (April 8, 1455–August 6, 1458) *Alfonso de Borja (Borgia)*. Died from gout, in Rome, at age 70. His original tomb (covered by a marble slab with the inscription CALLISTUS PAPA III, "Pope Callistus III") was made of brick and located under the floor of the Chapel of St. Mary delle febbre (St. Mary of the Fevers—the more easterly of the two round chapels that stood outside St.

The original monument to Callistus III, St. Peter's, according to Ciacconius. By permission of the Houghton Library, Harvard University.

106. - STATO ORIGINARIO DELLA TOMBA DI CALLISTO III.
(disegno di G. Grimaldi nella Biblioteca Vaticana, Barb. Lat. 2733 f. 14)

The original tomb monument of Callistus III, St. Peter's, according to Giacomo Grimaldi.

Peter's), as is recorded by church canon and historian Giacomo Grimaldi:

> Callixtus III was buried beside the altar of St. Mary of the Fevers. A great marble tablet marked the place, with the inscription "Callistus Papa III." The noble and elegant marble sepulcher of Callixtus was constructed on the wall of the chapel by Rodrigo Borgia, cardinal vice-chancellor, Callixtus's nephew [*trans. Phyllis Jestice*].[292]

Callistus's nephew, Pope Alexander VI (1492–1503), commissioned Paolino di Antonio di Binasco to make a grand mausoleum with the inscription CALIXTUS TERTIUS PONT. MAX. ("Callistus III, Supreme Pontiff") to be placed in the chapel. This monument, decorated with statues of Saint Callistus I, St. Nicholas, St. Augustine, and St. Vincenzo Ferrer (who had predicted Callistus's papacy), was placed at a position behind the organ.

Interestingly, church historian Alphonso Ciacconius's illustration of Callistus's original tomb is much more ornate than Grimaldi's illustration, and one cannot be sure which portrait of the mausoleum is accurate. Regardless, the original monument was destroyed in the sixteenth century. Luckily the sarcophagus with the effigy of Callistus survived and can now be seen in the Vatican grottoes, as can bits of the original monument including the sculpture of the Suffering of Christ, and statues of St. Augustine and Gregory the Great.

In 1582, church historian Alpharanus wrote that the body of Callistus's nephew, Pope Alexander VI (1492–1503), was placed along with Callistus in a vaulted marble tomb which had been built into the wall of the oratory in honor of Saints Andrew and James, in the Chapel of Santa Maria delle

Top: The original sarcophagus from the monument of Callistus III, Vatican grottoes. *Right:* The vaulted marble tomb that contained the remains of Popes Callistus III and Alexander VI (d. 1503) From H.K. Mann, *Tombs and Portraits of the Popes.*

febbre. In 1586, when the Oratory of Saints Andrew and James was destroyed during the destruction of St. Peter's, the remains of the Borgia popes were placed in a tomb with a small pyramid at the top. (See Appendix 4 for picture.) Grimaldi goes on to describe the reinterment of both Callistus and Alexander VI:

> In 1586, in Lent, it was taken apart and the bones of Callixtus and Alexander were honorably moved to behind the organ in the old basilica, where they remained until 1605 [*trans. Phyllis Jestice*].[293]

The epitaph was recorded by the historian Forcella (Forcella III 706):

OSSA / CALLISTI III ALEXANDRI VI / E GENTE BORGIANA SVMMORVM PONTIFICVM / ALEXANDRI CORPVS IN SACRARIO / BASILICAE CVM SACELLVM

VBI / QVIESCEBAT OCCVPARET IN CALLI / STI PATRVI SEPVLCRVM MARMO / REO OPERE E REGIONE SCVLPT V / A BASILICANIS ILLATVM EST / DEINDE IN OBELISCI TRANSLA / TIONE SVB SIXTO V PROPTER / MACHINAS CALLISTI SEPVLCRO / DISIECTO AMBORVM PONTIFICVM / OSSA SVB LAPIDE REPERTA IOAN / NES BAPTISTA VIVES VALENTINVS / APOSTOLICAE SEDIS PROTONOTARIVS / DE NVMERO ET SVBDIACONVS / IN BASILICA VETERI DECENTER / PONI CVRAVIT IN CVIVS DEMO / LITIONE SVB PAVLO V IDEM OB / HONOREM COMMVNIS PATRIAE / ET AD ANIMI SVI DEVOTIONEM / ATQVE OBSERVANTIAM ERGA /

Monument to Popes Callistus III and his nephew Alexander VI (d. 1503) in Santa Maria de Monserrato, Rome.

ILLVSTRISSIMAM GENTEM / BORGIAM
SIGNIFICANDAM / IN HVNC LOCVM TRANSTVLIT /
ANNO M DCV / PRESENTIBVS ILLVSTRISS. ET /
REVERENDISS. D D CARDINALE ZAPATA
AC EXCELLENTISS. / D MARCHIONE DE
BILLENA / ORATORE CATHOLICO[294]

("The bones of Callistus III and Alexander VI, the supreme pontiffs of the Borgia family. While the body of Alexander, in the sacristy of the church, occupied the chapel where it used to lie, it was brought into his uncle Callistus's sepulcher, which was sculpted directly out of marble. Thereafter in the translation of the obelisk under Sixtus V the bones of both pontiffs were discovered under a gravestone as Callistus's sepulcher had been laid in ruin. Valentinus, the living John the Baptist outstanding in rank, fittingly deacon of the Apostolic See in the old church, by the order of Paul V took care to have it displayed in its demolished form in return for public honor. For the devotion and respect for their souls and to make known the most illustrious Borgia family, it was transferred to the tomb in this place in the year 1515. By a Catholic orator in the presence of the most illustrious and reverent Cardinal Zapata, doctor of divinity, and most excellent Lord Marchion of Billena."—*Trans. Ruth Yeuk Chun Leung*)

Later in 1605, the tomb was moved to the angle made by the dividing wall and the outer left aisle of St. Peter's. On February 13, 1610, the pyramidal tomb was broken up and the urn containing the bones of both popes was taken to the Spanish national church of Rome, Santa Maria di Monserrato (as they were of Spanish descent), and placed in a wooden box behind the altar in the sacristy. In 1881, the remains were placed within the small monument sculpted by Filippo Moratilla in the chapel of St. Diego, which is located immediately to the right at the entrance of the church. The names are transposed under their portraits. Papal tomb historian Ferdinand Gregorovius, however, claims that the remains of the Borgia popes are in the sacristy, contained in a wooden chest with the following inscription:

LOS HUESOS DE LOS PAPAS ESTAN
EN ESTA CASETA, Y SON CALISTO Y
ALEXANDER VI. Y ERAN ESPANOLES.

("The bodies of the popes are in this case, and they are Callistus and Alexander VI, and they were Spanish.")

For further information and pictures on the tombs and burials of Callistus III, see Alexander VI (1492–1503).

FURTHER READING: M. Armellini, *Le chiese di Roma*, 1889; E. Tormo, *Monumentos de Espanoles en Roma, etc.*, I, Madrid, 1942; A. Signoretti, "Il sonno dei Borgia," in *Il Momento*, Rome, Feb. 4, 1949; Virgilio Cardinal Noe, *Le Tombe e i Monumenti*, Rome, 2000.

Pius II (August 19, 1458–August 15, 1464) *Enea Silvo Piccolomini*. Died at age 59 of fever at the seaport of Ancona, Italy. Pius was waiting anxiously at the port of Ancona for the enthusiastic masses to show up for his crusade against the infidels, but only a few people appeared, and he died depressed and heartbroken. Pius's heart was enshrined in the Duomo of Ancona, in the Temple of San Ciriaco, while the rest of his body was returned to Rome. The heart reliquary inscription reads:

MCCCCLXIIII XIX KLS SEPT / PII II /
PONT MAX PRAE / CORDIA TVMV /
LANTVR / CORPVS ROMAM / TRANSLATVM
ANCO (nae) / MORITVR DVM /
IN TVRCAS BELLVM / PARAT[295]

("The 19th of September, 1464, the heart of the supreme pontiff Pius II was translated to Ancona and buried. His body was buried in Rome. He died while he was preparing for the war against the Turks."—*Trans. Ruth Yeuk Chun Leung*)

In Rome, Pius's body was placed in an ancient marble sarcophagus with the inscription PIVS II PONTIFEX MAXIMVS ("Pius II, Supreme Pontiff). (Douglas Sladen, in *Old Saint Peter's*, claims that his body was never placed in that particular sarcophagus, yet he does not say where the body would have gone.[296]) Pius's tomb monument, done by either Pasquino Politiano, Niccolo della Guardia, Pietro Paulo da Todi, or Pasquino da Montepulciano, was erected by Pius's uncle, Cardinal Francesco of Siena (later Pope Pius III), in 1464. Above the sarcophagus is the Blessed Mother and Child, with St. Peter presenting the kneeling pope to her; on her other side the archangel Michael presents Pius as a cardinal. In the side niches are the allegorical figures of Science, Strength, Prudence, Justice, Truth, and Charity, while the bas-relief under the sarcophagus depicts the translation of the head of St. Andrew. Some fragments of the tomb broke off during the move from St Peter's and can now be found in the Louvre in Paris.

Pius was originally buried, as he had wished, in the Chapel of St. Andrew in St. Peter's. His is one of the earliest epitaphs written in prose (previous epitaphs were in verse). His original monument epitaph read:

PIUS II PONTIFEX MAXIMUS, NATIONE TUSCUS, /
PATRIA SENENSIS, GENTE PICCOLOMINEA. / SEDIT
ANNOS VI. BREVIS PONTIFICATUS INGENS FUIT
GLORIA. / CONVENTUM CHRISTIANORUM
MANTUAE PRO FIDE HABUIT, OPPUGNATORIBUS /
ROMANAE SEDIS INTRA ATQUE EXTRA ITLAIAM

RESTITIT, / CATHARINAM SENENSEM INTER
SANCTOS CHRISTI RETULIT, PRAGMATICAM / IN
GALLIA ABROGAVIT, FERDINADUM ARAGONENSEM
IN REGNUM / SICILIAE CIS FRETUM RESTITUIT,
REM ECCLESIA AUXIT, FODINAS / INVENTI TUM
PRIMUM ALUMINIS APUD TOLFAM INSTITUIT,
CULTOR / IUSTITAE ET RELIGIONIS, ADMIRABILIS
ELOQUIO. VADENS IN BELLUM / QUOD TURCIS
INDIXERAT, ANCONAE DECESSIT. IBI ET CLASSEM
PARATAM / ET DUCEM VENETORUM CUM SUO
SENATU COMMILITONES CHRISTI HABUIT. /
RELATUS IN URBEM EST PATRUM DECRETO,
ET HIC CONDITUS UBI CAPUT / ANDREAE
APOSTOLI AD SE EX PELOPONNESO
ADVECTUM COLLOCARI IUSSERAT. / VIXIT
ANNOS LVIII MENSES IX DIES XXVII. /
FRANCISCUS CARDINALIS SENENSIS AVUNCULO
SANCTISSIMO FECIT / ANNO MCCCCLX IIII.[297]

("Pius II, the supreme pontiff, a Tuscan from Siena, of the family of the Piccolomini. He held the chair for six years. His brief papacy was great in glory. He held a council of the Christians at Mantua in defense of faith, fought the enemies of the Roman seat inside and outside Italy, placed Caterina of Siena among the Saints of Christ, abolished the pragmatic sanction in France, reinstated Ferdinand of Aragon in the kingdom of Sicily this side of the strait, and enlarged the wealth of the church. He set up the mines of aluminum recently found at Tolfa. He was a friend of justice and religion, admirable in eloquence. Going to the war which he had declared on the Turks, he died at Ancona. There he found a navy prepared, as well as the Doge of Venice, with his senate as brothers in arms for Christ. He was brought back to Rome at the order of the cardinals and buried here where the head of the Apostle Andrew, brought to him from Peloponnesus, had been placed by his command. He lived for 58 years, 9 months, 27 days. Francesco, the cardinal of Siena, built this tomb for his most blessed uncle in the year 1464."[298])

A literary epigram, written in classical hendecasyllables, was composed by the Bishop of Terni for Pius[299]:

ECCE HOC IN TUMULO PIUM SECUNDUM / NE TU
CREDE: PIUS PETIVIT ASTRA / TERRIES GLORIA
NOMINIS VAGATUR / PRAETERQUAM OSSA NIHIL
RELIQUIT URNAE[300]

The tomb monument of Pius II, San Andrea della Valle, Rome.

("Do not believe Pius the Second to be lying in this sepulcher: Pius has ascended to the stars. The glory of his name has spread all over the world, in the urn he has left nothing but his bones."[301])

The monument was moved from St. Peter's in 1614 to the church of San Andrea della Valle, Rome, and remained the same, although the original epitaph was replaced with another very similar epitaph:

PIVS P̄P̄ II / PIVS II PONT. MAX. NATIONE TVSCVS PATRIA SENEN. GENTE PICO / LOMINEA SEDIT AN. VI AVGVSTA IN ANGVSTO PONTIFICATV GLORIA / CONVENTVM CHRISTIANORVM MANTVAE PRO FIDE HABVIT / OPPVGNATORIBVS ROM. SEDIS INTRA ATQ. EXTRA ITALIAM RESTITIT / CATHARINAM SENEN. INTER SANCTAS CHRISTI RETVLIT IN GALLIA / PRAGMATICAM ABROGAVIT FERDINANDVM ARAGONEN. IN REGNVM / SICILIAE CIS FRETVM RESTITVIT REM ECCLESIAE AVXIT FODINAS / INVENTI TVM PRIMVM ALVMINIS APVD TOLFAM INSTITVIT CVLTOR / IVSTITIAE ET RELIGIONIS ELOQVIO ADMIRABILIS PARATA CLASSE / AC VENETORVM DVCE CVM SVO SENATV COMMILITONIBVS CHRISTI HABITIS / IN BELLO TVRCIS INDICTO ANCONAE DECESSIT EX PATRVM DECRETO IN VRBEM / RELATVS IN BASILICA S. PETRI AN. MCCCCLXIIII CONDITVR TVM RELICTO / IBIDEM CAPITE S. ANDREAE APOST. VBI AD SE EX PELOPONESO ADVECTVM COLLOCARAT / ALEXANDRI PERETTI CARD. MONTALTI PIETATE HVC CVM PII III NEPOTIS OSSIBVS / SVMMO TRANSLATVS HONORE HIC HONORIFICE TVMVLATVR / KAL FEBR. AN. MDCXXIII / ALEXANDER PERETTVS / S. R. E. VICE CANCELL / CARD. MONTALTVS / IN PICCOLOMINEORVM DOMO / A CONSTANTIA AMALPHI DVCE / CLERICIS REGVLARIB. DONO DATA / B. ANDREAE TEMPLVM AEDIFICAVIT / PIO II P. M. MONVMENTVM / RESTITVIT ET ORNAVIT / AN. SAL. M D C L XIIII[302]

("Supreme Pontiff Pius II, from the Piccolomini family of Sienna in Tuscany, was enthroned for six years with magnificent glory in his brief pontificate. He held the assembly of Christians in Mantua in favor of their faith and resisted against the assailants of the Roman See inside and outside Italy. He brought Catherine of Siena among the saints of Christ. In Gaul he repealed the Pragmatic Sanction. He restored Ferrante of Aragon to kingship on this side of the Sicilian Strait. He increased church prop-erty. He then set up mines of aluminum first discovered near Tolfa. Admirable advocate of justice and piety in speech, supported by a well-equipped force and a general of the Venetians with his senate as his fellow-soldiers of Christ, he died in the war against the Turks in Ancona. By the decree of the fathers he was brought back to the city, and was buried in the church of St. Peter in the year 1464. Then his head was left in the same place as St. Andrew the Apostle, where he had settled upon his arrival from the Peloponnese, by the piety of Alexander Perettus, Cardinal of Montaltus, with the bones of his nephew Pius III. He was translated with greatest honor and buried honorably in the month of February, in the year 1623. Alexander Perettus of the Most Holy Roman Church.

"In the house of the Piccolomini, by the agreement with General Amalphus. Dedicated to the regular clerics in the church of St. Andrew, he built this sanctuary. This monument of Pius II he restored and adorned in the Year of our Savior 1614."—Trans. *Ruth Yeuk Chun Leung*)

Like previous epitaphs, this one mentions nothing of the pope's failures during his tenure and concentrates only on his good points.

FURTHER READING: R. Papini, "Un disegno del sepolcro di P. II in Roma," in *L'Arte*, Rome, XIII, 1910; E. Lavagnino, "Andrea Bregno e la sua bottega," in *L'Arte*, XXVII, 1924.

Paul II (August 30, 1464–July 26, 1471)

Pietro Barbo. Died at age 54 from an apoplectic fit brought on by indigestion as a result of gorging himself on melons. Papal historian Platina (who had no love for Paul) claimed that the melons were poisoned, and yet another theory claims he died of a stroke with no melons involved. The people of Rome, always happy for a scandalous story, whispered that Paul was strangled by a spirit trapped in one of his rings.[303]

Paul had felt fine on the day of his death, but he began to feel ill toward nightfall and so retired to bed. His chamberlain came to check on him after about an hour, only to find Paul foaming at the mouth. The cham-

The original tomb monument of Paul II, from Ciacconius, *Vitae....*

Sarcophagus of Paul II, Vatican grottoes.

berlain ran for help, but by the time he returned with the doctor, the pope had died.[304] Always one to plan ahead, Paul had ordered the huge sarcophagus of Saint Constantia, daughter of Constantine the Great, taken from the church of San Constanza and brought to his palace of San Marco so that when the time came, he could be buried in it — and so he was.[305] Paul's original monument featured his sarcophagus and his effigy by Giovanni Dalmata in the middle, with the figures of Matthew, Mark, Luke, and John carved by Mino da Fiesole in the side niches. Of the five bas-reliefs below the sarcophagus, Mino carved Strength, the Creation of Eve, Charity, and the Original Sin while Dalmata sculpted Hope. Atop the monument in the lunette is the Universal Judgment, by Mino, while below are reliefs of the Resurrection of Christ and the Glory of Eternity by Dalmata. Finished in 1477, the monument was originally located against the outer left wall (not far from the transept) of St. Peter's, but in 1544 was moved to the eastern portion

of the basilica. It was torn down in the seventeenth century; today all that remains is the sarcophagus, which can be seen in the Vatican grottoes. Church canon and historian Giacomo Grimaldi describes the monument as follows:

This sepulcher was most elegant and very tall, with marble statues or images of Faith, Hope, and Love, the work of Giovanni Dalmata (which can be seen today affixed to the wall in the ambit of the holy Confession), along with Adam and Eve (which were taken away before the demolition), along with a tree and serpent, along with the coat of arms of Marco, cardinal Barbo, cardinal and patriarch of Aquileia. Above these images rose columns of white marble sculpted with flowers, with architraves and ornaments. In the middle of this monument stood the sarcophagus, with the image of Paul II resting on it, wearing the triple tiara and pontifical vestments and made very elegantly, as can be seen now under the vault of the new pavement. Above the image of the pope was carved the resurrection of Christ (which is now also attached to the wall in the ambit of the holy Confession). The tomb was ornamented with the pontifical coat of arms: a lion rampant with an oblique spear. Above the capital of the column rose an arch, within which was carved the universal judgment with the images of our redeemer Jesus Christ judging from his throne of majesty, of Peter and Paul, of the archangel Michael, and of other saints to the number of 39, with Hell and demons at the left hand, and on the right of Jesus Christ Paul II, garbed in cope and tiara with clasped hands, and Emperor Frederick III in imperial garb and crown, the two offering the just, led by John the Baptist, for the judgment of God. Above the Judgment was a marble image of God the eternal father, crowned, with eight angels (which, along with the Judgment, can now be seen affixed to the wall under the vault of the new pavement in the ambit of the holy Confession) [*trans. Phyllis Jestice*].[306]

Interestingly, Grimaldi names Faith, Hope, and Love as the Virtues, whereas Renzo Montini, in *Le Tombe dei Papi*, lists the Virtues as Strength, Charity, and Hope. Grimaldi notes that the mausoleum was "constructed of Parian marble by Marco Barbo, cardinal of St. Mark's."

The original epitaph read:

PAULUS II VENETUS PONT(ifex) MAX(imus) E VETUSTA BARBORUM FAMILIA, PRAECLARIS NATURAE DOTIB(us) AVUNCULO EUGENIO IIII NON INFERIOR, IUSTITIAE, PIETATIS DIVINAR(um)QUE CAERIMONIAR(um) CULTOR RELIGIOSISS(imils), ECCLESIASTICAE LIBERTATIS MAIESTATISQUE DEFENSOR CONSTANTISS(itnus), PRAECIPUO PACIS SERIVANDAE STUDIO ET SINGULARI OMNIS GENERIS MUNERUM ABSTINENTIA, FORMIDANDA ETIAM LEGE MAGISTRATIB(us) INDICTA CLARISS(imus), IN PRINCIPES MUNIFICENTIA, IN PAUPERES MISERICORDIA INSIGNIS. PATRIO AMORE ANNONAE COPIAM URBI DEDIT, PATRIMONIUM BEATI PETRI ERRATIS POPULOR(um) INDULGENTISS(inii) PARENTIS AFFECTU EMENDATIS ET CONSERVAVIT ET AUXIT. FURENTES ARMIS HAERETICOS REPRESSIT, ET QUOD PER DIFFICILEM RER(um) TEMPOR(um)VE CONDITIONEM EFFICI CUM DIGNITATE NON POTERAT, MATURA CUNCTATIONE SALUBERRIME DISPOSUIT. V(ixit)

A(nnos) LIII M(enses) V D(ies) III, S(edit) A(nnos) VI M(enses) X D(ies) XXVI.[307]

("Paul II, high priest, of Venetian origin, from the ancient Barbo family. Not inferior in natural gifts to his uncle Eugene IV, he was a most religious promoter of justice, of piety and of sacred ceremonies. He was a strenuous defender of the freedom and preeminence of the Church, with great solicitude in preserving peace, with singular abstinence from every type of special favor, to be applied even by law to the magistrates. Distinguished for munificence toward rulers, known for mercy toward the poor, out of love for the fatherland he gave an abundance of produce to the city [of Rome]. After having reformed the errors of the people, with the most indulgent affection of a parent, he preserved and increased the patrimony of Blessed Peter. He put down with arms the furious heretics and disposed difficul matters in these troubled times with opportune patience. He lived 53 years, 5 months, 3 days. He held the seat 6 years, 10 months, 26 days. Mark Barbo, cardinal of Saint Mark, patriarch of Aquilea, placed [this monument] to his well-deserving relative in the year of salvation 1477." — *Trans. Father Tom Carleton*)

FURTHER READING: D. Gnoli, "Il monumento di P. II," in *Arch. St. dell'Arte*, Rome, III, 1890; G. de Nicola, "Il sepolcro di P. II," in *Boll. D'Arte*, Rome, II, 1908; Virgilio Cardinal Noe, *Le Tombe e i Monumenti* Rome, 2000.

Sixtus IV (August 9, 1471–August 12, 1484) *Francesco della Rovere*. Died from fever and severe gout in Rome at age 70, although the Romans liked to say his death was a result of having peace forced on him by the cities and princes of Italy.[308] Johann Burchard, the master of ceremonies for several popes including Sixtus, recorded what happened when the Romans heard that Sixtus had died:

When he died, groups of youths devastated the pope's nephew Count Giraolamo Riario palace, so badly that not a door or window was left in tact. Others went to the Castle Giubileo where they stole cows, goats, pigs, asses, geese, and roosters that belonged to the Countess, among which was a great amount of salted meat, and round Parmesan cheese. When they returned to Rome, they forced open the granaries of the churches of San Teodoro and Santa Maria Nuova. At Sant' Andrea delle Fratte, meanwhile, Battista Collerosso and his sons attacked the shop of a baker, killing him.[309]

A nasty little poem also circulated in Rome:

Sixtus, you're dead at last. Rome is full of
  bliss
Because of your reign's hunger, disaster and
  injustice.[310]

Burchard goes on to describe how even pontifical employees took part in the looting after the death of Sixtus:

The abbot of San Sebastiano, the sacristan, took the bed and all its adornments although, considering my office, these things properly belonged to me. Everything else was stolen, so to say, in an instant, no sooner than the corpse had been carried out of the room. And indeed, despite all my hunting from the sixth to the tenth hours, I was unable to find either oil or a handkerchief, or any sort of receptacle, in which to put the wine and the water scented with herbs to wash to corpse; and not even socks or a clean shirt to dress it.[311]

Penitentiaries placed his corpse, dressed in sacred vestments (Burchard admits that Sixtus should have been buried in a Franciscan habit, but mistakenly was not), on the bier so that it could be publicly displayed. Burchard describes the scene:

At first the corpse was set before the high altar, raised, then lowered a bit, with the head turned toward the altar, and the feet sticking out of a closed iron grate, in such a way that those who wanted to could kiss them. Later on the grate was opened, and the deceased was moved closer to the altar, so that everyone could enter and exit freely; nevertheless we posted some guards, so that no one could steal the ring or anything else. It remained there until about one at night.[312]

Sixtus's body was carried into the church on August 13 and immediately buried, although the obsequies began on August 17 and continued through August 25.

The Florentine Antonio Pollaiuolo took ten years to complete Sixtus's bronze floor tomb, finishing in 1453. The base of the tomb was made from green Lacedemonian marble. On either side of the death effigy are the Virtues (Charity, Truth, Prudence, Strength, Hope, Temperance, and Justice); and to represent Sixtus's considerable intellect and education, the Arts and Sciences (Arithmetic, Astrology, Dialectics, Rhetoric, Gram-

Floor tomb of Sixtus IV, Vatican treasury.

mar, Perspective, Music, Geometry, Philosophy, and Theology) cover the marble base of the tomb. Papal tomb historian H.K. Mann describes these female figures as "affected to the last degree, and their general want of naturalness is only equaled by their want of sufficient clothing."[313] On a more serious note, Mann describes the effigy itself as "one of the finest medieval monuments in St. Peter's…. The face, with its deep furrows and projecting chin, is full of character, and the very veins of his hands … are almost throbbing with warm blood."[314]

The epitaph is inaccurate in two places: The pope died on the 12th of August, not the 13th, and in the fourth, not fifth, hour of the night.[315] The epitaph (in classical form) reads:

SIXTO QUAR(to) PONT(ifici) MAX(imo) EX ORDINE MINORUM, DOCTRINA / ET ANIMI MAGNITUDINE OMNIS MEMORIAE PRINCIPI, / TURCIS ITALIA SUMMOTIS, AUCTORITATE SEDIS AUCTA, / URBE INSTAURATA TEMPLIS PONTE FORO VIIS. BIBLIO / THECA IN VATICANO PUBBLICATA, IUBILEO CELEBRATO, / LIGURIA SERVITUTE LIBERATA, CUM MODICE AC PLANO / SOLO CONDI SE MANDAVISSET, / IULIANUS CARDINALIS PATRUO B(ene) M(erenti) MAIORE PIETATE / QUAM IMPENSA F(aciundum) CUR(avit). / OBIT IDIB(us) SEXTIL(ibus) HORA AB OCCASU QUINTA AN(no) CHR(isti) MCDLXXXIIII, VIXIT / ANNOS LXX DIES XXII HORAS XII / OPVS ANTONI POLLAIOLI / FLORENTINI ARG. AVRO / PICT. AERE CLARI / AN. DO. MCCCCLXXXXIIII[316]

("To Sixtus IV, the supreme pontiff, of the orders of the Franciscans, by his doctrine and magnanimity an ever-remembered sovereign. He banished the Turks from Italy; increased the authority of the seat; renewed the city with churches, a bridge, a market-place, streets; opened the library in the Vatican to the public; celebrated the Jubilee; delivered Liguria from slavery. Because he had ordered that he should be buried modestly and on level ground, Cardinal Giuliano had this tomb erected to his well-deserving uncle, with greater piety than expense. He died on the ides of August in the fifth hour of the night in the year of Christ 1484. He lived for 70 years, 22 days, 12 hours."[317] ("The work of Antoni Pollaioli of

Florence, with silver and gold, embellished with shining copper in the year of the Lord 1493."—*Trans. Ruth Yeuk Chun Leung*)

The tomb was first located in the choir chapel that Sixtus had built in the southern part of St. Peter's, but it was moved in 1610 to the sacristy to spare it from the destruction of the basilica. At that time the coffin was opened and they found a sapphire (valued at 30 scudi), a brass medal with the pope's image on one side and the Madonna between St. Francis and St. Barnadine on the other, and 30 pieces of gold and silver money.[318]

In 1625 the tomb was moved to the Chapel del Coro in new St. Peter's, then in 1635 back to the Chapel of the Blessed Sacrament, when the following plaque was added:

SIXTI IV IVLII II ROMM PONTT / NATIONE LIGVR. P ATRIA SAONEN GENTE ROBORREA / GALEOTTI DE RVVERE / CARD S. PETRI AD VINCVLA / IVLII II SORORIS FILII ET / FATII SANCTORI / CARD S. SABINAE ET EPISC. CAESENATEN / DEPOSITI SVB HOC ELEGANTISSIMO AENEO MONVMENTO / VIII CALEND. SEPTEMBRIS MDCXXXV

("The mortal remains of Sixtus IV and Julius II, Roman pontiffs, of Liguria, from the city of Savona, of the Rovere family and of Galeotto of Rovere, titular cardinal of Saint Peter in Chains, son of the sister of Julian II, and of Fazio Santoro, titular cardinal of Santa Sabina and bishop of Cesena. Placed underneath the most elegant bronze monument. The eighth of September, 1635."—*Trans. Ruth Yeuk Chun Leung*)

In 1926 Sixtus's remains were removed and combined with those of his nephew Giuliano della Rovere (Julius II, d. 1513) inside St. Peter's (underneath the pavement in front of the monument to Clement X), where a marble plaque on the floor reads:

SIXTI IV IVLII II ROMM PONTT / NATIONE LIGVR. PATRIA SAONEN GENTE ROBOREA / GALEOTTI DE RVVERE / CARD S. PETRI AD VINCVLA / IVLII II SORORIS FILII ET / FATII SANCTORI / CARD S. SABINAE ET EPISC. CAESENATEN / LIPSANA HVC TRANSLATA / E. SACELLO SS SACRAMENTI / IDIBVS DECEMBRIS MCMXXVI

("The mortal remains of Sixtus IV and Julius II, Roman pontiffs, of Liguria, from the city of Savona, of the Rovere family and of Galeotto of Rovere, titular cardinal of Saint Peter in Chains, son of the sister of Julius II, and of Fazio Santoro, titular cardinal of Santa Sabina and bishop of Cesena, who was translated from the Blessed Sacrament Chapel, the 13th of December 1926." — *Trans. Father Tom Carleton*)

The tomb stayed in Blessed Sacrament Chapel until the late 1940s when it was moved to its own room in the newly redone crypt. Finally, in the latter half of the twentieth century, the treasury of St. Peter's was completed and the tomb moved there. It can now be seen by itself in a completely black, soulless room, unbefitting of such a fine monument.

FURTHER READING: G. Mauro Castro, "Il cenotafio di S. IV della Rovere nel Museo Petriano," in *Ill. Vaticana*, C.d.V., V, 1934; G. Beltrami, "Il monumento sepolcrale di S. IV e sue vicendi," in *Atti del III Congresso naz. di Studi romani*, Bologna, 1935; L. Gessi, "Il mausoleo di S. IV," in *Avvenire d'Italia*, Rome, 1950; L.D. Ettlinger, "Pollaiuolo's Tomb of Pope Sixtus IV," in *Journal of the Warburg and Courtauld Institutes*, London, XVI, 1953; Reardon, Wendy, *Humanism in the Tomb of Sixtus IV*, unpublished master's thesis, Center for Medieval Studies, the University of Reading, England; Virgilio Cardinal Noe, *Le Tombe e i Monumenti* Rome, 2000.

Innocent VIII

Innocent VIII (August 29, 1484–July 25, 1492) *Giovanni Battista Cibo*. Died at age 60 from digesting a potion of powdered and roasted emeralds that were to help reduce his fever. The rogue monk Savonarola had accurately predicted Innocent's death, although Innocent had actually been on his deathbed for about a year. He often went into deep trances and appeared dead, but was not. During his illness he received several blood transfusions from three young boys (who later died as a result of "donating" their blood). Innocent's last request was for the cardinals to elect someone better than him, and at 6 P.M., on July 25, he had a choking fit

and lost consciousness. He died at vespers that night after being anointed by Bishop Gamboa.[319] The historian Ferdinand Gregorovius said of Innocent's death: "Then he died — a weak and worthless character, devoid of genius or strength of will."[320] His obsequies began on July 28 and lasted until August 5, although his body was not interred until Antonio Pollaiuolo unveiled his monument on January 30, 1498. This is the first papal tomb whose ornaments include a depiction of a live pope rather than a deathbed effigy, which had been the norm for papal tombs up until then. The 4,000 ducat monument features Innocent holding the Holy Lance (with which Longinus had pierced the side of Christ) that the Sultan Bajet had given Innocent in life.[321] On either side of the sitting pope the niches are filled with theological and moral virtues — Prudence, Strength, Justice, and Temperance — while Truth and Hope are in the lunette above, with Charity in the center medallion.

The original bronze and marble monument was first located in the oratory to Our Lady (located near the west end of the left side of the nave in St. Peter's) that Innocent had restored during his pontificate, where he had placed the head of the Holy Lance. On September 5, 1606, during the demolition of St. Peter's, the monument was moved to the sudarium, or outer right aisle of the basilica. The coffin was opened on this occasion (when, according to papal tomb historian Renzo Montini, his body was removed to the polyandrum, or common tomb of the popes, under the high altar in St. Peter's) and once again on September 10, 1621, when a bronze medal representing the true likeness of the pope was discovered.

The original sarcophagus inscription read:

IN INNOCENTIA MEA INGRESSUS SUM. / REDIME ME DOMINE ET MISERERE MEI.[322]

("I will walk in mine integrity: redeem me, and be merciful unto me." — Psalm 25:2[323])

Also on that date in 1621 the monument's structure was inverted to create a

The original bronze and marble monument of Innocent VIII, St. Peter's Basilica. Drawing based on photograph in Renzo Montini, *Le Tombe dei Papi*.

more balanced look than the original placement of the sarcophagus and sitting pope. Now, from the chapel opposite the tomb, when the priest celebrated mass, he would celebrate it facing the sitting image of the pope instead of the deathbed image. A new epitaph was written when the tomb was inverted:

INNOCENTIVS VIII CIBO / IANVENSIS PONT OPT. MAX / VIXIT ANNOS VIII M X DI XXV / OBIIT AN DNI MCDIIIC M IVLII / D O M / INNOCENTIO VIII CIBO PONT. MAX. / ITALICAE PACIS PERPETVO CVSTODI / NOVI ORBIS SVO AEVO INVENTI GLORIA / REGI HISPANIARVM CATHOLICI NOMINE IMPOSITO / CRVCIS SACROSSANCTE REPERTO TITVLO / LANCEA QVAE CHRISTI HAVSIT LATVS / A BAIAZETE TVRCARVM TYRANNO DONO MISSA / AETERNVM INSIGNI / MONVMENTVM E VETERE BASILICA HVC TRANSLATVM / ALBERICVS CIBO

MALASPINA / PRINCEPS MASSAE / FERENTII DVX MARCHIO CARRARIAE ETC. / PRONEPOS / ORNATIVS AVGVSTIVQ. POSVIT ANNO DOM. MDCXXI

("Innocent VIII, Cibo, Genoese, high priest, reigned eight years, 10 months, 25 days. Died in the year of the Lord 1492, in the month of July." To God the greatest and best. In honor of Innocent VIII of the Cibo family, high priest, who continually guarded the peace of Italy; the glory of the new world was discovered in his age. He granted the title of "Catholic" to the king of Spain, restoring the claim of the most holy cross. He received as a gift from the Turkish tyrant Bayezid the lance that pierced Christ's side. Eternally distinguished Alberic Cibo Malaspina, prince of Massae, duke of Ferenza and the marche of Carrara, etc., his great-grandson, moved the monument from the old basilica to this place, making it more ornate and venerable. Placed here in the year of the lord 1621."—*Trans. Father Tom Carlton and Phyllis Jestice*)

Tomb monument of Innocent VIII, St. Peter's basilica.

FURTHER READING: E. Muntz, "La tomba di I. VIII," in *Arch. St. dell'Arte*, Rome, IV, 1891; Virgilio Cardinal Noe, *Le Tombe e i Monumenti*, Rome, 2000.

Alexander VI   (August 11, 1492–August 18, 1503) *Roderigo Borgia*.

Died from either poison or malaria at age 73 in the Borgia apartments in the Vatican. On the morning of August 6, 1503, Alexander watched the funeral of his very obese grand-nephew, Juan Borgia Lanzol (who had just died of malaria), from a window in the Vatican. "This is a bad month for fat men," he said, and just at that moment an owl flew through the window and flopped dead at his feet. "Bad omen! It's a bad omen!" he cried, and ran back to his apartments.

Alexander and his son, Cesare Borgia (an alleged poisoner), went to dine soon afterward at the vineyard of Cardinal Adriano Castellesi da Corneto.[324] Cesare had allegedly instructed a servant to serve a particular wine (some accounts claim it was sweetmeats) to his father and himself, while another particular bottle of wine was to be served to the cardinal. As the servant was pouring the wines, Alexander realized that he had forgotten his consecrated host that he carried with him at all times (an astrologer once told him that as long as he carried this host in a golden box, he could not die).

Alexander called to the same servant that Cesare had ordered to serve the wine and told him to run back to the Vatican to get the gold box. The poor servant had no choice but to go, while in the meantime, another servant came along and served the allegedly poisoned wine to the pope and Cesare.

During the next week both Cesare and the pope became very sick with vomiting and stomach pains (Cardinal Coroneto also became sick but recovered). The pope was bled, while Cesare was dipped alternately in ice water and warm mule entrails (which made his skin peel all over his body) and eventually recovered. After almost a week the pope felt well enough to play cards with some of his cardinals in his apartment, but on the seventeenth of August he became sick again. His master of ceremonies, Johann Burchard, wrote of Alexander's death in his diary. According to Burchard, the next morning Don Pietro Gamboa, Bishop of Carinola, heard Alexander's last confession and served him the Host as five cardinals stood by. That evening, at the hour of Vespers, Alexander received Extreme Unction.

As he was dying, Alexander called out, "Wait a just a little longer, I am coming, I am coming," to no one in particular. Then it was said that an ape appeared in the room, and a cardinal almost caught it as it leaped from the window but Alexander said, "No, it is the devil, let him go."

At the exact moment that Alexander died, people on the street reported seeing seven devils fly from his room. The Romans also whispered that after the death of the previous pope, Innocent VIII, Alexander had made a pact with the devil: In exchange for his soul, he would be pope for twelve years (which he was) with an addition of six days.

The stoic Burchard omitted both rumors in his journal, but recorded the traditional post-papal looting. Burchard writes that Cardinal Jacopo Casanova, when sealing the papal apartments, was forced at knife point by Cesare's henchman Michelotto to surrender the keys to the treasury or be tossed out the window. He surrendered, and Michelotto managed to steal 100,000 ducats for Cesare. Servants then looted everything they could, leaving "nothing with the papal arms except the papal throne and some cushions and hangings on the walls."

Buchard recorded only the facts, which in themselves are astonishing, and continued in his journal to report on the treatment of the corpse. Burchard and other attendants carried the pope's body through his apartments and laid it on a makeshift bier—a table covered with "a crimson cloth and piece of fine tapestry." They placed cushions under the pope's head and shoulders and covered the body with another tapestry; then they left the body for its ritual night alone, with two candles burning.

Burchard sent a messenger to command that all Rome's clergy assembly at five the next morning for the funeral procession. When morning arrived, Burchard stood by while four confessors recited the Office of the Dead, then oversaw the placing of the body in the Sistine Chapel, "whither came the monks of the city, the clery of St. Peter's and the canons bearing the cross." These men formed the funeral procession that carried the body to the basilica of St. Peter's.

The bier was placed toward the end of the basilica as the clergy chanted, "Free Me, O Lord." Suddenly some of the palace guards grabbed the tapers, and when the priests fought back, they brandished their weapons and the priests fled the sacristy, abandoning Alexander's body.

Burchard took action, moving the bier between the high altar and papal seat, although he changed his mind when it was brought to his attention that someone might climb up and desecrate his body. Therefore he moved the bier into the chapel so that Alexander's feet were close enough to the iron door to be touched by the faithful.

There the body stayed day and night, the candles burning down as the corpse's complexion "became increasingly foul and black." And by that afternoon it "had changed to the color of mulberry and of the blackest cloth and it was covered in blue-black spots. The nose was swollen, the mouth distended where the tongue was doubled over, and the lips seemed to fill everything." It was, Burchard says, a horror without precedent.

Later that day, Alexander was carried to his final resting place: the Chapel of Santa Maria della Febbre. Burchard tells us that "six labourers, or porters, making blasphemous jokes about the pope or in contempt of his corpse, together with two master carpenters," were to place the body in its coffin. But "the carpenters had made the coffin too narrow and short, and so they placed the pope's miter at his side, rolled his body up in an old carpet, and pummeled and pushed it into the coffin with their fists."[325]

A verse was found on the funeral bier:

Quis jacet hic. Sextus-Quis funera plangit?
  Erymus.
Quis comes in tanto funere obit? Vitium.
Et quae causa necis? Virus pro homina, virus,
Humane generi vita salusque fuit.

("Who lies here? The sixth. Who bewails his death? Erymus. Who dies as his companion in such a burial? Vice. And what is the cause of death? Poison for a man, poison. For the human race it was life and health." — *Trans. Alan Friedlander*)

A nasty little diptych was posted on the statue named Pasquino (which even to this day is used to post anonymous statements in Rome):

"Torments, perils, violence, fury, rage, lust
You are a horrendous sponge of blood and cruelty."[326]

Sannazzaro, a sixteenth-century historian, wrote the following inscription for Alexander:

FORTASSE NESCIS, CUIUS HIC TUMULUS SIET /
ADSTA VIATOR, NI PIGET. / TITULUM QUEM
ALEXANDRI VIDES, HAUD ILLIUS / MAGNI EST, SED
HUIUS, QUI MODO / LIBIDINOSA SANGUINIS
CAPTUS SITI / TOT CIVITATES INCLYTAS / TOT
REGNA EVERTIT, TOT DUCES LETHO DEDIT, /
NATOS UT IMPLEAT SUOS. / ORBEM RAPINIS,
FERRO ET IGNE FUNDITUS / VASTAVIT, HAUSIT,
ERUIT. / HUMANAN IURA, NEC MINUS
COELESTIA / IPSOSQUE SUSTULIT DEOS. / UT
SCILICET LICERET, HEU SCELUS! PATRI / NATAIE
SINUM PERMINGERE / NEC VENERANDIS
ABSTINERE NUPTIS / TIMORE SUBLATO SEMEL.[327]

("Perhaps you do not know whose tomb this is. Stay, traveler, if you aren't ashamed. The name Alexander that you see inscribed is not at all that of the great, but the name of him who lately, seized by the lustful thirst for blood, has destroyed so many famous cities, so many kingdoms, has slaughtered so many dukes, in order to fill up their places with his own offspring. He has laid waste the world completely with pillage, with sword and fire; he has drained it dry, he has demolished it. He upheld neither human laws nor, even less, the laws of Heaven, and upraised his own gods, so that he, the [Holy] Father, might be allowed—alas, what a crime!—to defile the natal bosom and not to abstain from honored marriage, having cast away all fear, once and for all."—*Trans. Alan Friedlander*)

Alexander's corpse was dressed in a vestment of white cloth with no train, a rochet, red brocade vestments with a short silken undergarment, chasuble, and crimson velvet slippers with golden crosses. He was initially buried in a simple brick vault close to the wall (in the angle to the left of the altar) in the oratory of Saints Cosmas and Damian, in the round chapel of Santa Maria de Febribus (St. Mary of the Fevers) of St. Peter's. Under Pius V (1566–1572) his monument was moved to a new place beside his uncle Callistus III, since his tomb was blocking the entrance to the chapel. The inscription read simply:

ALEXANDRI SEXTI PONTIFICIS
CINERES HIC CLAUDUNTUR

("The ashes of Pope Alexander VI are enclosed here."[328])

As with Alexander's uncle, Callistus III (d. 1458), two illustrations of what is purported to be the original tomb have surfaced: one detailed drawing from Ciacconius, and one simple sketch from Grimaldi. There is no evidence to suggest either is, or is not, the original.

Epitaph on the monument in St. Peters according to Grimaldi:

ΑΙΩΝΙΩ ΘΕΩΝ ÁVΤΟΚΡΑΤΟΡΙ

INGENTES TIBI GRATIAS AGO MORS /
FAVSTVS HOMINVM SEVERA VINDEX /
QVAE ME TERRICVLIS MINACIS ORCI /
VIVENTEM BENE NACTA LIBERASTI /
NEC VERO ES MALA TV SED HERME IN
ASTRIS / IN TERRA SIMILIS

CHAMAELEONTI / NAM FVLVIS NIGRA FVLGIDIS QVOD ATRA ES / ALEXANDER VI PONT. MAX. / PETRO CARANZA PROTONOT APOST ARCHIDIACONO / EX CALATRAVA AB ARCANO / CVBICVLO SVO BENE M. POS AVRA VITALI / FVNCTO ANNO LXVII M V D XIIII / EADEM DEFUNCTO IDIB NOVEMB MDI[329]

("Pope Alexander VI—O stern death, favorable punisher of men, I give you great thanks. While I lived, you came at me with the bogeymen of menacing death, but now you have set me free. Yet neither are you bad, O Death, but

The original monument to Alexander VI in St. Peter's, according to Ciacconius. From H.K. Mann, *Tombs and Portraits of the Popes.*

ΑΙΩΝΙΑ ΘΕΩΝ ΑΥΤΟΚΡΑΤΟΡΙ
INGENTES.TIBI GRATIAS. AGO. MORS.
FASTVS.HOMINVM.SEVERA.VINDEX.
QVAE.ME.TERRICVLIS.MINACIS.ORCI
VIVENTEM.BENE.NACTA.LIBERASTI
NEC VERO.ES.MALA.TV.SED.HERME.IN.ASTRIS
IN.TERRA.SIMILIS.CHAMAELEONTI
NAM.FVLVIS.NIGRA.FVLGIDIS.QVOD.ATRA

ALEXANDER.VI.PONT.MAX.
PETRO.CARANZA.PROTONOT.APOST.AR
CHIDIACONO.EX.CALATRAVA.AB ARCANO
CVBICVLO.SVO.BENE.M.POS.AVRA.VITALI
FVNCTO ANNO.LXVIII.M.V.D.XIIII.
EADEM.DEFVNCTO.IDIB.NOVEMB.MDI.

The original monument to Alexander VI, according to Grimaldi. From *Codex Barbarini Latinus 2733*.

like Mercury among the stars, like a chameleon on earth; for compared to the glittering golden stars you are dark, because you are black. Alexander VI, supreme pontiff, Pietro Caranza, protonotary apostolic, archdeacon, from Calatrava, being his privy chancellor, placed well this marble tablet on his resting place, having finished breathing in his 67th year, 5th month, 14th day, the Ides of November (Nov. 13) 1501 [*sic*; the correct date is 1503, but all recorded versions of this epitaph give the date as MDI, or 1501."—*Trans. Father Thomas Buffer*)[330]

In 1582, church historian Alpharanus wrote that Alexander's uncle, Pope Callistus III (d. 1458), was placed in a vaulted marble tomb along with Alexander which had been built into the wall of the oratory in honor of Saints Andrew and James, in the Chapel of Santa Maria delle Febbre. In 1586, when the oratory of Andrew and James was destroyed during the destruction of St. Peter's, the

remains of the Borgia popes were placed in a tomb with a small pyramid at the top. (See Appendix 4 for picture.) Grimaldi goes on to describe the reinterment of both Callistus III and Alexander VI:

> In 1586, in Lent, it [the tomb monument] was taken apart and the bones of Callistus and Alexander were honorably moved to behind the organ in the old basilica, where they remained until 1605 [*trans. Phyllis Jestice*].[332]

The epitaph was recorded by the historian Forcella (Vol. III, p. 706)[333]:

OSSA / CALLISTI III ALEXANDRI VI / E GENTE BORGIANA SVMMORVM PONTIFICVM / ALEXANDRI CORPVS IN SACRARIO / BASILICAE CVM SACELLVM VBI / QVIESCEBAT OCCVPARET IN CALLI / STI PATRVI SEPVLCRVM MARMO / REO OPERE E REGIONE SCVLPTV / A BASILICANIS ILLATVM EST / DEINDE IN OBELISCI TRANSLA / TIONE SVB SIXTO V PROPTER / MACHINAS CALLISTI SEPVLCRO / DISIECTO AMBORVM PONTIFICVM / OSSA SVB LAPIDE REPERTA IOAN / NES BAPTISTA VIVES VALENTINVS / APOSTOLICAE SEDIS PROTONOTARIVS / DE NVMERO ET SVBDIACONVS / IN BASILICA VETERI DECENTER / PONI CVRAVIT IN CVIVS DEMO / LITIONE SVB PAVLO V IDEM OB / HONOREM COMMVNIS PATRIAE / ET AD ANIMI SVI DEVOTIONEM / ATQVE OBSERVANTIAM ERGA / ILLVSTRISSIMAM GENTEM / BORGIAM SIGNIFICANDAM / IN HVNC LOCVM TRANSTVLIT / ANNO M DCV / PRESENTIBVS ILLVSTRISS. ET / REVERENDISS. D D CARDINALE ZAPATA AC EXCELLENTISS. / D MARCHIONE DE BILLENA / ORATORE CATHOLICO

("The bones of Callistus III and Alexander VI, the supreme pontiffs of the Borgia family. While the body of Alexander, in the sacristy of the church, occupied the chapel where it used to lie, it was brought into his uncle Callistus's sepulcher, which was sculpted directly out of marble. Thereafter in the translation of the obelisk under Sixtus V the bones of both pontiffs were discovered under a gravestone as Callistus's sepulcher had been laid in ruin. Valentinus, the living John the Baptist outstanding in rank, fittingly deacon of the Apostolic See in the old church, by the order of Paul V took care to have it displayed in its demolished form in return for public honor. For the devotion and respect for their souls and to make known the most illustrious Borgia family, it was transferred to the tomb in this place in the year 1515. By a Catholic orator in the presence of the most illustrious and reverent Cardinal Zapata, doctor of divinity, and most excellent Lord Marchion of Billena." — *Trans. Ruth Yeuk Chun Leung*)

Later in 1605, the tomb was moved to the angle made by the dividing wall and the outer left aisle of St. Peter's. On February 13, 1610, the pyramidal tomb was broken up and the urn containing the bones of both popes was taken to the Spanish national church of Rome, Santa Maria di Monserrato (as they were of Spanish descent), and placed in a wooden box behind the altar in the sacristy with the following inscription:

LOS GUESOS DE LOS PAPAS ESTAN
EN ESTA CASETA, Y SON CALISTO Y
ALEXANDER VI. Y ERAN ESPANOLES.

("The bodies of the popes are in this case, and they are Callistus and Alexander VI, and they were Spanish.")

In 1881, the remains were placed within the small monument sculpted by Filippo

Moratilla in the Chapel of St. Diego, which is located immediately to the right at the entrance of the church. The names however, are transposed under their portraits.

FURTHER READING: M. Armellini, *Le chiese di Roma*, 1889; E. Tormo, *Monumentos de Espanoles en Roma, etc.*, I, Madrid, 1942; A. Signoretti, "Il sonno dei Borgia," in *Il Momento*, Rome, Feb. 4, 1949.

Pius III (September 22–October 18, 1503) *Francesco Todeschini-Piccolomini*. Died from gout, at age 64, only 26 days after he was elected. His election was due mostly to his failing health, because the cardinals knew he wouldn't last long and they could spend his short reign playing politics for the next papal election. In fact, Pius was so sick that they omitted several ceremonies just so he could live through his coronation. Johann Burchard, the master of ceremonies, recorded the following after Pius died:

The pope was washed, dressed, and carried into the antechamber where, on a bed, the mattress of which had been covered with green velvet, he was dressed in the sacred

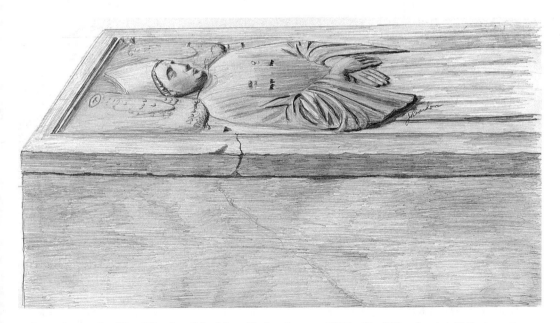

Sarcophagus that Pius III ordered for himself when he was still Cardinal Piccolomini, Vatican grottoes. Drawing by Joan Reardon.

vestments, with the sole exception of the pectoral cross, which was not there, and for which I substituted a cross made with the dangling cinctures, held in place with four pins. He was then transferred to the Hall of the Parrot, and placed upon the table. Meanwhile, in the antechamber and in the Hall of the Parrot, the penitentiaries said the office of the dead without interruption. The cardinals had convened in the Hall of the Pontiffs, then they passed into the Hall of the Parrot, reciting the "Our Father" ... and they kissed the pope's feet.[333]

While he was a cardinal, Pius had had a tomb slab carved for himself with the following epitaph:

FRAN(ciscus) PICCOLOMINEUS CAR(dinalis) SENENSIS, PII II / PONT(ificis) MAX(imi) NEPOS, VIVENS HIC AD AVUNCULI / SANCTISS(imi) PEDES SEPULCHRUM SIBI ET AUGUS(tino) / NEPOTI POSUIT CAPELLAMQ(ue) HANC ORNAVIT / AC PROPRIO AERE DOTAVIT. / VIXIT ANNIS MENS(ibus) DIEB(its)[334]

("Francesco Piccolomini, cardinal of Siena and nephew of Pope Pius II, erected, while living, a sepulcher for himself and for his nephew Agostino, at the feet of his most holy uncle. He also decorated this chapel and endowed it with his own money. He lived for [_] years [_] months [_] days."[335])

Pius was originally buried in the floor of the Chapel of St. Andrew, St. Peter's (in front of where his monument stood), next to Pius II and near the southern wall, close to the entrance of the old basilica. The epitaph slab described above was inverted and used to cover his floor tomb. Pius's monument was carved by Niccolo della Guardia and Pietro Paulo da Todi, crafted of Parisian marble, and gilded and adorned with sculptures. Above the sarcophagus effigy in the center is the Virgin and Child, on either side of which are two apostles (most likely Peter and Paul) presenting Pius as a pope to the Virgin on the left, and as a cardinal on the right. In the side niches are the saints Romualdo, Francis, Pius, Gregory the Great, Andrew, and Giacomo, while the bas-relief is a scene of Pius's coronation. This monument

also has the distinction of being the last entire monument erected in St. Peter's before the demolition began. The original epitaph from St. Peter's (which was replaced when the monument went to San Andrea delle Valle) read:

PIUS III PONTIFEX MAXIMUS, A PIO II AVUNCULO DUOS ET VIGINTI ANNOS NATUS ILL CARDINALIUM COLLEGIUM ASCITUS, URBIS ET PICAENI LEGATIONE INTEGERRIME FUNCTUS, A PAULO II AD FEDERICUM III INISSUS, UT GERMANORUM ARMA IN TURCAS CONCITARET, CONVENTURN FREQUENTISSIMUM PONTIFICIS MORTE DISSOLUTUM HABUIT. SUB INNOCENTIO VIII UMBROS DISSIDENTES PACAVIT, CAROLO GALLOREM REGE ITALIAM IRRUMPENTI AB ALEXANDRO VI SERO ADMODUM OBVIAM MISSUS, EO MORTUO DUO DE QUADRAGINTA PATRUM SUFFRAGIIS PONTIFEX CREATUS, DUM DE RESTITUENDA IN PRISTINAM MAIESTATEM CHRISTIANA REPUBLICA AC URBE AGIT, VI ET XX DIE E TANTA EXPECTATIONERERUM PUBLICO OMNIUM LUCTU DECESSIT, ELOQUIO, PRUDENTIA, RELIGIONE, INNOCENTIA ET GRAVITATE DOMI FORISQUE INSIGNIS, IN DICENDIS IN SENATU SENTENTIIS LIBER ET GRAVISSIMUS. VIXIT ANNOS LXIIII MENSES V DIES X, OBIIT AN(NO) SALUTIS CHRISTI MDIII (ANTE DIEM) XV KAL(ENDAS) NOVEMBRIS. IACOBUS ET ANDREAS FRATRI SANCTISSIMO POSUERE.[336]

("Pius III, the supreme pontiff. Elected by his uncle Pius II into the college of the cardinals at the age of 22, he acted as the legate of Ancona and Rome with great integrity and was sent by Paul II to Frederick III to urge the Germans to take up arms against the Turks. He presided over a great council which had been dissolved at the death of the pope. During the papacy of Innocent VIII he subdued the rebellious Umbrians. Sent by Alexander VI, rather late, to Charles, King of France, who was invading Italy, he was, on the death of Alexander, created pope with 38 votes of the cardinals. While trying to revive the former majesty of the Christian republic, after 26 days he passed away and, disappointing great hopes, was publicly mourned by all. He was remarkable in Rome as well as abroad for eloquence, prudence, piety, honesty, and dignity. At the meetings of the cardinals he expressed his opinions freely and with great dignity. He lived for 58 years, 5 months, 10 days and died in the year of salvation 1503, on the 18th of October. Giacomo and Andrea [dedicated this monument] to their most saintly brother."[337])

Church canon and historian Giacomo Grimaldi recorded the opening of Pius's tomb in 1610 during the demolition of St. Peter's:

> Then the tomb of Pius III was opened. The tomb was at the feet of Pius's uncle Pius II. It had on it: "Pius III Pontifex Maximus." He was buried in the tomb he had chosen as cardinal, with his image carved on the marble, dressed as a deacon, closing the tomb and turning away. It bore the inscription: "Francis Piccolomini, cardinal of Sens, nephew of Pope Pius II here lies buried at the feet of his most holy uncle. *an _____, mens_____, dies.*"
>
> The body of this highest pontiff Pius III, which was completely consumed, was clothed in a very fine chasuble of gold brocade with the figures of saints, and the bones of the body with the holy vestments were conveyed to the marble sarcophagus between Pius II and Hadrian IV [*trans. Phyllis Jestice*].

Pius's body was then placed in an ancient sarcophagus which had been found deeply buried near the choir. The front of the sarcophagus bore the monogram of Christ, and when it became Pius's tomb they simply carved his name in.

In 1614 Pius's monument was transferred to San Andrea della Valle, Rome, by Cardinal Alexandro Peretti, and was placed opposite Pius II at the end of the nave near the transept. A new epitaph replaced the old one.

PIUS III / PIVS TERTIVS PONT. MAX / NATIONE TVSCVS PATRIA SENE / GENTE PICOLOMINEA / SEDIT DIES XXVI / PIO III PONT. MAX. PII II NEPOTI / CVNCTIS VIRTVTIBVS ORNATISSIMO / POST LEGATIONES VRBIS PICENI GALLIAE / ATQVE GERMANIAE INTEGERRIME OBITAS / AD SVMMVM PONTIFIC. EVECTO VI ET XX DIE. / PVBLICO OMNIVM LVCTV VI MORTIS ABREPTO / IACOBVS ET ANDREAS FRATRI SANCTISS. POSS. / VIXIT AN. LXIIII M. V D. X / OBIIT AN. SAL. M C IIII XV KAL. NOVEM. / ALEXANDER PERETTVS / S. R. E. VICE CANCELL. / CARD. MONTALTVS / SEPVLCHRVM PII III PONT. MAX. / ET PII II EX ADVERSO POSITVM / PAVLO V P.M. CONCEDENTE / E VATICANO TRANSLATVM / MAGNIFICENTIVS REPONENDVM / CVRAVIT / AN. SAL. M D C XIIII[338]

("Supreme Pontiff Pius III, from Siena of Tuscany, of the Piccolomini family, was enthroned for 26 days. Supreme Pontiff Pius III, nephew of Pius II, most splendid in all virtues, after his legations in the town of Picenum Gaul and in

Sarcophagus housing the body of Pius III, Vatican grottoes.

Monument to Pius III, San Andrea della Valle, Rome.

Germany were most nobly executed. He was exalted to pontificate and was snatched away on the 26th day while all mourned for his death. The brothers James and Andrew [are now] most holy possessors [of his soul]. He lived for 64 years, five months, and ten days and died in the year of our Savior 1503, on the 15th of November. Alexander Perettus, vice chancellor of the Holy Roman Church, Cardinal Montaltus, caused the sepulcher of Supreme Pontiff Pius III and Pius II to be placed side by side. By the permission of Supreme Pontiff Paul V, it was translated from the Vatican to be preserved most magnificently in the year of our Savior 1614."—*Trans. Ruth Yeuk Chun Leung*)

FURTHER READING: E. Piccolomini, *Alcuni documenti inediti intorno a Pio II ed a Pio III*, Siena, 1871; Virgilio Cardinal Noe, *Le Tombe e i Monumenti*, Rome, 2000.

Julius II (November 1, 1503–February 21, 1513) *Giuliano della Rovere*. "The Warrior Pope," as he was often called, died of fever at age 70. During his last hours, mendicant friars kept watch over him and recorded that he called himself a sinner who had not ruled the church as he should have. After he died, his master of ceremonies, Parride de Grassis, wrote in his diary that he never saw such a crowd at the funeral of a pope. Julius was embalmed and his praecordia deposited in the Vatican grottoes, though it is unclear if they are still there.

He was the only pope of medieval and Renaissance history to discuss his burial with his master of ceremonies because he had seen in the past that dead popes were ignored by everyone and set upon by greedy servants, who sometimes left the corpse "with their private parts exposed." Julius didn't want this to happen to him, so he paid de Grassis in advance to make sure his dignity would be preserved after he died. De Grassis suggested that he would have Julius's corpse wrapped in a white shirt, as was tradition, to which Julius replied that the white cloth should be gilded with gold.[339]

An anecdote circulated in Rome after Julius died, claiming that when Julius approached the gates of heaven, St. Peter told him that because he was so rich he had to go build his own paradise. Julius gave him an ultimatum: Either St. Peter must surrender amicably within three weeks or Julius would bring 60,000 men and take heaven by storm.[340]

While in Avignon, Julius had become inspired by the idea of building an entire church around a tomb, as Clement VI (d. 1352) had done. Julius wanted his glorious tomb in the Cappella Maggiore of St. Peter's, but it didn't quite turn out that way. His massive tomb monument ended up in his titular church of San Pietro in Vincoli, Rome, although his body rests where it was originally deposited in a simple sarcophagus inscribed with "DEPOS(itum) IULII PONTIFIS MAXIMI"[341] ("burial site of Julius, supreme pontiff"; the word "depositum" at that time could have meant "temporary burial," the original intention for that burial site[342]). A simple plaque marks the spot (in front of the tomb of Clement X [d. 1606] in St. Peter's) where Julius rests with his uncle Pope Sixtus IV, who died in 1484 (see Sixtus IV for the plaque marking).

When the great artist Michelangelo Buonarotti was designing Julius's tomb in Bologna, he asked Julius if his outstretched hand of the pontiff was signifying a blessing or a curse. (There is no word on Julius's answer.) Buonarotti also asked Julius if he should place a book in his left hand on the monument, and Julius replied, "No, give me a sword, for I am no Scholasticus!"[343]

The famous cenotaph that was to be Julius's tomb can still be seen in the church of San Pietro in Vincoli. It includes a statue of a horned Moses. The reason Moses—the only sculpture in the cenotaph done by Michelangelo—has horns is because of a mistake in the Latin translation. The Hebrew text says that a radiance shone about Moses' face when he came down from Mount Sinai (Exodus 34: 29), but in Latin, the word for radiance, or "halo," could also be translated as "horns." It is said that when the cenotaph was set up, Jews flocked to it in great num-

Cenotaph to Julius II, San Pietro in Vincoli, Rome. From Ferdinand Gregorovius, *Tombs of the Popes*.

bers to venerate the statue of Moses. In good light and from the correct angle, it is possible to see portraits of Michelangelo and Julius II in Moses' beard.

FURTHER READING: C. Tolnay, *The Tomb of Julius II*, Princeton, 1954; E. Panofsky, "The First Projects of Michelangelo's Tomb of Julius II," in *The Art Bulletin*, New York, XIX, 1937.

Leo X   (March 11, 1513–December 1, 1521)

Giovanni de' Medici. Died at age 46 of either malaria or (as thought by the papal court) poison. Some claim he died of "excessive joy" at the defeat of the French and fall of Milan. The master of ceremonies, Parride de Grassis, had trouble getting enough candles for Leo's funeral because Leo had so completely depleted the papal treasury. Even Raphael's tapestries were pawned to raise money for the funeral. Finally de Grassis was forced to reuse candles from the recent funeral of a cardinal.[344] When Leo died, even his sister Lucrezi Salviati ransacked the Vatican in order to pilfer its treasures.

Leo had survived an earlier poisoning attempt when Cardinal Petrucci arranged to have a surgeon treat the pope's anal fistula with poisoned bandages—but Leo preferred his own doctor, who discovered the plot. Petrucci was strangled with a rope of crimson silk.[345]

At any rate, Leo, who had been warned by a monk that there might be further attempts on his life, was stricken and died of a "mysterious disease." De Grassis recalled that the night before Leo died, he had complained to his cupbearer at supper that the wine tasted bad and bitter. Early in the morning after Leo died, his cupbearer appeared with his dogs at the Porta Castello, saying that he was going hunting, but the alert sentry had him arrested and imprisoned.[346] Francis I of France is cited as the instigator of this poisoning plot against Leo as his revenge for having been abandoned by the pope as a political ally. It was believed Francis bribed the papal cellarer (who retrieved the wine to be poisoned) and the cupbearer (who would give the deadly goblet to Leo), although some say it was the cellarer himself who had a grudge against the pope.

Parride de Grassis thought he saw some signs of poisoning because the corpse soon became swollen with large black spots, and so Leo was autopsied:

> Yet this fever, since it had troubled him periodically, neglected for a long time either by doctors who were fawners or those misguided in judgment, at last lay so heavily upon him that only shortly before his death was it able to be diagnosed, the fatal hour perceived, and with a troubled mind he was snatched. Nevertheless, a few hours before he departed from life, he fell on his knees, joined with stretched hands, his eyes closed in prayer.... There have been those who speculated that he had been taken up by a poisonous draught put into his cup; for his heart displayed spots of dark bluish color, and his spleen was found to be of unnatural thinness, as though the power of this peculiar and secret poison had devoured his entire viscera.... A certain fetial priest, a scoundrel, augmented the suspicion since before sunrise, at the seventh hour of the night when the pontiff expired, this man, in the guise of going hunting with his hounds, went forth through the Vatican gate, so much so that the fugitive was captured by the praetorian guard[34] [*trans. Ruth Yeuk Chun Leung*].

Leo was originally buried in a simple brick tomb in St. Peter's with the inscription: LEONIS X PONT. MAX. DEPOSITVM ("Leo X, High Priest, is buried here").

In 1536 he was moved to an elegant monument carved by Raffaelle da Montelupo in Santa Maria Sopra Minerva, Rome. A likeness of Leo sits in the center of the tomb, while the side niches are occupied by Saints Peter and Paul. Above the figure of the pope is a bas-relief of Leo and Francis I of France, while to the left side is the Baptism of Christ and on the right is the Miracle of St. Julian. The monument bears no inscription, although the poet Pietro Bembo composed a literary epigram for his good friend:

Tomb monument to Leo X, Santa Maria Sopra Minerva, Rome. Drawing based on Montini, *Le Tombe dei Papi.*

DELICIAE HUMANI GENERIS, LEO MAXIME, / TECUM / UT SIMUL ILLUXERE, INTERIERE SIMUL.[348]

("Very great Leo, the delights of humanity, which began to shine with you, also passed away with you."[349])

A poem was posted on the statue named Pasquino (which is used even to this day to post anonymous statements):

> O musicians with your little jokes, weep, O violinists, weep, and weep, Florentines, beating plates and boxes. Weep, thin clowns and flirts, weep, mimes and hammy actors, gluttonous friars, cast into debt by your appetites, weep for your Lord, tyrants, weep, Florence, and all your bankers, and all other official fools. Weep, God's clerics, weep for Peter, weep, all of you, weep for your sins, for Leo the Tenth is dead.[350]

FURTHER READING: U. Middeldorf, "Two Sansovino Drawings," in *Burlington Magazine*, London, LXIV, 1934; J.J. Berthier, *L'eglise de la Minerve a Rome*, Rome, 1910.

Hadrian VI (January 9, 1522–September 14, 1523). *Adrian Dedal (Adrian of Utrecht).* Died at age 64 from stress and heat exhaustion, as well as the lingering effects of an unsuccessful poisoning attempt a month earlier. His death was celebrated by the Romans because he had dispensed with all the artistry and pomp of the papacy that Leo X had encouraged and that the Romans liked. Some Romans were so thankful for Hadrian's death that they sent flowers to the papal doctor who couldn't save him. The cardinals looted his apartments for papal treasure but found only two tiaras, a few chalices, worthless silver vessels, 12 rings, and barely 2000 ducats. They did, however, pawn the silver ring that Hadrian had brought with him from Utrecht, paying the Swiss guards with the proceeds.

Hadrian was originally buried in the Chapel of Santa Andrea in St. Peter's, between Pius II and Pius III. One of the original epitaphs from St. Peter's read:

QUO ROMANORUM SEXTUS PATER, / ANTE SACERDOS HOC ETIARN PIETAS CONDITUS IN TUMULO[351]

("In the very same sepulcher, where the sixth father of the Romans, formerly a priest, is laid to rest, piety is also buried."[352])

The second original epitaph from St. Peter's read:

HADRIANUS SEXTUS HIC SITUS EST, / QUI NIHIL SIBI INFELICIUS IN VITA, / QUAM QUOD IMPERARET, DUXIT[353]

("Here lies Hadrian VI, who thought his sovereign power to have been his greatest misfortune."[354])

Historian Giovio records an epigram in sappheric meter which he maintains was written on the temporary tomb. Actually, it was nothing more than mocking graffiti:

QUARN POTES MERITO OPTIMOQUE IURE INTER PONTIFICES PIOS IACERE MAXIMAE PIETATIS HADRIANE. INSIGNIS PIETAS TUA, HADRIANE, VIVENTI TIBI PROFUIT, DECUSQUE AUREI DIADERNATIS PARAVIT. IURE ID MEHERCULE, AT AEQUIUS TUAEQUE CERTIUS PIETATIS HOC

Tomb monument to Hadrian VI, Santa Maria dell'Anima, Rome. From Ferdinand Gregorovius, *Tombs of the Popes*.

TROPHAEURN EST, DEFUNCTUS QUOD HONORIBUS
TOT, INTER DUOS CONTIGERIT PIOS IACERE.[355]

("Very pious Hadrian, you are lying here between the two Popes Pius by dint of your great
merits. Your outstanding piety, oh Hadrian, did
you great service in your lifetime by gaining
for you the honor of the golden diadem. This
is, by Hercules, quite right. Still, a juster tro-
phy, and one more indicative of your piety, is
the fact that, dying after so honorable a career,
you are allowed to lie between the two Popes
Pius."[356])

And yet another poem about Hadrian
made the rounds in Rome:

Hadrian, treacherous as the sea,
Hypocrite, cruel envious, miserly,
Hateful to all, dear to none,
Enchanter, magician, idolater, hollow,
Rustic, disgraceful, inhuman,
Liar, deceiver, thief, poultry-keeper,
Solitary, bestial and a sorcerer.[357]

In 1533 the body of Hadrian was translated to Santa Maria dell'Anima, the national
German church in Rome, and placed in a
monument (located behind the altar on the
right) commissioned by Cardinal Wilhelm
Enkefortk, designed by Baldasarre Peruzzi,
and carved by Michelangelo of Siena and
Niccolo Tribolo. In the lunette above the
sleeping effigy are the Blessed Virgin and
Child with Saints Peter and Paul. Below the
sarcophagus is a bas-relief of Hadrian's entrance into Rome, while the niches on the
sides hold the figures of Temperance, Strength,
Justice, and Prudence. The epitaph here was
allegedly written by Tranquillus Molossus.

On the sarcophagus:

ADRIANVS / VI PP

Below the sarcophagus:

PROH DOLOR, QVANTUM REFERT IN
QVAE TEMPORA VEL OPTIMI CVIVSQ(ve)
VIRTVS INCIDAT.

Epitaph proper, in bas-relief:

HADRIANO VI PONT(ifici) MAX(imo) EX
TRAIECTO INSIGNI INFER(ioris) GERMANIAE
VRBE, / QUI DUM RERUM HUMANAR(um)
MAXIME AVERSATUR SPLENDOREM / ULTRO A

PROCERIB(us) OB INCOMPARABILEM SACRAR(uni)
DISCIPLINAR(um) SCIENTIAM AC PROPE DIVINAM
CASTISSIMI ANIMI MODERATIONEM / CAROLO V
CAES(ari) AUG(usto) PRAECEPTOR, ECCLE(siae)
DERTUSENSI ANTISTES, SACRI SENATUS PATRIBUS
COLLEGA, HISPANIAR(um) REGNIS PRAESES, /
REIPUB(licae) DENIQ(ue) CHRIST(ianae)
DIVINITUS PONTIF(ex) ABSENS ADSCITUS. VIX(it)
ANN(os) LXIIII MEN(ses) VI D(ies) XIII, /
DECESSIT XVIII K(a)L(endas) OCTOB(ris)
AN(no) A PARTU VIRG(inis) MDXXIII /
PONT(ificatus) SUI ANNO II / WILHELMVS
ENCKENVOIRT ILLIVS BENIGNITATE ET AUSPICIIS
T(i)T(uli) S(ancti) / IO(hannis), / ET PAVLI
PRESB.(yter) CARD(inalis) DERTVSEN(sis)
FACIVNDUM CVR(avit).[358]

("Pope Hadrian VI.—Alas, how much does it
mean in which age the sterling qualities of even
the best of men show themselves.—To Hadrian
VI, supreme pontiff, of Utrecht, the famous city
of Lower Germany. While he utterly renounced
the pomp of the present world, the leading people, recognizing his incomparable learning in
the sacred disciplines and the almost divine
moderation of his most pure soul, of their own
accord made him tutor to Emperor Charles V,
bishop of the church of Tortosa, colleague of
the fathers of the sacred senate, ruler of the
kingdom of Spain and finally, by divine inspi-
ration, in his absence pope of the Christian
republic. He lived for 64 years, 6 months, 13
days, and died on the 14th of September in the
year 1523 after the Nativity of the Virgin and
in the second year of his papacy. This tomb has
been erected by Wilhelm Enckenvoirt, who by
the goodwill and favor of the pope had been
made the presbyter cardinal of the church of St.
John and Paul at Tortosa."[359])

FURTHER READING: J. Schmidlin, "Hadrians
Grab," in Geschicte der deutsch Nationalkirche
in Rom S. Maria dell'Anima, Freiburg, 1906.

Clement VII (November 19, 1523–September 25, 1534) *Giulio de'Medici.* Died at
age 59 of either fever, eating poisoned mush-
rooms, or inhaling smoke from a poisoned
candle during a procession.[360] He was originally buried in a brick tomb in St. Peter's
with the following inscription:

Tomb monument to Clement VII, Santa Maria Sopra Minerva, Rome. Drawing based on photograph in Renzo Montini, *Le Tombe dei Papi*.

CLEMENTI VII PONT. MAX / CVIVS INVICTA
VIRTVS SOLA CLEMENTIA SVPERATA EST[361]

("[The tomb of] Clement VII, supreme pontiff,
whose unconquerable courage was second only
to his clemency."[362])

Clement's monument features the central figure of the pope himself, carved by
Nanni di Baccio Bigio, and flanked by statues of (most likely) Saints Peter and Paul.
Above the pope in bas-relief is the coronation of Carlos V, while to the right of that is
"The Battle Before the Turks" and to the left
is a relief of S. Benedict and Totila. The epitaph reads:

CLEMENTI SEPTIMO PONT(ifici) MAX(imo), /
CUIUS INVICTA VIRTUS / SOLA CLEMENTIA
SUPERATA EST. OBIIT ANNO DOMINI MDXXXIV, /
(ante diem) VI KAL(endas) OCTOB(ris), /
SEDIT ANNOS X M(enses) S D(ies) VIII.[363]

("Clement VII, supreme priest, of high virtues
and clemency, died on the 16th of September
and occupied the chair for 10 years, 10 months,
and 8 days."[364])

The poet Francesco Berni wrote an epigram in memory of Clement VII:

His reign was rich in seeking every way,
In change of mind and trying to be wise,
In if's and but's and no's and ayes,
With nothing ever done, but always much to
say.[365]

Paul III (October 13, 1534–November 10, 1549) *Alessandro Farnese.*

Died at age 81 of a
violent fever in Rome. His last words were
prayers and forgiveness for his grandson,
who was a liar and a thief. Paul was originally
buried in a brick tomb behind the organ in
St. Peter's with the inscription PAULO III
PONT(ifici) MAX(imo)[366] ("Supreme Pontiff
Paul III").

Commissioned by his nephew Cardinal
Alessandro Farnese and sculpted by Guglielmo della Porta at a cost of 24,000 scudi, the
tomb, originally designed to be freestanding,
was finished 25 years after it was begun. The
historian Schrader (Laurentio Schradero)

visited Rome in the late sixteenth century
and copied an epitaph from the tomb before
it had been relocated (from an area near the
transept of St. Peter's). Church canon and
historian Giacomo Grimaldi claims that this
epitaph could only have been carved on the
temporary tomb behind the organ (the
canons Grimaldi spoke to claimed there had
always been only a name, with no epitaph).[367]
Whatever the case, the epitaph recorded by
Schrader is as follows:

DISCITE MORTALES FLUXA UT SIT GLORIA
MUNDI, / UT TERRENA BREVI TEMPORE REGNA
RUANT. / QUI PETRI NUPER SACRATA IN SEDE
SEDEBAM, / DUM TEGERET NOSTRUM SACRA
THIARA CAPUT, / QUI POTUI DUDUM
DARE IURA SUBACTIS, / ANTE MEOS REGES
PROCUBUERE PEDES, / MAXIMUS ET CAESAR
PEDIBUS DEDIT OSCULA NOSTRIS, / NUMEN UT IN
TERRIS IAM VENERATUS ERAM, / TERTIUS HIC
GELIDO CONDOR SUB MARMORE PAULUS, /
CONTINET HAEC CINERES NUNC BREVIS URNA
MEOS. / PONTIFICEM GESSI SUMMUM TER
QUINQUE PER ANNOS, / TEMPESTIVA SENEM
ME LIBITINA RAPIT. / FUNERA NON LACRYMIS
MEA SUNT SPARGENDA, PEREGI / NATURAE
CURSUM, MORS NOVA VITA FUIT.[368]

("Learn, O mortals, how fleeting is the glory of
the world, how the earthly kingdoms fall in
brief time. I, only a short time ago, sat on the
chair of Peter, while the sacred tiara covered
my head. Just a short time ago I could govern
subjects, and before my feet kings bowed down.
Even the greatest caesar kissed my feet; as if a
divinity, I was already venerated on earth. I,
Paul III, am buried under this cold marble; this
little urn now contains my ashes. I held the
high priesthood for 15 years. A sudden death
took me — by now an old man — away. Now
upon my tomb, they shed tears. I have finished
the course of natural life; death was new
life." — *Trans. Father Tom Carleton*)

Paul's monument was moved to its
present place (to the left of the altar of the
canonized popes at the far end of the nave)
in 1599. The wall niche was too small for the
two figures of Mildness and Plenty, so they
are now preserved in a room of the Palazzo
Farnese, Rome. The figure of Prudence that
reclines in front of the pope is a likeness of

Tomb monument to Pope Paul III, St. Peter's Basilica. From Ferdinand Gregorovius, *Tombs of the Popes*.

Paul's mother, Giovanna Gaetani of Sermoneta, while Justice, also reclining in front of the pope, is allegedly the pope's sister Gulia Farnese.[369] Both figures were originally nude, but in 1594, in the Counter Reformation, the sculptor was Bernini was forced to cover them with a metal mantle. Inscription:

PAVLO III / FARNESIO PONT / OPT MAX /
F. GVLIELMVS DELLA PORTA DE
PORLETIA MEDIOLANEN FACIEBAT

("To Paul III, Farnese, supreme pontiff. Put in place by F. William of the Milan Gate of Portlezza." —*Trans. Father Tom Carleton*)

The following verse (it rhymes in the original Italian) was posted on the statue named Pasquino (which is used even to this day as a place to post anonymous statements):

> In this tomb there lies
> A greedy and rapacious vulture.
> That was Paolo Farnese,
> Who never gave, but only took.
> Pray for him, poor thing:
> Died of indigestion.[370]

FURTHER READING: Montini, Renzo, *Tomve di Sovrani in Roma*, Rome, 1957; L. Cadier, "Le tombeau du pape Paul III Farnese de Guglielmo della Porta," in *Mélanges de l'Ecole franc. de Rome*, Paris, 1889; K. Escher, "Zur Geschichte des Grabmals Pauls III. im St. Peter in Rom," in *Repertorium f. Kunstwissensch*, Berlin, XXXII, 1909; E. Steinmann, *Das Grabmal Pauls III in St. Peter in Rom*, Rome, 1912.

Julius III (February 8, 1550–March 23, 1555). *Giovanni Maria del Monte*. He died of gout at age 68 and was originally interred in a red stone sarcophagus in the chapel of San Andrea of St. Peter's. In 1608 his body was reinterred in a simple ancient sarcophagus inscribed only with IVLIVS PAPA III. The sarcophagus was reopened two years later during the demolition of the basilica, as is recorded by church canon and historian Giacomo Grimaldi:

> Afterwards, the next tomb over, that of Pope Julius III, was opened. He was in a

Sarcophagus of Julius III, Vatican grottoes. Drawing by Joan Reardon.

wooden coffin, the body reduced to bones, but the sacred garments still mostly whole. He was moved to beside Urban VI [*trans. Phyllis Jestice*].

No monument was erected for him in the basilica proper. His sarcophagus can still be seen in the crypt.

FURTHER READING: Virgilio Cardinal Noe, *Le Tombe e i Monumenti*, Rome, 2000.

Marcellus II (April 9–May 1, 1555) *Marcello Cervini*. Died at age 54 of a massive stroke, having been pope only 22 days. He was buried in a fourth century sarcophagus with a depiction of Jesus between Saint Peter and Saint Paul and the following inscription:

MARCELLVS II CERVINVS POLI / TIANVS PONT.
MAX. SEDIT DIES XXII / VIXIT ANNOS LIV
OBIIT KL. MAII MDLV[371]

("Marcellus II, Cervini of Montepulciano, High Priest; sat 22 days, lived 54 years, died the 1st of May 1555." —*Trans. Father Tom Carleton*).

The following is an eyewitness account of the opening of Marcellus's tomb and the exhumation of his body as recorded by church canon and historian Giacomo Grimaldi:

Sarcophagus of Marcellus II, Vatican grottoes.

Thursday, 15 September 1606, at the 22nd hour. In the presence of the most illustrious and reverend lord Robert Bellarmine of Montepulciano, cardinal priest of the holy Roman Church, cardinal priest, nephew of Pope Marcellus II through his sister, the sepulcher of this same Marcellus, situated in a marble sarcophagus between Nicholas V and Innocent IX, was opened. The body, clothed in sacred vestments, was whole, except that the head had been reduced to bone. The body having been raised, it was placed in a new fir coffin, under the vault of the new pavement. The miter was made of cloth of gold... [Grimaldi then takes refuge in "etc." instead of providing more details].

Grimaldi then describes the exhumation of the body on Monday, 16. October 1606. The marble sarcophagus to which he refers would have enclosed the fir coffin described in the quote above.

In the presence of the reverend lord Germanicus Fidelis, canons, and the greater sacristans, the body of Pope Marcellus II of happy memory was revealed in its marble sarcophagus. This sarcophagus had on its front an image of the Savior standing above the four rivers of Paradise, between the apostles Peter and Paul, and had been dug up in the preceding days in the old basilica. On its front the words are newly inscribed: "Pope Marcellus II." On the cover is the coat of arms of the same pontiff, namely deer lying among new ears of grain, with this inscription:

Marcellus II Cervinus
from Montepulciano, supreme pontiff.
He held office 22 days, lived 54 years.
Died on the 1st of May, 1555.

The fir coffin with the body of the pontiff having been placed within the aforementioned sarcophagus and the lid fastened down with iron bands, it was interred between Innocent VI and Innocent IX under the vault of the new pavement of St. Peter's [*trans. Phyllis Jestice*].[372]

Marcellus is memorialized in Palestrina's *Missa Papae Marcelli P.* because of his great singing ability. His simple sarcophagus can be seen today in the Vatican grottoes. No monument was ever erected for him.

FURTHER READING: Virgilio Cardinal Noe, *Le Tombe e i Monumenti*, Rome, 2000.

Paul IV (May 23, 1555–August 18, 1559) *Giampietro Caraffa*. Died suddenly at age 83 of either gout, dropsy, or old age. A Domini-can claimed to have heard him say, in his dying words, that he had been no high priest but "a satan."[373] He was hated by the Romans for endorsing torture chambers, the Spanish Inquisition, and the *auto-da-fe* (public mass burnings), and by the Jews for forcing them to wear yellow hats. When he died the Roman mob plundered the palace of the Inquisition, burned records, destroyed the hideous torture devices, freed the prisoners (after making them swear to honor the Church), and attempted to burn down the Dominican cloister of Minerva. They also put a yellow hat over Paul's tiara on his statue in the capitol before they smashed it to bits. Children kicked the mitered head of the statue around the city and threw it in the Tiber, while the City of Rome decreed that removal of all the Carafa coats of arms and inscriptions. Yet the next day the Romans all kissed his feet while he lay in state.[374]

Paul was secretly buried in the Vatican crypt until his tomb in Santa Maria sopra Minerva, Rome, was ready. Paul's simple monument in Santa Maria was designed by Pirro Ligorio, while the actual figure of the seated pope was sculpted by Giacomo da Castignola, Tommaso della Porta, Gian Pietro Annon, and Rocco da Montefiascone. The epitaph reads:

Tomb monument to Paul IV, Santa Maria sopra Minerva, Rome. Drawing by Joan Reardon.

IESV CHRISTO SPEI ET VITAE FIDELIVM / PAVLO IIII CARRAFAE PONT. MAXIMO / ELOQVENTIA DOCTRINA SAPIENTIA SINGVLARI / INNOCENTIA LIBERALITATE ANIMI MAGNITVDINE PRAESTANTI / SCEL-ERVM VINDICI INTEGERRIMO / CATHOLI-CAE FIDEI ACERRIMO PROPVGNATORI / PIVS V PONTIFEX MAXIMVS / GRATI ET PII ANIMI MONVMENTVM / POSVIT / VIXIT AN. LXXXIII MENS. I D. XX OBIIT MDLIX / XVIII KAL. SEPT. PONT. SVI ANNO V

("In the hope of Jesus Christ and faith-ful in life, in honor of Paul IV Carafa, supreme pontiff. Eloquent in doctrine, singular in wisdom, innocent in liber-ality, distinguished in greatness of soul.

Wholly devoted to punishing evil, most passionate champion of the Catholic faith. Pius V, supreme pontiff, erected this monument with a thankful and pious spirit. He lived 83 years, 1 month, 20 days. He died in 1559 on the 18th day before the calends of September, in the fifth year of his pontificate."—*Trans. Phyllis Jestice*)

FURTHER READING: F. Cerasoli, "Il monumnto di Paolo IV," in *Studi e documenti di Storia e di Diritto*, Rome, XV, 1894; A. Bertolotti, *Artisti Lombardi a Roma nei secoli XV, XVI, e XVII*, Milan, 1881.

Pius IV (December 25, 1559–December 9, 1565) *Giovanni Angelo Medici*. Died of gout or fever at age 64. Originally buried in St. Peter's, he was moved in 1583 to the Church of Santa Maria degli Angeli, Rome, and buried under the altar. The original marble sarcophagus inscription read simply: PIVS PAPA IIII. The epitaph read:

Wall plaque to Pius IV, Santa Maria degli Angeli, Rome.

D. O. M. / PIVS IIII PONT. MAX. / MEDICES MEDIOLANENSIS / SEDIT ANN. V MENS. XI DIES XV / VIXIT ANN. LXVI MENS. IX / OB. V ID. DECEMB. MDLXV / IOANNES ANTONIVS SORBELLONVS / EPISCOPVS PRAENESTINVS / CONSOBRINO / CAROLVS BORROMEVS S. PRAEXEDIS / MEDIOLANENSES / M. SITICVS DE ALTAEMPS GERMANVS / CONSTANTIEN. S. MARIAE TRANSTIB. / TITT. PRESBB. / AVVNCVLO / S. R. E. CARDDD. POSVERE[375]

("To God, best and greatest. Supreme Pontiff Pius IV, of the Medici of Milan, was enthroned for 5 years, 11 months, and 15 days. He lived for 66 years and 9 months. Died on the 5th on the ides of December, 1565. Joannes Antonius Sorbellonus, bishop of Praeneste Consorbrino, Charles Borromeo the patron saint of Milan, M. Siticus of Altaemps German, constantien of St. Mary beyond the Tiber. Cardinal Posvere of the Most Holy Roman Church laid him here."—*Trans. Ruth Yeuk Chun Leung*)

FURTHER READING: A. Pasquinelli, "Le vicende edilizie di S. Maria degli Angeli," in *Roma*, Rome, XIII, 1935; A. Meliu, *S. Maria degli Angeli alle terme di Diocleziano*, Rome, 1950.

St. Pius V (January 7, 1566–May 1, 1572) *Michele Ghislieri*. Died at age 68 of gravel (kidney stones). His last words were "O Lord, increase my sufferings and my patience!" An anonymous historian of the sixteenth century described Pius's death, "In the end, heaped with merits, he was suddenly taken by a crushing pain from his kidney stones, on the first day of May 1572, and forced to succumb after six years and three months of a glorious pontificate."[376]

Pius was originally buried in St. Peter's with the following epitaph:

PIVS QVINTVS GENTE GHISLERIA BOSCHI IN LIGVRIA NATVS / THEOLOGVS EXIMIVS A PAVLO TERTIO IN INSVBRIA HAERETICAE PRAVITATIS INQVISITOR / A IVLIO III S. INQVISITIONIS OFFICII COMMISSARIVS GENER. A PAVLO IV EPISCOPVS SVTRINVS / DEINDE S. R. E. TITT. S. MARIAE SVPER MINERVAM PRESB. CARD ET A PIO IV ECCLESIAE / MONTIS REGALIS IN SVBALPINIS ADMINISTRATOR FACTVS EO VITA FVNCTO / SVMMO CARDINALIVM CONSENSV PONTIF. MAX. CREATVR / QVI VETERES

Tomb monument of Pius V, Santa Maria Maggiore, Rome. From Ferdinand Gregorovius, *Tombs of the Popes.*

SANCTOS PONTIFICES AEMVLATVS CATHOLICAM
FIDEM PROPAGAVIT / ECCLESIASTICAM
DISCIPLINAM RESTITVIT TANDEM GESTARVM
RERVM GLORIA CLARVS / DVM MAIORA
MOLITVR TOTIVS CHRISTINAE REIPVBLICAE
DAMNO NOBIS ERIPITVR / KAL. MAI M. DLXXII
PONT. ANN. VII AETATISQ. SVAE LXVIII[377]

("Pius V of the Ghisleri family of Bosco in Liguria, exceptional theologian. By Paul III, he was made inquisitor of heretical perversity in Insubria, by Julius III, general commissioner of the Office of Inquisition, and by Paul IV, bishop of Sutri. Thereafter the cardinal priest of Santa Maria sopra Minerva of the Most Holy Roman Church and by Paul IV, administrator of the Church of Mount Regal in the Sub Alps, as he busied himself throughout life. By the greatest consensus of the cardinals, he was elected supreme pontiff, who, by following the example of ancient holy pontiffs, propagated the Catholic faith, restored ecclesiastical discipline, then illustrious of all things created, while the greater part of the entire Christendom was built. He was snatched away from us in grief in the month of May in 1572 in the sixth year of his pontificate at age 68." — Trans. Ruth Yeuk Chun Leung)

In 1583 he was moved to the Sistine Chapel of Santa Maria Maggiore, Rome, and interred in a grand monument designed by Dominico Fontana that depicts scenes from Pius's reign. Leonardo Sormani carved the papal effigy, while the bas-relief on the left, "The Consigning of the Standard to Marcantonio Colonna," and the bas-relief on the right, "The Consigning of the Baton to the Command of the Count of St. Fiora" were done by Nicholas Cordier. Silla Longhi da Viggiu sculpted the center bas-relief, "The Coronation of the Pope." The sarcophagus inscription read:

CORPVS / S. PII V / PONT. MAX. /
EX ORD. FF. PRAED.[378]

("The body of St. Pius V, supreme pontiff, from the Dominican order.")

The new epitaph in Santa Maria Maggiore read:

PIO V PONT. MAX. / EX ORD. PRAEDIC. / SIXTVS V
PONT. MAX. / EX ORD. MINOR. / GRATI ANIMI

MONVMENTVM / POSVIT / SELIMVM TVRCARVM
TYRANNVM / MVLTIS INSOLENTEM VICTORIIS
INGENTI PARATA CLASSE / CYPROQ EXPVGNATA
CHRISTIANIS EXTREMA MINITANTEM / PIVS V
FOEDERE CV PHILIPPO II HISPANIAR. REGE / AC
REP. VEN INITO / M. ANTONIVM COLVMNA
PONTIFICIAE CLASSI PRAEFICIES / AD ECHINADAS
HOSTIBVS XXX MILL. CAESIS X MILL. / IN
POTESTATEM REDACTIS TRIREMIBVS CLXXX
CAPTIS / XC DEMERSIS XV MILL. XPIANIS A
SERVITVTE LIBERATIS / PRECIBVS ET ARMIS
DEVICIT / GALLIAM CAROLO IX REGE
PERDVELLIVM / HAERETICORVMQ. NEFARIIS ARMIS
VEXATAM VT DE REGNO / DEQ. RELIGIONE ACTVM
VIDERETVR / PIVS V SFORTIAE COMITIS SANCTAE
FLORAE DVCTV / MISSIS EQVITVM PEDITVMQ.
AVXILIARIBVS COPIIS / PERICVLO EXEMIT /
HOSTIBVSQ. DELETIS VICTORIAM REPORTAVIT /
REGI REGNVM CVM RELIGIONE RESTITVIT
SIGNA / DE HOSTIBVS CAPTA AD LATERAN.
BASILICAM / SVSPENDIT[380]

("For Supreme Pontiff Pius V of the Dominican order, Supreme Pontiff Sixtus V of the Franciscan order laid here the monument of his gracious soul. In alliance with the king of Spain, Philip II, and the Venetian state from the beginning, Pius V, by appointing Marcantonio Colonna as general of the pontifical troops, with prayers and arms, defeated Solyman the tyrant of the Turks, who, insolent for his many victories, threatened the Christian borders when he attacked Cyprus with his vastly equipped armed forces. In Echinas 300,000 enemies were slain, 10,000 brought down in power, 1,800 warships seized, 90 sunk, and 15,000 Christians freed from servitude. With the leadership of his partner Sforza, Pius V, by dispatching auxiliary means of horsemen and foot-soldiers, released Gaul from danger when it was troubled by Charles IX, king of enemies and heretics with his abominable arms, so that it appeared to be an act of royal power and of religious piety. When the enemies had been destroyed, he reported victory to the king, restored the kingdom with religion, and hung the banner, taken from the enemies, at the Lateran Church." — Trans. Ruth Yeuk Chun Leung)

The following poem was written in honor of Pius V by a poet who has remained unidentified:

Tomb of Pius V, Santa Maria Maggiore. From R.P. Mortier, *Saint-Pierre de Rome.*

Zealous defender of the Holy Faith,
Of danger had he not the slightest fear.
He was a Cardinal in the Holy See,
Divine counsel his sole guiding star.
The princes there who kissed the Holy Foot
Saw a true son of humility.
And now ye listen who beseech his name
And love him, sainted, upon the holy
    altars.[381]

Pius was beatified on May 1, 1672, by Clement X and canonized by Clement XI on May 22, 1712. In 1904 a silver mask for the pope's face was made from his death mask, and it is possible to see his "remains" in a crystal coffin in the monument. Pius V's feast day is April 30 (formerly May 5).

FURTHER READING: G. B. Nasalli-Rocca, *Pio V e le sue reliquuie nella basilica liberiana*, Rome, 1904; G. Blanci, *De translatione Pii V e Vaticano in Esquilinum*, Rome, 1587.

Gregory XIII (May 14, 1572–April 10, 1585) *Ugo Boncompagni*. Died at age 84, probably of a heart attack. Gregory's death and burial was recorded in "A Letter lately written from Rome, by an Italian Gentleman, to a friend of his in Lyons in France" by John Florio. It is an accurate and rather amusing account of a papal funeral in the late sixteenth century:

On the ninth there was a rumble in his breast, with such violence that in two hours it dispatched him…. Yet was not his death so grievous unto the number of Cardinals, unto whom it seemed that he had proffered this seat too long, and that it was more than time for him to give place to others, aspiring to that dignity…. Commonly the day after the pope is dead, they are wont to convey his "carkas" in a litter … attended on by his mounted Garde of Switzers and light horsemen to the Consistorial chamber in St. Peter's Palace, where being Pontifically apparelled, all in white garments, even as if he should celebrate the sacred service, he is layd upon the beare, covered with a cloth of gold, and silk, with letters about it saying Gregorius 13. Pont Max. and two cardinal's hats at his feete, and so he is left untill the evening, at which time the Whole College of Cardinals being assembled there, with all the Bishops and Prelates that then are in Rome, and with all the Cannons of Saint John Lateran, and of S. Peter with their richest capes on, he is carried into the Popes Chappel before the high Altar, where the Bishops, Prelates and such people as be there do kiss his feete, after which ceremonie he is carried by the Canons of S. Peters, and laid before

the Sacrament chappel, his Pensioners going before … the head downeward, accompanied with the Cardinals apparelled in purple (which maketh a goodly show) where being led, the … funerall ceremonies unto the dead carkas are celebrated by one of the Canons of the said Church, after that he is carried into the S. Sixtus Chappell, where for three days space he is left, with his feete towards the grate, to the end, that the whole that wish may kiss his feet, he being attended as I have said before, with many Torches burning day and night about him, with a multitude of Priests tending on him, for fear he should run away. Three days being ended, he is buried in the said Church, where it pleaseth best his kinsman, where nine days after continually, many Torches are burning, for so long his funerals last, and therefore they are called Novendalie, which importeth in English, nine days work. A very high scaffold in the form of a Pyramid, being made in the middle of the Church, covered all over with black cloth, with his armes round about, but without the keys, with letters saying Pope Gregorie the 13, which pyramid is upheld by many pillars, under which doth appear an Hearce, all covered with cloth of gold, with cushions of the same, where every morning there is a mass sung by some Cardinal, created by the last pope, which mass being ended, he with four Cardinals more in black velvet robes, and Subdeane having said the Epistle, taking the cross in hand, the master of the ceremonies, and other his officers assisting, all the other Cardinals following, they go about the scaffold, or pyramid. The dead pope's whole household sitting about … all in mourning apparel, with burning torches in their hands, some bigger then other some, according to the degrees of the men: at each corner of the said scaffold, is placed a stool covered with black, upon which the four Cardinals in black velvet too sit, and he that hath sung Mass sitting upon another stool, in the midst of the side that looketh toward the Altar. Then he that sitteth at the right hand, beginneth to give holy water to the bier lying under the scaffold, and then Frankinsense, and so doeth he to all other Cardinals, this done he sayeth a prayer, and so do the other four Cardinals. Then they go up into the choir, where the whole College of the Cardinals doth resort, with burning torches in their handes, a great one standing in the midst unkindled. This being ended, they all withdraw themselves into S. Peter's Sextrie, where they keep a congregation for the space of two hours at least. The … Temple is hanged round about with black cloth, with vulgar letters saying, Gregorius Papa 13, in which there are many torches, that burn so long as the funerals last, which commonly are two hours long every day and thus they run nine mornings one after the other, which being ended, the morning following, the Mass of the holy Ghost is sung by the Cardinall Deane, after this is sung Veni creator spiritus, and so singing with the pensioners and other offi-cers, the singing men with the rest of the Cardinals going before, they all go towards the Conclave….

Gregory's original tomb, designed by Ciro Ferri and executed by Prospero Antichi, was located where Gregory XIV was to be buried and so was moved in 1591 to another niche in St. Peter's when Gregory XIV died. This original tomb, featuring the pope bestowing his blessing, with Charity and Strength (?) seated at his feet and two other Virtues in niches on either side of the pope, was either destroyed by Bramante in the early seventeenth century during the demolition of the basilica, or destroyed when the

The original tomb of Gregory XIII. Drawing based on Montini, *Le Tombe dei Papi.*

tomb had to be moved in 1591. At any rate, Clement XI (d. 1721) urged Cardinal Buoncompagni (a cousin of Gregory's) to commission a new tomb monument for him. That monument was begun in 1719 and took sculptor Camillo Rusconi four years to complete.

The Rusconi monument features the pope sitting upon his throne and giving his blessing while the figure of Religion (on the left) holds the bible and a tablet inscribed NOVI/OPERA/EIUS/ET/FIDEM/APOC. CAP.2/V.19 (The reference is to Revelation 2: 19: "I know your works, your love, faith, service, and endurance, and that your last works are greater than the first"). Strength, on the other side (in the guise of Minerva), draws back a covering from the coffin and exposes the bas-relief by Carlo Mellone of the "Promulgation of the Gregorian Calendar." Creeping out from under the coffin is a dragon, symbol on the pope's Boncompagni family coat of arms. Epitaph:

GREGORIA XIII PONT. MAX. / IVSTITIAE CVSTODI
PIETATIS CVLTORI RELIGIONIS VINDICI /
ET PROPAGATORI IN VTROQVE ORBE
MVNIFICENTISSIMO / IACOBVS TIT. S. MARIAE IN
VIA PRESB. S. R. E. CARD. BONCOMPAGNVS /
ARCHIEPISCOPVS BONONIAE ABNEPOS POSVIT /
ANN. SAL. MDCCXXIII[381]

("To Gregory XIII, High Priest, guardian of justice, defender and magnificent propagator of the faith in two worlds. Ugo Boncompagni, cardinal priest of the Holy Roman Church, titular of Saint Mary in Via, great-grandnephew and archbishop of Bologna placed [this monument] in the year of salvation 1723."— *Trans. Father Tom Carleton*)

FURTHER READING: U. Donati, *Artisti ticinesi a Roma*, Bellinzona, 1942; A. de Rinaldis, *L'arte in Roma dal Seicento al Novecento*, Bologna, 1948; Virgilio Cardinal Noe, *Le Tombe e i Monumenti*, Rome, 2000.

Sixtus V (April 24, 1585–August 27, 1590)

Felice Peretti. Died at age 70 of either stroke, malaria, or poison in the Quirinal Palace, Rome, in a sudden attack so violent that he

"New" (seventeenth century) tomb monument of Gregory XIII, St. Peter's Basilica, Rome.

died without making confession.[382] Sixtus began the tradition of placing papal viscera in terra cotta jars behind the walls—although some sources say the viscera are kept in the basement—in the Church of Saints Vincenzo e Anastasio, Rome. (See Appendix 6 for more information on this practice.)

The Romans hated Sixtus and his enthusiasm for the Inquisition. When they heard of his death, they toppled his statue on the Capitol. According to Claudio Rendina's *The Popes: Histories and Secrets* (p. 482), they also circulated a rumor that he had made a pact with the devil to get the papacy, and that the devil would therefore take his soul during a storm. (Sixtus died during a major hurricane.)

Sixtus's monument, designed by Domenico Fontana, is in the same chapel as Pius V (1566–1572) in Santa Maria Maggiore. The figure of the pope himself was carved by the

Tomb monument of Sixtus V, Santa Maria Maggiore, Rome. From Ferdinand Gregorovius, *Tombs of the Popes.*

famed sculptor Vasoldo, as was the left lower bas-relief entitled "The Rich Against the Poor in Rome" and the upper central relief, "The Coronation of the Pope." Nicola Mustaert and Nicola Pippe da Arras were responsible for the relief on the bottom right of the monument, "Against the Bandits of the Roman Campagna," which shows the figures of Justice and Strength confronting Turkish bandits in the Romagna who are grasping newly severed Christian heads by the hair. "The Canonization of St. Diego" on the upper left of the tomb and "The Peace of Austria and Poland" on the upper right of the monument were done by Egidio de la Riviere. The epitaph reads:

SIXTO V PONT. MAX / EX ORDINE. MINOR. / ALEXANDER PERETTVS / S. R. E. CARD. VICECAN / EX SORORE PRONEPOS / PERFECIT / SIXTVS V PONT. MAX / CVPRIS AD LITTVS SVPERI MARIS IN PICENO NATVS MONTALTI EDVCATVS / F. FELIX PERETTVS EX ORD. MINOR. THEOLOGVS ET CONCIONATOR INSIGNIS / HAERETICAE PRAVITATIS INQVISITOR SVI ORD. PROC. ET VIC. GENERALIS / A PIO IV PONT. MAX. CVM VGONE BONCOMPAGNO CARD / LEGATO APOSTOLICO IN HISPANIAM MISSVS / PIO V PONT. MAX. OB SPECTATVM FIDEI ZELVM EXIMIE CHARVS AB EOQVE / EPISCOPVS S. AGATHAE ET S. R. E. CARD. FACTVS MAGNISQ. NEGOTIIS ADHIBITVS / SVMMO SACRI COLLEGI CONSENSV PONT. MAX. CREATVS TOTO PONTIFICATV / IVSTITIAE PRVDENTIAE ANIMIQ. MAGNITVDINIS LAVDE FLORVIT / BEATVM DIDACVM HISPANVM EX ORD. FRATRVM MINORVM / PHILIPPO REGE CATHOLICO SVPPLICANTE / IN SANCTORVM NVMERVM RETVLIT / CAPTIVIS REDIMENDIS / PAVPERIBVS IN CVSTODIA INCLVSIS / AD AES ALIENVM DISSOLVENDVM / VIRGINIBVS DOTANDIS / FRVCTVS ANNVOS ATTRIBVIT / VICTVM PER VRBEM OSTIATIM QVAERENTIBVS / DOMVM IN QVA ALERENTVR AEDIFICAVIT / HIPPOLYTO CARD. ALDOBRANDINO LEG. IN POLON. MISSO / CONTROVERSIAS INTER AVSTRIACAM DOMVM / ET SIGISMVNDVM POLONIAE REGEM COMPOSVIT / EXVLVM ET PERDITORVM HOMINVM / LICENTIAM COERCVIT / PVBLICAM TRANQVILLITATEM RESTITVIT / VRBEM AEDIFICIORVM MAGNIFICENTIA / IN PRIMISQ. VATICANA TESTVDINE ORNAVIT / AQVAM FELICEM / OPERE SVMPTVOSO ADDVXIT[383]

("In honor of Sixtus V, supreme pontiff, of the order of Minorites, Alessandro Peretto, cardinal and vice chancellor of the holy Roman Church, his great nephew, completed this monument.

("Sixtus V, supreme pontiff, born in Piceno on the shore of the upper lake, educated at Montalto, became Brother Felice Peretto of the Franciscan order, theologian and distinguished orator. Inquisitor of heretical depravity and provincial vicar general of his order, he was sent as apostolic legate to Spain by supreme pontiff Pius IV, along with Cardinal Hugo Boncampagno. [He was] made bishop of St. Agatha and cardinal of the holy Roman Church by Pius V for the sake of his exceptional zeal for the faith, and invited with great pains. With the consent of the sacred college he was created supreme pontiff. He flourished with justice, prudence, and the praise of a great soul. At the petition of the Catholic king Philip, he raised to the number of the saints the blessed Didacus of Spain, from the order of Friars Minor. He gave his income to redeeming captives, caring for paupers, discharging debts, giving dowries to virgins, seeking the needy from door to door through the city. Having sent Hippolyto Cardinal Aldobrandino as his legate to Poland, he settled the disputes between the house of Austria and Sigismund, king of Poland. He restrained the license of exiles and men of perdition, and restored public tranquility. He adorned the city with magnificent buildings, above all the dome of the Vatican, and brought the Acqua Felice into the city with sumptuous work."—*Trans. Phyllis Jestice*)

FURTHER READING: R. Cecchetelli-Ippoliti, *La tomba di papa S. V nella basilica Liberiana*, Rome, 1923.

Urban VII (September 15–27, 1590) *Giambattista Castagna*. Died at age 69 of malaria. He became ill the day after he was elected pope and died before he was consecrated. However, he is officially a pope, and his praecordia were interred in the Church

The tomb of Urban VII, Santa Maria sopra Minerva, Rome.

of SS. Vincenzo e Anastasio, Rome (see Appendix 6 for more information on this practice). Urban left his large personal fortune of 32,000 scudi for the provision of dowries for the marriages of impoverished girls.[384] He was originally buried in a lead coffin in St. Peter's (see Appendix 4 for original shape of the tomb), with the following epitaph:

HOC PLVMBEO LOCVLO CONDITVM EST /
VENERABILE CORPVS / D. VRBANI PAPAE SEPTIMI
ROMANI / DE FAMILIA CASTANEA PONT. MAX. /
QVI SEDIT IN PONTIFICATV / DIES DVODECIM
MIGRAVIT AD DOMINVM / XXVII SEPT. FERIA V
HORA XII ANNO MDXC / NON SINE MAXIMO VRBIS
DOLORE / ANTE SVAE CORONATIONIS INSIGNIA /
VIXIT ANNOS LXVIII MEN. I DIES XXII / HIC IN
PACE DEPOSITVS EST / SODALITAS DEIPARAE
VIRGINIS ANNVNCIATAE / SVPRA MINERVAM EX
TESTAMENTO HAERES / OPTIMO BENEFACTORI
POSVIT / ET E VETERI IN NOVAM BASILICAM /
TRANSFERRI CVRAVIT / ANNO MDCVI DIE XXII
SEPTEMBRIS / PAVLI V PONTIFICATVS SECVNDO[385]

("Under this lead marker rests the venerable body of blessed Pope Urban VII of Rome, from the Castagna family, supreme pontiff, who, having held the pontificate twelve days, ascended to the Lord on Thursday the 27th of September, at the 12th hour, in the year 1590, not without the greatest grief in the city, before his coronation. He lived 68 years, 1 month, 22 days, and is here laid in peace. By his will, his heir was the sodality of the Virgin Mother of God of the Annunciation sopra Minerva, from the best of benefactors. His body was moved from the old to the new basilica in the year 1606 on the 22nd of September, in the second year of the pontificate of Paul V." — *Trans. Phyllis Jestice*)

Church historian Giacomo Grimaldi recorded the reburial of Urban VII in St. Peter's:

Replacing the body of Urban VII in a cypress coffin in the year 1606, on Sunday the 24th of September, at the 22nd hour. In the presence of the reverend lords Timocrato Aloysio, secretary Pietro Francisco of Nobilibus, and Ludovico Rivaldo, priest of Limoges, and on the advice of the venerable society of the most holy Annunciatio sopra Minerva, in the name of the confraternity, the body of Pope Urban VII of happy memory, supreme pontiff elect, was placed in a lead coffin and clothed in pontifical vestments, except for the maniple and the pallium, because he had not been crowned, and placed within a new cypress coffin provided by the already-mentioned society [*trans. Phyllis Jestice*].

Ambrogio Buonvicino sculpted Urban's simple monument, although a new epitaph was written when he was moved to Santa Maria sopra Minerva:

D. O. M. / VRBANO VII / CHRISTIANAE REIPVBLICAE
BONO NATO / CVI QVICQVID IN EGREGIVM
HOMINEM LAVDIS DICI POTEST / FVIT BENEFICIO
NATVRAE COLLATVM / AD SVMMI PONTIFICATVS
APICEM EO TARDIVS EVECTO / QVO CELERIVS
INVIDA MORTE PRAEREPTO / INCONSOLABILI
VRBIS ET ORBIS MOERORE AETAT. AN. LXX PONT.
DIE XII / ARCHICONFRATERNITAS SANCTISSIMAE
ANNUNTIATAE / OB AMPLIFICATOS SINE EXEMPLO
REDDITVS / IN PAVPERVM VIRGINVM DOTES

EROGANDOS / HAERES EX ASSE PROTECTORI
MVNIFICENTISSIMO / MVNVS SINGVLARI
RELIGIONE DEBITVM / DEDICAVIT[386]

("To God the best and greatest. In memory of
Urban VII, well born in the Christian republic. If something can be said in praise of this
excellent man, he was devoted in kindness by
nature. [He was] raised late to the apex of the
highest pontificate, whence quickly he was carried off by envious death, leaving the city and
the world inconsolable, at the age of 70, having been pontiff 12 days. He dedicated his fortune to the confraternity of the most holy
Annunciation, to provide dowries to poor virgins."—*Trans. Phyllis Jestice*)

Gregory XIV (December 5, 1590–October 16, 1591) *Niccolo Sfondrati*. Died of a large
(2.5 ounce) gallstone at age 56. His praecordia are in the Church of SS. Vincenzo e
Anastasio in Rome (see Appendix 6 for more
information on this practice), although there
is no word on whether the gallstone is interred with them. Prospero Antichi executed
a surprisingly simple monument in St.
Peter's for him. The monument features an
empty space where one would expect the
statue of the pope; humble Gregory did not
want a likeness of himself on his tomb. The
figure of Religion is to the left of the tomb
while Justice is on the right. Inscription:

GREGORIVS XIIII / PONT. MAX.

FURTHER READING: Virgilio Cardinal Noe, *Le
Tombe e i Monumenti*, Rome, 2000.

Innocent IX (October 29–December 30,
1591). *Giovanni Antonio Fachinetti*. Died at
age 72 of an illness (most likely pneumonia)
after he insisted on making a pilgrimage to
the seven major churches of Rome as the new
pope. On December 18, he caught the chill
that would kill him only 12 days later. His
praecordia were interred in the Church of
SS. Vincenzo e Anastasio, Rome (see Appendix 6 for more information on this practice).
No monument was erected in his memory,
although his simple sarcophagus was moved

Tomb of Gregory XIV, St. Peter's, Rome.

from St. Peter's proper to the Vatican grottoes in 1606.

Church canon and historian Giacomo
Grimaldi witnessed and recorded the opening of Innocent's tomb on September 13,
1606, and the reburial of his body on September 25 of the same year. Of the exhumation, Grimaldi wrote:

> The body was wrapped in a gold chasuble
> with other papal insignia, with a gold miter,
> ring, and crucifix on his chest. The body was
> whole, but the head is now decomposed
> [*trans. Phyllis Jestice*].

And of the reburial:

> The body of Pope Innocent IX of happy
> memory was placed in a lead coffin enclosed
> within new cypress, at the expense of the
> lord's great-nephew, with these letters
> piously inscribe on a marble tablet: "INNO-
> CENTUS. PAPA IX." The following inscription,
> carved on a lead plate, remains upon the

Sarcophagus of Innocent IX, Vatican grottoes.

cypress coffin: "A brief rule, but eternal remembrance. Borne in this lead coffin is the venerable body of the lord Innocent Pope, the Ninth, formerly from Bologna, Giovanni Antonio Fachinetti, who held the pontificate 2 months. He lived 73 years, 6 months, passing to the Lord on the 29th day of December, in the year 1591. Giovanni Antonio, whose memory be blessed." The great-nephew Antonio, Cardinal of SS. Quator Maior, agreed to removal of his body to the new basilica" [*trans. Phyllis Jestice*].[387]

Innocent's epitaph read:

BREVIS IMPERII MEMORIAE AETERNAE / IN HAC
PLVMBEA CAPSA CONSITVM / EST VENERABILE
CORPVS D INNOCENTTII / PP IX BONONIENSIS
ANTEA IO / ANTONII E DOMO FACHENETA QVI /
SEDIT IN PONTIFICATV MENSES / DVOS VIXIT
ANNOS / LXXIII MENS / VI MIGRAVIT AD DOMINVM
DIE / XXVIIII DECEMB IN AVRORA ANNO / MDXCI
CVIVS MEMORIA SIT IN / BENEDICTIONE IO
ANTONIVS / VTR SIGNATVRAE S D N PP REFER /
PROTONOT DE NVM ET SACRAE CON / SVLTATIONIS
AVDITOR AC LODOVICVS / MARCHIO VIANINI

FRATRES DE FACHENETIS / ET EIVSDEM
INNOCENTII / PRONEPOTES QVOD ANTONIVS
CARDINALIS / SS QVATVOR MAIOR NATV FRATER /
SI NON ESSET FATO PRAEVENTVS / FACERE
STATVERAT E VETERI IN NOVAM / BASILICAM
TRANSFERRI ET / DEPONI CVRARVNT ANNO
MDCVI / DIE XXV SEPTEMBRIS PAVLI PAPAE /
QVINTI ANNO SECVNDO.[388]

("In this leaden casket is guarded, to the eternal memory of a brief reign, the venerable body of the Pontiff Innocent IX, Bolognese; in the world, John Anthony of the Facchinetti family, who pontificated for two months. He lived 73 years and six months. He returned to the Lord on the dawn of the 29th of December of the year 1591. May his memory be in benediction. John Anthony, reporter of both signatures of Our Lord's Holiness, protonotary of number, and hearer of the sacred council, and Louis marquis Vianini, brothers of the Facchinetti family and great-grandnephew of the same Innocent, took care of the transferring from the ancient to the new basilica, the 25th day of September in 1606, the second year of the pontificate of Pope Paul V, insofar as the older brother

Anthony, cardinal of the Four Holy Crowned [martyrs] had arranged thus, in case, dying first, he might not be present."—*Trans. Father Tom Carleton*)

FURTHER READING: Virgilio Cardinal Noe, *Le Tombe e i Monumenti*, Rome, 2000.

Clement VIII (January 30, 1592–March 5, 1605) *Ippolito Aldobrandini*. Died at age 69 from gout and was originally buried in the Borghese chapel of St. Peter's. Church canon and historian Giacomo Grimaldi recorded the original epitaph:

HIC REQUIESCIT VENERABILE CORPUS SOMINI CLEMENTIS PAPAE OCTAVI ALDOBRANDINI, QUI VIXIT ANNOS 69, SEDIT IN PONTIFICATU ANNOS XIII, MENS. I, D. IIII. MIGRAVIT AD DOMINUM FERIA V POST DOMINCAM PRIMAM QUADRAGESIMAE DIE III MENSIS MARTII PAULO POST HORMA V NOCTIS, CUIUS MEMORIA IN BENEDICTIONE SIT. DEPOS. EST EIUSDEM MENSIS DIE VII IN FESTO B. THOMAE AQUINATIS, ANNO CHRISTI MDCV[389]

("Here rests the honorable body of Pope Clement VIII Aldobrandini, who lived 69 years, and sat on the papal throne for 13 years, 1 month, and 4 days. He departed to the Lord on the Thursday after the first Sunday of Lent, March 3, a little past the fifth hour of the night. May his memory be blessed. He was buried the seventh day of the same month on the feast of Blessed Thomas Aquinas, in the year of Christ 1605."—*Trans. Father Thomas Buffer*)

Clement's praecordia joined the ranks of his papal predecessors by being interred in the Church of SS. Vincenzo e Anastasio, Rome (see Appendix 6 for more information on this practice). His monument, designed by Flaminio Ponzio, was moved in 1646 to the Borghese Crypt in the Pauline Chapel in the basilica of Santa Maria Maggiore, Rome. Silla da Viggiu carved the figure of the pope, while Ippolito Buzi carved "The Peace of Henry IV and Phillip III" in the upper left of the monument. The upper center, "The Coronation of Clement VIII," and the cornice figures were carved by Pietro Bernini. The upper right relief, "The Canonization of

St. Giacinto and St. Raimondo," was carved by Giovanni Antonio Valsoldo; on the left bottom side, "The Occupation of Ferrara," by Ambriogio Bonvicino; and on the right bottom, "Invitation of the Troops in Hungary," by Camillo Mariani.

In 1942, when the crypt was being restored, Clement's actual sarcophagus was found, upon which was the following inscription:

CLEMENS V̅I̅I̅I̅ PONT. MAX. / MDXXXVI
HIPPOLYTVS ALDOBRANDINVS MDCV

("Clement VIII, supreme pontiff, 1536–1605, Hippolytus Aldobrandini")

The epitaph in Santa Maria Maggiore reads:

CLEMENTI VIII PONT. MAX / PAVLVS V PONT. MAX. ROM / GRATI ANIMI MONVMENTVM / POSVIT / CLEMENS VIII FLORENTINVS EX ALDOBRANDINA FAMILIA / POST. ROM. ROTAE IVDICIVM ET DATARIAE PRAEFECTVRAM / PVRPVRA DONATVS / ET MAIORIS POENITENTIARII MVNERE AVCTVS / POST SEDATAS IN POLONICA LEGATIONE INTER SIGISMVNDVM REGEM / ET AVSTRIACAM DOMVM ORTAS IN COMITIIS REGNI DISCORDIAS / AD PONTIFICATVS APICEM EVECTVS / PATRIARCHA ALEXANDRINO ET RVTHENIS EPISCOPIS / A SCHISMATE IN ROM. ECCLESIAE COMPLEXVM ADMISSIS / HENRICO IV APOSTOLICA CHARITATE RECEPTO / GALLIARVM REGNO CVM MAGNO RELIGIONIS BONO POST DIVTVRNA BELLA PARATO / INTER EVMDEM REGEM IAM ALPIBVS INSIDENTEM ET DVCEM SABAVDIAE / POST PETRVM ALDOBRANDINVM LEGATVM PACE FIRMATA / SAECVLARI ANNO IVBILAEI MIRAE PIETATIS DOCVMENTIS CVMVLATO / PONTIFICIA MAIESTATE VBIQVE CONSTANTER ASSERTA / SEDIT ANNOS XIII MENSEM I DIES IV OBIIT NON. MARTII MDCV AETATIS LXVIII / CORPVS E TEMPORARIO VATICANI TVMVLO HVC TRANSFERRI CVRAVIT DIE XXIII APR. MDCXLVI / M. ANTONIVS BVRGHESIVS PRINCEPS SVLMONIS PAVLI V E FRATRE NEPOS / LEGATO IN GALLIAS ALEXANDRO MEDICEO S. R. E. CARD. / PACEM INTER POTENTISSIMOS REGES / MAGNA TEMPORVM FELICITATE COMPOSVIT / FERRARIENSEM DITIONEM EXERCITV CELERRIME COMPARATO / SINE SANGVINIS EFFVSIONE VICTOR / SEDI APOSTOLICAE RECVPERAVIT / HIACYNTHVM POLONVM ET RAYMVNDVM HISPANVM / EX PRAEDICATORVM FAMILIA /

Cenotaph of Clement VIII in Santa Maria Maggiore, Rome.

VIRTVTE ET MIRACVLIS CLAROS SANCTORVM
NVMERO ADSCRIPSIT / IO. FRANCISCVM
ALDOBRANDINVM CVM VALIDISSIMIS COPIIS / AD
OTHOMANICAS EXPEDITIONES COERCENDAS / TER
IN PANNONIAM MISIT

("Paul V, supreme pontiff of Rome, erected this monument with a thankful soul in honor of Clement VIII, supreme pontiff. Clement VIII of Florence, from the Aldobrandini family. After serving as judge of the Roman rota and datary of the prefecture, he was given the purple and held the office of greater penitentiary. Afterwards [he was] sent as legate to Poland to resolve the discord that arose between King Sigismund and the house of Austria. Raised to the apex of the pontificate, he admitted the patriarch of Alexandrovo and bishop of Russia from schism into the Roman Church, and received in apostolic charity Henry IV, king of France, with great good to religion, prepared after long war. Between the same kingdom, now holding the Alps, and the duke of Savoy, he confirmed a peace after the legation of Pietro Aldobrandini. In the jubilee year he heaped up documents of marvelous piety, asserting with

constancy the majesty of the pontificate. He held office 13 years, 1 month, 4 days, and died on the nones of March 1605 at the age of 68. Antonio Burghese, prince of Sulmona, nephew of Paul V, transferred his body to this place from a temporary tomb in the Vatican on April 23, 1646, with the legate to France, Alessandro Medici, cardinal of the holy Roman Church. He made peace among the most powerful kings, in a great time of happiness. He regained Ferrara for the Apostolic See, swift victor without bloodshed. He added to the number of the saints Hyacinth of Poland and Raymund of Spain, from the family of preachers, for the brilliance of their virtues and miracles. He sent Giovanni Francesco Aldobrandini three times with great supplies to the expeditions against the Ottomans in Pannonia [or Hungary]."— Trans. Phyllis Jestice)

Leo XI (April 1–27, 1605) *Alessandro Otta- viano de'Medici.* Died at age 70 from an ill- ness he contracted while ritually taking possession of the Lateran. His praecordia

Tomb monument of Leo XI, St. Peter's Basilica.

were deposited in the church of SS. Vincenzo e Anastasio with those of his papal predecessors (see Appendix 6 for more information on this practice). Leo's family was extremely upset when, after such a long wait to see one of their own ascend to the papal seat, Leo died almost immediately, preventing them from reaping the lucrative benefits of having a pope as a family member. He was buried in the left nave of St. Peter's in a tomb monument by Alassandro Algardi, who carved the relief of the pope on the sarcophagus. Prudence and Liberty, located on either side of the pope, were sculpted by Ercole Ferrata and Giuseppe Peroni, respectively. The epitaph reads:

D. O. M. / LEONI XI MEDICI FLORENTINO PONT.
OPT. MAX. / QVI AD SVMMAM ECCLESIAE DEI
FELICITATEM / OSTENSVS MAGIS QVAM DATVS /
CHRISTIANVM ORBEM BREVI XXVII DIERVM
LAETITIA / ET LONGO ANNORVM MOERORE
COMPLEVIT / ROBERTVS CARDINALIS VBALDINVS
EX SORORE PRONEPOS / GRATI ANIMI
MONVMENTVM P. / OBIIT AN. AETATIS SVAE
LXIX QVINTO KAL. MAII / M. D. C. V.

("To God, the best and greatest. To Leo XI Medici, Florentine, supreme pontiff, who for the highest happiness of the Church of God, having demonstrated more than having been given, filled the Christian world with a brief joy lasting 27 days and with a long plan of years. Robert Ubaldino, great-grandnephew from his sister, placed this monument with grateful affection. He died at the age of 69 years, the 27th of April 1605."—*Trans. Father Tom Carleton*)

FURTHER READING: Virgilio Cardinal Noe, *Le Tombe e i Monumenti*, Rome, 2000.

Paul V (May 16, 1605–January 28, 1621) *Camillo Borghese*. Died of stroke at age 69 during a procession to celebrate a victory over the Protestants. His praecordia are located in the Church of SS. Vincenzo e Anastasio, Rome (see Appendix 6 for more on this practice). He was originally interred in the Borghese Chapel of St. Peter's but was reinterred in the crypt of Santa Maria Maggiore. The sarcophagus inscription reads:

PAVLVS V PONT. MAX. /
MDLII CAMILLVS BVRGHESIVS MDCXXI

("Paul V, supreme pontiff; 1552 Camillus Borghese 1621")

His tomb monument, located in the Pauline chapel, was designed by Flaminio Ponzio and features the figure of the praying pope (by Silla da Viggiu), flanked on the left by Stefano Moderna's relief, "Invasion against Turkey and Hungary," and on the right Ambrogio Bonvicinio's "Construction of the Fortification of Ferrara." Above the kneeling pope is the scene of his coronation carved by Ippolito Buzi. To the right is Cristoforo Stati's "The Pope Receiving the Persian Ambassador," while the left shows a relief of "The Canonization of St. Charles Borromeo and St. Francesa Romana" by Giovanni Antonio Valsoldo. The cornice figures are by Pompeo Ferucci. The monument epitaph reads:

PAVLVS V PONT. MAX. / MORTIS MEMOR / VIVENS
SIVI POSVIT / SCIPIO CARDINALIS BVRGHESIVS
AVVNCVLO / IVSTA SOLVI CORPVS INFERRI
CVRAVIT / PAVLVS V PONT. MAX. PATRIA ROMANVS
EX BVGHESIA FAMILIA / CVI PERPETVA VITAE
INNOCENTIA ET SPECTATA VIRTVS / AD INSIGNES
QVOSQVE HONORES GRADVM FECIT / BONONIAE
PROLEGATO PRAEFVIT MOX A GREGORIO XIV /
CAVSARVM CAM. APOST. AVDITOR CREATVS ET A
CLEMENTE VIII AD PHILIPPVM II / HISPANIARVM
REGEM DE GRAVISSIMIS REBVS LEGATVS / IN
AMPLISSIMVM ORDINEM COOPTATVS INTER
GENERALES INQVISITORES ADSCRIPTVS / ET VRBIS
VICARIVS ELECTVS CVM OMNES TANTORVM
MVNERVM PARTES / SVMMA CVM LAVDE OBIVISSET
AD SVMMVM PONTIFICATVM LEONE XI E. VIVIS
EREPTO / FLORENS ADHVC AETATE INCREDIBILI
PATRVM CONSENSV EVECTVS EST / CVMQVE VIGILI
SOLLICITVDINE SECVRITATEM ANNONAE COPIAM /
IVSTITIAM ET QVIETEM POPVLIS ECCLESIASTICAE
DITIONIS / CONCORDIAM VERO ET PACEM
VNIVERSO CHRISTIANO ORBI SEMPER
PRAESTITISSET / RELIGIONEM SVMMA PIETATE
COLVISSET / VRBEM MAGNIFICENTISSIMIS
AEDIFICIIS ORNASSET ATQ. EGREGIIS / OMNIVM
VIRTVTVM OFFICIIS ADITVM SIBI AD
IMMORTALITATEM APERVISSET / E MORTALIBVS
RAPTVS GRAVE CVNCTIS SVI DESIDERIVM
RELIQVIT / SEDIT IN PONTIFICATV ANNOS XV

MENSES VIII DIES XIII / OBIIT ANNO SAL.
MDCXXI DIE XXVIII IANVARII /
FRANSCISCAM VIDVAM ROMANAM ET
CAROLVM BORRHOMEVM / S. R. E.
CARDINALEM VITAE INNOCENTIA ET
MIRACVLIS CLAROS / RITE IN SANCTORVM
ALBVM RETVLIT / RODVLPHVM ROMANVM
IMPERATOREM ELECTVM / ADVERSVS
CHRISTIANI NOMINIS HOSTES / IN
HVNGARIA BELLVM GERENTEM
AVXILIARIBVS COPIIS ADIVVIT / CONGI
PERSIDISQVE REGVM ET IAPONIORVM / AD
SEDEM APOSTOLICAM DE RE CHRISTIANA
LEGATOS / HONORIFICENTISSIME
EXCEPIT / FERRARIAM VRBEM DITIONIS
ECCLESIASTICAE / NOBILE
PROPVGNACVLVM / EXTRVCTA
VALIDISSIMA ARCE MVNIVIT

Sarcophagus of Paul V, crypt of Santa Maria Maggiore, Rome. Drawing by Joan Reardon.

("Paul V, supreme pontiff. Remembering the living in death, Scipio Cardinal Borghese took care to enshrine the body and place this monument for his uncle, justly released [from this life]. Paul V, supreme pontiff of Roman birth from the Borghese family, whose perpetual innocence of life and visible virtue led him to distinguished honors. He presided over the legateship of Bologna under Gregory XIV, and for the sake of the apostolic camera was made an auditor and sent by Clement VIII as legate dealing with the gravest affairs to Philip II, king of Spain. He was coopted to the highest level among general inquisitors and elected vicar of the city with full share in this great office. Earning praise, he reached the heights of the highest pontificate when Leo XI was torn from among the living. Flourishing thus, at an incredible age he became father by general consent, and with vigilant care provided abundant grain, security, justice, and quiet for the people of the church under his authority. Truly he always offered concord and peace to the universal Christian world, cultivating what remained with highest benevolence. He adorned the city with magnificent and distinguished buildings. Approaching his offices with all virtues, he revealed immortality; carried off from among the living, he left behind deep grief for such a man. He was pontiff 15 years, 8 months, 13 days, and died in the year of salvation 1621, on the 28th of January. He brought into the ranks of the saints the Roman widow Francesca and Charles Borromeo, cardinal of the holy Roman Church, innocent in life and brilliant in miracles. He offered great assistance in aiding Rudolph, Roman emperor elect against the enemies of the Christian name in war in Hungary. He received the Christian legates of the kings of Congo, Persia, and Japan with highest honor to the Apostolic See. He fortified the city of Ferrara, under the sovereignty of the Church, with a noble rampart, and erected a very mighty citadel."—*Trans. Phyllis Jestice*)

Gregory XV (February 9, 1621–July 8, 1623) *Alessandro Ludovisi*. Died at age 70 from fever in the Quirinal Palace, Rome. Because they abhorred his financial extravagances, the Romans celebrated when he died by mass looting and pillaging until finally Prince Savelli took charge and placed soldiers all over Rome to control the mob. After that, anyone caught looting was immediately hanged. Gregory's praecordia are entombed in the Church of Sts. Vincenzo e Anastasio

Tomb monument of Gregory XV, San Ignazio, Rome.

in Rome (see Appendix 6 for more information on this practice).

Originally buried in the Quirinal Palace, Gregory was moved in 1634 to the right of the altar in San Ignazio, Rome. His monument, designed by Orazio Grassi, features two angels holding back the curtains of eternity to reveal the seated pope bestowing his blessing, which was sculpted by Pietro le Gros the Younger and Pietro Stefano Monnet. Camillo Rusconi carved the cardinal virtues Religion and Magnificence that flank the sides. The epitaph reads:

ALTER IGNATIVM / ARIS / ALTER ARAS IGNATIO / GREGORIVS XV / PONT. MAX. / LVDOVICVS CARD. / LVDOVISIVS[390]

("A second Ignatius to the tomb, a second tomb to Ignatius. Gregory XV, supreme pontiff. [Erected by] Ludovico cardinal Ludovisi."— *Trans. Phyllis Jestice*)

Church historian Alfonso Ciacconius recorded another epitaph:

GREGORIO XV / PONTIFEX TER MAXIMVS / TERRARVM ORBIS BENEMERENTISSIMVS / MVLTA BREVI IACVLATVS IMPERIO / QVOT MENSIVM TOT LVSTRORVM AEQVAVIT ANNOS / IMMORTALI DIGNVS NOMINE / REBVS PRAECLARE GESTIS / ROMAE PRO ROMA / PIETATEM AVXIT NOVO CVLTV RELIGIONIS / RELIGIONI ARAS EXTRVXIT / NOVA SANCTORVM APOTHEOSI / INTER QVOS / IGNATIVM SOCIETATIS IESV FVNDATOREM / FRANSISCVM XAVERIVM ANTESIGNANVM / GEMELLVM NVMEN / COELI ALBO / VTRIVSQ. ORBIS GEMELLVM VELVTI CASTOREM / FESTA OMNIVM ACCLAMATIONE / INTVLIT / FECISSET PLVRA / NI. / FATO ABREPTVS PRAEPOREO / OBIISSET / LVGENDVS SEMPER QVOD IMPERASSET PARVM / AN. SAL. M. DC. XXIII

("Gregory XV, supreme pontiff. Most meritorious in the lands of the world. He strove after much in his brief rule, in lustrous months that were equal to years. Worthy of immortal name, preeminent in Roman deeds for Rome, he aided piety in the new cult of religion. He built up altars of religion, and presided over new apotheoses of saints, among them Ignatius, founder of the Society of Jesus, and Francis Xavier, who marched before the standards, twins by divine will, bright in heaven, twins in both worlds; he instituted their festivals with all acclamation. Having done many things, he died, snatched away ahead of time by fate. He mourned continually that he commanded too little. In the year of salvation 1623."—*Trans. Phyllis Jestice*)

FURTHER READING: F. Smouse Ingersoll, "Pierre le Gros Il et les sculpteurs français à Rome vers la fin du XVII siècle," in *Gazette des Beaux Arts*, Paris, 1913.

Urban VIII (August 6, 1623–July 29, 1644) *Mafeo Barberini*. Died at age 76. A cleric whispered to him on his deathbed, "You'll not see Peter's years," to which the pope replied, "It is not an article of faith." Urban was not very popular when he died because he was an extreme nepotist and ardent patron of the arts, which was fine until he drained the papal coffers and attempted to fill them again by imposing a tax on the Romans. His praecordia are in the church of SS. Vincenzo e Anastasio (see Appendix 6 for more information on this practice). Famed sculptor Gian Lorenzo Bernini began his tomb in 1623, although it was not completed until 1647. The pope is seated atop a pedestal, bestowing his blessing, while below him a golden winged skeleton inscribes the pope's name in the *Liber Mortis*, or Book of the Dead. Charity stands to the left with her children, while Justice looks dreamily on on the right of the monument.

The monument inscription reads:

URBANVS VIII / BARBERINVS / PONT. MAX.

("Urban VIII, Barberini, supreme pontiff")

To the right of the statue of Charity is a sign with the following inscription:

ANGELI CARDINALSI GIORII PROBATATAE FIDEI EN SPECTATORE VIRTUTI SEPULCHRALE HOC OPUS SIBI EXTRUENDUM MANDAVIT URBANUS PAPA VIII.

("The faithful probate Cardinal Giorii ordered this sepulcher for the virtuous Pope Urban VIII.")

FURTHER READING: Munoz, "L'amante del Bernini sul monumento di U. VIII" in *Strenna dei Romanisti*, XV, Rome, 1954; Louise Rice, *The Altars and Altarpieces of New St. Peter's: Outfitting the Basilica, 1621–1666*, Cambridge University Press, 1998.

Tomb monument of Urban VIII, St. Peter's Basilica, Rome. From Ferdinand Gregorovius, *Tombs of the Popes.*

Innocent X (September 15, 1644–January 1, 1655) *Giambattista Pamfili*. Died at age 80 (after a long illness) in the Quirinal

Monument to Innocent X, Sant' Agnese in Agone, Rome. Drawing based on Montini, *Le Tombe dei Papi.*

Palace. The Romans hated Innocent because of his nepotism for his sister-in-law, Donna Olympia Maldachini, and her greedy family. They had good reason; indeed, Innocent lay dead for three days before he was discovered because Donna Olympia didn't want to give up her power. Innocent's remains were laid out in St. Peter's, but none of his family would pay for his burial, not even Donna Olympia, who claimed she was just a poor widow and couldn't afford to pay for a burial. As a result the body was unceremoniously stored in a masons' workroom in St. Peter's. One worker felt bad for the dead pope, so he lit a coarse tallow candle at the pope's head; another observant mason suggested that the corpse might get gnawed by mice, so perhaps they should start a collection for a guard. After another lonely day for Innocent, the majordomo, Monsignor Scotti, took pity on the dead pope and ordered a coffin of poplar wood. Monsignor Segni, a

canon of St. Peter's (who had once been Innocent's majordomo but who had been fired), actually ended up paying for Innocent's very cheap, simple burial in St. Peter's. Innocent's praecordia were at least interred in the church of SS. Vincenzo e Anastasio, Rome, without a fuss (see Appendix 6 for more information on this practice). In 1730, his body was moved by a distant nephew, Cardinal Camillo Pamfili, to the Pamfili family crypt in Sant' Agnese in Agone (in the Piazza Navona, Rome). The inscription to the right of the altar in the crypt reads:

INNOCENTIVS. X. PAMPHILIVS / PONTIFEX.
MAXIMVS / VIXIT . ANN. $\overline{\text{LXXX}}$. MENS. $\overline{\text{VIII}}$ /
PONTIFICATVS . SVI. ANN. $\overline{\text{X}}$ /
MENS. III. DIE. XXIII / DECESSIT. VII.
IDVS. IANVAR / AN. CHR. $\overline{\text{MDCLV}}$ [391]

("Innocent X Pamfili, supreme pontiff. Lived 80 years and eight months. Died after ten years, three months, and 23 days in the pontificate, on the seventh day before the ides of January, in the year of Christ 1655." —*Trans. Phyllis Jestice*)

In 1730, a cenotaph by G. Valvassori and G.B. Maini was erected over the main doorway on the inside of the church. It features the Virtues Truth on the left and Strength on the right. The inscription on the cenotaph over the door reads:

INNOCENTIVS X PAMPHILIVS /
ROMANVS PONT. OPT. MAX.

("Innocent X Pamphili, Roman, supreme pontiff")

FURTHER READING: F. Cancellieri, *Il mercato, il lago dell'acqua Vergine ed il Palazzo Panfiliano nel Circo Agonale detto volgarmente Piazza Navona*, Rome, 1811.

Alexander VII (April 7, 1655–May 22, 1667) *Fabio Chigi*. Died at age 66 from kidney failure. He kept his coffin in his bedroom, and a skull (carved by famed sculptor Gian Lorenzo Bernini) on his writing table, because he was always aware that he would someday die.[392]

A seventeenth century pamphlet credited to Philip Ayres, titled *A Short Account of the Life and Death of Pope Alexander VII*, contains many fascinating details about Alexander's passing. According to this pamphlet, Alexander, although bedridden, wanted to celebrate the Passion to ready himself for his impending death. Neither his surgeon nor his confessor was able to persuade him to save his strength. He blessed the large crowd of people on Easter day, the last time they would ever see him alive.

Three days later the pains became more violent, but Alexander remained cheerful because he hoped "to enjoy eternal felicity." He himself called for the Viaticum, then assembled his cardinals and spoke to them in Latin because he felt he could convey his message better in Latin than in Italian. He begged their pardon for his frailty, apologized for "expending great sums for promoting the Church interest," told them to

use sincerity and "cleverness" in the next election, and added, "Consider that from the Church you have received the most honorable part of what you possess; that if you were constrained to leave that which you received from the Church, to the offerings of others, how much more contentedly, (without any other appetite) should you then enjoy that which you do now possess." He then asked them to pray for his cardinal nephew, his older brother, the rest of his family, and himself. He blessed them by lifting his weak hands. Each cardinal then kissed his hand and departed, each "with tears in his eyes." When everyone had left, he began to pray, often repeating, "*Cupio disolvi,*" and "*Effe cum christo.*" He also read spiritual books, particularly the penentential psalms. Although he was in great pain, he never showed any "discomposed countenance."

A priest gave him a picture of hearts, each one representing one of the Mysteries of the Passion, so that when he was hurting most he could remember the pain that Jesus suffered on the cross. He put this picture behind his pillow, so he could lay his head on it, although sometimes he asked that it be placed at the foot of his bed so he could meditate on it.

The pope received the eucharist and the sacrament of Extreme Unction, and prepared himself for his "transit." One of the priests standing near him asked him for a final Act of Contrition, as well as to ask God pardon for his sins. Although the pope could barely speak, he answered, "*Ita.*" The priest then said that he should hope in the mercies of God, and the pope answered his last word "*certe.*"

On his own decaying, the pope had once said, "One's life should decay before one's death." He died on Sunday, May 22, about 10:00 in the morning. Later that night the cardinal lord chamberlain dressed his corpse, put it on a litter of crimson velvet, and, accompanied by the penitentiary fathers, guards and light horses, the artillery, and the rear guard of the curiaffiers, carried him to the Vatican.

Tomb monument of Alexander VII, St. Peter's basilica, Rome.

The next day Alexander was autopsied and his doctors found a black spot on one of his lungs, a wasted kidney containing "fleshy kernels" (kidney stones), and an ulcer of the kidneys, which was the worst of all his afflictions. He was embalmed (his praecordia are in the church of SS. Vincenzo e Anastasio, Rome — see Appendix 6 for more information on this practice) and pontifically clothed, then carried the next day to St. Peter's and placed in the Chapel of the Holy Sacrament, where scores of people came to kiss his feet and "take from him, whatsoever they could lay hands on, to preserve to themselves as Holy Reliquaries."

A great funeral machine (an apparatus for lifting the coffin into the crypt) was built in St. Peter's for the funeral of this pope, with inscriptions praising him for works he did around Rome while he was alive. His monument, by the great sculptor Gian Lorenzo Bernini, is located in St. Peter's basilica and features the praying pope (by Michele Maglia) surrounded by Charity (Giuseppe Mazzuoli), Truth (Lazzaro Morelli and Giulio Catani), Prudence (Giuseppe Baratta and Giulio Cartari), and Justice (Giulio Catani). Begun in 1672, it was completed in 1678, the same year that Innocent XI ordered that Charity's breasts be covered in a metal vest because they were too indecent for the Counter Reformation age. A skeleton appears to be emerging from the door below, as if rising from the papal tomb to grasp the pope and deliver him to life everlasting — but it's really just coming out of a broom closet. The monument inscription reads:

ALEXANDER VII / CHISIVS / PONT. MAX.

("Alexander VII, Chigi, supreme pontiff")

The poet John Flowre wrote a poem to Alexander, c. 1667:

Within this Marble doth Intombed lye,
Not One, but All a Noble Familie:
A Pearle of such a Price, that soon about
Possesion of it, Heaven, and Earth fell out;
Both could not have Him, So they did Devise
This Fatall Salvo, to divide the Prize:

Heaven Share's the Soul, and Earth his Body take's,
Thus we lose all, whilst Heaven, and Earth, part flakes:
But Heaven, not brooking that the Earth should share
In the least Attome, of a Piece so Rare,
Intents to Sue Out, by a new Revize
His Habeus Corpus, at the Grand Assize.[393]

FURTHER READING: G. B. Passeri, *Die Kunstlerbiographien*, Vienna, 1934; Virgilio Cardinal Noe, *Le Tombe e i Monumenti*, Rome, 2000.

Clement IX (June 20, 1667–December 9, 1669) *Giulio Rospigliosi*. Died of stroke at age 69 after hearing about the terrible loss of life on Crete. Popular with the Romans, he was sadly missed when he died. His praecordia are in the church of SS. Vincenzo e Anastasio in Rome (see Appendix 6 for more information on this practice). He was originally buried in St. Peter's but was moved in 1675 to Santa Maria Maggiore, Rome, where his body is interred under the pavement of the central nave. The floor marker inscription:

CLEMENS NONVS / PONTIFEX MAXIMVS /
LIBERIANAE BASILICAE / OLIM CANONICVS ET
VICARIVS / HIC IACENS / EIVS PRAESIDIVM /
QVAE IANVA COELI EST / ET FIDELIVM PRECES /
IMPLORAT / OBIIT DIE IX DECEMBRIS / ANNO
SALVTIS MDCLXIX / AETATIS SEXAGESIMO NONO /
VIXIT IN PONTIFICATV / ANNOS DVOS /
MENSES QVINQVE / DIES NOVEMDECIM

("Clement IX, supreme pontiff, once canon and vicar of the Liberian Basilica (St. Mary Major), lying here, begs the protection of him who is the gate of heaven, as well as the prayers of the faithful. He died the ninth day of December, in the year of salvation 1669, in the 69th year of his age. He reigned as pope for two years, five months, 19 days." — *Trans. Father Thomas Buffer*)

Clement's cenotaph, by Bernini's pupil, Ercole Ferrata, is located across from the monument of Nicolas IV and features the pope (carved by Girolamo Rainaldi) in the center niche, with Charity (Erocole Ferrata) on the left and underneath a medallion

Cenotaph of Clement IX, Santa Maria Maggiore, Rome.

showing "The Inauguration of a new Papal Altar." On the right Cosimo Fancelli carved Truth, which is underneath a medallion featuring "The Bridge of Sant' Angelo." Under the epitaph is the shell, symbolic of birth and resurrection. The cenotaph epitaph reads:

CLEMENTIS IX AETERNAE MEMORIAE
PONTIFICIS / MAGNI CINERES / NE
ABSQVE VLLO SEPVLCRALI HONORE SICVT
IPSE IVSSERAT / HVMI LATERENT /
CLEMENS X PONT. MAX. BENEFACTORI
SVO ET OB SPECTATVM FIDEI ZELVM / OB
EGREGIAM ERGA OMNES BENEFICENTIAM
ET CHARITATEM / DE RE CHRISTIANA
OPTIME MERITO GRATI ANIMI
MONVMENTVM / POSVIT /
ANNO DOMINI MDCLXXI

("The grateful Clement X, supreme pontiff, placed this monument to his benefactor, both because of his concern for the zeal of the faith, and because of his outstanding beneficence and charity toward all, on account of his Christian merit, lest the great ashes of Clement IX, pontiff of everlasting memory, should lie hidden in the earth without the honor of a sepulcher, as he himself had commanded. In the year of Our Lord 1671."—*Trans. Fr. Thomas Buffer*).

FURTHER READING: Virgilio Cardinal Noe, *Le Tombe e i Monumenti*, Rome, 2000.

Tomb monument of Clement X, St. Peter's Basilica, Rome. From R.P. Mortier, *Saint-Pierre de Rome*.

putti (by Filippo Carcani) hold up the inscription:

CLEMENS X / ALTERIVS ROMANVS / PONT. MAX.

("Clement X, Altieri, Roman, supreme pontiff")

Clement X (April 29, 1670–July 22, 1676) *Emilio Altieri*. Died at age 86 of dropsy followed by a malignant fever. His praecordia are in the Church of SS. Vincenzo e Anastasio in Rome (see Appendix 6 for more information on this pactice). His monument, designed by Mattia de' Rossi, is located in St. Peter's basilica and features the pope (by Ercole Ferrata) high atop the monument with Clemency (by Giuseppi Mazzuoli) and Goodness (by Lazzaro Morelli). Leonardo Reti carved the sarcophagus bas-relief, "The Beginning of the Jubilee of 1675." Two

Blessed Innocent XI (September 21, 1676–August 12, 1689) *Benedetto Odescalchi*. Died at age 78 from kidney stones (one reportedly weighing a remarkable seven ounces); there is no word on whether the stones were interred along with his praecordia in the Church of SS. Vincenzo e Anastasio in Rome (see Appendix 6 for more information on this practice). His praecordia are separated from those of the other popes: His are in the chapel of the Madonna, while his heart is in the chapel of the

Tomb monument of Blessed Innocent XI, St. Peter's basilica, Rome.

Venerated remains of Innocent XI, St. Peter's basilica, Rome.

Odescalchi Palace in Rome.[394] Innocent's monument, located in St. Peter's Basilica, was designed by C. Maratta and sculpted by Stefano Monnot. It features the pope with Truth and Strength, and a bas-relief on the sarcophagus entitled "The Liberation of Vienna." The monument inscription reads:

INNOCENTIO XI / PONT. MAX / LIVIVS
ODESCHALCVS NEP. / AN. IVB. MDCC

("To Innocent XI, high priest, the nephew Livius Odescalchi in the jubilee year 1700."— *Trans. Father Tom Carleton*)

The French aborted his canonization process in 1744, but Innocent was beatified by Pius XII on October 7, 1956, and his remains placed under the altar of Saint Sebastian in St. Peter's. The inscription on the glass sarcophagus reads:

B. INNOCENTIVS XI PONT. MAX

("Blessed Innocent XI, Supreme Pontiff")

The feast day of Innocent XI is August 12.

FURTHER READING: B. Odescalchi, "La tomba d'I. XI," in *Impressioni di storia e d'arte*; A. Castan, *Le sculpteur francais Pierre-Etienne Monnot*, Besancon-Cassel, 1888; Virgilio Cardinal Noe, *Le Tombe e i Monumenti*, Rome, 2000; Louise Rice, *The Altars and Altarpieces of New St. Peter's : Outfitting the Basilica, 1621–1666*, Cambridge University Press, 1998.

Alexander VIII (October 6, 1689–February 1, 1691) *Pietro Ottoboni*. Died at age 81. He sent a letter to Louis XIV from his deathbed opposing the extension of the regalia (the royal prerogative allowing the state to share in the administration and, especially, the income of the church) that almost led to a new French schism. Arrigo of St. Martin designed Alexander's monument in St. Peter's; Giuseppe Bertosi sculpted the bronze statue of the pope, while Angelo de Rossi sculpted the marble figures of Religion and Prudence as well as the bas-relief, "The Canonization of 1690."

Tomb monument of Alexander VIII, St. Peter's basilica, Rome. From R.P. Mortier, *Saint-Pierre de Rome*.

PATRVO MAGNO / ALEXANDERO VIII OTTHOBONO / VENETO P.O.M. / PETRVS CARD. EPVS. SABIN. S.R.E. VIC. CANC. / ANNO IVB. MDCCXXV

("To the eminent great uncle, Alexander VIII Ottoboni, Venetian, great high priest, Peter, cardinal bishop of Sabina, vice chancellor of the Holy Roman Church, year of the Jubilee 1725."—*Trans. Father Tom Carleton*)

FURTHER READING: R. Ippoliti Cecchetelli, *La tomba di Alessandro VIII nella basilica Vaticana*, Rome, 1921; Virgilio Cardinal Noe, *Le Tombe e i Monumenti*, Rome, 2000.

Innocent XII (July 12, 1691–September 27, 1700) *Antonio Pignatelli*. Died at age 87. His praecordia are in the Church of SS.

Vincenzo e Anastasio, Rome (see Appendix 6 for more information on this practice), although his heart, encased in silver, was brought to Naples and placed in a monument that was erected in his honor in 1696. Originally this cenotaph was located in the tribune, but Cardinal Giuseppe Spinelli had it transferred to its present location in the left transept in the late eighteenth century. The epitaph reads:

INNOCENTIO XII PONT. MAX PIGNATELLO / DE CHRISTIANA RE OPTIME MERITO / MUNIIS PLURIMIS APUD CATHOLICOS PRINCIPES ET IN AULA ROMANA MIRE PERFUNCTO / PER GRADUS HONORUM OMNES / AB ARCHIEP. NEAPOLITANO SANCTE ET EFFUSA IN EGENOS CHARITATE GESTO / AD SUPREMUM PONTIFICATUS MAXIMI APICEM EVECTO / INDICTA ABOLITI NEPOTISMI LEGE NORMAQUE PRAEMONSTRATA / ECCLESIA AC TOTO TERRARUM ORBE PLAUDENTE / PAUPERIBUS PERPETUO CENSU DITATIS ET IN LATERANO / MAGNI GREGORII EXEMPLO MUNIFICENTISSIME ALITIS / PARAECIARUM REDDITIBUS UT EGESTATI UBIQUE OCCURRATUR EX INTEGRO RESTITUTIS / MAGNO CUM ECCLESIARUM EMOLUMENTO NEAPOLITANI REGNI EPISCOPIS / SPOLIORUM ONERE SUPRA VOTUM CONDONATO LEVATIS / INTER PRAECLARISSIMA LIBERALITATIS MUNERA / QUAMVIS EXHAUSTO AERARIO OB EXTINCTAM CAMERALIS QUAESTURAE VENALITATEM / DATIS SACRO IN TURCAS FOEDERE SUBSIDIIS / SANCTISSIMIS LEGIBUS / ECCLESIASTICAE DISCIPLINAE IUSTITIAE ET POPULORUM TUTELA STRENUE ASSERTA / PASTORALI SOLICITUDINE EXIMIOQUE ZELO IN TOTA CHRISTIANA REPUBLICA PACANDA / ET RELIGIONE AMPLIFICANDA COMMENDATISSIMO / JACOBUS CARDINALIS CANTELMUS ARCHIEPISCOPUS NEAPOLITANUS /

Tomb monument of Innocent XII, St. Peter's basilica, Rome.

ANNO SAL. HUM. M DC XCVI / PONTIFICATUS
VERO VI MAIORA DATURI / P.

("Supreme Pontiff Innocent XII, of the Pignatello family. With greatest merit in the affairs
of Christianity; with many gifts among
Catholic leaders and in the Roman court per-
forming wonderfully through every grade of
honor; from the holy archbishopric of Naples,
in which he spent himself freely in charitable
deeds to the needy, he reached the apex of the
supreme pontificate. You issued a law abolish-
ing nepotism and pointed out the right way, to
the applause of the Church and all lands of the
earth. You perpetually cared for the poor, even
in the Lateran, copying with greatest munificence the example of Gregory the Great. You
gave back so that those in poverty might be
completely restored. With great effort you
lightened the burdens of the despoiled churches
in the kingdom of Naples, as vowed. [You
were] among the most excellent in the gifts of
liberality, to the point of emptying the treasury
because the greed of the quaestorial office had
been abolished. You gave holy subsidies to
the confederation against the Turks. You
strenuously asserted pastoral care and
exceptional zeal in all of Christendom with
most holy laws regarding ecclesiastical discipline, justice, and care of the populace, and
magnified all with most praiseworthy religion. Jacopo cardinal Cantelmo, archbishop
of Naples, gave this monument in the year
of human salvation 1696, in the sixth year of
his pontificate."—*Trans. Phyllis Jestice*)

Innocent was originally buried in a
simple marble sarcophagus located in the
Chapel of the Sacrament in St. Peter's, but
in 1746 Fillipo della Valle and Ferdinando
Fuga completed a grand monument that
features the sitting pope bestowing the
benediction, while Charity adores him on
the right and Justice looks longingly down
at her scales on the left. The monument
epitaph reads:

INNOCENTIUS XII / PIGNATTELLI / INNOCENTII
XII P.M. / INORNATUM MONUMENTUM / IN
HANC ELEGANTEM FORMAM REDIGI CURAVIT /
ADPROBANTE BENEDICTO XIV P. M. / VINCEN-
TIUS S. R. E. CARD. PETRA EP. PRAEN. / ET M:
POENITEN. / A.S. MDCCXLVI

("Vincent Petra, cardinal of the Holy Roman
Church, and chief penitentiary, with the
approval of Supreme Pontiff Benedict XIV, took
care to restructure in this elegant form the
unadorned tomb of Supreme Pontiff Innocent
XII, 1746."—*Trans. Father Tom Carleton*)

Clement XI (November 23, 1700–March 19,
1721) *Giovanni Francesco Albani*. Died at age
71 of stroke. His praecordia are sometimes
thought to be in the Church of SS. Vincenzo
e Anastasio, Rome (see Appendix 6 for more
information on this practice), but they are
actually in the Church of San Francesco in
Urbino, Italy.[395] In Rome Clement was interred under the pavement of Choro chapel
in St. Peter's, which was marked only a marble slab:

D.O.M. / CLEMENS XI PM / HVIVS SS. BASILICAE /
OLIM VICARIVS / ET POSTEA CANONICVS / SIBI
VIVENS PONI IVSSIT / OBIIT DIE XIX MARTII /

Cenotaph to Clement XI, Duomo of Ferrara.

ANNO SAL. MDCCXXI / AETATIS VERO SVAE LXXI / MENS. VII D XXV / SEDIT IN PONTIFICATV / ANNOS XX MENSES III / DIES XXIV / ORATE PRO EO

("To God, the best and greatest. Clement XI, high priest, of this sacrosanct basilica first vicar, and then canon, [while] still living, ordered this marble to be placed to himself. Died the 19th of March of the year of Salvation 1721, at the age of 71 years, 7 months and 25 days. He was Pope 20 years, 3 months and 24 days. Pray for him." — *Trans. Father Tom Carleton*)

There is also a cenotaph in Clement's honor in the Duomo of Ferrara, to the left of the high altar, exactly opposite the cenotaph of Pope Urban III (d. 1197).

FURTHER READING: I. Berni, "Tre cuori in un santuario di montagna," in *Amor di Roma*, Rome, 1956; Virgilio Cardinal Noe, *Le Tombe e i Monumenti*, Rome, 2000.

Innocent XIII (May 8, 1721–March 7, 1724) *Michelangelo dei Conti*. Died at age 69 of long illness. His last words were, "I am not of this world." His praecordia are in the Church of SS. Vincenzo e Anastasio, Rome (see Appendix 6 for more information on this practice). His heart, however, was transported to the sanctuary in Mentorella sul monte Guadagnolo, as a pilaster in the sanctuary states: CUORE INNOCENTII XIII DE COMITIBUS ("The heart of Innocent XIII adorns this"). His original sepulcher, made of stucco, was located in the right nave of St. Peter's,

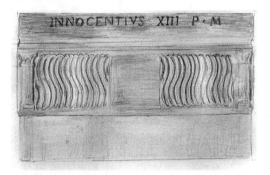

Sarcophagus of Innocent XIII, Vatican grottoes. Drawing by Joan Reardon.

although in 1836 he was reinterred in an ancient sarcophagus now located in the crypt.

The following epitaph for Innocent XIII was posted on the statue known as Pasquino, which is used to post anonymous messages even today:

> Pope Conti has died,
> He who did not do much good
> Because he didn't want to,
> And didn't do much bad
> Because he wasn't able to.[396]

FURTHER READING: Virgilio Cardinal Noe, *Le Tombe e i Monumenti*, Rome, 2000.

Benedict XIII (May 29, 1724–February 21, 1730) *Pietro Francesco Orsini*. Died at 81. His praecordia are in the Vatican grottoes, in a marble tabernacle along with those of Queen Christina of Sweden. After the restoration of the grottoes, the Rev. Fabbrica of St. Peter's moved the tabernacle to the chapel of Santa Maria de Pregnantibus, which is not open to the public. The Romans hated Benedict because he ignorantly surrounded himself with scheming greedy men from his home town of Benevento, Italy. When he died, therefore, the Romans celebrated by attacking the Beneventans, who were barely able to escape Rome alive.

Benedict was originally buried in St. Peter's, but because he had wished to be buried in Santa Maria sopra Minerva, his successor, Clement XII, had his remains moved there on February 22, 1738. Benedict's monument, designed by Marchionni and actually made during Benedict's lifetime, features the pope carved by Pietro Bracci, with Purity (also by Bracci) and Prayer (by Baccio Pincellotti) on either side of his sarcophagus. The bas-relief on the sarcophagus itself depicts a council presided over by Benedict. The monument inscription reads:

BENEDICTVS XIII VRSINVS / PONT. OPT. MAX. / EX ORDINE PRAEDICATORVM

("Benedict XIII Orsini. Best and greatest of pontiffs from the Order of Preachers." — *Trans. Phyllis Jestice*)

Tomb monument of Benedict XIII, St. Peter's basilica, Rome.

FURTHER READING: G. Rohault de Fleury, *Le Latran au moyen-age*, Paris, 1877.

Clement XII (July 12, 1730–February 6, 1740) *Lorenzo Corsini*.

Died at age 87 of bladder infection, although he was also blind and bedridden with gout. His praecordia are in the Church of SS. Vincenzo e Anastasio in Rome (see Appendix 6 for more information on this practice). His cenotaph, designed by Alessandro Galilei, is located in St. John Lateran and features Magnificence and Abundance (by C. Monaldi), with the pope (by G.B. Maini) giving his blessing. The inscription reads:

CLEMENS XII / PONT. MAX. /
ANNO IV / OBIIT ANNO X

("Clement XII, supreme pontiff, in year 4 [*sic*], died in his tenth year.")

Clement's actual remains are interred in an ancient bath that he had caused to be removed from the Pantheon and that is buried in his family mausoleum in the crypt of the church; it bears the following inscription:

D.O.M. / OSSA CLEMENTIS XII P.M. QVAE E VATIC.
BASILIC. TRANSLATA / HIC RECONDI CURAVIT VI
KAL. SEXTIL. A M DCC XLII / NERVES CARDINALIS
FRATRIS FILIVS

Monument to Clement XII, St. John Lateran, Rome. Drawing based on Montini, *Le Tombe dei Papi*.

("In the name of God, best and greatest. The bones of Clement XII pontifex maximus which were transferred from the Vatican basilica. Cardinal Nereo, his brother's son, had them placed here on the sixth day before the calends of August in the year 1742."—*Trans. Phyllis Jestice*)

He is the last pope to have been originally buried in the Lateran.

Sarcophagus of Clement XII, crypt of St. John Lateran, Rome. Drawing based on Montini, *Le Tombe dei Papi*.

Benedict XIV (August 17, 1740–midday May 3, 1758) *Prospero Lorenzo Lambertini*.

Died of kidney disease, fever, and inflamma-

Tomb monument of Benedict XIV, St. Peter's basilica, Rome.

tion of the lungs at age 83. His last words were, "Our Lord died under Pilate, I shall die under Pontius"[397] (Pontius was his doctor). Not only were his praecordia placed, as was custom, in the Church of SS. Vincenzo e Anastasio (see Appendix 6 for more information on this practice), but he had an underground chapel built beneath the high altar of the church to house all the praecordia, "in a well sealed mortuary vase," of the popes whose names were recorded in marble inscriptions placed in the walls of the high altar.[398] The 64 cardinals he created during his reign paid for the marble monument in St. Peter's, on which the pope, carved by Pietro Bracci, stands majestically above a doorway while Knowledge (also Bracci) looks up at him longingly on the left and Temptation (by Gaspare Sibilla) sits on the right. Benedict's right hand is extended in a gesture that he never used, and his left hand is behind him, holding a cherub by the hair — although the Romans like to say that he's shaking off the remnants of his last pinch of snuff, to which he was addicted.

BENEDICTO XIV / PONT. MAX. /
S.R.E. CARDINALES / AB EO CREATI

("To Benedict XIV, supreme pontiff, [by] the Cardinals of the Holy Roman Church, created by him."—*Trans. Father Tom Carleton*)

FURTHER READING: C. Maes "Tabacco in chiesa probito," in *Cracas*, Rome, n. s., VI, 1893; Virgilio Cardinal Noe, *Le Tombe e i Monumenti*, Rome, 2000.

Clement XIII (July 6, 1758–February 2, 1769) *Carlo della Torre Rezzonico*. Died suddenly at age 75 from a heart attack which was hastened by stress concerning the decision to dissolve the Jesuits. His praecordia are in the Church of SS. Vincenzo e Anastasio (see Appendix 6 for more information on this practice). His

monument, by Antonio Canova, in St. Peter's was unveiled on April 4, 1795, to good reviews. Religion stands on the left, holding a cross with her right hand, while the Angel of Death, with an inverted torch, stands on the other side. Small bas-reliefs of Charity and Hope flank either side of the inscription. Canova injured himself with a drill while working on the tomb and suffered extremely severe stomach pains for the rest of his life. Eventually he died from the effects of his injury.

Clement's monument inscription reads:

CLEMENTI XIIII / REZZONICO /
P. M. / FRATRIS FILII

Tomb monument of Clement XIII, St. Peter's basilica, Rome.

("To Clement XIII, Rezzonian, supreme pontiff, [by the] sons of your brother"—*Trans. Father Tom Carleton*)

FURTHER READING: G.G. de Rossi, *Lettera sul depostio di C. XIII nella Basilica Vaticana*, Bassano, 1792; Munoz, "Le prime opere di A. Canova in Roma," in *Capitolium*, Rome, VII, 1931.

Clement XIV (May 19, 1769–September 22, 1774) *Lorenzo Ganganelli.* Died at age 69 from either lung cancer or poison in the Quirinal Palace, Rome. In 1773 he annulled the Order of Jesus, and soon afterwards he began complaining of pains and wasting away. He also suffered from depression, herpes, and bad acne. Not long after the dissolution of the Order of Jesus, he began showing signs of mental disturbance: His mouth would slaver as his eyes darted about in their bulging sockets; he shuffled from room to room, always keeping close to the walls for fear of being assassinated by a Jesuit. Visionary nuns had correctly predicted that he would die in September of 1774, and his last words were, "I am passing into eternity, and I know the reason why." His body became black immediately and decayed so rapidly that it was impossible to lay him out for the ceremony of kissing his feet. Although supporters of the Jesuits were suspected of poisoning the pope, no signs of poison were seen at the autopsy, leading to the ruling that his death was by natural causes. The Spanish ambassador said that Clement died of a natural illness; both the lungs were inflamed and cancerous. However, the French ambassador claimed that he knew for a fact that the pope *did not* die from natural causes. The next pope, Pius VI, once said to Cardinal de Bernis that he knew what Clement had died of, and he was "therefore loath to risk a similar death."[399]

Clement's praecordia are in the Church of SS. Vincenzo e Anastasio, Rome (see Appendix 6 for more information on this practice). Antonio Canova's monument for Clement which features

Tomb monument of Clement XIV, Church of Santi Apostoli, Rome.

the seated pope ominously bestowing his blessing while Temperance collapses in anguish on his sarcophagus and Mildness sits forlornly at the base of the monument, was moved in 1802 to the Church of Santi Apostoli, Rome (which is, ironically, near two Jesuit colleges). The following epitaph was recorded in 1863:

HEIC SITVM EST IN PACE / CORPVS / CLEMENTIS XIV / PONTIFICIS MAXIMI / ORDINIS FRATR. MINOR. CONVENTVAL / VENIA PII VII / PARENTIS OPTIMI INDVLGENTISSIMI / E LOCO SEPVLTVRE PONTIFICIAE / AD VATICANVM / VBI QVIERAT / ANN. XXVI MENSIB. IV DIEB. XXVII / IN HANC BASILICAM SS. XII APOSTOLOR. / XII KAL. FEBR. MDCCCII TRANSLATVM / BONAVENTVRA BARTOLO / INTERAMNATE / EIVSDEM ORDINIS / GENERALI MINISTRO XCIII / VIXIT ANN. LXVIII MENSIB. X DIEB. XXII / CREATVS XIV KAL IAN. MDCCLXIX / IN PONTIFICATV / ANNOS V MENSES IV DIES III / OMNIVM VIRTVTVM GENERE ENITVT / PRINCIPI PIENTISSIMO / MNEMOSYNON DIVTVRNI AMORIS / ANNO M DCCC LXIII D.[400]

("Here is placed in peace the body of Clement XIV, supreme pontiff, of the order of Friars Minor (Conventual). [It was] brought by Pius VII, best and most indulgent of fathers, from the place of pontifical entombment at the Vatican, where it rested 26 years, 4 months, 27 days, to this basilica of the holy twelve apostles. Transferred on the twelfth day before the calends of February 1802, by Bonaventura Bartolo of Teramo, 93rd general minister of that same order. He lived 68 years, 10 months, 22 days. On the fourteenth day before the calends of January 1769 he was made pontiff, serving 5 years, 4 months, 3 days. He strove for all the virtues of a most pious prince. A memorial of eternal love, in the year 1863."—*Trans. Phyllis Jestice*)

It is the custom of American seminarians studying at the Pontifical Gregorian University to place flowers at the tomb of Clement XIV after difficult exams from their Jesuit professors.

Pius VI (February 15, 1775–August 29, 1799) *Giovanni Angelo Brachi*. Died at age 82 from a collapsed heart in a fortress at Valence on the Rhone. Napoleon demanded the abolition of the papacy, but Pius refused to submit and was therefore taken prisoner and forced to march over the Alps to France. When Pius asked Napoleon if he could die in Rome, Napoleon said, "You can die anywhere." On the morning of August 29 Pius lay dying, yet for the first time in eleven days he "recovered his perfect senses," and bade all those around him come closer. He took each man's hand and gave them his blessing. He then told the Bishop of Corinth (who had stayed by his side through all the troubles), "Recommend above all things to my Successor, to forgive the French, as I most sincerely forgive them from my heart."[401] With his last strength he raised his crucifix and gave a triple blessing; then he clasped it to his breast and died.[402] Pius's fisherman's ring was left unbroken and a new inscription added for his successor, Pius VII. In the eyes of the world Pius died a martyr, and he wished to be buried as close as possible to St. Peter.

According to the pamphlet "Death of the Pope!" the Spanish ambassador tried to claim Pius's remains to bring back to Rome, but he was refused. The body was then "burnt with quick-lime,"[403] a common practice in Europe at the time, especially for people who died far from the place they were to be interred. Quick-lime dissolved the flesh, leaving only the bones, which were easy to store and transport.

In December of that year one of Napoleon's earliest decrees as first consul called for funeral honors for the bones of Pius VI, which were still lying unburied in a sealed coffin in the cemetery of Santa Caterina in Valence. The local constitutional clergy, however, refused Pius a Christian burial so the town prefect registered the death of "Citizen Braschi, Exercising the Profession of Pontiff."

Napoleon raised a monument (sculpted by Massimiliano Laboureur) in the cathedral of Valence, France, to house Pius's heart. A bust of the pope sits atop the reliquary, underneath which is the allegorical figure of Religion presenting the cross as a symbol of restoring the church to France.[404] The epitaph is located behind the reliquary:

PIVS VI PONT. MAX / DIE 29 AVGVSTI 1799 /
VALENTIAE ALLOBROGVM PIENTISSIME OBIIT /
CVIVS CORPVS IN COEMETERIO S. CATHARINAE
DEPOSITVM / ROMAM DIE 29 DECEM. 1802
TRANSLATVM / IN BASILICA VATICANA IVXTA B.
PETRI CONFESSIONEM / REQVIESCIT / PRAECORDIA
EIVS PII VII MVNIFICENTIA / VALENTINAE
CATHEDRALI DIE 29 MARTII 1803 CONCESSA /
IN HOC MARMORE DIE 25 OCT. 1811 INCLVSA /
RELIGIOSE SERVANTVR / CLERICIS MAIORIS
SEMINARII AB ANNO 1791 EXSVLIS / ET SAEVIENTE
ITERVM PERSECVTIONE A. D. / 1906 A PIO VI
NVNCVPATI / IN CIVITATEM EPISCOPALEM
FELICITER REDEVNTIBVS / ANNO REPARATAE
SALVTIS IVBILARI 1934 / HOC PIETATIS
MONVMENTVM / ILL. AC RR. DD. CAMILLO PIC
VALENTINENSI PRAESVLE / IN NOBILIORI HAC
CHORI PARTE / COLLOCATVM EST[405]

("Pius VI, supreme pontiff. Died most piously in Valence on the 29th of August 1790 [actually 1799]. Whose body, having been deposited in the cemetery of St. Catherine, was transferred to Rome on 29 December 1802, that it might rest in the Vatican basilica beside the confession of St. Peter. His heart was conceded to the cathedral of Valence on 29 March 1803, through the munificence of Pius VII, and enclosed in this marble on 25 October 1811. [Pius was] served religiously by the clerics of the greater seminary, who were exiled in the year 1791 and repeatedly suffered savage persecution. In the year 1906 they happily returned to the episcopal city named by Pius VI. In the jubilee year of restored salvation 1934, this monument of piety was placed in the more noble part of the choir by the illustrious and most reverend lord Camillo Pic, bishop of Valence."—*Trans. Phyllis Jestice*)

Cardinal Spina, who was with Pius in exile, added the following:

SANCTA PII SEXTI REDEUNT PRAECORDIA GALLIS /
ROMA TENET CORPUS NOMEN UBIQUE SONAT /
CARD. SPINA.[406]

("Returned from France, the holy heart of Pius VI. Rome conserves the body; while everywhere the name resounds."—*Trans. Father Tom Carleton*)

On December 29, 1802, the French consulate said the body of Pius VI could be taken back to Rome, which it was, and placed to the left of the main altar of St. Peter's. In 1822, Antonio Canova erected a simple monument on which Pius is shown kneeling in prayer, looking to the heavens. The monument was originally placed in the confession of St. Peter's, although it is now in the grottoes of the basilica near the sarcophagus of Innocent VII. Inscription:

PIVS VI BRASCHIVS CAESENAS / ORATE PRO EO

("Pius VI, Braschi of Cesea. Pray for him.")

His praecordia were entombed in the Church of SS. Vincenzo e Anastasio, Rome (see Appendix 6 for more information on this practice), with this inscription:

(praecordia) TRANSLATA SVNT
VALENTIAM APVD RHODANVM /
UBI DECESSIT DIE XXIX AVGVSTI MDCCIC[407]

("[Heart] transferred to Valence on the Rhone where he died on 29 August 1799."—*Trans. Phyllis Jestice*)

In 1949, Piux XII rearranged the Vatican crypt and placed Pius's remains in an ancient sarcophagus that features a bas-relief of the Adoration of the Magi. The inscription reads:

MORTALES PII VI EXVVIAS QVEM INIVSTVM
CONSVMPSIT EXILIVM / PIVS XII PONT. MAX. HEIC
DIGNE COLLOCARI / AC MARMOREO ORNAMENTO
ARTE HISTORIAQVE PRAESTANTISSIMO / DECORARI
IVSSIT A. MCMXXXXIX[408]

("Pius XII, High Priest, in the year 1949, arranged that the mortal remains of Pius VI, worn out by unjust exile, might be here worthily located and might have the embellishment of this marble ornament distinguished by art and history."—*Trans. Father Tom Carleton*)

On the Roman statue named Pasquino (an old, broken statue on which people to this day post anonymous messages) appeared this couplet, which rhymes in Italian:

A Pius loses his faith
To hang on to his throne.[409]

Sarcophagus of Pius VI, Vatican grottoes.

FURTHER READING: G. Anichini, "Di una singolare scultura scoperta nelle Grotte Vaticane," in *Boll. Degli Amici delle Catacombe*, Rome, XII, 1942; A. Tadolini, *Ricordi autobiografici*, Rome, 1900; Virgilio Cardinal Noe, *Le Tombe e i Monumenti*, Rome, 2000.

Pius VII   (March 14, 1800–July 20, 1823)

Luigi Barnabus Chiaramonte. Died at age 81 of a "weakened heart"[410] in the Quirinal Palace, Rome. He was physically, emotionally and spiritually anguished and suffered from depression fits during which he would say, "I shall die insane like Clement XIV." On July 6, 1823, he fell in his apartment, fractured his thigh, and was placed in his bed, where he would stay for the remainder of his life. He died a few weeks later with his faithful secretary of state, Cardinal Consalvi, at his side to hear his last words, "Savona and Fontainebleau."

Consalvi later sold his own personal objects to have Alberto Thorwaldsen create a monument for Pius. The monument was erected in St. Peter's and features the pope bestowing his blessing, with the angels of Time and History on either side. Two small putti hold Pius's coat of arms beneath the inscription, while Wisdom stands on the right side and Strength stands on the left. His praecordia are in the Church of SS. Vincenzo e Anastasio (see Appendix 6 for more information on this practice). The inscription reads:

PIO VII CLARAMONTIO CAESENATI
PONTIFICI MAXIMO / HERCVLES CARD.
CONSALVI ROMANVS AB EO CREATVS

("To Pius VII, Chiaramonti of Cesena, supreme pontiff. Cardinal Hercules Consalvi, Roman, created [cardinal] by him [Pius VII]."— *Trans. Father Tom Carleton*)

FURTHER READING: M.K. Norvegaard, "Thorwaldsen e il monumento di P. VII in S. Pietro," in *Illustr. Vaticana*, C.d. V., IX 1938; Virgilio Cardinal Noe, *Le Tombe e i Monumenti*, Rome, 2000.

Tomb monument of Pius VII, St. Peter's basilica.

Leo XII   (September 28, 1823–February 10, 1829) *Annibale Sermattei della Genga*. Died at age 69 from a botched operation to remove his crippling chronic hemorrhoids. When elected, he had protested to the cardinals: "Do not insist. You are electing a corpse." He was so sickly that he was given his last rites 17 times.[411] He was very unpopular with the Romans when he died because he took a very clerical view of things and refused to acknowledge the changing world around him. His praecordia are in the Church of SS. Vincenzo e Anastasio (see Appendix 6 for more information on this process).

Gregory XVI ordered Giuseppe Fabris to execute a monument for Leo, which was unveiled in 1837 and located in the right nave of St. Peter's basilica. The monument, above a doorway, features the standing pope in a niche bestowing his blessing, while Religion and Justice, in bas-relief above the niche, gaze upon the papal tiara. The monument inscription reads:

MEMORIAE LEONIS XII P. M. GREGORIVS XVI P. M.

("To the memory of Leo XII, supreme pontiff. Pope Gregory XVI, supreme pontiff.")

The following inscription, set in a circle of marble, marks the spot under the pavement of St. Peter's (near the altar of Leo the Great) where the body of Leo XII is buried:

LEONI MAGNO PATRONO COELESTI / ME SVPPLEX
COMMENDANS / HIC APVD SACROS EIVS CINERES /
LOCVM SEPVLTVRAE ELEGI / LEO XII HVMILIS
CLIENS / HAEREDVM TANTI NOMINIS MINIMVS /
VIXIT AN. LXVIII M. V D. VIII / OBIIT IV ID. FEBR.
A. M.D.CCCXXVIIII / PONTIFICATVS SVI
ANNO V M. IV D. XIII / HIC POSITVS EST NON.
DECEMBR. / AN. M. D. CCCXXX[412]

("As a suppliant I commend myself to the heavenly patronage of Leo the Great. Here by his holy ashes I chose the place of my burial. Leo XII, humble client, least heir of such a great name. He lived 68 years, 5 months, 8 days. He died on the fourth day before the ides of February in the year 1829, in the fifth year, 4th month, and 13th day of his pontificate. Placed here on the nones of December in the year 1830."—*Trans. Father Tom Carleton*)

FURTHER READING: G. Servi, *Il monumento fatto innalzare … all'augusta memoria di L. XII nella basilica Vaticana*, Rome, 1837.

Pius VIII   (March 31, 1829–November 30, 1830) *Francesco Saverio Castiglione*. Died at age 69 from an unknown illness, although he suffered many convulsions in the days leading to his death. Because they suspected poison, his doctors secretly performed an autopsy but simply found "the organs healthy; the only thing noticed was some weakness in the lungs and some said his heart was weak."[413] Originally buried in the Vatican grottoes, he was reinterred in 1857 in a monument commissioned by Cardinal Albani and sculpted by Pietro Tenerani. It features the kneeling pope with the full figure of Christ seated above him. St. Peter admires Christ on the left while St. Paul looks on from the right. Base reliefs with Prudence on the left and Justice on the right flank the door to the sacristy (which is also the entrance to the Vatican treasury). The inscription reads:

PIO VIII PONTIFICI MAXIMO /
IOSEPHVS ALBANIVS CARDINALIS

("To Pius VIII, high priest. Cardinal Joseph Albani.")

FURTHER READING: G. De Ferrari, *Il sepolcro di P. VIII nella basilica vaticana*, Rome, 1866; Virgilio Cardinal Noe, *Le Tombe e i Monumenti*, Rome, 2000.

Gregory XVI   (February 2, 1831–June 1, 1846) *Bartolomeo Albert Cappellari*. Died, probably of cancer, at age 81. He had been visibly wasting away for some time but called no doctor because he didn't want to burden the state treasury. His praecordia were interred with those of his predecessors in the Church of SS. Vincenzo e Anastasio, Rome (see Appendix 6 for more information on this practice). He was originally buried in the grottoes of St. Peter's but was moved in 1853 to the basilica proper to be interred in a fine mausoleum by Luigi Amici. On the tomb

Tomb monument to Pius VIII, St. Peter's basilica.

Tomb monument to Gregory XVI, St. Peter's Basilica.

monument, the pope is seated on a throne bestowing the benediction while underneath in the bas-relief, he blesses the Catholic missionaries. Prudence stares in contemplation on the right side while Wisdom extends her left arm over the inscription:

GREGORIO $\overline{XVI}$ PONT. MAX / S. R. E. CARDINALES
AB EO CREATI / ANNO $\overline{MDCCCLIV}$

("To Gregory XVI, supreme pontiff. The cardinals of the Holy Roman Church created by him,1854."—*Trans. Father Tom Carleton*)

FURTHER READING: L. Moreschi, *Relazione sul monumento sepolcrale ... di G. XVI*, Rome, 1857; E. Pucci, "Il monumento a G. XVI e lo scultore Luigi Amici," in *L'Urbe*, Rome, VI, 1941; Virgilio Cardinal Noe, *Le Tombe e i Monumenti*, Rome, 2000.

Blessed Pius IX (June 16, 1846–February 7, 1878) *Giovanni Maria Mastai-Ferretti*. Died from fever at the age of 86 (with the honor of having held the longest papal reign in history). He became sick in January, and one Roman newspaper went so far as to publish a report that he had died. By February 6, the pope had suffered several bouts of severe fever and had become delirious. At noon on February 7, Pius sent for Cardinal Bilio so he could begin the recitation of prayers for the dying. When Cardinal Bilio began the prayer, "Depart, Christian soul," Pius spoke his last words: "Yes, depart." Pius died at 5:40 P.M. Immediately afterward Cardinal Pecci lifted the veil covering the pope's face and said, "Giovanni, Giovanni, Giovanni." Receiving no answer, Pecci declared the pope dead.[414]

On February 9, Pius's body was exposed in the Chapel of the Blessed Sacrament in St. Peter's so that the people could kiss his feet. On February 13 he was laid in the tribune of St. Peter's for the novena celebration.

Originally Pius was interred in Sta. Maria Maggiore,[415] although his viscera were enshrined in the grottoes of St. Peter's[416] (there is an empty space for Pius in the list of popes on the plaque in the Church of SS.

Vincenzo e Anastasio— see Appendix 6 for more information on this practice). His body was then provisionally buried in St. Peter's until his tomb in San Lorenzo fuori le Mura could be completed. On July 13, 1881, as his funeral cortege was taking his body from St. Peter's to San Lorenzo fuori le Mura for its final reinterment, an angry anticlerical Roman mob disrupted the procession and unsuccessfully tried to toss his body into the Tiber river.

Although Pius desired only a simple stone sarcophagus, he was buried in an ornate white sepulcher that was placed in the niche of the crypt thought once to have held the remains of Pope St. Sixtus III (d. 440). In 1882, Pope Leo XIII had wrought-iron gates installed to protect the sarcophagus of Pius IX, as is evident by the inscription in the railing:

HYPOGEO TVTANDO—LEO XIII PONT. MAX—
ANNO DOM. MDCCCLXXXII

("Placed in the protection of the underground chamber—Supreme Pontiff Leo XIII—A. D. 1882."—*Trans. Phyllis Jestice*)

On October 25, 1956, Pius's coffin was opened to gather bones for an ossuary, but his corpse was found perfectly preserved. His face and hands were therefore covered with silver and his body put on display in a crystal coffin in front of his tomb. The tomb inscription reads:

OSSA ET CINERES / PII PAPAE $\overline{IX}$ / VIXIT A. $\overline{LXXXV}$
IN PONT. A. $\overline{XXXI}$ M. VII D. XXII / ORATE PRO EO.

("The bones and ashes of Pope Pius IX. He lived 85 years, and was pope for 31 years, seven months, and 22 days. Pray for him."—*Trans. Phyllis Jestice*)

The beatification process began on February 11, 1907, although it wasn't until 1985 that it continued under John Paul II who wanted to officially recognize Pius's "heroic virtue." Pius was finally beatified on September 3, 2000.

FURTHER READING: M. Meloni, *Intorno alla santita del Sommo Pontefice P. IX*, 2nd ed., Macerata, 1912; L. Ferretti, *La tomba di Pio IX*, Rome,

Sarcophagus and remains of Blessed Pius IX, San Lorenzo fuori le Mura, Rome.

1915; G.B. de Rossi, *Il sepolcro del S. P. Pio IX nella chiesa di S. Lorenzo f. le Mura*, Milan, 1890; Mariano da Alatri, "Il sepolcro di P. IX," in *Oss. Romano*, C.d.v. February 7, 1957.

Leo XIII (February 20, 1878–July 20, 1903) *Gioacchino Vincenzo Pecci*. He died as a result of a heart attack he suffered at 2:45 P.M. on Monday, July 20, 1903, at the age of 93. Two hours after the heart attack the majordomo of the papal palace, Gaetano Bisleti, asked Leo for a blessing. Leo raised his hand and said, "This is the end," and died four minutes later.[417] He was the last pope to have his viscera interred in the Church of SS. Vincenzo e Anastasio, Rome (see Appendix 6 for more information on this practice). Leo wrote a poem about his own death in 1897; it is reproduced in this book's front matter.

Leo was originally buried in St. Peter's but was moved on October 25, 1924, to the basilica of St. John Lateran, according to his wishes. His monument, by Giulio Tadolini, features the pope bestowing his blessing with the figures of St. Joseph on one side and (probably) the Blessed Virgin on the other. The epitaph is in several parts (all translated here by Phyllis Jestice):

LEONI XIII / CARDINALES—AB EO CREATI

("Leo XIII. [This tomb is] By the cardinals he created.")

On the left:

AD PATREM—FILJ EX OMNI REGIONE—
VENERATVRI CONVENIVNT

("To the father, sons from all lands come that he might be venerated.")

On the right:

ECCLESIA INGEMVIT—
COMPLORANTE—ORBE VNIVERSO

("The Church groaned, lamenting, with the whole world.")

Tomb monument of Leo XIII, St. John Lateran, Rome.

On the Roman statue named Pasquino (an old, broken statue on which people to this day post anonymous messages) appeared this poem after the pope's death:

Let's make peace, Holy Father
What's done is done ... let's shake hands
And all give thanks to God.[418]

St. Pius X (August 4, 1903–August 20, 1914) *Giuseppe Melchiorre Sarto*. Died at age 79 from depression brought on by the beginning of World War I. He wrote in his will: "I was born poor, I have lived poor, and I wish to die poor." On his deathbed he wished to die "for the soldiers on the battlefield."[419] At 8:00 P.M. on August 19, Pius was found in his room suffering from a severe fever. Cardinal Merry del Val rushed to his bedside at 10:00 P.M. and grasped his hands while the pope cried out, "Eminence, Eminence...." The pope was immediately given the rites of the dying, to which he replied, "I resign myself completely." He died in his sleep at 1:15 in the morning.[420]

Pius had left instructions that he not be embalmed, which is the cause of a rumor (persisting today) that popes cannot be embalmed. He was interred in the crypt of St. Peter's in a temporary tomb until his final tomb was ready. That tomb, located in the Chapel of the Presentation of the crypt, was large but modest, bearing only his name. A short epitaph was laid in the floor in front of it:

PIVS X PAVPER ET DIVES / MITIS ET HVMILIS CORDE / REIQVE CATHOLICAE VINDEX FORTIS / INSTAVRARE OMNIA IN CHRISTO / SATAGENS PIE OBIIT / DIE XX AVG. A. MCMXIV.

("Pius was poor and rich, meek and humble of heart, strong defender of the Catholic faith, employing himself in every way to restore everything in Christ. Died piously the 20th of August 1914."—*Trans. Father Tom Carleton*)

Pius's bronze memorial monument in St. Peter's, sculpted by Pier Enrico Astorri and Florestano Di Fausto, was erected in 1923 and displays a statue of the standing pope in a niche with both arms outstretched. Below the towering statue on the left side of the door is a bas-relief of "The Consecration of 15 French *viscovi* in St. Peter's," "The Inauguration of the New Vatican Library," and the following inscription:

INSTAVRARE / GALLIAE LABORANTI PASTORES DATI FELICITER / PINACOTHECAE VATIC. NOVA SEDES DATA / MCMIII / STVDIIS SCRIPTVRAE SACRAE PROVEHENDIS / OMNIA IN CHRISTO / IVRIS ECCLESIASTICI LEGES EMENDATAE AC DIGESTAE / CONCERTVS SACRI IN PRISTINAM FORMAN RESTITVTI / MCMXIV /

 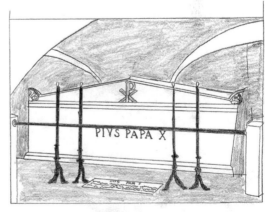

Left: The temporary tomb of St. Pius X in the Vatican crypt. Drawing by author based on a photograph in Nello and Matt, *St. Pius X*. *Right:* The tomb of Pius X, Vatican grottoes. Drawing based on Nello and Matt, *St. Pius X*.

The sainted remains of Pius X, beneath the Altar of the Presentation, St. Peter's basilica.

CALABRIAE AC SICILIAE ORPHANIS
ADIVTOR ET PATER

("To renew.* In 1903 the blessed laborers of Gaul provided a new home for the Vatican gallery. Advancing the study of holy scripture, the laws of the Church were assimilited, amended, and restored by holy effort to their pristine form in the law of Christ 1914. Helper and father of the orphans of Calabria and Sicily."— Trans. Phyllis Jestice)

Despite immediate calls for canonization right after his death, not until June 3, 1951, was Pius X beatified (by Pius XII). At that time he was placed in the major altar of the crypt dedicated to Christ the King, which was decorated with a bas-relief of the Redemption (attributed to Giovanni Dalmata). In February of 1952 he was placed in a crystal coffin underneath the Altar of the Pre-sentation (the second chapel on the left of the nave of St. Peter's), and a copper mask was placed over his face while his hands remained exposed. Because he wished not to be embalmed, his praecordia were not removed, thus ending the tradition of papal viscera interment at the Church of Sts. Vincenzo e Anastasio (see Appendix 6 for more information on this process). Pius XII canonized him on May 29, 1954, and his feast day is now August 21 (formerly September 3).

FURTHER READING: A. Lancellotti, *Concorso per il monumento a P. X*, I Emporium, XLV, 1917. Virgilio Cardinal Noe, *Le Tombe e i Monumenti*, Rome, 2000; Frances Burkle-Young, *Passing the Keys: Modern Cardinals, Conclaves, and the Election of the Next Pope*, Madison Books, 2001.

*A major achievement of Pius X was a sort of internal renovation of the Church, including a revision of Canon law and a raising of the spiritual and moral level of the clergy. His official motto was "To Restore All Things in Christ." The word "Instaurare" or "To Renew," as the beginning of this epitaph, echoes that motto.

Benedict XV (September 3, 1914–January 22, 1922) *Giacomo Della Chiesa*. Died at age 88 from flu or pneumonia, or possibly poison. Church historian Friedrich Gontard, in his book *The Chair of Peter*, claims that he was most likely poisoned because he was in perfect health yet died after only three days of sickness after having suffered many mysterious "attacks."[421]

Benedict had been ill for a few days, slipping in and out of lucidness. When it was obvious that he was finally dying, the blessed sacrament was brought into the sickroom by a procession headed up by the Swiss Guards, followed by papal grooms with burning candles, and finally the commandant of the Noble Guard. The pope's sacristan carried the Holy of Holies, followed by 21 cardinals. The majordomo read the creed while the pope whispered along with him. Benedict then received communion, struck his chest three times, and said the communion prayer.[422] He tried to get up twice while in a state of delirium but had to be gently forced back to bed, where he said, "We offer our life to God on behalf of the peace of the World."[423] The gathered cardinals, knowing the end was near, vested him with a rochet, pectoral cross, and mula. Benedict asked what time it was, and was told it was 11:15 P.M. The pope said, "Well, there is plenty of time before six o'clock."

At two o'clock A.M. Cardinal Oreste Giorgi, the major penitentiary, who had read the profession of faith, approached the pope and shouted, "Holiness, bless your relatives!" The pope barely moved his right hand in response. The death rattle could clearly be heard from the dying pontiff's throat when Giorgi shouted again, "Holiness, now bless your household!" Benedict tried but could not move his hand. Giorgi shouted at the pope one more time: "Holiness, bless those who desire peace!" The pope sat straight up

Sarcophagus of Benedict XV, Vatican crypt.

Monument to Benedict XV, St. Peter's basilica.

in bed, eyes wide open, cried out with his last bit of strength, "May the blessing of Almighty God, Father, Son, and Holy Spirit, descend on you now and remain forever!" He slowly made the sign of the cross three times in the air before collapsing back into the pillows. And just as he had predicted, Benedict gave one last sigh and died precisely at 6 A.M. Cardinal Gasparri put a candle near the lips of the pontiff, but the flame didn't waiver. The cardinal then lifted the veil over the pope's face, and whispered, "Giacomo, Giacomo, Giacomo." When he received no response, he declared the pope officially dead.[424]

In 1924, Benedict's body was placed in a white marble sarcophagus with a bronze effigy by Giulio Barbieri which was placed in the crypt of St. Peter's. His memorial monument, by Pietro Canonica, was unveiled on November 22, 1928. It features in bas-relief the Madonna and Child; the child is holding an olive branch, over a scene of devastation, which was most likely a reference to World War I. The pope himself is shown in profile, kneeling on what appears to be a sarcophagus.

FURTHER READING: Virgilio Cardinal Noe, *Le Tombe e i Monumenti*, Rome, 2000.

Pius XI (February 6, 1922–February 10, 1939) *Ambrogio Damiano Achille Ratti*. Died at age 82 from either thrombosis and fever or poison (because it was rumored he was on the verge of condemning fascism in 1939, and his doctor was a relative of the Italian foreign minister). Although those touting the poison theory claim he died suddenly, Pius's health actually deteriorated over several days. He began his real downturn on February 6, 1939, with exhaustion, fever, and bouts of delirium. The Vatican claimed that Pius had only a cold, but rumor spread around Rome that he had gone insane and that he was dying. On February 9 he complained of severe bladder pain, and around 4:00 that day he went limp during his doc-

tor's examination. His pulse could hardly be detected, but he was still alive.

The doctor summoned Eugenio Pacelli (soon to be the next pope Pius XII); the pope's favorite nephew, Franco Ratti; Carlo Confalonieri, the pope's secretary; and several members of the papal court into the pope's room. Pius had chosen his final prayer, and Confalonieri began to recite it: "Jesus, Mary and Joseph, I give you my heart, my mind, and my soul. Jesus, Mary, and Joseph, help me in my last agony. Jesus, Mary, and Joseph, may…," but the secretary couldn't finish as he was too upset. Pius himself finished the prayer: "May I breathe forth my soul in peace with thee." These were the last words the pope would ever utter. By 10:00 P.M., the pope could not recognize anyone around him as he slipped in and out of consciousness. At 5:15 in the morning, Pacelli called out for the pope's final act: "Holy Father, give us your blessing." Pius could only mumble as he tried to lift his right hand. He died sixteen minutes later.

Candles were placed around the pope's death bed while Pacelli donned his violet mozzetta and mantelletta, as was custom. He lifted the veil on the pope's face and whispered softly, "Achille, Achille, Achille." With no response, he officially announced that the pope was dead. The Vatican bells rang as the cardinal vicar of Rome began the first mass for Pius's soul. The secretary of apostolic briefs began drafting the pope's death certificate.

That next Sunday morning the pope's body was brought to St. Peter's for viewing, and by Tuesday, February 14, the last of the three requiem masses was said. At 4:30, the members of the papal household, along with 37 cardinals, gathered in St. Peter's for the burial of the pope. There were recitations of prayers for the dead and a reading of the act of burial, after which the ten *sediari* lifted the bier and lowered it into the innermost coffin of wood. Pius's robes were too bulky for the coffin, however, so they had to be folded under his feet. Antonio Bacci gave a eulogy, a copy of which was put into a brass

Sarcophagus of Pius XI, Vatican grottoes.

cylinder in that innermost coffin. Also added were three bags of coins—one of silver, one of gold, and one of copper. Each contained seventeen coins, one for each year of the pope's reign. Pius's secretaries covered his face and hands with a veil of white silk, and the body was finally covered with a crimson pall. Then the wood coffin was sealed and encircled with three ribbons and placed into a bronze casket, but the workmen soldering the bronze casket ran out of material and had to go into town to get more. When that was finally done, ribbons were also wrapped around the bronze casket, and it was lowered into the outermost coffin, which was made of lead.

Interestingly, workmen had discovered earlier that day a forgotten recess where Pius had chosen to be buried (this would later lead to the discovery of St. Peter's original tomb). The lead coffin was placed in this forgotten recess, which had remained sealed since the sixteenth century. The cardinals then went down to the crypt to wait for the half-ton coffin to be lowered. When it came down, the cardinals and the pope's family simply had the coffin placed in a niche in the Chapel of St. Sebastian without any ceremony.[425]

On February 9, 1941, Pius's remains were placed in the Vatican crypt in a beautiful Candoglia marble sarcophagus topped by the deathbed effigy of the pope, which was sculpted by Giannino Castiglioni. The back wall of the niche is a beautiful gold mosaic

The death agony of Pius XII. By permission of Jon N. Austin and Jason Meyers of the Museum of Funeral Customs, Springfield, Illinois.

featuring a Byzantine-style Christ, over which can be read REX REGVM PRINCEPS PACE ("king of kings, prince of peace"). The mosaic at the pope's head contains St. Ambrose (a fellow Milanese), and at his feet the figure of St. Theresa and the Baby Jesus, because of Pius's special devotion to the Carmelite nun.

Eight years later, on December 18, 1949, Pietro Canonica unveiled his monument to Pius XI. The monument shows the pope on his throne, raising his right hand in benediction. The inscription read:

PIO XI / PONT. MAX. / S. R. E. CARDINALES /
AB EO CREATI

("Pius XI, supreme pontiff. The cardinals of the Holy Roman Church created by him.")

PIVS XI PON. MAX / CVIVS EPISOCPALE INSIGNE /
TOTIVSQVE VITAE RATIO / ATQVE PROPOSITVM
FVIT / "PAX CHRISTI IN REGNO CHRISTI"

("To Pius XI, supreme pontiff, whose episcopal motto was the reason and purpose of life: 'Peace of Christ in the reign of Christ.'"—Trans. Father Tom Carleton)

FURTHER READING: M. Sarfatti, "Guanti di P. XI," in *L'Elefante*, Rome, 1950; Virgilio Cardinal Noe, *Le Tombe e i Monumenti*, Rome, 2000; Frances Burkle-Young, *Passing the Keys: Modern Cardinals, Conclaves, and the Election of the Next Pope*, Madison Books, 2001.

Pius XII   (March 2, 1939–October 9, 1958)
Eugenio Maria Giovanni Pacelli. Died at age 82 from complications from pneumonia, which was a result of a torn stomach lining severely inflamed by intense hiccoughs. He died in the summer papal residence of Castel Gandolfo.

The pope had his first attack of hiccoughs in 1953, although they weren't as bad then as they would become five years later (for an extremely detailed account of the sickness of Pius XII, see Frances Burkle-Young's *Passing the Keys*, which provided much information for this entry). The pope had a massive stroke on October 5, 1958. He was not completely incapacitated, but the

next day while discussing music with his doctor, Riccardo Galeazzi-Lisi, the pope suffered an even more significant stroke and fell unconscious, despite the doctor's stimulant injections, which had worked the day before.

The doctor called in Dr. Antonio Gasbarrini, a gastroenterologist from Bologna, to help assess the pope's stomach ailments, which had plagued him for years and had increased in severity since the strokes. Pius was placed in an oxygen tent, and important curial and family members were contacted because the doctor felt that the end was near. Monsignor Van Lierde, the sacristan, administered the last rites to the dying pontiff as the doctor began to recognize the symptoms of pneumonia. The room soon became crowded with those who had to be there for ceremonial reasons: Cardinal Eugene Tisserant, dean of the Sacred College, and Clemente Micara; the sacristan Pieter Canisius van Lierde; the pope's confessor, Father Augustin Bea, S.J.; and the *maestro di camera*, Federico Callori di Vignale; the pope's sister, Contessa Elisabetha Pacelli Rossignani; his three nephews, the princes Carlo, Giulio, and Marcantonio Pacelli; and Sister Pasqualina, who had taken care of him since his early days in Bavaria. The archbishop Domenico Tardini, Pius's closest assistant, began saying a mass for him later that evening that was broadcast all over the world. In his death agony he yelled out, "To work! Files! Documents! To Work!"[426]

Around 3:30 that morning Pius's death rattle and quick panting could be heard throughout the whole room, although he clung to what precious little life he had left. At that moment, a Swiss doctor who, by Pius's request, had long ago administered near-fatal injections from the adrenal glands of monkeys to the pope in hopes of rejuvenating him, began snapping pictures, much to the horror of those present.

At 3:52 A.M., after a particularly loud death rattle, Gasbarrini felt for a pulse in the pope's wrist and, feeling nothing, rose and announced that the pope was dead. Galeazzi-

Lisi approached the pope and claimed he was still alive, but Cardinal Tisserant agreed with Gasbarrini that Pius was dead. Four minutes later, a small trickle of blood dribbled from the right side of Pius's mouth, and his head drooped forward. Galeazzi-Lisi stepped forward again, examined the pope, and declared that the Holy Father had died. Cardinal Alfredo Ottaviani checked Pius himself with the stethoscope, then nodded to Tisserant, confirming the pope's death.

A moment of silence passed in the room but was broken when someone opened the door and a throng of people who had gathered outside stampeded into the bedroom. Sister Pasqualina took charge, and everybody who did not have to be there was hastily removed. Tisserant, acting as the interim camerlengo, performed the ceremony of the cloth by calling out the pope's Christian name three times—"Eugenio, Eugenio, Eugenio"—and declaring that the pope had died.

Vatican radio announced at 3:56 that the pope had died at 3:52. Frances Burkle-Young writes in the wonderfully detailed book *Passing the Keys*:

> When the small crowd had left the bedroom, four penitentiarii (by tradition Conventual Franciscans) entered to prepare the body for dressing. To do this they sponged Pius' body with alcohol and shaved his beard with an electric razor.... Because Pius had wished not to be embalmed Pius' doctor, Galeazzi-Lisi, took this as a chance to try out his own "spray on" embalming fluid for the pontiff. The procedure, which had been developed by Oreste Nuzzi, a surgeon and crony of the pope's doctor, consisted of spraying the corpse with a compound of resins, oils, and other chemical compounds which were supposed to produce a deoxidizing effect that would prevent decay—Nuzzi called this "aromatic osmosis." Then the body was robed in a white cotton cassock, scarlet mozetta, and scarlet camauro.[427]

When this was done two Noble Guards took their place at the head of the bed, and several important prelates were allowed in to pray. Later that day the body was placed in the great hall and the doors were opened for the residents of Gandolfo to venerate the remains of their beloved pope. Meanwhile a death mask of Pius was being made, and Tisserant was in Rome, sealing the papal apartments and preparing for the upcoming conclave. He soon received word that the embalming hadn't gone exactly as planned and that the pope's remains were not holding up very well in the warm October weather. Therefore he cancelled the viewing of the body in the Chapel of the Blessed Sacrament and ordered a five-foot-high catafalque for the pope's body so it could not be seen close-up by the throngs of mourners. The cardinals decided that because his body was decomposing so rapidly that they would cut short the public viewing by three days, although they would continue the novena, which would conclude on October 25.

A motorcade of 20 cars escorted the hearse to Rome to the Lateran Palace for the first of the official funeral ceremonies, and during the quiet of the mass a loud crack was heard—the seal on the coffin had broken from the pressure of escaping gasses from the badly embalmed body. At the conclusion of the mass, Pius's body was escorted to St. Peter's by a hundred *cabarini* walking nine abreast. The pope was brought into the basilica and rerobed in anticipation of the crowds who would come to venerate his remains.

The basilica was opened the next day at 6:00 A.M. for the first truly public viewing of Pius as the first of the nine requiem masses was said in the Chapel of the Choir. More than 500 people per minute passed the bier at St. Peter's over the next three days and nights, moving rapidly in two files, five deep. The stench of the rotting corpse was so bad that one of the guards stationed at the bier fainted, and the other had tears streaming down his face from the odor. Those witnessing this display of emotion from the guard assumed it was because of his intense grief for the passing of the pontiff. Finally Pius's nose went black and fell off before his final interment.

Sarcophagus of Pius XII, Vatican grottoes.

Despite the unfortunate embalming incident, L'Osservatore Romano said his funeral was the greatest in the long history of Rome, "surpassing even that of Julius Caesar." The body lay on a catafalque beneath the baldachino; to the right were the three coffins that he would be buried in. In his eulogy, Monsignor Antonio Bacci declared that "with his death a great light went out on earth, and a new star lit in heaven." The requiem was televised live on Eurovision.

For final burial, Pius was laid in the first casket, his face covered with white silk and his entire body wrapped in a crimson shroud. The text of the eulogy was placed in a brass tube alongside a purse containing gold, silver, and bronze coins minted during his pontificate; then this inner coffin was secured with silk ribbons attached with seals before being placed in the protective lead case. The outer elm coffin was then secured with golden nails and wheeled before the high altar. It was lowered on pulleys from a scaffold into the grottoes below.

Pius's memory is often tarred by accusations that he did not do enough to help the Jews during the Holocaust, but after his passing, Golda Meir, Israel's foreign minister, said of Pius, "When fearful martyrdom came to our people in the decade of Nazi terror, the voice of the Pope was raised for the victims. The life of our times was enriched by a voice speaking out on the great moral truths above the tumult of daily conflict. We mourn a great servant of peace."[428]

Pius's plain, white marble sarcophagus rests in the Vatican crypt, where it can be seen today. His imposing, grand bronze funeral monument in the basilica of St. Peter's was sculpted by Francesco Messina. The inscription on the funeral monument reads:

PIO XII / PONT. MAX /
S. R. E. CARDINALES / AB EO CREATI

("To Pius XII, supreme pontiff. The cardinals of the Holy Roman Church created by him." — *Trans. Father Tom Carleton*)

FURTHER READING: Virgilio Cardinal Noe, *Le Tombe e i Monumenti*, Rome, 2000; Frances Burkle-Young, *Passing the Keys: Modern Cardinals, Conclaves, and the Election of the Next Pope*, Madison Books, 2001.

Blessed John XXIII (October 28, 1958–June 3, 1963) *Angelo Giuseppe Roncalli*.

Died at age 82 from stomach cancer. He had been hemorrhaging on and off for days, but he refused an operation to remove the cancerous tumors from his stomach. On the night of May 29 he suffered a massive, painful hemorrhage due to the rupture of a tumor and so was placed in an oxygen tent with the papal sacristan, Bishop Pieter Canisius van Lierde, who gave John the sacrament of extreme unction. But van Lierde was so upset that he forgot the order of anointing the five senses, so the pope himself had to direct him. John fell in and out of consciousness but was happy to see his brothers and sisters at his bedside. His last coherent words were, "Lord, you know that I love you," although it was thought that he tried to declare his motto, "*Ut unum sint*" ("That all may be one"). John died at 7:49 that evening. The crowd in the Piazza of St. Peter's had been watching the pope's bedroom for days; when they saw the bedroom light go out, they knew their pope was dead.

Following John's wishes, his camerlengo, Benedetto Aloisi Masella, ordered that the death certificate be drawn up and that the body of the pope be washed and dressed for a simple viewing by close family and friends. A Vatican car was sent for Professor Gennar Goglia, who, along with his colleagues, would embalm the pontiff. After waiting an hour for the artist Giacomo Manzu to make a bronze death mask and cast of John's right hand, Goglia injected ten liters of embalming fluid into the pope's wrist and stomach to neutralize any putrification. The entire process took about five hours to complete.

An hour before the funeral rites began John's body was lifted from its catafalque and brought to the steps of St. Peter's for public viewing. Pericle Felici conducted the funeral ceremonies, with Monsignor Nicola Metta reading the act of burial. When that was done the portable bier on which the pope was lying was lowered into the innermost wood coffin (which was inside the lead coffin, which itself was inside a sarcophagus). Monsignor Amleto Tondini read a cold, formal eulogy clearly demonstrating that he wasn't very fond of Pope John. Regardless, a copy was sealed in a brass cylinder and placed in the wood coffin, along with two velvet bags of coins and medals that had been printed during John's reign. Each cardinal came forward to bless the dead pope before the pope's face and hands were covered by veils and a crimson pall laid over his body. When this was done, the coffins were lowered into the crypt, where they were swiftly soldered together. Only a few cardinals and some of John's family — his brother, sister, three nephews and two nieces — were in the crypt to receive the sarcophagus.

The next morning thousands of people solemnly made their way by John's tomb to pray for his soul. He was posthumously awarded the United States Presidential Medal of Freedom. John XXIII was beatified by Pope John Paul II in September of 2000 and was consequently exhumed in January 2001 to be restored for viewing in June of the same year. Before being placed in a crystal, bulletproof, ultraviolet ray–blocking coffin, the pope was dressed in a white silk cassock and red cape with a fur-lined bonnet. His face and hands were covered in wax, although the original embalmer, Goglia, commented, "It made me think of Madame Tussauds's. It could have been handled better."[429]

In May of 2002, John Paul II presented an unspecified relic of John XXIII to the new Sophia Cathedral[430] in Bulgaria (John XXIII is revered in Bulgaria because of his priestly work there between 1929 and 1934). The body of Blessed John XXIII now rests in St. Peter's basilica and can be easily viewed by the public.

FURTHER READING: Frances Burkle-Young, *Passing the Keys: Modern Cardinals, Conclaves, and*

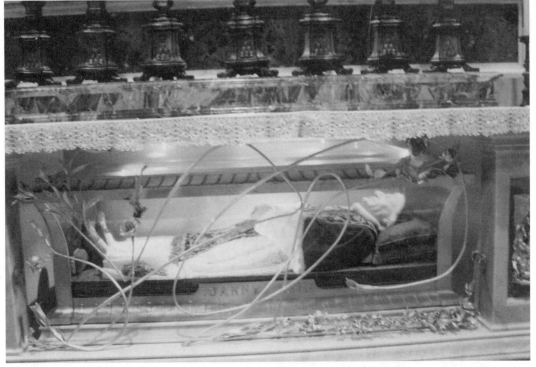

Top: The original tomb of John XXIII, Vatican grottoes. *Bottom:* The venerated remains of Blessed John XXIII, St. Peter's basilica.

the Election of the Next Pope, Madison Books, 2001; Louise Rice, The Altars and Altarpieces of New St. Peter's: Outfitting the Basilica, 1621–1666, Cambridge University Press, 1998; Virgilio Cardinal Noe, Le Tombe e i Monumenti, Rome, 2000.

Paul VI   (June 21, 1963–August 6, 1978) *Giovanni Battista Montini*. Died at age 81 at Castel Gandolfo from a massive heart attack, which was brought on by news that his close friend Italian politician Aldo Moro (who had been kidnapped) had been murdered. After receiving that news, Paul lapsed in and out of consciousness for days. Finally, a little after 9:00 P.M. on August 6, he began to faintly recite the Lord's Prayer. He died at 9:41 that night, and immediately afterwards his alarm clock — which was not set for that time — began to ring. The Swiss Guard hung

Floor tomb of Paul VI, Vatican grottoes.

a heavy black chain on the doorway to the villa as a sign to the pilgrims who were praying for the dying pope that he had indeed died. In Rome, the bell of the Arco delle Campani rang the death knell.

Paul was not wearing his fisherman's ring when he died, so the first order of business was to find that ring and destroy it, lest anyone use it to forge the pope's seal. Paul himself had expressed his wishes: "I want my funeral to be as simple as possible and I want neither tomb nor special monument. A few offerings (prayers and good works)."[431]

The pope died on a Sunday, and the next day his body was embalmed and dressed in a white simar, white alb, cincture, amice, and red and gold chasuble. His pectoral cross lay across his chest and a golden miter was placed on his head. Swiss Guards at Castle Gandolfo guarded his body as it lay in state for pilgrims to pay their last respects as three Franciscans chanted the Office of the Dead.

The next Wednesday evening his body was brought to St. Peter's, via St. John Lateran, for recitation of the prayers for the dead during which time the coffin remained in the hearse. When it arrived at St. Peter's, priests, Third Order Franciscans and 40 cardinals carrying lighted candles accompanied the body to the steps of St. Peter's because Paul had requested his funeral be outside so that everyone could witness it, not just those privileged enough to be in St. Peter's.

The funeral was not without mishap. A deacon, and only a deacon, can recite the solemn liturgy of the reception of the dead into St. Peter's. Unfortunately, all the deacons of Rome were on vacation to escape the dreadful summer heat. Finally, the Reverend Stephen DiGiovanni, of Bridgeport, Connecticut, was ordained deacon by officials at the North American College so that the novena, or nine days of mourning, could commence with an official deacon.[432]

On Thursday and Friday the public were allowed to view the body (Vatican Radio estimated 10,000 people per hour passed the coffin[433]), although by Friday evening Paul's ears began to turn black from decomposition in the heat. Nevertheless, his body was again displayed on Saturday morning while the cardinals were receiving representatives of other religions in honor of Paul — something that had never been done before. The simple wood coffin (the coffin of a beggar, as Paul wished) was closed at 2:00 P.M., and the book of the Gospels was placed on top of it for the duration of the funeral. Paul had requested only one Paschal candle instead of the usual 24 that surrounded the coffin of a pope.

At 5:00 the coffin was carried out to the steps of St. Peter's, where 103 cardinals celebrated mass. When the mass was finished, the coffin was brought back into St. Peter's, placed in the other two coffins and lowered into a vault under the floor in the crypt. [434] It had been Paul's wish to be buried in the ground, rather than in an above-ground sarcophagus. Some 60 million people watched the funeral on television.

FURTHER READING: Virgilio Cardinal Noe, *Le Tombe e i Monumenti*, Rome, 2000; Frances Burkle-Young, *Passing the Keys: Modern Cardinals, Conclaves, and the Election of the Next Pope*, Madison Books, 2001.

John Paul I (August 26–September 28, 1978) *Albino Luciani*. Died at age 65 of either a coronary embolism (heart attack) or poison. John Cornwell, in *The Thief in the Night*, writes of John Paul's death, "John Paul almost certainly died of a pulmonary embolus due to a condition of abnormal coagularity of the blood. He required rest and monitored medication. If these had been prescribed he would almost certainly have survived. The warnings of a mortal illness were clear for all to see; the signs were ignored."[435]

Yet reliable sources, notably the Abbé de Nantes and David Yallop, investigative reporter and author of *In God's Name: An Investigation into the Murder of Pope John Paul I*, contend that the pope was murdered. Although the Abbé de Nantes heartily disagrees with what Yallop claims were some of John Paul I's policies (such as possible

women priests in the church and advocation of birth control), he is in complete agreement with idea that the pope was murdered.

Why would someone want to murder the pope? The answer, according to Yallop, lies in the Vatican bank scandal. The night before he died, the 29th of September, John Paul had tea with Cardinal Jean Villot in a meeting in which the pope revealed that Villot would be replaced. Also, John Paul disclosed that he was going to have the corrupt Cardinal Cody of Chicago removed and that he was going to expose the Vatican Bank scandal and clean out the *Mafioso*, Freemasons, and members of P-2 (a secret European organization) who had infiltrated the bank and turned it into a huge international money laundering institution.

Yallop contends that Villot could not allow this to happen, for if the pope exposed the major players in the scandal, Villot and Cody among the group, many important and dangerous people would go down. The pope had to be silenced ... and it had to be covered up.

The first official story from the Vatican is as follows: John Paul's secretary, John McGee, found the pope at 5:00 A.M. propped up in his bed with *The Imitation of Christ* in his hands, as if he had been reading it when he died. No autopsy was done because no matter what the doctors would find, the press would somehow twist the facts so that it looked like a murder. The Vatican also claimed that it was either a heart attack that killed him, or, as Villot hinted, maybe the pope killed himself by accidentally (or intentionally) taking too many of his blood pressure pills before he went to bed because he couldn't handle the stress of evil in the world.

In short, the murder-conspiracy theory would not have gained such momentum had it not been for Villot himself, who perpetuated proven mistruths and was largely responsible for some of the questionable circumstances surrounding the pope's death. Those circumstances, along with basic facts about the pope and the procedures that took place after his death, raised a lot of understandable suspicion:

- John Paul had a medical checkup two weeks before he was elected pope and he was reportedly in excellent health.

- Each morning at 4:45, Sister Vincenza, John Paul's trusted housekeeper, would leave the pope's coffee on a tray outside his bedroom door. When he didn't retrieve it on the morning of the 29th, she let herself into the room and found John Paul dead with "an expression of agony on his face."

- Sister Vincenza told a group of French priests that morning that she found the pope dead in the bathroom, not in the bed as Villot ordered the reports should read.

- Villot imposed a vow of silence on Sister Vincenza, and she was sent to a far-off convent after the funeral.

- The pope's bottle of Efforil (a medication to raise blood pressure), his slippers, his glasses, his will, and the papers that outlined his changes regarding Villot, Cody, and the Vatican Bank scandal, all disappeared and have never been seen since. Yallop suspects this is because there could have been vomit on these articles which could prove the pope was poisoned.

- The embalmers arrived at 5:00 A.M., before the other cardinals or doctors were summoned. Italian law states that a body cannot be embalmed for 12 hours after death. Although the Vatican is not required to follow Italian law, the rapid embalming was still highly unusual because Catholic tradition dictates that 24 hours pass from the death of the pontiff to his embalming.

- Villot called Dr. Buzzonati, deputy head of the Vatican's health service, instead of Professor Fontana, the head of that service, or John Paul's personal doctor to declare him dead.

- Dr. Buzzonati declared that the pope died from a heart attack just by looking at him and without an autopsy.

- Villot ordered that no blood or organs whatsoever were to be removed from the body during the embalming — yet that is a standard practice, even for popes, due to the quick decomposition of organs and the need to pump embalming fluid through the veins so that the body can be put on display for a few days without decomposing.

- The death certificate, if one was ever drawn up, has never been made public.

- By 6:00 that evening all 19 rooms in the papal apartments were thoroughly cleaned and scrubbed down, as if John Paul I never existed.

Why not autopsy the pope to determine his cause of death? Popes had been autopsied in the past, the most recent having been Pius VIII in 1830, so there was a precedent for autopsying a pope. The College of Cardinals voted against autopsy despite the protests of Cardinal Felici, who was almost always with the pontiff during his short reign. Their reasoning was that even if there was an autopsy the scandalmongers wouldn't be satisfied no matter what the outcome, and two other doctors who examined the body agreed with the findings of the first doctor, Buzzonati, that the pope had died from a heart attack.

Meanwhile, the pope's body had to be pulled out of rigor mortis by ropes, and he was dressed and made up, including powder for his wrists where the ropes had been tied. After the papal dignitaries had visited the body, it was transported to the Sala Clementina for viewing by world dignitaries, many of whom sent representatives to the funeral in their place because, as a CBS executive said, "We did this show last month."[436]

That Saturday night, the body of the pope was transported on the shoulders of the papal throne bearers across the piazza to St. Peter's, amidst a crowd of 100,000 people. Ninety-four cardinals celebrated the 90-minute funeral mass on the steps of St. Peter's in the pouring rain on Wednesday, October 4. The mass ended just before 6:00 P.M. John Paul lay in a plain coffin of a beggar, as he had stipulated in his will. On top of the closed coffin Holy Bible lay open to the Gospel of John, and a single Paschal candle

Sarcophagus of John Paul I, Vatican grottoes.

flickered. After the mass the coffin was brought back into the basilica and lowered into the crypt, then placed in a sarcophagus across the aisle from Marcellus II (1555), whose pontificate lasted only 21 days.

The prophet Nostradamus supposedly predicted the "murder" (if indeed it was a murder) of John Paul I in three of his quatrains[437]:

Century 3 Quatrain 65

When the sepulchre of the great Roman is found,
The day after a Pope shall be elected:
The Senate (Conclave) will not approve of him.
His blood is poisoned in the sacred chalice.

Century 10 Quatraine 12

The one elected Pope will be mocked by his electors,
This enterprising and prudent person will suddenly be reduced in silence,
They cause him to die because of his too great goodness and mildness,
Stricken by fear, they will lead him to his death in the night.

Century 4 Quatraine 11

He who will have the government of the great cape
Will be led to execute in certain cases.
The twelve red ones will spoil the cover.
Under murder, murder will come to be perpetrated.

On Monday, August 26, 2002, in the parish of Canale d'Agordo, a holy mass in memory of the 24th anniversary of John Paul I's election as pope was celebrated by the Bishop of Belluno, Monsignor Vincenzo Savio. At the end of the mass, a bishop's declaration was read in which, among other things, it was announced that a postulator would be appointed and a diocesan priest would be at his side to start "the preliminary research necessary to pick up the informations regarding life and work of Pope Luciani, indispensable premise to every request of introducing a Cause of Canonisation."

A very important statement came to this author in the form of a personal email from the Belgian priest Father Johan Goosens, who is working with the promulgator for the success of this cause. Father Goosens wrote:

A lot of stories accompany John Paul I's death. Stories were told as if he would have been murdered. I have a good relationship with his close family (brother, niece…) and these people brought me into contact with the nearest fellow-workers of Albino Luciani. All of them assured me the pope could not have possibly been murdered. They are sure he died a natural death. He possibly died in his bed while working (probably preparing speeches), as he used to do when he couldn't sleep. But as this isn't a "beautiful death" for a pope, they sent another message to the world. And this created some guesses.

For information regarding the Cause of Beatification of Pope Luciani, email the Diocese of Belluno: *vescovado@diocesi.it*. One can even sign a petition for the cause by going to *www.albinoluciani.com*.

Pope John Paul I also has a fan club started by Massimiliano Piovesan, at *www. amicipapaluciani.it/*. There is also a website by Father Johan Goossens: *www.albino luciani.com*.

FURTHER READING: Virgilio Cardinal Noe, *Le Tombe e i Monumenti*, Rome, 2000; Frances Burkle-Young, *Passing the Keys: Modern Cardinals, Conclaves, and the Election of the Next Pope*, Madison Books, 2001. John Cornwell, *A Thief in the Night*, 1982; David Yallop, *In God's Name: An Investigation into the Murder of Pope John Paul I*, Bantam Books, 1984.

Notes

1. Agostino Paravicini-Bagliani, *The Pope's Body* (Chicago: University of Chicago Press, 2000), 115.

2. Quoted in Paravicini-Bagliani, 134.

3. Paravicini-Bagliani, 115.

4. James Lees-Mine, *St. Peter's*. Boston: Little, Brown, 1967.

5. Sergio Bertelli, *The King's Body*, (University Park: Pennsylvania State University Press, 2001), 43. Bertelli attributes this information to Amion.

6. H.P.V. Nunn, *Christian Inscriptions* (New York: Philosophical Library, 1952), 57–58. Both the Latin epitaph and its translation are drawn from this source.

7. John Curran, "The Bones of St. Peter?" Originally published in *Classics Ireland* **3** (1996). Reprinted by permission of John Curran.

8. Tomb historian H.K. Mann writes that the church of St. Clement "was really on a headland in the harbor of Sebastopol, and was marked in Russian maps as late as 1772." Mam, *Tombs and Portraits of the Popes of the Middle Ages* (London: Sheed & Ward, 1928), 7.

9. Renzo Montini, *Le Tombe dei Papi* (Rome: Istituto di Studi Romani, 1957), 66.

10. Montini, 66.

11. Montini, 67.

12. Montini, 68.

13. *Catholic Encyclopedia*, Online Edition Copyright © 2003 by Kevin Knight.

14. J.N.D. Kelley, ed., *The Oxford Dictionary of Popes*, (Oxford: Oxford University Press, 1986), 15.

15. Montini, 80.

16. Montini, 80.

17. Nunn, 63.

18. Montini, 23.

19. Orazio Marucchi, *Christian Epigraphy*, trans. J. Armine Willis (Cambridge: Cambridge University Press, 1912), 234.

20. Marucchi, 181.

21. Nunn, 65.

22. Mann, *Tombs and Portraits*, 10.

23. Marucchi, 162.

24. Nunn, 60.

25. Marucchi, 163.

26. Montini, 90.

27. Montini, 90.

28. Montini, 10.

29. The only scholar I have found who refers to the combing of Silvester, Vigilius, and Adrian IV is Renzo Montini in his 1957 *Le Tombe dei Papi*, page 110. Nor can I find mention of an altar to St. Silvester in any other books, old or new.

30. Montini, 92.

31. Deutsche Zeitschrift für Geschichtswissenschaft, N. S., **I** (1896–1897), 176.

32. Historisches Jahrbuch, **V** (1884), 424–436.

33. Montini, 95.

34. Montini, 95.

35. Nunn, 50.

36. Nunn, 50.

37. Nunn, 50.

38. Kelley, 36.

39. Montini, 96.

40. Montini, 98.

41. Montini, 98.

42. Montini, 99–100.

43. Nunn, 72.

44. Nunn, 72.

45. Montini, 100.

46. Montini, 103.

47. Giacomo Grimaldi, *Descrizione della Basilica Antica di S. Pietro in Vaticano: Codice Barberini*

Latino 2733, ed. Reto Niggl (Vatican City: 1972), 234–235.

48. Montini, 105.

49. Iiro Kajanto, *Papal Epigraphy in Renaissance Rome*, (Helsinki: Suomalainen tiedeakatemia, 1982), 13.

50. Kajanto, 13.

51. Montini, 106.

52. Montini, 107.

53. Montini, 108.

54. Montini, 109.

55. Montini, 110.

56. Montini, 110–111.

57. The only scholar I have found that refers to the combining of Silvester, Vigilius, and Adrian IV is Renzo Montini in his 1957 *Le Tombe dei Papi*, page 110. Nor can I find mention of an altar to St. Silvester in any other books, old or new.

58. Kajanto, 14.

59. Grimaldi.

60. Memmo Caporilli, *The Popes*, (Rome: Euroedit–Trento, 1999), 24.

61. P.G. Maxwell-Stuart, *Chronicle of the Popes*, (London: Thames and Hudson, 1997), 60.

62. Montini, 114.

63. Montini, 114–115.

64. Montini, p. 115.

65. Montini, p. 137.

66. Montini, 118.

67. Grimaldi, 97.

68. Montini, 116.

69. The altar belonged to Boniface IV and had nothing to do with St. Thomas, but in the new St. Peter's, paintings were often haphazardly placed over altars until a suitable altarpiece was found. In this case, a painting of St. Thomas ended up over Boniface IV, and over time the altar simply became referred to as the Altar of St. Thomas. From Louise Rice, *The Altars and Altarpieces of New St. Peter's*, (Cambridge: Cambridge University Press, 2000), 241.

70. Montini, 118–119.

71. Montini, 119–120.

72. Grimaldi, 391.

73. Grimaldi, 392.

74. Grimaldi, 392.

75. Montini, 121.

76. An exarch sent to arrest Martin, Olympian, was allegedly struck blind and converted to Christianity while in Rome. Subsequently he turned on his emperor in support of Martin.

77. Kelley, 75.

78. Grimaldi, 393.

79. Montini, 124.

80. Montini, 126.

81. Montini, 127.

82. Montini, 127.

83. Grimaldi, 393.

84. Montini, 151.

85. Grimaldi. ch. 80.

86. Montini, 129.

87. Grimaldi. ch. 237.

88. Montini, 129.

89. Montini, 130.

90. Montini, 131.

91. Montini, 132.

92. Mann, *Tombs and Portraits*, 22.

93. Ferdinand Gregorovius, *Tombs of the Popes* (London: Archibald Constable, 1903), 21–22.

94. Grimaldi, 392.

95. Kelley, 100.

96. Montini, 138.

97. Grimaldi, 236.

98. R. Lanciani, (Reprint, Manchester NH: Ayer, 1968), chapter 5.

99. Grimaldi, ch. 202.

100. Montini, 139.

101. Montini, 140.

102. Grimaldi, 397.

103. Montini, 141.

104. Montini, 142.

105. Montini, 144.

106. Montini, 145.

107. Montini, 146.

108. Montini, 147.

109. Montini, 147–148.

110. Montini, 148.

111. Montini, 149.

112. Montini, 149–150.

113. Chris Nyborg, *The Churches of Rome*, online at http://home.online.no/~cnyborg/popes.html.

114. Montini, 150.

115. Grimaldi, 400.

116. Mann, 25.

117. Montini, 152.

118. Montini, 152–153.

119. Mann, *Tombs and Portraits*, 25.

120. Mann, *Tombs and Portraits*, 25.

121. Montini, 156.

122. Montini, 134.

123. According to Lanciani, Crescenzio died peacefully in the monastery of S. Alessio on the Aventine in 964. His tomb inscription is in the cloisters of the monastery: "Here lies the body of Crescentius, the illustrious, the honorable citizen of Rome, the great leader, the great descendant of a great family…. Christ the Saviour of our souls made him infirm and an invalid, so that, abandoning any further hope of worldy success, he entered this monastery, and spent his last years in prayer and retirement." Lanciani, chapter 5.

124. Montini, 161.

125. Montini, 162.

126. Montini, 162.

127. Gregorovius, 30–31.

128. Gregorovius, 30–31.

129. Mann, *Tombs and Portraits*, 25.

130. Raymond Davis, *Lives of the Tenth-Century Popes (Liber Pontificalis)*. (Liverpool: Liverpool University Press, 1997).

131. Gregorovius, 33–34.

132. Rasponi, "De Basilica et Patriarchio Lateranensi," Rome 1656, p. 76.

133. Lanciani, chapter 5.

134. Montini, 168.

135. Mann, *Tombs and Portraits*, 25.

136. Montini, 170.

137. Montini, 170.

138. Mann, *Tombs and Portraits*, 25.

139. Montini, 173.

140. His uncle put him on the papal throne when he was about twenty years old. In 1044 the Romans, disgusted with Benedict, removed him and elected Silvester III in his place (hence Silvester is an antipope). Benedict in turn ejected Silvester that same year, but then decided he wanted to marry and so sold the papacy to John Gratian, who became Pope Gregory VI (and an antipope). Benedict then thought better of this and deposed Gregory. Weary of the chaotic situation, Henry III called the Council of Sutri in 1046 and deposed all three popes. Abbot Suidger of Bamberg, Germany, became Pope Clement II, but he died fairly soon thereafter (murdered by lead poisoning, as his autopsy in 1942 proved), and Benedict IX once again claimed he was pope in November of 1047. Benedict was at last driven away exactly one year later by pope Damasus II.

141. *The Catholic Encyclopedia* (New York: McGraw-Hill, 1967).

142. Montini, 176.

143. Montini, 176.

144. Montini, 178.

145. Mann, *Tombs and Portraits*, 27.

146. Gregorovius, 37.

147. Montini, 181.

148. Charles John Samuel Thompson, *Poisons and Poisoners: With Historical Accounts of Some Famous Mysteries in Ancient and Modern Times* (London: Harold Shaylor, 1931), 76.

149. Mann, *Tombs and Portraits*, 29.

150. Paravicini-Bagliani, 138.

151. Montini, 183–184.

152. Montini, 186.

153. Mann, *Tombs and Portraits*, 29.

154. Gregorovius, 43.

155. Gregorovius, 43.

156. Mann, *Tombs and Portraits*, 25.

157. Caporilli, 49.

158. Mann, *Tombs and Portraits*, 25.

159. Mann, *Tombs and Portraits*, p. 25.

160. Joachim Prinz, *Popes from the Ghetto* (New York: Horizon, 1966), 237.

161. Montini, 193.

162. Montini, 193–194.

163. Joachim Prinz, *Popes from the Ghetto* (New York: Horizon, 1966), 237.

164. Mann, *Tombs and Portraits*, 25.

165. Mann, *Tombs and Portraits*, 25.

166. Montini, 196.

167. Caporilli, 51.

168. Brenda Bolton, *Hadrian IV* (Aldershot, Hants., England: Ashgate, 2003).

169. Bolton.

170. The only scholar I have found who refers to the combining of Silvester, Vigilius, and Adrian IV is Renzo Montini in his 1957 *Le Tombe dei Papi*, page 110. Nor can I find mention of an altar to St. Silvester in any other books, old or new.

171. Mann, *Tombs and Portraits*, 31.

172. Mann, *Tombs and Portraits*, 25.

173. Montini, 202–203.

174. Gregorovius, 47.

175. Gregorovius, 47.

176. Montini, 203.

177. Montini, 205.

178. Julian Gardner, *The Tomb and the Tiara*, (New York: Oxford University Press, 1992), 29.

179. Montini, 205.

180. Montini, 206.

181. Montini, 206.

182. Mann, *Tombs and Portraits*, 25.

183. Mann, *Tombs and Portraits*, 25.

184. Paravincini-Bagliani, 144.

185. Paravincini-Bagliani, 122; Bertelli, 43.

186. Paravincini-Bagliani, 103.

187. Paravicni-Bagliani, 139.

188. P.G. Maxwell-Stuart, *Chronicle of the Popes* (London: Thames and Hudson, 1997).

189. Bertelli, 43.

190. Gregorovius, 50.

191. Gregorovius, 50.

192. Gregorovius, 51.

193. Gregorovius, 51.

194. Paravicini-Bagliani, 140.

195. Gregorovius, 52.

196. Gregorovius, 52.

197. Montini, 217–218.

198. Gardner, 69.

199. Paravincini-Bagliani, 141.

200. Montini, 218.

201. Gregorovius and Mann attribute the tomb to Margaritone of Arrezzo; Montini claims they are wrong but is vague about who sculpted the tomb.

202. Gregorovius, 53.

203. Gregorovius, 53.

204. Montini, 220.

205. Mann, *Tombs and Portraits*, 25.

206. Gardner, 72.

207. Paravincini-Bagliani, 136.

208. Montini, 226.
209. Montini, 226.
210. Montini, 227.
211. Montini, 229.
212. Mann, *Tombs and Portraits*, 33–44.
213. Montini, 230.
214. Montini, 230.
215. Paravicini-Bagliani, 140, 309 n. 83.
216. Paravicini-Bagliani, 145.
217. Montini, 216.
218. Mariangela Rinaldi and Mariangela Vicini, *Buon Appetito, Your Holiness: The Secrets of the Papal Table* (Milan, 1998), 89.
219. Gardner, 103.
220. Montini, 236–238.
221. Kelley, 77.
222. Montini, 240–241.
223. E.R. Chamberlain, *The Bad Popes* (New York: Barnes & Noble, 1993), 122.
224. Malachi Martin, *The Decline and Fall of the Roman Church*, (New York: G.P. Putnam's Sons, 1981), 63.
225. George Frederick Kunz, *Rings of the Finger*, (1917; reprint, New York: Dover, 1973), 306.
226. Grimaldi, 97.
227. Grimaldi, 403.
228. Paravicini-Bagliani, 137.
229. Kunz, 273.
230. Paravicini-Bagliani, 118.
231. Montini, 245, 247.
232. Mann, *Tombs and Portraits*, 53.
233. www.avignon-et-provence.com/avignon/popes/gb/index.html.
234. Maxwell-Stuart.
235. Paravicini-Bagliani, 140.
236. Mann, *Tombs and Portraits*, 55.
237. Mann, *Tombs and Portraits*, 56.
238. Montini, 248.
239. Mann, *Tombs and Portraits*, 56.
240. Mann, *Tombs and Portraits*, 56.
241. Mann, *Tombs and Portraits*, 57.
242. Mann, *Tombs and Portraits*, 58.
243. Mann, *Tombs and Portraits*, 58.
244. Mann, *Tombs and Portraits*, 58.
245. Paravicini-Bagliani, 134.
246. Anne Morgenstern, "Art and Ceremony in Papal Avignon: A Prescription for the Tomb of Clement VI" (Gesta XL/I, 2001).
247. Paravicini-Bagliani, 135.
248. Maxwell-Stuart, 134.
249. Not in Notre dom des Doms, as reported by the *Catholic Encyclopedia*.
250. Urban had been abbot of Marseilles, which is why he was buried there.
251. Mann, *Tombs and Portraits*, 61.
252. Mann, *Tombs and Portraits*, 61.
253. Mann, *Tombs and Portraits*, 60.
254. Montini, 255–256.
255. Paravicini-Bagliani, 314.
256. Montini, 258.
257. Gregorovius, 66–67.
258. Gregorovius, 66–67.
259. Sladen, 56.
260. Grimaldi, 219.
261. Douglas Sladen, *Old St. Peter's and St. Peter's Crypt at Rome with a List of the Popes* (London: Hurst and Blackett, 1907), 57.
262. Gardner, 156.
263. Kelley, 232.
264. Kajanto, 21.
265. Montini, 264.
266. Kajanto, 23.
267. I am grateful to my friend Chad Underkoffler, who first made me aware of the theft of the skull.
268. Grimaldi, 219.
269. Montini, 267.
270. Montini, 267–278.
271. Mann, *Tombs and Portraits*, 66.
272. Robert Wesley Habenstein and William Mathias Lamers, *History of American Funeral Directing*, rev. ed. (Milwaukee: Bulfin, 1962).
273. Mann, *Tombs and Portraits*, 69.
274. Mann, *Tombs and Portraits*, 68.
275. Mann, *Tombs and Portraits*, 69.
276. Roberta J.M. Olson, *Italian Renaissance Sculpture* (London: Thames and Hudson, 1992), 75.
277. Kajanto, 31.
278. Montini, 273.
279. Kajanto, 32.
280. Kelley, 243.
281. Paravicini-Bagliani, 157.
282. Paravicini-Bagliani, 158.
283. Grimaldi.
284. Kajanto, 44.
285. Montini, 50.
286. Kajanto, 50.
287. Kajanto, 51.
288. Kajanto, 52.
289. Kajanto, 52.
290. Grimaldi, 403.
291. Grimaldi, 403.
292. Grimaldi, 271.
293. Grimaldi, 271.
294. Kajanto, 63.
295. Montini, 289.
296. Sladen, 56.
297. Kajanto, 64.
298. Kajanto, 65.
299. Kajanto, 67.
300. Kajanto, 67.
301. Kajanto, 67.
302. Montini, 288–289.
303. Rinaldi and Vicini, 160.
304. Maxwell-Stuart, 149.

305. Sladen, 59.

306. Grimaldi, ch. 192.

307. Kajanto, 70.

308. Kelley, 251.

309. Paravicini-Bagliani, 104.

310. Rinaldi and Vicni, 179.

311. Paravicini-Bagliani, 128.

312. Paravicini-Bagliani, 157.

313. Mann, *Tombs and Portraits*, 79.

314. Mann, *Tombs and Portraits*, 9.

315. Kajanto, 75.

316. Kajanto, 75.

317. Kajanto, 75.

318. Mann, *Tombs and Portraits*, 79–80 n. 4.

319. Friedrich Gontard, *The Chair of Peter*, trans. A.J. and E.F. Peeler (New York: Holt, Rinehart and Winston, 1964), 369.

320. Gregorovius, 87.

321. The sultan had given Innocent the lance in return for the pope holding the Sultan's brother Djem hostage in Rome so that he wouldn't be able to overthrow the sultan.

322. Kajanto, 86.

323. Kajanto, 86.

324. It had been rumored that when the pope needed more money he went to dinner at a cardinal's home, and the cardinal often ended up dead from a dose of *La Cantarella*, the notorious Borgia poison allegedly made from a base of arsenic. The cardinal's estate would then go to the coffers of the pope.

325. Johann Burchard, *At the Court of the Borgia*, ed. and trans. by Geoffrey Parker (London: Folio Society, 1963), 147.

326. Rinaldi and Vicini, p. 195.

327. Gregorovius, 90.

328. Kajanto, 87.

329. Grimaldi.

330. The inscription is incorrect, as Alexander died in his seventy-third year.

331. Grimaldi, 271.

332. Kajanto, 63.

333. Paravicini-Bagliani, 129.

334. Kajanto, 89.

335. Kajanto, 89.

336. Kajanto, 90.

337. Kajanto, 90–91.

338. Montini, 300–301.

339. Paravicini-Bagliani, 127.

340. Gontard, 369.

341. Kajanto, Iiro, 92.

342. Kajanto, Iiro, 92.

343. Gregorovius, 91.

344. Gontard, 393.

345. Maxwell-Stuart, 175.

346. Gontard, 393.

347. Francis Burkle-Young, *Passing the Keys* (New York: Madison, 1999), 61.

348. Kajanto, 96.

349. Kajanto, 96.

350. Rinaldi and Vicini, 210–211.

351. Kajanto, 102.

352. Kajanto, 102.

353. Kajanto, 102.

354. Kajanto, 102.

355. Kajanto, 103.

356. Kajanto, 103.

357. Peter and Margaret Hebblethwaite, *The Next Pope* (San Francisco: HarperSanFrancisco, 2001), 65.

358. Kajanto, 104.

359. Kajanto, 104.

360. Thompson, 117.

361. Kajanto, 106.

362. Kajanto, 106.

363. Kajanto, 106.

364. Kajanto, 106.

365. Kelley, 88.

366. Kajanto, 108.

367. Kajanto, 109.

368. Kajanto, 109–110.

369. Paul owed his pontificate to his sister, who was the mistress of Pope Alexander VI (d. 1503). Alexander made Paul a cardinal for that reason alone, and so he was commonly referred to as the "Petticoat Cardinal."

370. Rinaldi and Vicini, 224.

371. Montini, 326.

372. Grimaldi, chs. 182, 187.

373. Gontard, 430.

374. Paravicini-Bagliani, 73.

375. Montini, 332.

376. Rinaldi and Vicini, 239.

377. Montini, 334.

378. Montini, 334.

379. Montini, 336.

380. Rinaldi and Vicini, 240.

381. Montini, 337.

382. Gontard, 251.

383. Montini, 341–342.

384. Kelley, 273.

385. Montini, 344.

386. Montini, 344, 348.

387. Grimaldi, ch. 78.

388. Cardinal Virgilio Noe, *Le Tombe e i Monumenti Funerebri dei Papi nella Basilica di San Pietro in Vaticano* (Modena: F.G. Industrie Grafiche, 2000), 209.

389. Grimaldi.

390. Montini, 360.

391. Montini, 365.

392. Lees-Milne, 169.

393. Philip Aryes, *A Short Account of the Life and Death of Pope Alexander the VII* (London: Moses Pitt, 1667).

394. Montini, 378.

395. Montini, 385.

396. Claudio Rendina, *The Popes: Histories and Secrets*, trans. Paul D. McCusker (Santa Ana CA: Seven Locks, 2002), 526.

397. Lees-Milne, 300, 302.

398. Paravicini-Bagliani, 143.

399. Gontard, 447.

400. Montini, 396.

401. *Death of the Pope! (Pius V.)*

402. Gontard, 486.

403. George Aislabie Procter, "The Death of Pecci" (pamphlet, 1903).

404. Eamon Duffy, *Saints and Sinners* (New Haven: Yale University Press, 1997), 203.

405. Montini, 402.

406. Montini, 402.

407. Montini, 100.

408. Montini, 398.

409. Rinaldi and Vicini, 279.

410. Gordon Thomas and Max Morgan-Witts, *Pontiff* (New York: Doubleday, 1983), 335.

411. Rendina, 555.

412. Montini, 405–406.

413. Thomas and Morgan-Witts, 336.

414. Burkle-Young, 3.

415. Montini, 112.

416. Sladen, 70.

417. Burkle-Young, 6.

418. Rinaldi and Vicini, 318.

419. Gontard, 530.

420. Burkle-Young, 11–12.

421. Gontard, p. 530.

422. Gontard, p. 537.

423. *Catholic Encyclopedia*, online edition, "Benedict XIV."

424. Burkle-Young, p. 17–20.

425. Burkle-Young, p. 30–40.

426. John Cornwell, *Hitler's Pope: The Secret History of Pius XII* (New York: Viking, 1999), 366.

427. Burkle-Young, 86.

428. Cornwell, 355.

429. Rory Carroll, "Pope Welcomes Embalmed Predecessor on a Saintly Mission," *The Guardian*, June 4, 2001.

430. Fortean Times **163**, 20.

431. Burkle-Young, 237.

432. James-Charles Noonan, *The Church Visible* (New York: Viking, 1996), 27.

433. Noonan, 27.

434. Burkle-Young, 240–243.

435. John Cornwell, *A Thief in the Night: The Death of Pope John Paul I* (New York: Penguin, 1990), 265.

436. Thomas and Morgan-Witts, 343.

437. John Hogue, *Nostrodamus: The Complete Prophecies* (Shaftesbury, England: Element, 1997).

Appendix 1:
Alphabetical List of Popes

Antipopes are listed in italics.

A(da)lbert *1101*
Adeodatus II 672–6
Agapitus I 535–6
Agapitus II 946–55
Agatho 678–81
Alexander I .... c. 109–c. 116
Alexander II 1061–73
Alexander III 1159–1181
Alexander IV 1254–61
Alexander V *1409–10*
Alexander VI 1492–1503
Alexander VII 1655–67
Alexander VIII 1689–91
Anacletus .... c. 79–c. 91
Anacletus II *1130–8*
Anastasius Biblio. *855*
Anastasius I 399–401
Anastasius II 496–8
Anastasius III 911–3
Anastasius IV 1153–4
Anicetus .... c. 155–c. 166
Anterus 230–236
Benedict I 575–9
Benedict II 684–5
Benedict III 855–8
Benedict IV 900–3
Benedict V .... 964 dep
Benedict VI 973–4
Benedict VII 974–83

Benedict VIII 1012–24
Benedict IX 1032–44; 1045; 1047–8
Benedict X *1058–9*
Benedict XI 1303–4
Benedict XII 1334–42
Benedict (XIII) *1394–1417*
Benedict XIII 1724–30
Benedict (XIV) *1425*
Benedict XIV 1740–58
Benedict XV 1914–22
Boniface I 418–22
Boniface II 530–2
Boniface III 607
Boniface IV 608–15
Boniface V 619–625
Boniface VI 896
Boniface VII 984–5
Boniface VIIII 1294–1303
Boniface IX 1389–1404
Callistus I 217–22
Callistus II 1119–24
Callistus (III) *1168–78*
Callistus III 1455–8
Celestine I 422–432
Celestine (II) 1124–5/6
Celestine II 1143–4
Celestine III 1191–8
Celestine IV 1241
Celestine V 1294

John XII	955–64	*Nicholas (V)*	*1328–30*
John XIII	965–72	Nicholas V	1447–55
John XIV	983–4	*Novatian*	*251–8*
John XV	985–96	*Paschal*	*687*
John XVI	*997–8*	Paschal I	817–24
John XVII	1003	Paschal II	1099–1118
John XVIII	1003–9	*Paschal III*	*1164–8*
John XIX	1024–32	Paul I	757–67
John XXI	1276–7	Paul II	1464–71
John XXII	1316–34	Paul III	1534–49
John XXIII	*1410–15*	Paul IV	1555–9
John XXIII	1958–63	Paul V	1605–21
John Paul I	1978	Paul VI	1963–78
John Paul II	1978–	Pelagius I	556–1
Julius I	337–352	Pelagius II	579–90
Julius II	1503–13	Peter	d. *c.* 64
Julius III	1550–5	*Philip*	*768*
Lando	913–4	Pius I	c. 142–c. 155
Lawrence	*498–9*	Pius II	1458–64
Leo I The Great	440–61	Pius III	1503
Leo II	682–3	Pius IV	1559–65
Leo III	795–816	Pius V	1566–72
Leo IV	847–55	Pius VI	1775–99
Leo V	903–4	Pius VII	1800–23
Leo VI	928	Pius VIII	1829–30
Leo VII	936–9	Pius IX	1846–78
Leo VIII	963–5 dep	Pius X	1903–14
Leo IX	1049–1054	Pius XI	1922–39
Leo X	1513–21	Pius XII	1939–58
Leo XI	1605	Pontian	230–235
Leo XII	1823–9	Romanus	897
Leo XIII	1878–1903	Sabinian	604–6
Liberius	352–366	Sergius I	687–701
Linus	c. 66–c. 78	Sergius II	844–7
Lucius I	253–4	Sergius III	904–11
Lucius II	1144–5	Sergius IV	1009–12
Lucius III	1181–5	Severinus	640
Marcellinus	296–304	Silverius	536–7
Marcellus	306–8	Silvester I	314–31
Marcellus II	1555	Silvester II	999–1003
Marinus I	882–4	Silvester III	1045–63
Marinus II	942–6	*Silvester IV*	*1105–11*
Mark	336	Simplicius	468–83
Martin I	649–55	Siricus	384–99
Martin II (*see* Marcellus I)		Sisinnius	708
Martin III (*see* Marcellus II)		Sixtus I	c. 116–c. 125
Martin IV	1281–5	Sixtus II	257–8
Martin V	1417–31	Sixtus III	432–40
Miltiades	311–4	Sixtus IV	1471–84
Nicholas I	858–67	Sixtus V	1585–90
Nicholas II	1058–61	Soter	c. 166–c. 174
Nicholas III	1277–80	Stephen I	254–257
Nicholas IV	1288–92	Stephen I (II)	752

Appendix 2:
Papal Death, Burial and Reburial Chart

Arrangement is chronological. Antipopes are listed in italics.

Papal Name	Mode of Death	Church Buried	Reburied in
St. Peter (Apostle) (d. c. 64)	Crucified	Vatican Area, Rome	
St. Linus (c. 66–c. 78)	*Martyred	Vatican Area, Rome	
St. Anacletus (c. 79–c. 91)	*Martyred	Vatican Area, Rome	
St. Clement I (c. 91–c. 101)	*Drowned	unknown area, Crimea	San Clemente, Rome
St. Evaristus (c. 100–c. 109)	*Martyred	Vatican Area, Rome	
St. Alexander (c. 109–c. 116)	Beheaded	Via Nomentana, Rome	
St. Sixtus (c. 116–c. 125)	*Martyred	Duomo of Alatri, Alatri	
St. Telesphorus (c. 125–c. 136)	Martyred	Vatican Area, Rome	
St. Hyginus (c. 138–c. 142)	*Martyred	Vatican Area, Rome	
St. Pius I (c. 142–c. 155)	*Martyred	Vatican Area, Rome	
St. Anicetus (c. 155–c. 166)	*Martyred	Vatican Area, Rome	Altemps Palace, Rome
St. Soter (c. 166–c. 174)	*Martyred	Vatican Area, Rome	San Martino ai Monte, Rome
St. Eleuther(i)us (c. 174–c. 89)	*Martyred/ raked over coals	Santa Susanna, Rome	Santa Susanna, Rome
St. Victor I (189–98)	*Martyred	Vatican Area, Rome	
St. Zephyrinus (198/9–217)	*Martyred	Cemetery of Callistus, Rome	
St. Callistus (217–22)	Drowned	Cemetery of Caledipus	Sta. Maria in Trastevere, Rome
St. Hippolytus (217–35)	Harsh prison	Cemetery of Hippolytus, Rome	
St. Urban (222–30)	*Beheaded	Cemetery of St. Praetextatus, Rome	
St. Pontian (230–235)	Beaten	Papal crypt, Cemetery of Callistus, Rome	

*—Allegedly
†—San Silvestro was built above the Cemetery of Priscilla

Papal Name	Mode of Death	Church Buried	Reburied in
St. Anterus (230–236)	*Martyred	Papal crypt, Cemetery of Callistus, Rome	San Silvestro in Capite, Rome
St. Fabian (236–250)	Beheaded	Papal crypt, Cemetery of Callistus, Rome	San Sebastiano, Rome
St. Cornelius (251–253)	Beheaded	Crypt of St. Lucina, Rome	Sta. Maria Trastevere
Novatian (251–8)	–	–	
St. Lucius I (253–4)	*Beheaded	Papal crypt, Cemetery of Callistus, Rome	Sta. Ceceilia in Trastevere
St. Stephen I (254–257)	*Beheaded	Papal crypt, Cemetery of Callistus, Rome	SS Capite/Cavalieri. Pisa
St. Sixtus II (257–8)	Beheaded	Cemetery of Callistus, Rome	San Sisto Vecchio, Rome
St. Dionysius (260–8)	–	Papal crypt, Cemetery of Callistus, Rome	San Silvestro in Capite
St. Felix I (269–274)	*Beheaded	Papal crypt, Cemetery of Callistus, Rome	
St. Eutychian (275/7–283)	–	Papal crypt, Cemetery of Callistus, Rome	Sarzana Cathedral, Sarzana
St. Gaius (283–296)	–	Cemetery of Callistus, Rome	S.S. Capite/chpl Barbarini, Rome
St. Marcellinus (296–304)	Beheaded	Cemetery of Priscilla, Rome	
St. Marcellus (306–8)	Overworked in a stable	Cemetery of Priscilla, Rome	San Silvestro in Capite
St. Eusebius (310)	*Harsh treatment	Cemetery of Callistus, Rome	
St. Miltiades (311–4)	–	Cemetery of Callistus, Rome	
St. Silvester (314–335)	–	San Silvestro†, Rome	S.S. Capite/Ab.of Nonantola, Italy
St. Mark (336)	–	Cemetery of Balbina	San Marco, Rome
St. Julius I (337–352)	–	Cemetery of Calepodius, Rome	Sta. Maria Trastevere
Liberius (352–366)	–	San Silvestro†, Rome	
St. Felix II (355–365)	Beheaded	Church on Via Aurelia	
St. Damasus I (366–384)	–	Cemetery of Callistus, Rome	San Lorenzo in Damaso
Ursinus (366–7)	Murdered	Gaul	
St. Siricus (384–99)	*Martyred	San Silvestro†, Rome	Sta. Prassade, Rome
St. Anastasius I (399–401)	–	Pontian Cemetery, Rome	San Martino ai Monte
St. Innocent I (401–17)	–	Pontian Cemetery, Rome	San Martino ai Monte
St. Zosimus (417–8)	Illness	S. Lorenzo al Verano, Rome	San Silvestre in Capite
Eulalius (418–9)	–	–	
St. Boniface (418–22)	Old age	St. Felicitias, Rome	
St. Celestine (422–432)	–	San Silvestro†, Rome	Santa Prassade, Rome
St. Sixtus III (432–40)	–	S. Lorenzo al Verano, Rome	
St. Leo I The Great (440–61)	–	St. Peter's, Rome	
St. Hilarus (461–8)	Old age	S. Lorenzo al Verano, Rome	
St. Simplicius (468–83)	Illness	St. Peter's, Rome	
St. Felix III (II) (483–92)	–	St. Paul's Fuori la Mura, Rome	
St. Gelasius (492–6)	–	St. Peter's	
Anastasius II (496–8)	"Divine judgement"	St. Peter's	
St. Symmachus (498–514)	–	St. Peter's	
Lawrence (498–9)	–	–	
St. Hormisdas (514–6)	–	St. Peter's	
St. John I (523–6)	Starvation (martyr)	St. Peter's	
St. Felix IV (III) (526–30)	–	St. Peter's	
Dioscorus (530)	–	–	
Boniface II (530–2)	–	St. Peter's	

Papal Name	Mode of Death	Church Buried	Reburied in
John II (533–5)	–	St. Peter's	
St. Agapitus I (535–6)	–	St. Peter's	
St. Silverius (536–7)	Harsh prison	Monastery on Isle of Ponza, Italy	
Vigilius (537–55)	*Murdered/ gallstones	San Silvestro†, Rome	St. Peter's
Pelagius I (556–1)	Old age	St. Peter's	
John III (561–574)	–	St. Peter's	
Benedict I (575–9)	Illness	St. Peter's	
Pelagius II (579–90)	Plague	St. Peter's	
St.Gregory I (590–604)	Gout/Illness	St. Peter's	
Sabinian (604–6)	*Ghost of Gregory I	St. Peter's	
Boniface III	–	St. Peter's	
St. Boniface IV (608–15)	–	St. Peter's	
Deusdedit (615–8)	–	St. Peter's	
Boniface V (619–625)	–	St. Peter's	
Honorius I (615–38)	–	St. Peter's	
Severinus (640)	Harsh prison	St. Peter's	
John IV (640–2)	–	St. Peter's	
Theodore I (642–9)	*Poison	St. Peter's	
St. Martin I (649–55)	Starvation	Church of Our Lady, Chersonesus	
St. Eugene I (654–7)	–	St. Peter's	
St. Vitalian (657–72)	–	St. Peter's	
Adeodatus II (672–6)	–	St. Peter's	
Donus (676–8)	–	St. Peter's	
St. Agatho (678–81)	Illness	St. Peter's	
St. Leo II (682–3)	–	St. Peter's	
St. Benedict II (684–5)	–	St. Peter's	
John V (685–6)	Illness	St. Peter's	
Conon (686–7)	Illness	St. Peter's	
Theodore (687)	–		
Paschal (687)	–		
St. Sergius I (687–701)	–	St. Peter's	
John VI (701–5)	–	St. Peter's	
John VII (705–7)	*Murder	St. Peter's	
Sisinnius (708)	Gout	St. Peter's	
Constantine (708–15)	*Illness	St. Peter's	
St. Gregory II (715–31)	–	St. Peter's	
St. Gregory III (731–41)	–	St. Peter's	
St. Zacharias (741–52)	–	St. Peter's	
Stephen (II) (752)	Stroke	St. Peter's	
Stephen II (III) (752–7)	–	St. Peter's	
St. Paul I (757–67)	Heat exhaustion	S. Paulo fuori le mura	St. Peter's
Constantine (766–8)	Harsh prison		
Philip (768)	–		
Stephen III (IV) (768–72)	–	St. Peter's	
Hadrian I (772–95)	–	St. Peter's	
St. Leo III (795–816)	Illness	St. Peter's	
Stephen IV (V) (816–7)	–	St. Peter's	
St. Paschal I (817–24)	–	St. Peter's	
Eugene II (824–7)	–	St. Peter's	

Papal Name	Mode of Death	Church Buried	Reburied in
Valentine (827)	"Bodily troubles"	St. Peter's	
Gregory IV (827–44)	–	St. Peter's	
John (844)	–		
Sergius II (844–7)	–	St. Peter's	
St. Leo IV (847–55)	–	St. Peter's	
Benedict III (855–8)	–	St. Peter's	
Bibliothecarius (855)	–	–	
St. Nicholas I (858–67)	Illness	St. Peter's	
Hadrian II (867–72)	–	St. Peter's	
John VIII (872–82)	Poison & clubbed	St. Peter's	
Marinus I (882–4)	–	St. Peter's	
St. Hadrian III (884–5)	*Poison	Abbey of Nonantola, Nonantola, Italy	
Stephen V (VI) (885–91)	–	St. Peter's	
Formosus (891–6)	Illness	St. Peter's	
Boniface VI (896)	*Murdered	St. Peter's	
Stephen VI (VII) (896–7)	Strangled	St. Peter's	
Romanus (897)	*Poison	St. Peter's	
Theodore (897)	"Foul play"	St. Peter's	
John IX (898–900)	*Murdered	St. Peter's	
Benedict IV (900–3)	"Mysterious causes"	St. Peter's	
Leo V (903–4)	Strangled	St. Peter's	
Christopher (903–4)	Strangled	St. Peter's	
Sergius III (904–11)	"Mysteriously"	St. Peter's	
Anastasius III (911–3)	*Poisoned	St. Peter's	
Lando (913–4)	*Murdered	St. Peter's	
John X (914–28)	Smothered	St. Peter's	
Leo VI (928)	*Murdered	St. Peter's	
Stephen VII (VIII) (928–31)	*Murdered	St. Peter's	
John XI (931–6)	Poison	St. Peter's	
Leo VII (936–9)	Heart attack	St. Peter's	
Stephen VIII (IX) (939–42)	Mutilation	St. Peter's	
Marinus II (942–6)	"Suspiciously"	St. Peter's	
Agapitus II (946–55)	"Mysteriously"	St. Peter's	
John XII (955–64)	Strangled	St. Peter's	
Leo VIII (963–5 dep)	"Suspiciously"	St. Peter's	
Benedict V (964 dep)	Beaten	Cathedral of Hamburg, Germany	unknown location, Rome
John XIII (965–72)	–	St. Paul fuori le Mura, Rome	
Benedict VI (973–4)	Strangled	St. Peter's, Rome	
Benedict VII (974–83)	–	Sta. Croce in Gerusalemme, Rome	
John XIV (983–4)	Starved	St. Peter's, Rome	
Boniface VII (984–5)	Poison	–	
John XV (985–96)	Fever	St. Peter's, Rome	
Gregory V (996–999)	*Poison/malaria	St. Peter's, Rome	
John XVI (997–8)	Mutilation	–	
Silvester II (999–1003)	*Poison	Lateran, Rome	
John XVII (1003)	–	St. Paul fuori le Mura or Lateran	
John XVIII (1003–9)	–	St. Paul fuori le Mura or Lateran, Rome	

Papal Name	Mode of Death	Church Buried	Reburied in
Sergius IV (1009–12)	*Murdered	Lateran	
Benedict VIII (1012–24)	–	St. Peter's, Rome	
Gregory (VI) (1012)	–	*Hamburg, Germany	
John XIX (1024–32)	–	St. Peter's, Rome	
Benedict IX (1032–44)	*Illness	Abbey of Grottaferrata, Grotteferrata, Italy	
Silvester III (1045–63)	–	*Sabina, Italy	
Gregory VI (1045–6 dep)	Illness	St. Peter's, Rome	
Clement II (1046–7)	Poison	Cathedral of Bamburg, Germany	
Damasus II (1048)	*Poison/malaria	San Lorenzo fuori le Mura, Rome	
St Leo IX (1049–54)	Illness	St. Peter's, Rome	
Victor II (1055–7)	*Poison/fever	Mausoleum of Theodoric, Ravenna, Italy	
Stephen IX (X) (1057–8)	Malaria	San Reparata, Florence	
Benedict X (1058–9)	–	San Agnese in Agone, Rome	
Nicholas II (1058–61)	–	San Reparata, Florence	
Alexander II (1061–73)	Illness	Lateran or St. Peter's	
Honorius (II) (1061–4)	–		
St. Gregory VII (1073–85)	Despair	Church of St. Matthew, Salerno, Italy	Salerno Cathedral
Clement III (1080)	–	–	
BL. Victor III (1086–7)	Illness	Abbey of Grottaferrata, Monte Cassino	St. Paul fuori le Mura, Rome
BL. Urban II (1088–99)	–	St. Peter's, Rome	
Paschal II (1099–1118)	Harsh prison or street riot	Lateran, Rome	
Theodoric (1100–1)	–	La Cava, Italy	
A(da)lbert (1101)	–	San Lorenzo, Aversa, Italy	
Silvester IV (1105–11)	–	–	
Gelasius II (1118–9)	Pleurisy	Abbey Church, Cluny, France	
Gregory (VIII) (1118–21)	Mob beating	–	
Callistus II (1119–24)	Roman fever	Lateran	
Honorius II (1124–30)	Roman fever	Lateran	
Celestine (II) (1124–5/6)	Severe beating	–	
Innocent II (1130–43)	–	Lateran, Rome	Sta. Maria in Trastevere, Rome
Anacletus II (1130–8)	–	Sta. Maria in Trastevere	
Victor IV (1138)	–	–	
Celestine II (1143–4)	Old age	Lateran, Rome	
Lucius II (1144–5)	Hit on head by rock	Lateran, Rome	
BL. Eugene III (1145–53)	Violent fever	St. Peter's, Rome	
Anastasius IV (1153–4)	Old age	Lateran, Rome	
Hadrian IV (1154–9)	Illness	St. Peter's, Rome	
Alexander III (1159–1181)	Illness	Lateran, Rome	
Victor IV (1159–64)	Illness	Monastery in Lucca, Italy	
Paschal III (1164–8)	–	–	
Callistus (III) (1168–78)	–	–	
Innocent (III) (1179–80)	–	Abbey of Trinita in La Cava, Italy	
Lucius III (1181–5)	–	Verona Cathedral, Verona	

Papal Name	Mode of Death	Church Buried	Reburied in
Urban III (1195–7)	Illness	Duomo of Ferrara, Ferrara	
Gregory VIII (1187)	Illness	Duomo of Pisa, Pisa	
Clement III (1187–91)	–	Lateran, Rome	
Celestine III (1191–8)	Illness	Lateran, Rome	
Innocent III (1198–1216)	Fever	San Lorenzo,Perugia, Italy	St. John Lateran, Rome
Honorius III (1216–27)	Old age	Sta. Maria Maggiore, Rome	
Gregory IX (1227–41)	Heat exhaustion	St. Peter's	
Celestine IV (1241)	Harsh conclave	St. Peter's, Rome	
Innocent IV (1243–7)	–	San Januarius, Italy	
Alexander IV (1254–61)	–	St. Lawrence, Italy	
Urban IV (1261–4)	–	Cathedral of Perugia, Italy	
Clement IV (1265–8)	–	San Francesco, Italy	
BL. Gregory X (1271–6)	Fever	Duomo of Arrezo, Arezzo	
BL. Innocent V (1276)	Fever	Lateran, Rome	
Hadrian V (1276)	Illness	San Francesco, Viterbo	
John XXI (1276–7)	Ceiling collapse	St. Lawrence, Viterbo	
Nicholas III (1277–80)	Stroke/apoplexy	St. Peter's, Rome	
Martin IV (1281–5)	Choked on pickled eels	Perugia Cathedral	
Honorius IV (1285–7)	Stroke/gout	St. Peter's, Rome	Sta. Maria in Aracoeli, Rome
Nicholas IV (1288–92)	–	Sta. Maria Maggiore, Rome	
Celestine V St. Peter (1294)	Infected abcess	St. Anthony, Ferentino	Sta. M. Collamagio, L'Aquila, Italy
Boniface VIII (1294–1303)	Depression/kidney stones	St. Peter's, Rome	
BL. Benedict XI (1303–4)	*Poisoned figs/ dysentery	San Dominico Cathedral, Perugia	
Clement V (1305–14)	Ate crushed emeralds	Parish Church, Uzeste, FR.	
John XXII (1316–34)	Old age	Notre–Dom–Des–Doms, Avignon, FR.	
Nicholas (V) (1328–30)	–	*Avignon	–
Benedict XII (1334–42)	"Tibial pain"	Notre–Dom–Des–Doms, Avignon, FR.	
Clement VI (1342–52)	Illness	Benedictine Abbey, La Chaise-Dieu, FR.	
Innocent VI (1352–62)	Stress	Villeneuve–les–Avignon, France	
BL. Urban V (1362–70)	Illness	St. Marziale, Avignon	Abbey of St. Victor, Marseilles, France
Gregory XI (1370–8)	Exhaustion	Sta. Maria Nuova, Rome	
Urban VI (1378–89)	*Poison	St. Peter's, Rome	
Clement (VII) (1378–94)	Apoplexy	Choir, Notre-Dame-des-Doms	
Boniface IX (1389–1404)	Kidney stones	St. Peter's, Rome	
Benedict (XIII) (1394–1417)	Old age	Chapel crypt, Pensicola	Castle of Illeuca, Spain
Innocent VII (1404–6)	Common cold	St. Peter's	
Gregory XII (1406–15)	Old Age	St. Flaviano, Pecanati, Italy	
Alexander V (1409–10)	*Poison	St. Francis, Bologna, Italy	
John XXIII (1410–15)	Illness	Baptistery, Florence Cathedral	
Martin V (1417–31)	Apoplexy	Lateran, Rome	
Clement (VIII) (1423–9)	Apoplexy	Chapel of Piety, Cathedral of Palma, Spain	

Papal Name	Mode of Death	Church Buried	Reburied in
Benedict (XIV) (1425)	–	Under a rock in Aramagnoc, Spain	
Eugene IV (1431–47)	Plague	St. Peter's, Rome	S. Salvatore in Lauro, Rome
Felix V (1439–49)	–	*Ripaille, France	
Nicholas V (1447–55)	Depression & gout	St. Peter's, Rome	
Callistus III (1455–8)	Gout	St. Peter's, Rome	S.M. Monserrato, Rome
Pius II (1458–64)	Fever	St. Peter's, Rome	S.M. delle Valle, Rome
Paul II (1464–71)	*Poison melons/ apoplexy	St. Peter's, Rome	
Sixtus IV (1471–84)	Fever/gout	St. Peter's, Rome	Vatican Treasury
Innocent VIII (1484–92)	Ate roasted emeralds	St. Peter's, Rome	
Alexander VI (1492–1503)	*Poison/malaria	St. Peter's, Rome	S.M. Monserrato, Rome
Pius III (1503)	Gout	St. Peter's, Rome	S.M. delle Valle, Rome
Julius II (1503–13)	Fever	St. Peter's, Rome	
Leo X (1513–21)	*Poison/malaria	St. Peter's, Rome	S.M. sopra Minerva, Rome
Hadrian VI (1522–3)	Stress/Heat exhaustion	St. Peter's, Rome	S.M. delle Anime, Rome
Clement VII (1523–34)	*Poisoned mush-rooms/*smoke from poison candle/ fever	St. Peter's, Rome	S.M. sopra Minerva, Rome
Paul III (1534–49)	Violent fever	St. Peter's, Rome	
Julius III (1550–5)	Gout	St. Peter's, Rome	
Marcellus II (1555)	Stroke	St. Peter's, Rome	
Paul IV (1555–9)	Gout/dropsy/old age	St. Peter's, Rome	S.M. sopra Minerva, Rome
Pius IV (1559–65)	Gout/fever	St. Peter's, Rome	S.M. degli Angeli, Rome
St. Pius V (1566–72)	Illness	St. Peter's, Rome	S.M. Maggiore, Rome
Gregory XIII (1572–85)	*Heart attack	St. Peter's, Rome	
Sixtus V (1585–90)	*Poison/stroke/ malaria	Sta. Maria Maggiore, Rome	
Urban VII (1590)	Malaria	St. Peter's, Rome	
Gregory XIV (1590–1)	2.5 oz. gallstone	St. Peter's, Rome	
Innocent IX (1591)	Pneumonia	St. Peter's, Rome	
Clement VIII (1592–1605)	Gout	St. Peter's, Rome	S.M. Maggiori, Rome
Leo XI (1605)	Illness	St. Peter's, Rome	
Paul V (1605–21)	Stroke	St. Peter's	Sta. Maria Maggiore, Rome
Gregory XV (1621–3)	Fever	Quirinal Palace, Rome	San Ignazio, Rome
Urban VIII (1623–44)	–	St. Peter's, Rome	
Innocent X (1644–55)	Illness	St. Peter's, Rome	San Agnese in Agone, Rome
Alexander VII (1655–67)	Kidney failure	St. Peter's, Rome	
Clement IX (1667–9)	Stroke	St. Peter's, Rome	S.M. Maggiore, Rome
Clement X (1670–6)	Fever/dropsy	St. Peter's, Rome	
BL. Innocent XI (1676–89)	7 oz. kidney stone	St. Peter's, Rome	
Alexander VIII (1689–91)	–	St. Peter's, Rome	
Innocent XII (1691–1700)	–	St. Peter's, Rome	
Clement XI (1700–21)	Stroke	St. Peter's, Rome	
Innocent XIII (1721–4)	Illness	St. Peter's, Rome	
Benedict XIII (1724–30)	–	St. Peter's, Rome	
Clement XII (1730–40)	Bladder infection	Lateran, Rome	
Benedict XIV (1740–58)	Kidney disease	St. Peter's, Rome	
Clement XIII (1758–69)	Heart attack	St. Peter's, Rome	
Clement XIV (1769–74)	*Poison/lung cancer	St. Peter's, Rome	Sancti Apostoli, Rome

Papal Name	Mode of Death	Church Buried	Reburied in
Pius VI (1775–99)	Collapsed heart	Valence, France	St. Peter's, Rome
Pius VII (1800–23)	"Weakened heart"	St. Peter's, Rome	
Leo XII (1823–9)	Botched operation to remove chronic hemorrhoids	St. Peter's, Rome	
Pius VIII (1829–30)	Long illness	St. Peter's, Rome	
Gregory XVI (1831–46)	Cancer	St. Peter's, Rome	
Pius IX (1846–78)	Fever	St. Peter's, Rome	San Lorenzo fuori le Mura, Rome
Leo XIII (1878–1903)	Heart attack	St. Peter's, Rome	Lateran, Rome
St. Pius X (1903–14)	Depression	St. Peter's, Rome	
Benedict XV (1914–22)	*Poisoned/flu	St. Peter's, Rome	
Pius XI (1922–39)	Fever/*poison	St. Peter's, Rome	
Pius XII (1939–58)	Hiccoughing & pneumonia	St. Peter's, Rome	
John XXIII (1958–63)	Stomach cancer/ heart attack	St. Peter's, Rome	
Paul VI (1963–78)	Heart attack	St. Peter's, Rome	
John Paul I (1978)	*Poison/heart attack	St. Peter's, Rome	

Appendix 3:
Existing Papal Monuments, Tombs and Other Funerary Objects, Listed by Location

Antipopes are listed in italics.

France

Benedict XII (1334–42). Avignon: Calvet Museum. Fragments.

Clement VI (1342–52). Avignon: La Chaise-Dieu. Fragments.

Gelasius II (1118–9). Cluny. Fragments.

Clement V (1305–14). Uzeste Parish Church. Fragments.

Pius VI (1775–99). Valence Cathedral. Praecordia monument.

Innocent VI (1352–62). Villeneuve-les-Avignon. Fragments.

BL. Urban V (1362–70). Marseilles: St. Victor. cenotaph.

Spain

Benedict (XIII) (1394–1417). Castle of Illueca. Skull.

Clement (VIII) (1423–1426). Palma Cathedral, Majorca. Tomb monument.

Germany

Clement II (1046–7). Cathedral of Bamburg. Free-standing tomb.

Benedict V (964). Hamberg: Cathedral. Cenotaph.

Italy (outside Rome)

BL. Gregory X (1271–6). Arezzo Duomo. Body and sarcophagus.

Alexander V (1409–10). Bologna: San Francisco. Wall tomb.

Urban III (1195–7). Ferrara Cathedral. Cenotaph.

Clement XI (1700–1721). Ferrara Cathedral. Cenotaph.

John XXIII (1410–15). Florence: Baptistery. Wall tomb.

Celestine V (1294). L'Aquila: Sta. Maria Collemaggio. Body and tomb monument.

Innocent IV (1243–7). Naples: Cathedral of Naples. Tomb monument.

St. Silvester (314–31). Nonantola: Abbey of Nonantola. Sarcophagus.

St. Hadrian III (884–5). Nonatola: Abbey of Nonantola. Altar.

BL. Benedict XI (1303–4). Perugia: S. Dominico. Wall tomb and ossurary.

Urban IV (1261–4). Perugia: St. Francis of Assisi. Sarcophagus.

Martin IV (1281–5). Perugia: St. Francis of Assisi. Sarcophagus.

St. Silverius (536–7). Ponza Island. Shrine.

Gregory XII (1406–15). Recanati Duomo. Sarcophagus.

St. Gregory VII (1073–85). Salerno Cathedral. Body and tomb.

Lucius III (1181–5). Verona Duomo. Wall cenotaph.

John XXI (1276–7). Viterbo: Duomo. Sarcophagus and fragments.

Hadrian V (1276). Viterbo: San Francesco. Wall tomb.

Clement IV (1265–8). Viterbo: San Francesco. Wall tomb.

Rome

Innocent III (1198–1216). Lateran. Tomb monument.

Sergius IV (1009–12). Lateran. Cenotaph.

Alexander III (1159–1181). Lateran. Cenotaph.

Martin V (1417–31). Lateran. Floor tomb.

Clement XII (1730–40). Lateran. Tomb monument.

Leo XIII (1878–1903). Lateran. Tomb monument.

Silvester II (999–1003). Lateran. Wall cenotaph.

St. Anicetus (c. 155–c. 166). Altemps Palace. Sarcophagus.

St. Lucius I (253–254). Sta. Cecilia in Trastevere. Sarcophagus.

Pius III (1503). San Andrea delle Valle. Cenotaph.

Pius II (1458–64). San Andrea delle Valle. Tomb monument.

Julius II (1503–13). San Pietro in Vincoli. Cenotaph.

Eugene IV (1431–47). San Salvatore in Lauro. Wall tomb.

Benedict X (1058–9). San Agnese in Agone-crypt. Sarcophagus.

Innocent X (1644–55). San Agnese in Agone. Monument.

Damasus II (1048). St. Lawrence Outside the Walls. Sarcophagus.

Pius IX (1846–78). St. Lawrence Outside the Walls. Body and sarcophagus.

Benedict VII (974–83). Sta. Croce in Gerusalemme. Epitaph Inscription.

Pius IV (1559–65). Sta. Maria degli Angeli. Wall memorial.

Hadrian VI (1522–3). Sta. Maria delle Anima. Wall tomb.

Alexander VI (1492–1503). Sta. Maria di Monserrato. Wall memorial.

Callistus III (1455–8). Sta. Maria di Monserrato. Wall memorial.

Honorius IV (1285–7). Sta. Maria in Arecoeli. Wall tomb.

Innocent II (1130–43). Sta. Maria in Trastevere. Sarcophagus.

Nicholas IV (1288–92). Sta. Maria Maggiore. Tomb monument.

St. Pius V (1566–72). Sta. Maria Maggiore. Body and tomb monument.

Sixtus V (1585–90). Sta. Maria Maggiore. Tomb monument.

Clement VIII (1592–1605). Sta. Maria Maggiore. Tomb monument.

Paul V (1605–21). Sta. Maria Maggiore. Tomb monument.

Clement IX (1667–1669). Sta. Maria Maggiore. Tomb monument.

Gregory XI (1370–8). Sta. Maria Nuova. Tomb monument .

Leo X (1513–21). Sta. Maria sopra Minerva. Tomb monument.

Clement VII (1523–1534). Sta. Maria Sopra Minerva. Tomb monument.

Paul IV (1555–1559). Sta. Maria Sopra Minerva. Tomb monument.

Urban VII (1590). Sta. Maria Sopra Minerva. Wall tomb.

Gregory XV (1621–1623). San Ignazio. Tomb monument.

St. Peter's

St. Leo I The Great (440–61). St. Peter's Basilica. Altar.

St.Gregory I The Great (590–604). St. Peter's Basilica. Altar.

St. Boniface IV (608–15). St. Peter's Basilica. Altar.

St. Leo II (682–3). St. Peter's Basilica. Altar.

St. Leo III (795–816). St. Peter's Basilica. Altar.

St. Leo IV (847–55). St. Peter's Basilica. Altar.

Bl. Innocent XI (1676–1689). St. Peter's Basilica. Altar and body.

St. Pius X (1903–1914). St. Peter's Basilica. Altar and body.

Bl. John XXIII (1958–1963). St. Peter's Basilica. Altar and body.

Sixtus IV/Julius II (1471–1484). St. Peter's Basilica. Floor marker.

Innocent VIII (1484–92). St. Peter's Basilica. Tomb monument.

Paul III (1534–49). St. Peter's Basilica. Tomb monument.

Gregory XIII (1572–85). St. Peter's Basilica. Tomb monument.

Gregory XIV (1590–1). St. Peter's Basilica. Tomb monument.

Leo XI (1605). St. Peter's Basilica. Tomb monument.

Urban VIII (1623–44). St. Peter's Basilica. Tomb monument.

Alexander VII (1655–67). St. Peter's Basilica. Tomb monument.

Clement X (1670–6). St. Peter's Basilica. Tomb monument.

BL. Innocent XI (1676–89). St. Peter's Basilica. Tomb monument.

Alexander VIII (1689–91). St. Peter's Basilica. Tomb monument.

Innocent XII (1691–1700). St. Peter's Basilica. Tomb Monument.

Clement XI (1700–21). St. Peter's Basilica. Floor marker.

Benedict XIII (1724–30). St. Peter's Basilica. Tomb monument.

Benedict XIV (1740–58). St. Peter's Basilica. Tomb monument.

Clement XIII (1758–69). St. Peter's Basilica. Tomb monument.

Clement XIV (1769–74). St. Peter's Basilica. Tomb monument.

Pius VII (1800–23). St. Peter's Basilica. Tomb monument.

Leo XII (1823–9). St. Peter's Basilica. Floor marker and monument.

Pius VIII (1829–30). St. Peter's Basilica. Tomb monument.

Gregory XVI (1831–46). St. Peter's Basilica. Tomb monument.

St. Pius X (1903–14). St. Peter's Basilica. Monument.

Benedict XV (1914–1922). St. Peter's Basilica. Monument.

Pius XI (1922–39). St. Peter's Basilica. Monument.

Pius XII (1939–58). St. Peter's Basilica. Monument.

John XXIII (1958–63). St. Peter's Basilica. Monument.

St. Peter (d. *c.* 64). St. Peter's Crypt. Tomb.

Hadrian IV (1154–1159). St. Peter's Crypt. Inscription and sarcophagus.

Nicholas III (1277–80). St. Peter's Crypt. Sarcophagus.

Boniface VIII (1294–1303). St. Peter's Crypt. Sarcophagus.

Urban VI (1378–89). St. Peter's Crypt. Sarcophagus.

Innocent VII (1404–6). St. Peter's Crypt. Sarcophagus.

Nicholas V (1447–55). St. Peter's Crypt. Sarcophagus.

Callistus III (1455–8). St. Peter's Crypt. Sarcophagus.

Paul II (1464–71). St. Peter's Crypt. Sarcophagus.

Julius III (1550–5). St. Peter's Crypt. Sarcophagus.

Marcellus II (1555). St. Peter's Crypt. Sarcophagus.

Innocent IX (1591). St. Peter's Crypt. Sarcophagus.

Innocent XIII (1721–1724). St. Peter's Crypt. Sarcophagus.

Pius VI (1775–1799). St. Peter's Crypt. Sarcophagus and monument.

Pius XI (1922–1939). St. Peter's Crypt. Sarcophagus.

Paul VI (1963–1978). St. Peter's Crypt. Floor tomb.

John Paul I (1978). St. Peter's Crypt. Sarcophagus.

Anastasius IV (1153–4). Vatican Museum. Sarcophagus.

Hadrian I (772–95). St. Peter's Porch. Epitaph plaque.

Sixtus IV (1471–84). St. Peter's Treasury. Floor cenotaph.

Appendix 4:
Papal Tombs During the
Reconstruction of St. Peter's

During the demolition and reconstruction of St. Peter's in the sixteenth century, the papal tombs, which had begun crowding not only the atrium but the nave itself, were moved around as each section of the basilica was torn down. It was during the moving of these tombs that most of the older sarcophagi or even many three-tiered tombs were destroyed, owing to architect Bramante's idea that the Basilica had to be completed post-haste. As a result, all that remains of the original papal tombs dating back thousands of years are some sarcophagi and pieces of sculpture.

Fortunately, church canon Giacomo Grimaldi took pains to sketch what the tombs looked like as they sat waiting for either their final placement or their final destruction. His illustrations not only show us the temporary placement of the tombs, but they show the various shapes of the tombs as well. Had Grimaldi not had the foresight to record the appearances of these tombs, we would never be able to see how the earlier papal tombs compared to the newer ones in shape or complexity.

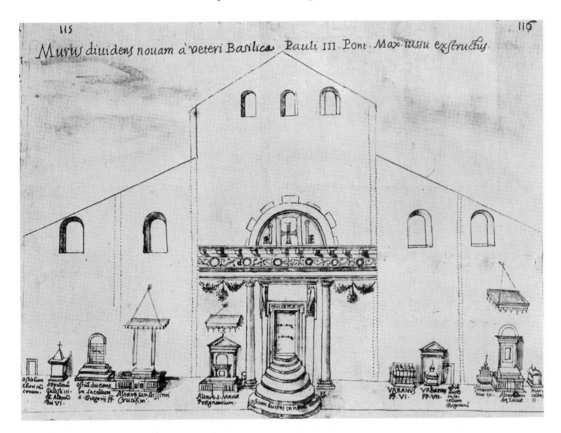

Church canon and historian Giacomo Grimaldi sketched the interior of St. Peter's during the reconstruction. Note the temporary placement of papal tombs, as well as the relative sizes and shapes of the tombs. By permission of the Houghton Library, Harvard University.

Appendix 5:
Old St. Peter's Tomb Map

This map by Tiberio Alfarano (c. 1590) shows what the original St. Peter's would have looked like complete with its original chapels and tombs dispersed throughout the basilica, which was built by Constantine in 320 over the spot where St. Peter is believed to have been buried. This church survived until the beginning of the Renaissance, around 1510, when Pope Julius II decided it should be rebuilt because it had fallen into such disrepair (and a new design would allow space for his own monstrous tomb). But to tear down St. Peter's would mean finding a solution to the problem of the overcrowded papal tombs that choked the portico and nave and were slowly encroaching on the small chapels as well. Some tombs and monuments were moved to other Roman churches, but most were simply broken up; their contents, if any were left, were catalogued and reburied.

Following pages: Grimaldi's map (with key) of old St. Peter's which includes the original altars and tomb placements (by permission of the Houghton Library, Harvard University). The map and keys have been trimmed and enlarged in order to enhance readability.

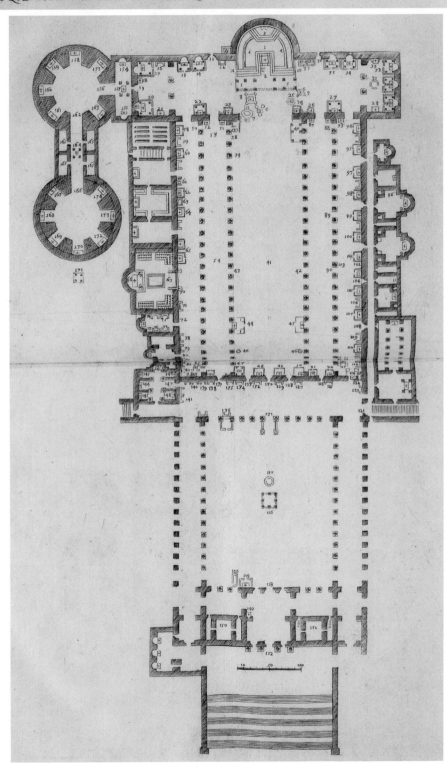

Declaratio Ichnographiæ Basilicæ veteris San-
Eti Petri in Vaticano, sacrorumque
ædificiorum prope illam con-
structorum.

1 ALTARE maius, vbi Apostolorum Petri, & Pauli corpora requiescunt.
2 Confessio Beati Petri ab Anacleto Papa exornata, Romanorum Pontificum sepultura, vbi sumuntur Pallia pro Archiepiscopis in signum plenitudinis Pontificalis officij.
3 Solium Romani Pontificis.) Sub quibus sunt sepulcra SS. Potificum Lini, Cleti, Anacleti, Euaristi, Thelesphori, Higini, Pij, Eleutherij, Victoris, & Ioannis I.
4 Subsellia S. R. E. Cardinalium.
5 Duodecim Columnæ elegantissimæ frontem maioris altaris complectentes, & sancta sanctorum constituentes.
6 Candelabrum eximium pro Cereo Paschali.
7 Suggestum marmoreum ad Euangelium decantandum.
8 Olim altare S. Sixti I. à Paschale II.
9 Altare de ossibus nuncupatum à Francisco de Tibaldeschis Cardinali.
10 Ostiolum ducens ad Oratorium post Confessionem.
11 Alterum Ostiolum præfati Oratorij, vbi ossa plurimorum congesta sunt.
12 Sepulchrum marmoreum N.
13 Porta Templi ad Occidentem.
14 Oratorium S. Leonis Papæ, vbi sunt Corpora SS. Leonum I. II. III. & IV.
15 Oratorium S. Hadriani I. Papæ.
16 Sepulchrum Vrbani II. Papæ.
17 Oratorium S. Mariæ de Cancellis à S. Paulo I. Papa.
18 Sacellum S. Mariæ à Io. Caietano de Vrsinis Cardinali.
19 Porta ad Meridiem, vbi multa Pontificum, & Cardinalium sepulchra.
20 Oratorium SS. Processi, & Martiniani à Paschali I.
21 Sacellum S. Catherinæ pro Cardinali Tyburtino.
22 Oratorium S. Mauritij, ad quod Imperator, & Imperatrix ab Episcopis Card. benedicuntur, & in brachio dextro oleo sacro vnguntur antequam à Romano Pontifice coronentur.
23 Altare S. Siluestri Papæ, vbi Vigilij, & Hadriani IV. sepulchra.
24 Altare S. Bartholomæi.
25 Columna sancta vna ex duodecim è Salomonis Templo.
26 Altare S. Antonij ab Antoniotto de Pallauicinis Card.
27 Altare S. Luciæ Virginis à Gregorio I.
28 Altare pro mortuis priuilegiatum.
29 Altare trium Regum Magorum.
30 Oratorium S. Ioannis ad fontes à Symmacho Papa.
31 Fons Baptismi à Damaso Papa versibus exornatus.
32 Altare S. Ioannis Euangelistæ à Symmacho Papa.
33 Altare B. Mariæ Virginis.
34 Altare S. Annæ Soc. Parafrenariorum S. R. E. Card.
35 Oratorium S. Crucis à Symmacho Papa.
36 Porta ad Occidentem.
37 Duo Sacella antiquissima SS. NN.
38 Altare B. Mariæ, & altare S. Gabinij Mart. à Greg. III. quæ Eugenius III. in vnum restituit, & Innocentius VIII. exornauit plurimorum Sanctorũ reliquijs reconditis.
39 Chorus, supra quem erat Organum.
40 Altare S. Pastoris ab Vrso de Vrsinis Cardinali.
41 Parietes veteris templi partem, à nouo diuidentes.
42 Altare SS. Processi, & Martiniani ex priori loco cum statua ænea S. Petri translatum.
43 Altare B. Mariæ translatum.
44 Sacellum SS. Apostolorum Simonis & Iudæ, vbi sanctissimum Eucharistiæ Sacramentum honorificè custoditur.
45 Olim Altare SS. Apostolorum Philippi, & Iacobi.
46 Fontes aquæ benedictæ, & Altare B. Mariæ Virginis ad Columnam ad dexteram templi.
47 Sacellum S. Bonifacij Mart. à Bonifacio VIII.
48 Altare mortuorum priuilegiatum, & sepulchrum Leonis IX.
49 Altare S. Antonij Abbatis, & S. Annæ.
50 Altare S. Vinceslai Mart. Regis Boemorum, atque S. Erasmi.

51 Altare S. Martialis à Neapolione de Vrsinis Cardin. & Vannotia de Sabellis, vbi cum suis maioribus requiescunt.
52 Altare S. N.
53 Sepulchrum Pauli III. eximium ab Alexandro Farnesio Cardinali.
54 Altare Sanctissimi Crucifixi, vbi est corpus S. Petronillæ.
55 Sepulchrum Bonifacij IV. & statua equestris Roberti Malatestæ.
56 Altare de Perrerijs, vbi sepultus Petrus Raymundoz Hierosolym. Hosp. Magister.
57 Altare S. N.
58 Altare Beatæ Mariæ ab Eugenio IV. & Petro Barbo Card.
59 Sepulchrum Eugenij IV. vbi ossa multorum sunt congesta.
60 Altare S. Marci Euangelistæ à Paulo II.
61 Altare S. Nicolai à Nicolao V.
62 Altare S. Blasij à Poncello de Vrsinis.
63 Sepulchrum Vrbani VI. & multorum Pontificum.
64 Altare Annunciationis B. Mariæ Virginis.
65 Duo Altaria SS. NN.
66 Altare B. Mariæ, & S. Francisci, & Antonij de Padua à Sixto IV.
67 Sepulchrum Sixti IV. æneum elegantissimum.
68 Sepulchra Iulij II. & Fatij Sanctorij Cardinalis.
69 Sepulchrum Franciotti de Ruuere Cardinalis.
70 Sepulchrum Carolæ Cypri, & Hierusalem Reginæ.
71 Sepulchrum Bernardi Heruli Narniensis Cardinalis.
72 Sepulchrum Stephani Nardini Foroliuiensis Cardinalis.
73 Altare S. Thomæ Apostoli, ante quod sunt sepulti Io. Podius Episcopus Bononien. & Matthiolus de Lampugnano Plocen. Episcopus, & Franciscus Barthelai Molopotanien. & Petrus Lundhus Episcopus Gaetanus.
74 Fons Baptismi, & sepulchrum Innocentij VII.
75 Sepulchrum Petri Fonsecæ Lusitani Card. & Nicolai Vicecomitis Mediolanen.
76 Sepulchrũ Ardicini Iunioris Nouarien. Card. della Porta.
77 Sepulchrum Ardicini Senioris Nouarien. Cardinalis, & Theobaldi de Rubeo Monte Archiepiscopi Bisun.
78 Sepulchrum Christophori Moroni Episcopi Isernien. Card.
79 Sepulchrum Gregorij V.
80 Altare S. N.
81 Sepulchrum Pij III. ante quod est sepultus Franciscus Bandinus Picolomineus Archiepiscopus Senensis.
82 Olim Sepulchrum Pij V. & Sixti V.
83 Olim Sepulchrum Hadriani VI. nunc Iulij III.
84 Sepulchrum Pij II. ante quod sunt sepulti Pius II. & III.
85 Altare S. Gregorij Papæ à Gregorio IV. supra quod est caput S. Andreæ Apostoli à Pio II.
86 Sepulchrum Agnetis de Columna Honorati Caietani vxoris.
87 Olim Altare SS. Laurentij, & Gregorij à Iacobo Caietano de Stephaneschis Cardinali.
88 Altare S. N. nunc Columna Sancta translata.
89 Sepulchrum Gregorij XIII. & Gregorij XIV.
90 Altare B. Mariæ, ante quod est sepulchrum Bernardini de Cruce Episcopi Nouocomensis, iuxta quod fuere translata ossa Callisti III. Alexandri VI. & Vrbani VI. & demum sepultus Vrbani VII.
91 Olim Altare S. Tridentij Mart. Nunc lapis, supra quem plures Sancti Martyrium subiere.
92 Olim Altare S. Antonini Mart. ab Odone Lotta de Amareschis, nunc lapis, supra quem fuerunt diuisa ossa SS. Apostolorum Petri & Pauli, à B. Siluestro Papa.
93 Altare S. N.
94 Sacellum S. Ægidij Abb. à Io. Tomacello Comite Ioræ Bonifacij IX.
95 Sacellum S. Nicolai à Nicolao III. vbi Nicolai, & Honorij IV. ac Francisci Buccamatij Card. sepulchra.
96 Altare Capellæ Gregorianæ, vbi est corpus S. Gregorij Nazianzeni à Gregorio XIII. translatum.
97 Altare S. Iacobi Apostoli ab Aut. de Caluis Card.
98 Altare S. Hieronymi.
99 Altare S. Augustini.
100 Altare S. Ambrosij.
101 Altare S. Martini à Io. Episcopo Hostiensi Card. Vitiarien.
102 Altare S. Agathæ nunc sepulchrum Marcelli II.
103 Altare S. Luciæ translatum, & sepulchrũ Innocentij IX.
104 Sepulchrum Nicolai V. translatum.
105 Altare S. Marci translatum.

106 Sepulchrum Pauli II.
107 Olim Altare S. Abundij Mansionarij Basilicæ, postea Leonis X. & Pij IV. sepulchra.
108 Olim aditus ad Ecclesiam S. Vincentij, nunc Sacellum Innocentij VIII. translatum, vbi omnes reliquiæ templi.
109 Sepulchrum Innocentij VIII. translatum.
110 Olim altare S. Laurentij, nunc sepulchrum marmoreum translatum N. Sum. Pont.
111 Sepulchrum Aloysij ex familia Rossiorum Cardinalis, postea Pauli IV.
112 Sepulchrum olim Franciotti de Vrsinis Cardinalis.
113 Porta paruula olim.
114 Altare olim Oratorij S. Mariæ ad Præsepe à Ioan. VII. nunc Porta Sancta.
115 Altare vultus sancti, vbi sanctissimum Sudarium, quo D.N. Iesus Christus ante passionem faciem suam extersit, & Lancea, qua eiusdem D.N. latus apertum fuit, custodiuntur.
116 Pinea ænea speciosissima à Symmacho Papa.
117 Fons magnus æneus pro Peregrinis à Symmacho Papa.
118 Tres portæ, supra quas est restituta de nouo Nauicula Principis Apostolorum fluctuans, ex musiuo elegantissimo, opere Iotti, impensis Iacobi Caietani Cardinalis de Stephaneschis olim Canonici.
119 Paruula ædicula multorum Sanctorum reliquias continens.
120 Sepultura Honorij I. Othonis II. & Placidij, & Valentiniani III. Augustorum Cæsarum.
121 Porta Palatij à Iulio II. restaurata.
122 Aula Regia Sacri Palatij, iuxta quam ab Occidente est Capella Sixti IV. ad Orientem, sacri Concistorij aulæ, & mœnia multiplicis ordinis, à Leone X. ad Meridiem Capella Pauli III. & ad Aquilonem amplissima Summorum Pontificum Cubicula.
123 Sepulchrum Benedicti IV.
124 Porta sancta, quæ vigesimo quinto Iubilæi anno per Romanum Pontificem aperitur & clauditur.
125 Sepulchrum Ioan. IX.
126 Porta dicta Guidonea, supra quam olim erant appensa multarum victoriarum insignia.
127 Sepulchra Stephani V. & VI.
128 Porta Romana, supra quam sunt appensæ vectes Portarum Tuneti à Carolo V. Imperatore missæ.
129 Sepulchra Benedicti III. & Io. XIX. & Bulla centesimi quoque Iubilæi anni à Bonifacio VIII.
130 Porta Meridiana olim argentea ab Honorio I. & Leone VII. nunc ænea ab Eugenio IV.
131 Valuæ æneæ antiquissimæ.
132 Olim sepulchrum Sergij I. nunc adest lapis numidicus, cui insculptum est epitaphium sepulchri Hadriani I. à Carolo Magno editum, ex priori loco translatum.
133 Porta Rauenniana, supra quam sunt appensa insignia, & catenæ Portus Smyrnæ à Sixto IV.
134 Tabulæ marmoreæ, in quibus sunt insculpta nomina Oliuetorum & fundorum à Gregorio Papa pro luminaribus Templi.
135 Sepulchrum Nicolai Papæ I.
136 Locus sepulchri Gregorij I. olim.
137 Porta Iudicij, per quam defuncti inferebantur.
138 Sepulchrum Ioannis VIII.
139 Sepulchrum Ioannis XIV.
140 Sepulchra Ioannis II. & III.
141 In hac parte porticus Templi sunt sepulti multi summi

A
B
C
D
E

Pontifices sanctissimi.
142 Sacellum principale secretarij, vbi translata fuit Imago Beatæ Mariæ, dicta de Febribus, & sepulchrum Benedicti I.
143 Altare Sancti Ioannis Baptistæ translatum de familia Vrsinorum.
144 Altare Sancti Sebastiani à Christophoro de Iacobatijs.
145 Altare S. N. & sepulchr. de Perbenedictis Card.
146 Altare ad quod fuit translata Imago Beatæ Mariæ ex intercolumnijs Porticus.
147 Aditus ducens ad Porticum.
148 Altare S. N.
149 Altare olim Sanctæ Mariæ in Turri, vbi electus in Imperatorem, à Canonicis sancti Petri recipitur in Canononicum, & in fratrem.
150 Palatium Archipresbyteri Basilicæ.
151 Turris Campanaria.
152 Tres portæ olim æneæ, in quibus erant insculpta nomina Regnouum, Prouinciarum, Ciuitatum, & Insularum Sedis Apostolicæ.
153 Altaria Sancti Andreæ, vbi summi Pontifices solemnia quædam peragebant.
154 Altare Sancti Angeli.
155 Altare S. N.
156 Transitus.
157 Altare Saluatoris dictum de Abundantia, à Thoma de Vrsinis Cardinali, & Neapolione Comite Manupelli.
158 Sacellum Beatæ Mariæ Annunciationis à Maria de Comitibus.
159 Sacellum S. N. multorumque nobilium sepulchra.
160 Olim Sacellum sanctæ Petronillæ virginis à Ludouico Rege Francorum dotatum, vbi erant sepultæ Agnes Henrici II. & Maria Thermantia Honorij Imperatoris Vxores.
161 Sacellum S.N. vbi ossa è diuersis sepulchris eruta congesta sunt.
162 Transitus ad alterum templum.
163 Sacellum S. N. vbi congesta sunt ossa veterum sepulchrorum.
164 Altare S. Ioannis Chrysostomi Archiepiscopi Constantinopolitani.
165 Aulæ sanctimonialium iugiter Deum laudantium.
166 Transitus.
167 Sacellum S. N. vbi est sepultus Oddo Ianuensis Episcopus Interamnensis.
168 Sacellum Sanctorum Lamberti, & Seruatij à Georgio de Cæsarinis Canonico, ad quod fuit translatum corpus S. Ioannis Chrysostomi, & est sepulchrum omnium Canonicorum Basilicæ.
169 Sacellum S. N. vbi conseruantur sedes, siue Cathedra S. Petri, & culcitra, siue stragulum Sanctorum Martyrum.
170 Sacellum, & sepulchrum Callisti III. & Alexandri VI. & quorundam Cardinalium, multorumque nobilium.
171 Obelisci Cæsaris in medio Circi, Caij, & Neronis primæuus locus.
172 Sacellum B. Mariæ de Febribus, ante quod sunt sepulti Bartholomæus Marascus Episcopus Castellanus, & Iacobus Breuccietti Episcopus Nucerinus.
173 Sacellum S. N. vbi erat sepulchrum Hugonis Lingles Nicosien. Regni Cypri Camerarij.
174 Sacellum Sanctissimæ Trinitatis, & SS. Cosmæ, & Damiani, vbi est sepulchrum Beneficiatorum, & Clericorum Basilicæ.

Appendix 6:
Papal Organ Burial in the Church of SS. Vincenzo e Anastasio

Vincenzo e Anastasio was traditionally the parish church of the Quirinal Palace, where many popes died. When Sixtus V died in 1590, his praecordia (vital organs, i.e., the heart and intestines, which were removed during embalming) were put in an earthen jar and placed in the basement of the church. This began a tradition which ended in 1914 with Pius X, who did not wish to be embalmed. (However, a part of John Paul II's lower intestine that had to be removed when he was shot in 1981 was placed in a jar and is now sealed behind the wall in the church with the other papal praecordia.) The reason for preserving the organs is so that the pope can be reunited with them on the day of the Resurrection, according to Catholic theology.

There are two plaques on either side of the main altar that commemorate the owners of the entombed praecordia:

FIRST PLAQUE

D.O.M. / SIXTVS V P.M. / PONTEFICIIS AEDIBVS / IN QVIRINALI AMPLIATIS / ET IN IISDEM / PRIWS SVPREMA MORTALIS VrrAE / EXPLETA PERIODO / AD HANC APOST. PAL. PAROCH. eccusum / VT EADEM EXIMIIS AVGERETVR HONORIBVS / EX SVIS PRAECORDIIS PORTIONE DELATA / ROMANORVM PONTIFICVM / MONVMENTA PRIMA RELIQVIT / DIE XXVII AVGVSTI MDXC

("To God the best and greatest. Sixtus V, supreme pontiff. He enlarged the pontifical buildings on the Quirinal, and in those same buildings he ended his mortal life. He gave his heart to the parish church of the apostolic palace so that it might be increased with exceptional honors. He left the Roman pontificate for this monument, 27 August 1590."—*Trans. Phyllis Jestice*)

PRAECORDIA

LEONIS XI P.M./OBIIT IN QVIRIN. DIE XXVII APRILIS MDCV

("Leo XI, supreme pontiff. Died in the Quirinal on the 27th of April, 1605.")

PAVLI V P.M. / OBIIT DIE XXVIII IANVARII MDCXXI

("Paul V, supreme pontiff. Died the 28th Day of January, 1621.")

GREGORII XV P.M. / OBIIT DIE VIII IVLII MDCXXIII

("Gregory XV, supreme pontiff. Died the eighth day of July, 1623.")

INNOCENTII X P.M. / OBIIT DIE VII
IANVARII MDCLV

("Innocent X, supreme pontiff. Died the 7th day
of January, 1655.")

ALEXANDRI VII P.M. / OBIIT DIE XXIII
MAII MDCLXVII

("Alexander VII, supreme pontiff. Died the 23rd
day of May, 1667.")

CLEMENTIS IX P.M. / OBIIT DIE VIII
DECEMBRIS MDCLXIX

("Clement IX, supreme pontiff. Died the eighth
day of December, 1669.")

CLEMENTIS X P.M. / OBIIT DIE XXII
IVLII MDCLXXVI

("Clement X, supreme pontiff. Died the 22nd day
of July, 1676.")

INNOCENTII XI P.M. / IN SACELLO B. VIRG.
OBIIT XXII AVGVSTI MDCLXXXIX

("Innocent XI, supreme pontiff. In the shrine of
the Blessed Virgin Died the 22nd of August, 1689.")

ALEXANDRI VIII P.M. / OBIIT DIE PRIMA
FEBRVARII MDCXCI

("Alexander VIII, supreme pontiff. Died the first
day of February, 1691.")

INNOCENTII XII P.M. / OBIIT DIE XXVII
SEPTEMBRIS MDCC

("Innocent XII, supreme pontiff. Died the 27th
day of September, 1700.")

CLEMENTIS XI P.M. / OBIIT DIE XIX
MARTII MDCCXXI

("Clement XI, supreme pontiff. Died the 19th day
of March, 1721.")

INNOCENTII XIII P.M. / OBIIT DIE VII
MARTII MDCCXXIV

("Innocent XIII, supreme pontiff. Died the seventh day of March, 1724.")

CLEMENTIS XII P.M. / OBIIT DIE IV
FEBRVARII MDCCXL

("Clement XII, supreme pontiff. Died the fourth
day of February, 1740.")

SECOND PLAQUE

BENEDICTVS XIV PONT. MAX / SVMMORVM PONTIF-
ICVM / PRAECORDIA / HVMILI ET OBSCVRO
LOCO / SITA / CONSTRVCTIS NOVIS
LOCVLAMENTIS / IN HONESTIOREM TVMVLVM /
INFERRI IVSSIT / ANNO MDCCLVI

("Benedict XIV, supreme pontiff, ordered that the
heart of the highest pontiff, which had been placed
in a humble and obscure place, be placed in a
more suitable tomb when the new place was constructed, in the year 1756. — *Trans. Phyllis Jestice*)

PRAECORDIA

BENEDCIT XIV P.M. / OBIIT DIE III MAII MDCCLVIII

("Benedict XIV, supreme pontiff. Died the 3rd
Day of May, 1758.")

CLEMENTIS XIII P.M. / OBIIT DIE SECVNDA
FEBRVARII MDCCLXIX

("Clement XIII, supreme pontiff. Died the second
day of February, 1769.")

CLEMENTIS XIV P.M. / OBIIT DIE XXII
SEPTEMBRIS MDCCLXXIV

("Clement XIV, supreme pontiff. Died the 22nd
day of September, 1774.")

PP VI PONT. MAX / TRANSLATA SVNT VALENTIAM
APVD RHODANVM / VBI DECESSIT
DIE XXIX AVGVSTI MDCCIC

("Pius VI, supreme pontiff. Translated here from
Valance near the Rhone, where he died on the 29th
day of August, 1799.")

PP VII PONT. MAX / OBIIT DIE XX
AVGVSTI MDCCCXXIII

("Pius VII, supreme pontiff. Died on the 20th of
August, 1823.")

LEONIS XII PONT. MAX. / OBIIT IV IDVS
FEBRVARII AN. MDCCCXXIX

("Leo XII, supreme pontiff. Died four [days be-
fore] the ides of February 1829.")

PP VIII PONT. MAX. / OBIIT PRIDIE
KALEN. DECEMB. AN. MDCCCXXX

("Pius VIII, supreme pontiff. Died the day before
the calends of December in the year 1830.")

GREGORII XVI P.M. / OBIIT KAL IVNII
MDCCCXXXXVI

("Gregory XVI, supreme pontiff. Died on the Calends of June 1846.")

[Here on the plaque is a space for the name of
Pius IX, although his praecordia are enshrined
in the grottoes of St. Peter's.]

LEONIS XIII P.M. / OBIIT DIE X
IVLII MDCCCCIII

("Leo XIII, supreme pontiff. Died the 20th day of
July, 1903.")

Appendix 7:
The Apostolic Constitution
(Universii Domini Gregis)

This is the apostolic constitution, written by Pope John Paul II, concerning the vacancy of the Apostolic See and the election of the new pope.

JOHN PAUL II
SUPREME PONTIFF
APOSTOLIC CONSTITUTION
UNIVERSI DOMINICI GREGIS
ON THE VACANCY
OF THE APOSTOLIC SEE
AND THE ELECTION
OF THE ROMAN PONTIFF

JOHN PAUL, BISHOP
SERVANT OF THE SERVANTS OF GOD
FOR PERPETUAL REMEMBRANCE

Introduction

The Shepherd of the Lord's whole flock is the Bishop of the Church of Rome, where the Blessed Apostle Peter, by sovereign disposition of divine Providence, offered to Christ the supreme witness of martyrdom by the shedding of his blood. It is therefore understandable that the lawful apostolic succession in this See, with which "because of its great pre-eminence every Church must agree," has always been the object of particular attention.

Precisely for this reason, down the centuries the Supreme Pontiffs have deemed it their special duty, as well as their specific right, to establish fitting norms to regulate the orderly election of their Successor. Thus, also in more recent times, my Predecessors Saint Pius X, Pius XI, Pius XII, John XXIII and lastly Paul VI, each with the intention of responding to the needs of the particular historical moment, issued wise and appropriate regulations in order to ensure the suitable preparation and orderly gathering of the electors charged, at the vacancy of the Apostolic See, with the important and weighty duty of electing the Roman Pontiff.

If I too now turn to this matter, it is certainly not because of any lack of esteem for those norms, for which I have great respect and which I intend for the most part to confirm, at least with regard to their substance and the basic principles which inspired them. What leads me to take this step is awareness of the Church's changed situation today and the need to take into consideration the general revision of Canon Law which took place, to the satisfaction of the whole Episcopate, with the publication and promulgation first of the Code of Canon Law and subsequently of the Code of Canons of the Eastern Churches. In conformity with this revision, itself inspired by the Second Vatican Ecumenical Council, I then took up the reform of the Roman Curia in the Apostolic Constitution *Pastor Bonus*. Furthermore, Canon 335 of the Code of Canon Law, restated in Canon 47 of the Code of Canons of the Eastern Churches, makes clear the need to issue and constantly update the specific laws regulating the canonical provision for the Roman See, when for any reason it becomes vacant.

While keeping in mind present-day requirements, I have been careful, in formulating the new discipline, not to depart in substance from the wise and venerable tradition already established.

It is in fact an indisputable principle that the Roman Pontiff has the right to define and adapt to changing times the manner of designating the person called to assume the Petrine succession in the Roman See. This regards, first of all, the body entrusted with providing for the election of the Roman Pontiff: based on a millennial practice sanctioned by specific canonical norms and confirmed by an explicit provision of the current Code of Canon Law (Canon 349), this body is made up of the College of Cardinals of Holy Roman Church. While it is indeed a doctrine of faith that the power of the Supreme Pontiff derives directly from Christ, whose earthly Vicar he is, it is also certain that this supreme power in the Church is granted to him "by means of lawful election accepted by him, together with episcopal consecration." A most serious duty is thus incumbent upon the body responsible for this election. Consequently the norms which regulate its activity need to be very precise and clear, so that the election itself will take place in a most worthy manner, as befits the office of utmost responsibility which the person elected will have to assume, by divine mandate, at the moment of his assent.

Confirming therefore the norm of the current Code of Canon Law (cf. Canon 349), which reflects the millennial practice of the Church, I once more affirm that the College of electors of the Supreme Pontiff is composed solely of the Cardinals of Holy Roman Church. In them one finds expressed in a remarkable synthesis the two aspects which characterize the figure and office of the Roman Pontiff: *Roman*, because identified with the Bishop of the Church in Rome and thus closely linked to the clergy of this City, represented by the Cardinals of the presbyteral and diaconal titles of Rome, and to the Cardinal Bishops of the suburbicarian Sees; *Pontiff of the universal Church*, because called to represent visibly the unseen Pastor who leads his whole flock to the pastures of eternal life. The universality of the Church is clearly expressed in the very composition of the College of Cardinals, whose members come from every continent.

In the present historical circumstances, the universality of the Church is sufficiently expressed by the College of one hundred and twenty electors, made up of Cardinals coming from all parts of the world and from very different cultures. I therefore confirm that this is to be the maximum number of Cardinal electors, while at the same time indicating that it is in no way meant as a sign of less respect that the provision laid down by my predecessor Pope Paul VI has been retained, namely, that those Cardinals who celebrate their eightieth birthday before the day when the Apostolic See becomes vacant do not take part in the election. The reason for this provision is the desire not to add to the weight of such venerable age the further burden of responsibility for choosing the one who will have to lead Christ's flock in ways adapted to the needs of the times. This does not however mean that the Cardinals over eighty years of age cannot take part in the preparatory meetings of the Conclave, in conformity with the norms set forth below. During the vacancy of the Apostolic See, and especially during the election of the Supreme Pontiff, they in particular should lead the People of God assembled in the Patriarchal Basilicas of Rome and in other churches in the Dioceses throughout the world, supporting the work of the electors with fervent prayers and supplications to the Holy Spirit and imploring for them the light needed to make their choice before God alone and with concern only for the "salvation of souls, which in the Church must always be the supreme law."

It has been my wish to give particular attention to the age-old institution of the Conclave, the rules and procedures of which have been established and defined by the solemn ordinances of a number of my Predecessors. A careful historical examination confirms both the appropriateness of this institution, given the circumstances in which it originated and gradually took definitive shape, and its continued usefulness for the orderly, expeditious and proper functioning of the election itself, especially in times of tension and upheaval.

Precisely for this reason, while recognizing that theologians and canonists of all times agree that this institution is not of its nature necessary for the valid election of the Roman Pontiff, I confirm by this Constitution that the Conclave is to continue in its essential structure; at the same time, I have made some modifications in order to adapt its procedures to present-day circumstances. Specifically, I have considered it appropriate to decree that for the whole duration of the election the living-quarters of the Cardinal electors and of those called to assist in the orderly process of the election itself are to be located in suitable places within Vatican City State. Although small, the State is large enough to ensure within its walls, with the help of the appropriate measures indicated below, the seclusion and resulting concentration which an act so vital to the whole Church requires of the electors.

At the same time, in view of the sacredness of the act of election and thus the need for it to be carried out in an appropriate setting where, on the one hand, liturgical actions can be readily combined with juridical formalities, and where, on the other, the electors can more easily dispose themselves to accept the interior movements of the Holy Spirit, I decree that the election will continue to take place in the Sistine Chapel, where everything is conducive to an awareness of the presence of God, in whose sight each person will one day be judged.

I further confirm, by my apostolic authority, the duty of maintaining the strictest secrecy with regard to everything that directly or indirectly concerns the election process itself. Here too, though, I have wished to simplify the relative norms, reducing them to their essentials, in order to avoid confusion, doubts and even eventual problems of conscience on the part of those who have taken part in the election.

Finally, I have deemed it necessary to revise the form of the election itself in the light of the present-day needs of the Church and the usages of modern society. I have thus considered it fitting not to retain election by acclamation *quasi ex inspiratione,* judging that it is no longer an apt means of interpreting the thought of an electoral college so great in number and so diverse in origin. It also appeared necessary to eliminate election *per compromissum,* not only because of the difficulty of the procedure, evident from the unwieldy accumulation of rules issued in the past, but also because by its very nature it tends to lessen the responsibility of the individual electors who, in this case, would not be required to express their choice personally.

After careful reflection I have therefore decided that the only form by which the electors can manifest their vote in the election of the Roman Pontiff is by secret ballot, in accordance with the rules set forth below. This form offers the greatest guarantee of clarity, straightforwardness, simplicity, openness and, above all, an effective and fruitful participation on the part of the Cardinals who, individually and as a group, are called to make up the assembly which elects the Successor of Peter.

With these intentions, I promulgate the present Apostolic Constitution containing the norms which, when the Roman See becomes vacant, are to be strictly followed by the Cardinals whose right and duty it is to elect the Successor of Peter, the visible Head of the whole Church and the Servant of the servants of God.

PART ONE
The Vacancy of the Apostolic See

CHAPTER I
The Powers of the College
of Cardinals During the Vacancy of the Apostolic See

1. During the vacancy of the Apostolic See, the College of Cardinals has no power or jurisdiction in matters which pertain to the Supreme Pontiff during his lifetime or in the exercise of his office; such matters are to be reserved completely and exclusively to the future Pope. I therefore declare null and void any act of power or jurisdiction pertaining to the Roman Pontiff during his lifetime or in the exercise of his office which the College of Cardinals might see fit to exercise, beyond the limits expressly permitted in this Constitution.

2. During the vacancy of the Apostolic See, the government of the Church is entrusted to the College of Cardinals solely for the dispatch of ordinary business and of matters which cannot be postponed (cf. No. 6), and for the preparation of everything necessary for the election of the new Pope. This task must be carried out in the ways and within the limits set down by this Constitution: consequently, those matters are to be absolutely excluded which, whether by law or by practice, come under the power of the Roman Pontiff alone or concern the norms for the election of the new Pope laid down in the present Constitution.

3. I further establish that the College of Cardinals may make no dispositions whatsoever concerning the rights of the Apostolic See and of the Roman Church, much less allow any of these rights to lapse, either directly or indirectly, even though it be to resolve disputes or to prosecute actions perpetrated against these same rights after the death or valid resignation of the Pope. All the Cardinals are obliged to defend these rights.

4. During the vacancy of the Apostolic See, laws issued by the Roman Pontiffs can in no way be corrected or modified, nor can anything be added or subtracted, nor a dispensation be given even from a part of them, especially with regard to the procedures governing the election of the Supreme Pontiff. Indeed, should anything be done or even attempted against this prescription, by my supreme authority I declare it null and void.

5. Should doubts arise concerning the prescriptions contained in this Constitution, or concerning the manner of putting them into effect, I decree that all power of issuing a judgment in this regard belongs to the College of Cardinals, to which I grant the faculty of interpreting doubtful or controverted points. I also establish that should it be necessary to discuss these or other similar questions, except the act of election, it suffices that the majority of the Cardinals present should concur in the same opinion.

6. In the same way, should there be a problem which, in the view of the majority of the assembled Cardinals, cannot be postponed until another time, the College of Cardinals may act according to the majority opinion.

CHAPTER II
The Congregations of the Cardinals in Preparation for the Election of the Supreme Pontiff

7. While the See is vacant, there are two kinds of Congregations of the Cardinals: *General* Congregations, which include the whole College and are held before the beginning of the election, and *Particular* Congregations. All the Cardinals who are not legitimately impeded must attend the General Congregations, once they have been informed of the vacancy of the Apostolic See. Cardinals who, by virtue of <u>No. 33</u> of this Constitution, do not enjoy the right of electing the Pope are granted the faculty of not attending these General Congregations, should they prefer.

   The Particular Congregation is made up of the Cardinal Camerlengo of Holy Roman Church and three Cardinals, one from each Order, chosen by lot from among the Cardinal electors already present in Rome. The office of these Cardinals, called Assistants, ceases at the conclusion of the third full day, and their place is taken by others, also chosen by lot and having the same term of office, also after the election has begun.

   During the time of the election, more important matters are, if necessary, dealt with by the assembly of the Cardinal electors, while ordinary affairs continue to be dealt with by the Particular Congregation of Cardinals. In the General and Particular Congregations, during the vacancy of the Apostolic See, the Cardinals are to wear the usual black cassock with piping and the red sash, with skull-cap, pectoral cross and ring.

8. The Particular Congregations are to deal only with questions of lesser importance which arise on a daily basis or from time to time. But should there arise more serious questions deserving fuller examination, these must be submitted to the General Congregation. Moreover, anything decided, resolved or refused in one Particular Congregation cannot be revoked, altered or granted in another; the right to do this belongs solely to the General Congregation, and by a majority vote.

9. The General Congregations of Cardinals are to be held in the Apostolic Palace in the Vatican or, if circumstances demand it, in another place judged more suitable by the Cardinals. At these Congregations the Dean of the College presides or, should he be absent or lawfully impeded, the Subdean. If one or both of these, in accordance with <u>No. 33</u> of this Constitution, no longer enjoy the right of electing the Pope, the assembly of the Cardinal electors will be presided over by the senior Cardinal elector, according to the customary order of precedence.

10. Votes in the Congregations of Cardinals, when more important matters are concerned, are not to be expressed by word of mouth but in a way which ensures secrecy.

11. The General Congregations preceding the beginning of the election, which are therefore called "preparatory," are to be held daily, beginning on the day which shall be fixed by the Camerlengo of Holy Roman Church and the senior Cardinal of each of the three Orders among the electors, and including the days on which the funeral rites for the deceased Pope are celebrated. In this way the Cardinal Camerlengo can hear the opinion of the College and communicate whatever is considered necessary or appropriate, while the individual Cardinals can express their views on possible problems, ask for explanations in case of doubt and make suggestions.

12. In the first General Congregations provision is to be made for each Cardinal to have available a copy of this Constitution and at the same time to have an opportunity to raise questions about the meaning and the implementation of its norms. The part of the present Constitution regarding the vacancy of the Apostolic See should also be read aloud. At the same time the Cardinals present are to swear an oath to observe the prescriptions contained herein and to maintain secrecy. This oath, which shall also be taken by Cardinals who arrive late and subsequently take part in these Con-

gregations, is to be read aloud by the Cardinal Dean or by whoever else presides over the College by virtue of <u>No. 9</u> of this Constitution, in the presence of the other Cardinals and according to the following formula:

We, the Cardinals of Holy Roman Church, of the Order of Bishops, of Priests and of Deacons, promise, pledge and swear, as a body and individually, to observe exactly and faithfully all the norms contained in the Apostolic Constitution Universi Dominici Gregis *of the Supreme Pontiff John Paul II, and to maintain rigorous secrecy with regard to all matters in any way related to the election of the Roman Pontiff or those which, by their very nature, during the vacancy of the Apostolic See, call for the same secrecy.*

Next, each Cardinal shall add: *And I, N. Cardinal N., so promise, pledge and swear.* And, placing his hand on the Gospels, he will add: *So help me God and these Holy Gospels which I now touch with my hand.*

13. In one of the Congregations immediately following, the Cardinals, on the basis of a prearranged agenda, shall take the more urgent decisions regarding the beginning of the election. In other words:

  a) they shall fix the day, hour and manner in which the body of the deceased Pope shall be brought to the Vatican Basilica in order to be exposed for the homage of the faithful;

  b) they shall make all necessary arrangements for the funeral rites of the deceased Pope, to be celebrated for nine consecutive days, determining when they are to begin, in such a way that burial will take place, except for special reasons, between the fourth and sixth day after death;

  c) they shall see to it that the Commission, made up of the Cardinal Camerlengo and the Cardinals who had formerly held the offices of Secretary of State and President of the Pontifical Commission for Vatican City State, ensures that the rooms of the *Domus Sanctae Marthae* are made ready for the suitable lodging of the Cardinal electors, that rooms suitable for those persons mentioned in <u>No. 46</u> of the present Constitution are also made ready, and that all necessary arrangements are made to prepare the Sistine Chapel so that the election process can be carried out in a smooth and orderly manner and with maximum discretion, according to the provisions laid down in this Constitution;

  d) they shall entrust to two ecclesiastics known for their sound doctrine, wisdom and moral authority the task of presenting to the Cardinals two well-prepared meditations on the problems facing the Church at the time and on the need for careful discernment in choosing the new Pope; at the same time, without prejudice to the provisions of <u>No. 52</u> of this Constitution, they shall fix the day and the time when the first of these meditations is to be given;

  e) they shall approve — at the proposal of the Administration of the Apostolic See or, within its competence, of the Governatorato of Vatican City State — expenses incurred from the death of the Pope until the election of his successor;

  f) they shall read any documents left by the deceased Pope for the College of Cardinals;

  g) they shall arrange for the destruction of the Fisherman's Ring and of the lead seal with which Apostolic Letters are despatched;

  h) they shall make provision for the assignment of rooms by lot to the Cardinal electors;

  i) they shall set the day and hour of the beginning of the voting process.

CHAPTER III
Concerning Certain Offices During
the Vacancy of the Apostolic See

14. According to the provisions of Article 6 of the Apostolic Constitution *Pastor Bonus*, at the death of the Pope all the heads of the Dicasteries of the Roman Curia — the Cardinal Secretary of State and the Cardinal Prefects, the Archbishop Presidents, together with the members of those Dicasteries — cease to exercise their office. An exception is made for the Camerlengo of Holy Roman Church and the Major Penitentiary, who continue to exercise their ordinary functions, submitting to the College of Cardinals matters that would have had to be referred to the Supreme Pontiff.

    Likewise, in conformity with the Apostolic Constitution *Vicariae Potestatis* (No. 2 § 1), the Cardinal Vicar General for the Diocese of Rome continues in office during the vacancy of the Apostolic See, as does the Cardinal Archpriest of the Vatican Basilica and Vicar General for Vatican City for his jurisdiction.

15. Should the offices of Camerlengo of Holy Roman Church or of Major Penitentiary be vacant at the time of the Pope's death, or should they become vacant before the election of his successor, the College of Cardinals shall as soon as possible elect the Cardinal, or Cardinals as the case may be, who shall hold these offices until the election of the new Pope. In each of the two cases mentioned, election takes place by a secret vote of all the Cardinal electors present, with the use of ballots distributed and collected by the Masters of Ceremonies. The ballots are then opened in the presence of the Camerlengo and of the three Cardinal Assistants, if it is a matter of electing the Major Penitentiary; if it is a matter of electing the Camerlengo, they are opened in the presence of the said three Cardinals and of the Secretary of the College of Cardinals. Whoever receives the greatest number of votes shall be elected and shall *ipso facto* enjoy all the relevant faculties. In the case of an equal number of votes, the Cardinal belonging to the higher Order or, if both are in the same Order, the one first created a Cardinal, shall be appointed. Until

the Camerlengo is elected, his functions are carried out by the Dean of the College or, if he is absent or lawfully impeded, by the Subdean or by the senior Cardinal according to the usual order of precedence, in conformity with No. 9 of this Constitution, who can without delay take the decisions that circumstances dictate.

16. If during the vacancy of the Apostolic See the Vicar General for the Diocese of Rome should die, the Vicegerent in office at the time shall also exercise the office proper to the Cardinal Vicar in addition to the ordinary vicarious jurisdiction which he already holds. Should there not be a Vicegerent, the Auxiliary Bishop who is senior by appointment will carry out his functions.

17. As soon as he is informed of the death of the Supreme Pontiff, the Camerlengo of Holy Roman Church must officially ascertain the Pope's death, in the presence of the Master of Papal Liturgical Celebrations, of the Cleric Prelates of the Apostolic Camera and of the Secretary and Chancellor of the same; the latter shall draw up the official death certificate. The Camerlengo must also place seals on the Pope's study and bedroom, making provision that the personnel who ordinarily reside in the private apartment can remain there until after the burial of the Pope, at which time the entire papal apartment will be sealed; he must notify the Cardinal Vicar for Rome of the Pope's death, whereupon the latter shall inform the People of Rome by a special announcement; he shall notify the Cardinal Archpriest of the Vatican Basilica; he shall take possession of the Apostolic Palace in the Vatican and, either in person or through a delegate, of the Palaces of the Lateran and of Castel Gandolfo, and exercise custody and administration of the same; he shall det ermine, after consulting the heads of the three Orders of Cardinals, all matters concerning the Pope's burial, unless during his lifetime the latter had made known his wishes in this regard; and he shall deal, in the name of and with the consent of the

College of Cardinals, with all matters that circumstances suggest for safeguarding the rights of the Apostolic See and for its proper administration. During the vacancy of the Apostolic See, the Camerlengo of Holy Roman Church has the duty of safeguarding and administering the goods and temporal rights of the Holy See, with the help of the three Cardinal Assistants, having sought the views of the College of Cardinals, once only for less important matters, and on each occasion when more serious matters arise.

18. The Cardinal Major Penitentiary and his Officials, during the vacancy of the Apostolic See, can carry out the duties laid down by my Predecessor Pius XI in the Apostolic Constitution *Quae Divinitus* of 25 March 1935, and by myself in the Apostolic Constitution *Pastor Bonus*.

19. The Dean of the College of Cardinals, for his part, as soon as he has been informed of the Pope's death by the Cardinal Camerlengo or the Prefect of the Papal Household, shall inform all the Cardinals and convoke them for the Congregations of the College. He shall also communicate news of the Pope's death to the Diplomatic Corps accredited to the Holy See and to the Heads of the respective Nations.

20. During the vacancy of the Apostolic See, the Substitute of the Secretariat of State, the Secretary for Relations with States and the Secretaries of the Dicasteries of the Roman Curia remain in charge of their respective offices, and are responsible to the College of Cardinals.

21. In the same way, the office and attendant powers of Papal Representatives do not lapse.

22. The Almoner of His Holiness will also continue to carry out works of charity in accordance with the criteria employed during the Pope's lifetime. He will be dependent upon the College of Cardinals until the election of the new Pope.

23. During the vacancy of the Apostolic See, all the civil power of the Supreme Pontiff concerning the government of Vatican City State belongs to the College of Cardinals, which however will be unable to issue decrees except in cases of urgent necessity and solely for the time in which the Holy See is vacant. Such decrees will be valid for the future only if the new Pope confirms them.

CHAPTER IV
Faculties of the Dicasteries of the Roman Curia During the Vacancy of the Apostolic See

24. During the period of vacancy, the Dicasteries of the Roman Curia, with the exception of those mentioned in No. 26 of this Constitution, have no faculty in matters which, *Sede plena,* they can only deal with or carry out *facto verbo cum Sanctissimo* or *ex Audientia Sanctissimi* or *vigore specialium et extraordinariarum facultatum* which the Roman Pontiff is accustomed to grant to the Prefects, Presidents or Secretaries of those Dicasteries.

25. The ordinary faculties proper to each Dicastery do not, however, cease at the death of the Pope. Nevertheless, I decree that the Dicasteries are only to make use of these faculties for the granting of favours of lesser importance, while more serious or controverted matters, if they can be postponed, shall be exclusively reserved to the future Pope. If such matters admit of no delay (as for example in the case of dispensations which the Supreme Pontiff usually grants *in articulo mortis*), they can be entrusted by the College of Cardinals to the Cardinal who was Prefect until the Pope's death, or to the Archbishop who was then President, and to the other Cardinals of the same Dicastery, to whose examination the deceased Supreme Pontiff would probably have entrusted them. In such circumstances, they will be able to decide *per modum provisionis,* until the election of the Pope, what they judge to be most fitting and appropriate for the preservation and defence of ecclesiastical rights and traditions.

26. The Supreme Tribunal of the Apostolic Signatura and the Tribunal of the Roman Rota, during the vacancy of the Holy See, continue to deal with cases in accordance with their proper laws, with due regard for the prescriptions of Article 18, paragraphs 1 and 3 of the Apostolic Constitution *Pastor Bonus.*

CHAPTER V
The Funeral Rites of the Roman Pontiff

27. After the death of the Roman Pontiff, the Cardinals will celebrate the funeral rites for the repose of his soul for nine consecutive days, in accordance with the *Ordo Exsequiarum Romani Pontificis,* the norms of which, together with those of the *Ordo Rituum Conclavis,* they are to observe faithfully.

28. If burial takes place in the Vatican Basilica, the relevant official document is drawn up by the Notary of the Chapter of the Basilica or by the Canon Archivist. Subsequently, a delegate of the Cardinal Camerlengo and a delegate of the Prefect of the Papal Household shall separately draw up documents certifying that burial has taken place. The former shall do so in the presence of the members of the Apostolic Camera and the latter in the presence of the Prefect of the Papal Household.

29. If the Roman Pontiff should die outside Rome, it is the task of the College of Cardinals to make all necessary arrangements for the dignified and reverent transfer of the body to the Basilica of Saint Peter's in the Vatican.

30. No one is permitted to use any means whatsoever in order to photograph or film the Supreme Pontiff either on his sickbed or after death, or to record his words for subsequent reproduction. If after the Pope's death anyone should wish to take photographs of him for documentary purposes, he must ask permission from the Cardinal Camerlengo of Holy Roman Church, who will not however permit the taking of photographs of the Supreme Pontiff except attired in pontifical vestments.

31. After the burial of the Supreme Pontiff and during the election of the new Pope, no part of the private apartment of the Supreme Pontiff is to be lived in.

32. If the deceased Supreme Pontiff has made a will concerning his belongings, bequeathing letters and private documents, and has named an executor thereof, it is the responsibility of the latter to determine and execute, in accordance with the mandate received from the testator, matters concerning the private property and writings of the deceased Pope. The executor will give an account of his activities only to the new Supreme Pontiff.

Appendix 8:
The Legend of Pope Joan

There is a legend that in the ninth century a woman became pope and was called by the name of Joan. During her coronation procession from the Lateran Palace to St. Peter's, she gave birth outside the church of San Clemente. Reportedly, the crowd was shocked more by the fact that she had had sex and given birth than by the fact that she was a woman. As for her death, some say she was tied to the tail of a horse, dragged through the streets of Rome, and finally stoned to death and buried at the spot where she died, where an inscription was posted:

PETRE PATER PATUM PAPISSAE PRODITO PARTUM.

("Peter the Father gave birth, revealing a female pope.")

Other legends claim that after she gave birth, Joan was immediately deposed and did penance for many years, while her son became the Bishop of Ostia and had her interred in Ostia after she died (year unknown.)

And some whisper that while giving birth she had a vision, in which she was given a choice between temporal disgrace or eternal punishment. She chose temporal disgrace and therefore died on the street where she gave birth.

Appendix 9:
The Cemetery of Callixtus:
The Crypt of the Popes

During the Christian persecutions of the first three centuries, Christians had to celebrate mass in secret in the catacombs that run underneath Rome. Likewise, when Christians died, they were buried in the miles of multi-storied underground niches that were the catacombs. Popes were no different, for to bury them in a public place would risk their desecration by the emperor's men. Therefore, they were buried in a special crypt in the Cemetery of Callixtus: The Crypt of the Popes. This was discovered by famed archeologist de Rossi in 1854. By that time the crypt had fallen into terrible decay, and the remains of the popes were not there, most having been transferred to other Roman churches to hide them from the invading Lombards in the ninth century.

Next page: The Crypt of the Popes in the Cemetery of Callixtus as it would have originally looked. From H.K. Mann, *Tombs and Portraits of the Popes.*

Bibliography

The main sources, the books I had surrounding me at all times, were H.K. Mann's Tombs and Portraits of the Popes, Iiro Kajanto's Papal Epigraphy in Renaissance Rome, Richard P. McBrien's Lives of the Popes, J.N.D. Kelley's Oxford Dictionary of Popes, and Renzo Montini's Le Tombe dei Papi. Of course I gathered information from many, many books; the list alone would comprise an entire volume all on its own. The works listed below represent a useful and broad-ranging selection.

Acta Sanctorum. 58 vols., Antwerp: 1643–1867; 2nd ed., 67 vols., Paris: 1863–1925.

Ambrosini, Maria Luisa. *The Secret Archives of the Vatican.* Boston: Little, Brown, 1969.

Aries, Phillip. *The Hour of Our Death.* New York: Knopf, 1981.

Aston, Margaret, ed. *Panorama of the Renaissance.* New York: Abrams, 1996.

Ayres, Philip. *A Short Account of the Life and Death of Pope Alexander the VII: With a Description of His Funeral Machine, and Elegies Erected in St. Peter's Church in Rome....* London: Moses Pitt, 1667.

Ball, Ann. *Catholic Book of the Dead.* Huntington IN: Our Sunday Visitor, 1995.

Barraclough, Geoffrey. *The Medieval Papacy.* Library of World Civilization. New York: Norton, 1979.

Bertelli, Sergio. *The King's Body.* University Park: Pennsylvania State University Press, 2001.

Binns, L. Elliot. *The Decline and Fall of the Medieval Papacy.* New York: Barnes & Noble, 1995.

Blouin, Francis X., general editor. *Vatican Archives.* New York: Oxford University Press, 1998.

Bolton, Brenda. *Hadrian IV.* Aldershot, Hants., England: Ashgate, 2003.

Brown, Peter. *The Cult of the Saints.* Chicago: University of Chicago Press, 1982.

Bunson, Matthew. *The Pope Encyclopedia: An A to Z of the Holy See.* New York: Crown, 1995.

Burchard, Johan. *At the Court of the Borgia.* Ed. and trans. by Geoffrey Parker. London: Folio Society, 1963.

Burkle-Young, Francis. *Passing the Keys.* New York: Madison, 1999.

Butler, Alban. *Lives of the Saints.* San Francisco: HarperSanFrancisco, 1991.

Caporilli, Memmo. *The Popes.* Rome: Euroedit-Trento, 1999.

Carlino, Andrea. *Books of the Body: Anatomical Ritual and Renaissance Learning.* Chicago: University of Chicago Press, 1994.

The Catholic Encyclopedia. New York: McGraw-Hill, 1967.

Chamberlin, E.R. *The Bad Popes.* New York: Barnes & Noble, 1993.

Cheetham, Nicolas. *A History of the Popes*. New York: Barnes & Noble, 1992.

Christian Inscriptions. New York: Philosophical Library, 1952.

Ciacconius, Alphonso. *Vitae, et res gestae pontificum romanorum et S.R.E. Cardinalium ab initio nascentis ecclesiae usque ad Clementem LY. P. O.M. Alphonsi Ciaconii Ordinis Fraedicatorum & aliorum opera descripte… Romae, Cura, et Sump. Philippi, et Ant. De Rubeis*. Vols. 1 and 2. 1677.

Cornwell, John. *Hitler's Pope: The Secret History of Pius XII*. New York: Viking, 1999.

_____. *A Thief in the Night: The Death of Pope John Paul I*. New York: Penguin, 1990.

Cruz, Joan Carrol. *Relics*. Huntington IN: Our Sunday Visitor, 1984.

Davies, John (of Kidwelly). *The New Pope, or, A true account of the ceremonies and proceedings in the conclave of Rome, upon the Pope's death, for the election of a new pope, according to the constitutions and ceremonials. Translated out of the French by John Davies. London: Printed, and are to be sold at the George in Fleet Street near Cliffords-Inns, 1677.*

Davis, Raymond. *Lives of the Eighth-Century Popes*. (*Liber Pontificalis.*) Liverpool: Liverpool University Press, 1992.

_____. *Lives of the Ninth-Century Popes*. (*Liber Pontificalis.*) Liverpool: Liverpool University Press, 1995.

_____. *Lives of the Tenth-Century Popes*. (*Liber Pontificalis.*) Liverpool: Liverpool University Press, 1997.

Death of the Pope! (Pius VI.) 1799.

de Rossi, Giovanni Battista. *Inscriptiones christianae Urbis Romae VIIsaeculo antiquiores*, Rome, 1861–1888.

De Voragine, Jacobus. *The Golden Legend*. Vols. 1 and 2. Trans. William Granger Ryan. Princeton: Princeton University Press, 1995.

Dionysius, P. *Sacrarum Vaticanae basilicae cryptarum monumenta*. 2nd ed. Rome, 1828.

Distincto racconto della traslazione del corpo di P. Benedetto XIII. Rome, 1733 (pamphlet).

Dollison, John. *Pope-Pourri*. New York: Fireside, 1994.

Duffy, Eamon. *Saints and Sinners*. New Haven CT: Yale University Press, 1997.

Durant, Will. *The Age of Faith*. New York: MJF, 1950.

_____. *The Renaissance*. New York: MJF, 1953.

Enciclopedia dei Papi. Rome: Istituto Isti della Culturo l'Italiano, 2000.

Ettlinger, L. D. "Pollaiulolo's tomb of Sixtus IV." in *Journal of the Warburg and Courtauld Institutes*, 1953.

Eusebius. *The History of the Church from Christ to Constantine*. Trans. G.A. Williamson. New York: Barnes & Noble, 1995.

Farrow, John. *Pageant of the Popes*. Lanham MD: Sheed and Ward, 1942.

Fiedler, Maureen. *Rome Has Spoken: A Guide to Forgotten Papal Statements, and How They Have Changed Through the Centuries*. New York: Crossroad/Herder & Herder, 1998.

Florio, John. *A Letter lately written from Rome, by an Italian gentleman to a friende of his in Lyons in France. Wherein is declared, the state of Rome: the suddaine death & sollemne buriall of Pope Gregory the thirteenth. The election of the newe Pope (Sixtus V.) and the race of life this newe Pope ranne before he was advanced…. Newly translated out of Italian into English by I.F.* London: John Charlewood, 1585.

Forcella, Vincenzo. *Inscizioni delle chiese d'altri edifici di Roma dal secolo Afino ai giori nostri*. 14 vols. Rome, 1869–1884.

Gail, Marzieh. *The Three Popes*. New York: Simon & Schuster, 1969.

Gardner, Julian. *The Tomb and the Tiara: Curial Tomb Sculpture in Rome and Avignon in the Later Middle Ages*. New York: Oxford University Press, 1992.

Gontard, Friedrich. *The Chair of Peter: A History of the Papacy*. Trans. A.J. and E.F. Peeler. New York: Holt, Rinehart and Winston, 1964.

Greeley, Andrew M. *The Making of the Popes 1978*. Kansas City: Andrews and McMeel, 1979.

Gregorovius, Ferdinand. *Tombs of the Popes*. London: Archibald Constable, 1903.

Grimaldi, Giacomo. *Descrizione della Basilica Antica di S. Pietro in Vaticano: Codice Barberini Latino 2733*. Ed. R. Niggl. Vatican City, 1972.

Habenstein, Robert Wesley, and Lamers, William Mathias. *The History of American Funeral Directory*. Rev. ed. Milwaukee: Bulfin, 1962.

Hebblethwaite, Peter, and Hebblethwaite, Margaret. *The Next Pope: A Behind-the-Scenes Look at How the Successor to John Paul II Will*

Be Elected and Where He Will Lead the Catholic Church. San Francisco: HarperSanFrancisco, 2000.

Hibbert, Christopher. *The Popes.* New York: Tree Communications, 1984.

Hintzen-Bohlen, Brigitte. *Rome and the Vatican City.* New York: Barnes & Noble, 2001.

Hogue, John. *Nostradamus: The Complete Prophecies.* Shaftesburg, England: Element, 1997.

Hook, Donald D. *Madmen of History.* New York: Barnes & Noble, 1996.

Iserson, Ken. *Death to Dust.* Tucson AZ: Galen Press, 1996.

Johnson, Paul. *The Papacy.* London: Weidenfeld & Nicolson, 1997.

Kajanto, Iiro. *Papal Epigraphy in Renaissance Rome.* Helsinki: Suomalainen tiedeakatemia, 1982.

Kastenbaum, Robert, and Kastenbaum, Beatrice. *The Encyclopedia of Death.* New York: Avon, 1989.

Kelley, J.N.D., ed. *The Oxford Dictionary of Popes.* Oxford: Oxford University Press, 1986.

Kunz, George Frederick. *Rings for the Finger.* 1917; Reprint. New York: Dover, 1973.

Lanciani, R. *Pagan and Christian Rome.* Reprint, Manchester NH: Ayer, 1968.

Lees-Milne, James. *St. Peter's.* Boston: Little, Brown, 1967.

Lisboa Camara Municipal. *Papa Joao XXI: Pietro Hispano.* Lisbon: Stampa Grafispaco, 2000.

Lo Bello, Nino. *The Vatican Empire.* New York: Trident, 1968.

_____. *The Incredible Book of Vatican Facts and Papal Curiosities: A Treasury of Trivia.* Liguori MO: Liguori, 1998.

Mann, H.K. *Tombs and Portraits of the Popes of the Middle Ages.* London: Sheed & Ward, [1928].

Mann, Horace Kinder. *The Lives of the Popes in the Early Middle Ages.* London: K. Paul, Trench, Trubner, 1902.

Martin, Malachi. *The Decline and Fall of the Roman Church.* New York: G.P. Putnam's Sons, 1981.

Marucchi, Orazio. *Christian Epigraphy.* Trans. J. Armine Willis. Cambridge: Cambridge University Press, 1912.

Maxwell-Stuart, P.G. *Chronicle of the Popes.* London: Thames and Hudson, 1997.

McBrien, Richard P. *Lives of the Popes.* San Francisco: HarperSanFrancisco, 1997.

McDowell, Bart. *Inside the Vatican.* Washington, D.C.: National Geographic Society, 1991.

Miller, J. Michael. *The Shepherd and the Rock.* Huntington IN: Our Sunday Visitor, 1995.

Mims, Cedric. *When We Die.* London: Constable & Robinson, 1998.

Montini, Renzo Umberto. *Le Tombe dei Papi.* Rome: Istituto di Studi Romani, 1957.

Morgenstern, Anne. "Art and Ceremony in Papal Avignon: A Prescription for the Tomb of Clement VI." Gesta XL/I, 2001.

Mortier, R.P. *Saint-Pierre de Rome: Histoire de la Basilique Vaticane et du Culte du Tombau de Saint Pierre.* Tours: Alfred Mame et Fils, 1900.

Nello, Vian, and Matt, Leonard von. *St. Pius X: A Pictorial Biography.* Trans. Sebastian Bullough. London: Longmans, Green, 1995.

Noe, Cardinal Virgilio. *Le Tombe e i Monumenti Funerebri dei Papi nella Basilica di San Pietro in Vaticano.* Modena: F.G. Industrie Grafiche, 2000.

Noonan, James-Charles. *The Church Visible.* New York: Viking, 1996.

Northecote, J. Spencer. *Roma sotterranea: or, An account of the Roman catacombs, especially of the cemetery of San Callisto; comp. from the works of commendatore de Rossi (Giovanni Battista de Rossi).* London: Longmans, Green, 1879–1880.

Nunn, H[enry] P[reston] V[aughn]. *Christian Inscriptions.* New York: Philosophical Library, 1952.

Oliphant, Mrs. *A History of Rome.* New York: Macmillan, 1897.

Olson, Roberta J.M. *Italian Renaissance Sculpture.* London: Thames & Hudson, 1992.

Panofsky, Erwin. *Tomb sculpture: Four Lectures on Its Changing Aspects from Ancient Egypt to Bernini.* 1964: Reprint. New York: Abrams, 1992.

Paperbrochii, D. *Conatus chronico-historicus ad catalogum Romanorum ontiflicum, in Propylaeum ad Acta Sanctorum.* Antwerp, 1685.

Paravicini-Bagliani, Agostino. *The Pope's Body.* Trans. David S. Peterson. Chicago: University of Chicago Press, 2000.

Pastor, Ludwig. *Lives of the Popes.* Vols. 1–36. St. Louis: Herder, 1949.

Perkins, Charles C. *Historical Handbook of Italian Sculpture.* London: Remington, 1883.

Pistolesi, Erasmo. *Funeral Oration on the Death of Pope Pius VII.* (No publishing information available.)

Plumb, J.H. *The Italian Renaissance.* Boston: Houghton Mifflin, 1961.

Pope-Hennessy, John. *Italian High Renaissance and Baroque Sculpture.* New York: Random House, 1985.

Prinz, Joachim. *Popes from the Ghetto.* New York: Horizon, 1966.

Procter, George Aislabie. "The Death of Pecci." Pamphlet. 1903.

Rasponi, Caesare. *De Basilica et Patriarchio Lateranensi Libri Quattuor: Ad Alexandrum VII, Pont. Max.* 1656.

Reese, Thomas. *Inside the Vatican.* Cambridge MA: Harvard University Press, 1998.

Rendina, Claudio. *The Popes: Histories and Secrets.* Trans. Paul D. McCusker. Santa Ana CA: Seven Locks, 2002.

Renouard, Yves. *The Avignon Papacy.* New York: Barnes & Noble, 1994.

Rice, Louise. *The Altars and Altarpieces of New St. Peter's: Outfitting the Basilica 1621–1666.* Cambridge: Cambridge University Press, 2000.

Richardson, Ruth. *Death, Dissection, and the Destitute.* Chicago: University of Chicago Press, 2000.

Rinaldi, Mariangela, and Vicini, Mariangela. *Buon Apetite, Your Holiness: The Secrets of the Papal Table* (Milan: 1998).

Scaglia, Sisto. *The Catacombs of Saint Callistus: History and Description with General View of the Christian Sepulchre, Epigraphy and Art.* Grottaferrata: Scola tip Italo-Orientale "S. Nilo," 1923.

Shaw, Christine. *Julius II: The Warrior Pope.* Cambridge: Blackwell, 1996.

Sladen, Douglas. *Old St. Peter's and St. Peter's Crypt at Rome with a List of the Popes.* London: Hurst and Blackett, 1907.

Spano, Pietro. *Papa Joao XXI, Pedro Hispano, Papa Giovanni XXI.* Lisbon: Lisboa Camara Municipal, 2000.

Strocchia, Sharon T. *Death and Ritual in Renaissance Florence.* Baltimore: Johns Hopkins University Press, 1992.

Thomas, Gordon, and Morgan-Witts, Max. *Pontiff.* New York: Doubleday, 1983.

Thompson, Charles John Samuel. *Poisons and Poisoners: With Historical Accounts of Some Famous Mysteries in Ancient and Modern Times.* London: Harold Shaylor, 1931.

W.B.; A.M. *A New History of the Roman Conclave Containing the Rites and Ceremonies Used and Observed at the Death, Election, and Coronation of the Pope.* London: Samuel Smith, 1691.

Wallace, William E., ed. *The Tomb of Julius 11 and Other Works in Rome.* Hamden CT: Garland, 1995.

Williams, George L. *Papal Genealogy: The Families and Descendants of the Popes.* Jefferson NC: McFarland, 1998.

Wintle, W. J. *A Popular Account of the Conclave at Rome.* London: London Magazine, June 1903.

Woodward, Kenneth L. *Making Saints: How the Catholic Church Determines Who Becomes a Saint, Who Doesn't, and Why.* New York: Simon & Schuster, 1996.

Yallop, David. *In God's Name: An Investigation into the Murder of Pope John Paul I.* New York: Bantam, 1984.

Websites

www.abruzzo2000.com (An excellent site on Abruzzo, with a service that will photograph any part of Abruzzo and send it to you.)

www.anneball.com (Anne Ball is an expert on Catholic death.)

www.catacombsociety.org (The International Catacomb Society, everything you ever wanted to know about catacombs.)

www.find-a-grave.com (Very useful site with wonderful photos of graves around the world.)

www.hidden-knowledge.com (A wonderful website full of useful tidbits of historic information.)

www.home.online.no/-cnyborg (Chris Nyborg's site lists every church in Rome and details about each church as well as Rome itself—a must for visiting Rome, and one of the best sites on Rome.)

www.italyworldclub.com (A comprehensive site highlighting the treasures of Italy.)

www.newadvent.com (Wonderfully informative site about everything Catholic, including the *Catholic Encyclopedia*.)

www.newyorkcarver.com (By far the best medieval site on the web, dealing in all things medieval by providing links to a plethora of topics.)

www.papaluciani.com (Site for Pope John Paul I.)

www.pope-charts.com (A very informative site

where one can buy posters of all the popes and learn fun facts about the papacy.)

www.romeartlover.it (A very detailed site on the monuments and art of Rome.)

www.stuardtclarkesrome.com (One of the best sites on Rome, a definite must for the study of Rome.)

www.the-popes.net (Run by Father Tom Carleton, this site offers insight into the papacy as well as the struggle to end abortion.)

www.ukans.edu/histoU/index/europe/ancient-rome/E/home.html (Bill Theyer's site about Rome and Italy, one of the best sites on papal and classical Rome with more web pages and links than any Roman related site.)

www.vatican.va (Vatican website.)

www.westgatenecromantic.com (The best site for beautiful death imagery.)

Index